QUEST INTO THE UNKNOWN

QUEST INTO THE UNKNOWN

TONY HOWARD

MY LIFE AS
A CLIMBING
NOMAD

Vertebrate Publishing, Sheffield
www.v-publishing.co.uk

To my mum and dad; my sister, Kathryn; my daughter, Tannith;
Di Taylor, my ever-undaunted companion on many years of exploration,
and now my wife; and all those who unquestioningly supported me along the way.

Thanks.

First published in 2019 by Vertebrate Publishing.

Vertebrate Publishing
Omega Court, 352 Cemetery Road, Sheffield S11 8FT United Kingdom.
www.v-publishing.co.uk

Front cover: Our first sight of the awesome Great Siq which splits Jebel Rum's summit plateau. Jordan, 1984.
Photography by Tony Howard unless otherwise credited.

Tony Howard has asserted his rights under the Copyright, Designs and Patents Act 1988
to be identified as author of this work.

This book is a work of non-fiction based on the life of Tony Howard. The author has stated
to the publishers that, except in such minor respects not affecting the substantial accuracy
of the work, the contents of the book are true.

A CIP catalogue record for this book is available from the British Library.

ISBN 978-1-911342-83-0 (Paperback)
ISBN 978-1-911342-84-7 (Ebook)
ISBN 978-1-912560-05-9 (Audiobook)

10 9 8 7 6 5 4 3 2 1

Design and production by Jane Beagley.
www.v-publishing.co.uk

Vertebrate Publishing is committed to printing on paper from sustainable sources.

Printed and bound in the UK by T.J. International Ltd, Padstow, Cornwall.

CONTENTS

PRECIS IX

PART ONE

1   EARLY DAYS – PART ONE 3
2   EARLY DAYS – PART TWO 8
3   EARLY DAYS – PART THREE 12
4   TEENAGE KICKS – PART ONE 14
5   TEENAGE KICKS – PART TWO 18
6   THE RIMMON 21
7   WHALING DAYS – SOUTH GEORGIA BOUND 25
8   WHALING DAYS – ANTARCTIC ADVENTURES 30
9   KEEP ON ROCKIN' 33
10   WINTER WANDERINGS 43
11   NORWAY – ARCTIC ADVENTURES 48
12   JOBS ON THE ROCKS 50
13   DOLOMITE DAYS 55
14   MOROCCAN MOUNTAINS 60
15   NORWAY – THE TROLL WALL AND OTHER ESCAPADES 66
16   LIFE ON THE OCEAN WAVE 73
17   NORWAY – THE ROMSDAL YEARS 77
18   THE TIMES THEY ARE A-CHANGING 88
19   ON THE ROAD AGAIN 91
20   CANADA – YUKON YARNS 93
21   CANADA – 'THE TRAIL OF '98' 98
22   HOMEWARD BOUND 108
23   BACK HOME 112
24   GREENLAND 117
25   LIFE AT TROLL 125
26   PERSIAN PERAMBULATIONS 128
27   AND THEN THERE WERE TWO 138
28   ATAKOR ADVENTURES 140
29   MEANWHILE, BACK AT WORK 148
30   SPANISH ROCK 155
31   MOROCCO – HERE COMES THE SUN 158
32   ALPINE ADVENTURES 166
33   ALL CHANGE 171

34	HARD ROCK DAYS	174
35	SUDAN SAGA – KASSALA MOUNTAINS	177
36	SUDAN SAGA – TICKET TO RIDE	185

PART TWO

37	EXPLORING JORDAN – WADI RUM DISCOVERY	203
38	EXPLORING JORDAN – RUM ROCK	212
39	EXPLORING JORDAN – PETRA'S SECRET CANYON	223
40	EXPLORING JORDAN – BEYOND PETRA	231
41	EXPLORING JORDAN – MORE RUM GOINGS ON	238
42	EXPLORING JORDAN – BEDOUIN ROCK	248
43	TRAVELS IN THAILAND	257
44	OMAN ODYSSEY – A SURPRISE CHRISTMAS	263
45	OMAN ODYSSEY – MUSANDAM TO DHOFAR	272
46	EXPLORING EGYPT – SINAI AND THE RED SEA MOUNTAINS	279
47	EXPLORING EGYPT – SOME YOU WIN, AND SOME YOU LOSE	287
48	INCREDIBLE INDIA – THE WESTERN GHATS AND BEYOND	289
49	INCREDIBLE INDIA – LADAKH AND BEYOND	297
50	EXPLORING ETHIOPIA – THE ROOF OF AFRICA	304
51	A LIBYAN INVITATION	312
52	MIDDLE EASTERN MEANDERINGS	321
53	EXPLORING JORDAN – THE LOWEST ADVENTURES ON EARTH	323
54	MADAGASCAR – MYSTICAL MOUNTAINS	333
55	WELCOME TO PALESTINE	341
56	EXPLORING EGYPT – IF AT FIRST YOU DON'T SUCCEED …	350
57	EXPLORING EGYPT – NUBIAN NEMESIS	356
58	INCREDIBLE INDIA – THE NORTH-EAST FRONTIER	361
59	INCREDIBLE INDIA – SARAMATI SURPRISE	367
60	PALESTINE – IS THERE ANYBODY OUT THERE?	371
61	EXPLORING JORDAN – THE KNIFE CANYON	376
62	MALI – MOUNTAINS, MAGIC AND MUSIC	381
63	EXPLORING JORDAN – NEW DISCOVERIES	389
64	EXPLORING JORDAN – THE JORDAN TRAIL	395
65	INCREDIBLE INDIA – A WALK ON THE WILD SIDE	399
66	EXPLORING JORDAN – BACK ON THE TRAIL	404
67	MEMORY LANE	411
68	THE END OF THE TRAIL	414

| POSTSCRIPT | 421 |
| ACKNOWLEDGEMENTS | 425 |

PRECIS

I had never intended to write my autobiography; a bit too narcissistic perhaps, or an admission that it's 'game over'. I even held publication of *Troll Wall* in abeyance until 2011 – forty-six years after simultaneous first ascents by a Norwegian team and us, 'the English'. I had written the story directly after the climb then shelved it to escape the limelight and get on with my life.

When it was finally published, people asked when I was going to write my autobiography. Matt Heason, for example, says in his review of the book that, 'the chapters either side of the ascent … are absolutely fascinating. I sincerely hope that he is, as I write, locked in a room somewhere typing up his full memoirs as they are destined to impress and inspire.' In similar vein, Andy Kirkpatrick commented, 'You'd hope that age would slow Tony enough so that he'd finally sit still and write a few more memoirs, so we might have a chance of more books like this.'

Then in 2014, despite it being a good summer, events transpired to ground me more than anticipated. My regular climbing mate Mick Shaw was struggling with a bad heel after smashing it in a bouldering fall. My shoulder was also playing up – 'Wear and tear, what do you expect at your age?', the doctor said unhelpfully – and my wife and climbing and trekking partner, Di, had a knee problem. 'Why don't you do some writing?' she suggested.

I do enjoy writing, so here I am: shut up in a room, sat at my computer while out of my window I can see the Peak District cliffs where I started climbing over sixty years ago. Di and I are still out every week, either walking or climbing. We had our annual six-week trip to Jordan in the spring and together with friends almost finalised one of our oldest ongoing projects, the 400-mile Jordan Trail. We were also walking and climbing in Shetland, even new routing on a sea cliff we found, and we will be out in Jordan for another six weeks in the autumn, hopefully putting the finishing touches to the trail.

I finally decided that writing up my stories might serve a purpose, in that it will hopefully entertain or be of interest. But more that it might inspire someone, somewhere, to live their dreams and escape the pre-ordained path of life that others may expect of them – just as I did. Though maybe having adventures was easier in my day. We were lucky. The climbing world was largely unexplored – even the cliffs surrounding my Peak District home were little known.

Since then the world has changed beyond imagination: we had no TVs, computers, mobile phones or GPS. No one we knew flew anywhere; travel was infinitely more difficult, as was gathering information on what were then considered 'remote destinations'. Even maps were often hard to come by. But my motto was always: 'you never know until you go'.

Places like Norway's Lofoten Islands were well off the beaten track, as was Morocco; no one had climbed in Tafraout when we went there in 1964 after a winter ascent of Jebel Toubkal and we were the first Brits to climb in the Taghia canyons in 1980. Now these places are easily accessible for climbing holidays in the sun. More amazingly, the now world-famous mountains of Wadi Rum in Jordan were also unknown other than in the writings of T.E. Lawrence until we traced his footsteps in 1984 and were welcomed by the Bedouin. And as recently as 2002 we were told that we were the first foreigners to report the existence of the Living Bridges of Meghalaya, and the following year to visit a Naga village on Mount Saramati on the India-Burma border, then a closed area.

Everywhere we went we were welcomed by the indigenous people, whose hospitality was always overwhelming. In particular the tribal peoples of Africa and the Middle East, the Qashqai and Kurds of Iran, the Tahltan up in the Yukon, the Greenland Inuit, the many and varied Malagasy, Sudanese and Ethiopian tribes, the Sherpas of Nepal and the Nagas and Bodos in the jungles of north-east India – all of whom had so little to give but gave so much. I owe the richness of my experiences to them and to my friends who accompanied me on these adventures to the world's wild places, and also to those of my family that I left behind but nonetheless accepted my idiosyncrasies. I hope this book will be some small repayment.

Meanwhile, as I have been writing this, Di has just reminded me that the sun is out. She has changed her mind.

'You can write again later,' she said. 'We should be out on the hills.'

She's right.

Tony Howard
Greenfield, September 2018

PART ONE

1

EARLY DAYS – PART ONE

*I belonged to that generation which saw,
by chance, the end of a thousand years' life.*
Cider with Rosie, Laurie Lee

The day I was born was a momentous day. Mum and Dad must have wondered anxiously about the world I was entering. It was Britain's darkest hour: the eve of the World War Two Dunkirk evacuation in May 1940. Over 7,000 men were rescued from the beaches of northern France on that first day, and over a third of a million on subsequent days. I, of course, knew nothing of it, but soon after my father was sent to work in London at the time of the Blitz, which lasted from September 1940 to May 1941. Bombs fell on London for seventy-six consecutive nights, killing over 20,000 civilians and destroying more than a million houses. Worrying days for Mum, though Dad wrote often and whenever possible came home to Greenfield, the village where we lived on the edge of the Pennine moors in the West Riding of Yorkshire.

Rationing of food and petrol was introduced the year I was born and continued throughout the war. Bread escaped rationing but was in such short supply that it had to be sold a day old when it would be going stale and could consequently be cut into thinner slices. The shortage of food was so great that on my fifth birthday – three weeks after the end of the war in Europe in 1945 – food rations were reduced even further. The weekly bacon allowance went down from four ounces to three ounces, cooking fat from two ounces to just one, and the meagre meat ration of 1/2 d (half an old penny) per family had to be taken in corned beef. Supplies of food continued to be so short that bread was finally added to the ration list a year later and was not removed until 1948.

Rationing of other foods continued until 1954 when I was fourteen and the last item, meat, was finally taken off the government's list. Mum used to make 'rag puddings' to make the meat go further. They consisted of chopped-up pieces of meat with onions and gravy, wrapped in suet pastry, tied in a 'rag' and boiled in a pan on the fire. Cheap, and saved electricity too. Raiding our pantry to make a swift treacle butty when no one was around, or sticking my finger in the jam jar, became habits. Mum never said anything. Dripping butties were another secret delight, the best bits of dripping being the dark brown bottom layer. Mum always knew I had been in the jar as the top crust had to be broken to get at the juicier layer underneath.

My sister Kathryn was born a couple of years after me, and with Dad still working away, Mum worked hard bringing us up. Despite the difficulties of life at that time, our home was a happy place, surrounded on three sides by fields. It seemed everyone knew everyone in the village. Nestled beneath the western edge of the Pennines, Greenfield is overlooked by the wild moors and jutting gritstone crags of Chew Valley. These cliff-rimmed hills – which I still think are the nearest thing to mountains between Snowdonia and the Lakes – were to become my childhood playground and had a huge influence on my life, but not before my formative years in the friendly warmth of the village community.

A cousin of my mum's lived just across the road with his family including a couple of lads about my age. My aunty lived down the lane with her family including two daughters, also of similar age to me. My uncle and his wife also lived nearby. Sadly, both my mum's parents died young and I never met them, but my dad's parents lived in an old stone cottage in a small hamlet just up the hill from us, across some fields. Other relations from both sides of the family also lived in the village where, as in many northern villages, our life revolved around the Methodist chapel.

Sundays were not my favourite days, as I had to wear 'Sunday best' and attend Sunday school. I could never relate to the Sunday school classes and hymns, though the pictures of desert scenes with their dunes, palm trees, camels and exotically garbed people always intrigued me. Nor did I enjoy the pantomimes in which I was a very reluctant actor dressed embarrassingly in anything from sailor suits to Hawaiian grass skirts, to perform on stage for parental admiration.

Otherwise, the village was a great place to grow up in and, for the most part, certainly for a young lad, was far from the war. Despite the mill in Chew Valley manufacturing gun-cotton and presumably being a potential bombing target, the nearest thing to a hit came one night in 1941 when a bomb accidentally landed on the cricket pitch. How dare they! I remember the rationing, the blackout blinds, my gas mask, the sirens and the drone of enemy planes going over in the night as they headed to and from Manchester and Salford docks just ten miles away. Two of Mum's brothers were killed in the wars, when both were in their teens. I often wonder what it must have been like for someone who had never previously travelled to die in such alien places so far from home and family. Everyone dreaded receiving a black-edged envelope from the Ministry of Defence. Mum's sister had been working in the Women's Land Army down south and had met an American soldier. They came up to see us and the rest of the family in Greenfield and were married soon after the war, moving to America where she stayed – a major step for a country girl in the 1940s.

I remember the first bananas and pineapples coming into the village in 1946 and everyone making such a fuss about it. The 'Dig for Victory' campaign was still promoted every week by the BBC and we worked in the school allotments one day a week, growing vegetables, just as my dad and everyone else did in their gardens at home. School dinners were good and I ate everything that was put on my plate.

What with the Great Depression of the 1930s and then the war and rationing, it's no wonder people with rickets were still a common sight, as were men in uniform, or with missing limbs and burnt faces. A large house at the entrance to Chew Valley was then a recuperation home for injured soldiers that we used to visit on special occasions such as Whit Fridays when the brass bands were out in full force and there were games and competitions in the field near the cricket pitch.

Primary school was just five minutes' walk down our lane; sometimes Mum would walk with us on her way to or from the shops, otherwise I would go with my sister or friends. There was no paranoia about kids being out without their parents in those days. School itself was fine, we all knew each other and enjoyed our time there, learning our 'three Rs', as well as art, music, history, geography, RE and PE. The map of the world on the classroom wall was predominantly pink, the colour of our empire 'on which the sun never set'. We used old-fashioned nibbed pens that were provided by the school and dipped into inkwells that were set in our desks and filled each day by an 'ink monitor'.

After school I would be off into the fields with my mates, damming streams or up trees and generally doing what boys do. Looking for birds' nests was a springtime hobby – frowned upon these days, I know. But we never damaged them; the fun was in finding them. Once, trying to climb a big sycamore with no low branches I hammered in some six-inch nails to make a ladder (I had discovered what aid climbing was, but didn't know it). Inevitably one of them came out and I tore my leg badly on the nails lower down resulting in a real telling off from my mum once she had recovered from the shock of all the blood and my ripped trousers. Autumn meant raiding orchards. The stolen apples were usually small and sour, but it was worth it for the fun. Inevitably I would arrive home dirty to be asked yet again by my long-suffering mum why I hadn't come home from school to put my old clothes on.

Washing clothes wasn't easy in those days: no washing machines, just a boiler, poss-tub or dolly tub and mangle. Weather permitting, it was then pegged out on the line, all of which I sometimes helped with, though often I had already managed to escape outdoors. Other chores included washing and drying the pots after meals, which Kathryn and I tried to avoid, usually without success. Chopping wood for lighting the fire was my dad's job, though that was something I always enjoyed. No one we knew had any form of central heating then, so the coal fire was essential in winter and lit by Mum to warm the living room before she made breakfast and packed us off to school.

On winter mornings the insides of the windows would often be covered in frost-feathers. Getting up and dressed was a chilly business. Then, as the room warmed with the heat of the fire, the frost would melt, sending trickles of water down the glass into small channels cut into the bottoms of the wooden window frames. From there, the water escaped outside through holes drilled specially in the wood … unless the hole was frozen up, which it usually was, then the water overflowed to form small pools on the window ledge. It was normal. I even had my tonsils taken out at home, while my two mates who lived next door tried to peep between the drawn curtains. I remember lying on the table in our living room and being chloroformed, then waking up just as the doctor was throwing my tonsils in the fire.

An everyday event was the delivery of milk and eggs by our local farmer, Billy Bradbury. He arrived by horse and cart with churns of milk from which he would fill a shiny gallon can to carry to the door, heralded by the clatter of his clogs on the path. Milk was then measured out into a pint or jill can for pouring into our jug. While all this was going on, his carthorse, Dolly, would amble down to the next house on his round and wait there for Billy to catch up. Another farmer who had fields around our avenue was known as Ernest o'Derby. Like Billy's farm and most others around the village, his dated back to the seventeenth century and was a wonderful place. His doors were never locked, which was not unusual at that time, and we would wander in and chat with him or his wife Minnie while hens clucked about our feet, in and out of the kitchen, pecking at crumbs and scraps. Ernest wore clogs and black leather spats, and if he went up the lane with his horse and cart when we were in the schoolyard at playtime, he sometimes stopped and did a clog dance for us.

Carts were more common than cars. All sorts of people used to peddle their wares around the village. The 'rag-and-bone man', calling out, 'Rag, bone, cream and white donkey stone', which I'm sure sounds mysterious to anyone not of that generation, 'rag-and-bone men' and 'donkey stone' now being things of the past. The rag-and-bone men were the scrap dealers of their day, exchanging donkey stone for old clothes or whatever unwanted items you might have. The 'stones', the size of a block of soap, were originally used in northern mills to clean greasy steps, but the idea soon caught on and they were used by housewives to give their doorsteps a clean and decorative finish. And woe betide a woman who didn't have a clean 'donkey-stoned' step outside her door. The knife-sharpener was another regular, also with his horse and cart. The crumpet lady came on foot with her large basket of delicious home-made crumpets, and gypsies or tinkers were not infrequent callers, with a ready curse if Mum didn't buy something.

Mum walked half a mile to the shops most days with her wicker shopping basket for fresh food: bread, butter, veg and the like. The village co-op was a great place; a barrel of butter was always open on the counter, as well as a side of ham for carving. There was always time for a friendly chat while purchases were weighed out, poured into paper packets then neatly folded, before the divvy and ration book were stamped and signed. There were also four baker- ies in the village and two fish and game shops with rabbits and grouse hang- ing outside. The aptly named Mrs Cotton owned the village's haberdashery shop, and a hardware store sold all the essentials for farming, gardening and household repairs. On the edge of the village, the blacksmith usually had a couple of carthorses tethered by the open door, and the sound of hammer- ing rung from inside the smithy as their shoes were shaped on the anvil.

There were four pubs too, though to my knowledge my parents never went in them. The nearest my mum ever came to drinking alcohol was a glass of sherry on Christmas Day, which she always said made her 'tiddly'.

2

EARLY DAYS – PART TWO

Greenfield was my whole world. Huddersfield was over the moors; Oldham and Manchester, though nearer, were also on the far side of hills and rarely visited unless new clothes had to bought. Mum and Dad were both from Greenfield – and most of their ancestors before them. Mum had lived just down the lane from Dad and was from a more middle-class family, her father being a manager in a village mill and choirmaster at the Methodists. Dad had a poorer upbringing, his father being a labourer and handyman, who, among other things, had worked on the construction of the Chew Reservoir, which, at 487 metres above sea level, is the highest in England.

Growing up in a seventeenth-century cottage, Dad had to carry water from the well and meals were cooked on the fire or in the oven of the old Yorkshire Range, which also had a small boiler for hot water. There was no bath, except for a tin tub that was placed in front of the fire on the rag rug that my grandad had made from shreds of old clothes. Their only washbasin was the kitchen sink, which was carved out of a slab of stone. The toilet was an outside closet. Dad told me he was one of the first people in Greenfield to build a crystal set, so they could listen to the radio – commercial radio broadcasting had only just started in the 1920s and radios were very expensive, so their neighbours used to come round and listen to this new miracle of science.

Dad had a superb sledge made for me at the local ironmongers in the magnificent winter of 1947. I don't think we have had as much snow since. The drift under the railway arch near the end of our lane was six metres deep. Our sledging track started up at Billy Bradbury's farm, went down two long, steep fields and then on to a narrow railway footbridge full to the top with hard-packed snow, with nothing to stop you going over the side. We went down that at break-neck speed; if you got it wrong, a twelve-metre plunge on to the tracks below awaited. If not, then it was down into another field, across our snow-covered lane and yet another field to the valley bottom. We were banned from doing the bridge run when our parents discovered what we were up to, though we still sneaked one in on our last run home at night.

In the summer we would go picnicking 'up Chew' with our family, walking up past the mill to Nut Bottom where the Chew and Greenfield brooks met to swim in rocky pools, though both valleys are now flooded by the reservoir. Above us were the moor-edge cliffs of Alderman, Dovestones and Wimberry, rising like battlements on the skyline. I was soon going up there with my young friends despite – or more likely because of – repeated warnings to 'Keep away from those cliffs and don't go on the moors, they're dangerous'.

My parents enjoyed walking and being outdoors. In our early years, Kathryn and I would go up on the moorland hillsides with Mum, collecting wimberries or blackberries with her, then coming home with purple fingers and mouths before helping to remove the leaves and bits of twigs so she could make pies. She, like most housewives those days, especially in the country, also used to make jam and bottled fruit for the winter.

Dad and I sometimes went fishing for sticklebacks and the like. In spring I would keep a jar of frogspawn on the windowsill, so I could watch it turn into tadpoles then metamorphose into frogs. We also went up on the moors, once walking twenty miles, quite a way for a young lad still at primary school. These were memorable days. I used to wonder how he knew his way around the wild places as he never had a map. He taught me the names of the cloughs and cliffs and the moorland birds. We also went up to Wimberry Rocks together in 1949, a few days after a Dakota crashed up there on its way to Manchester airport. There had been thirty-two people on board; twenty-four were killed. There was part of a wing lying in the clough near the crag and bits of debris everywhere. It was my first awareness of the fragility of life. On another walk we saw climbers at Laddow Rocks, on the far side of the moor from Greenfield overlooking Longdendale valley – a place I had never seen or heard of before. I had never seen climbers either, but these were definitely climbers. They had ropes and nailed boots, and I wondered how you went about becoming a climber … it looked exciting!

Whenever possible I was also out with my friends exploring our hills and neighbouring upriver Pennine villages that had changed little since their origins, their gritstone cottages hugging narrow lanes. The coming of the Industrial Revolution however had brought 'dark satanic mills' which stood alongside every river like great black carbuncles. Some once had waterwheels, but by my time all had huge mill chimneys and were powered by coal, the smoke blackening the old gritstone walls and the mill workers' terraced stone houses. Even the cliffs of the moor edges were grimy with soot.

Further upstream, steepening rocky cloughs and waterfall-filled canyons led to the wild moors. Up there, in the slate below the deep peat groughs, we found fossilised ferns, and above them, vestigial tree stumps, both of which told their tales of earlier times when forests covered the hills. Forests are once again returning due to cleaner air, changing farming practices and European conservation measures; tree by tree, birch, willow, rowan, pine, even alien Himalayan rhododendrons are now suddenly beginning to dot our moors where, in my childhood days, there was nothing other than peat bogs, sphagnum moss, cotton grass, wimberry and heather. We loved it up there, but we never passed beyond our known horizons. Our parents' warnings that 'people get lost up there' had been well and truly drummed into us.

Despite the pull of the hills, 'Sunday dinner' was just about inescapable. The wireless would usually be on, the BBC Light Programme having started after the war in 1945. On Sundays, Two-Way Family Favourites played record requests and linked families at home with British forces posted overseas. Mum was a Kathleen Ferrier fan, while Dad was more into Winifred Atwell and even Fats Domino. Maybe he was an early rocker, though no one would ever have suspected it, least of all me. He also enjoyed Dick Barton, Special Agent, which was on every night and hugely popular, a forerunner to James Bond.

As I got into my teens, music began to play a part in my life. I would stay up late after my parents and sister had gone to bed and listen to Radio Luxembourg where American DJ Alan Freed was introducing the new rock and roll music. I was at Oldham Hulme Grammar by then, where 'rock music' was frowned upon and considered a bad influence. The headmaster banned pupils from going to see films of that ilk such as *Rock Around the Clock*, starring Bill Haley and his Comets, and *The Girl Can't Help It*, starring Jayne Mansfield with music by, among others, The Platters, Fats Domino, Eddie Cochran, Gene Vincent and Little Richard. Both films were released in 1956 when 'Teddy Boys' with their fancy hairdos, long jackets, drainpipe trousers and 'brothel creeper' crepe-soled shoes were creating social havoc. Of course, being banned made the films essential viewing. Needless to say any dress or haircut that came remotely near Teddy Boy style at school was also banned. To emphasise this, one would-be 'Ted' got a public caning in the main hall by the headmaster who first of all peered inside the seat of the lad's trousers to make sure he hadn't put any padding in to cushion his bum. Like me, the victim was a Saddleworth lad, the head often referring to us disparagingly as 'that Saddleworth lot', as we came from Yorkshire rather than Lancashire where Hulme Grammar was, so we weren't fee payers.

My irresistible curiosity about the dreaded cane finally led me to the receiving end. How stupid can you get? Sent to the head's study, I was first lectured on the importance of good behaviour before he opened his glass-fronted case that was positioned prominently on the wall behind his desk, and in which he kept an array of canes on display, each of which he would flex and whisk though the air dramatically and repeatedly with a dreadful swishing sound, testing their feel and hoping to terrify you before he actually made a suitable choice and got down to the real thing. 'Bend over boy', he said. Then swish-whack, swish-whack, swish-whack – up to six times, dependent on the punishment. It wasn't fun. In fact it hurt, but it was a challenge. For me, the important thing was to stand up afterwards as though nothing had happened and say with an impertinent smile, 'Is that it, sir?' before being dismissed, hoping I had annoyed him by not bursting into tears.

I enjoyed school. Lessons were for the most part interesting and I did reasonably well in most of them. PE was fun, I always looked forward to the regular cross-country runs, usually arriving back tired and muddy but in the first half dozen, which wasn't bad as I was among the youngest in my year having sat the eleven-plus exam when I was ten. I also joined the school Cadet Force, mainly because it had outdoor activities and taught map reading, but also because the alternative was religious education with the headmaster.

In later years at school I became increasingly rebellious. I didn't like the discipline and felt it was designed to crush the *me* out of me, and mould me into one of them. While most of my schoolmates knew what careers they were hoping to follow, I hadn't a clue. I toyed with the idea of going on to university to study forestry or geology just to meet expectations and please my parents while hopefully getting some time in the mountains, but in reality all I wanted to do was climb, and as far as I knew climbing wasn't a career.

3
EARLY DAYS – PART THREE

Early summers were always a time for haymaking. I couldn't wait for Billy Bradbury to tell my mum they were starting the mowing. The hay would need cutting, turning, windrowing and housing. In the early years there were sometimes itinerant Irish farmworkers who would work in unison, scything then turning the hay into rows with long wooden hay-rakes. Whenever I got the chance I would work with them – not easy for a young lad; they were fit and worked hard and I would get home with blistered hands and aching muscles but it felt good. As I got further into my teens I was allowed to drive the horse, pulling the big rake to and fro across the fields, gathering the rows of drying hay.

Those were good days, working hard, enjoying the camaraderie of the men, sitting in the shade of a hawthorn hedge eating sandwiches and drinking sweet tea brought to the fields by Billy's wife, Olive. I still remember the sweet smell of new-mown grass and sun-dried hay in the summer breeze; the scrape of metal against a whetstone as a scythe was sharpened, the whinny of Dolly the mare as I harnessed her in the stable, ready for the day's work. None of us realised that this traditional rural scene would soon be gone from the English countryside to be replaced by mechanisation, leaving huge bales of ugly plastic-wrapped hay in the fields.

At the end of the day I would fetch the cows in from a distant meadow. On arriving at the shippon, they would each go to their habitual places between the boskins and wait patiently to be tethered, ready for milking. I remember the warm smell, the contented lowing of the cattle, the rattle of their chains, the sound of Billy's clogs and the swish, swish of milk splashing into the bucket as he worked his way along the rows with his milking stool, his brown, sinewy, veined hands making easy work of this twice-daily task.

The milk was taken down to the dairy, still warm from the cows, to be poured through a sieve and a cooler and into the churns to be kept cold in the trough ready for the milk round. There was no pasteurised milk in those days. Additionally, the eggs had to be collected and hens put in their pens for the night because of foxes. Today these eggs would be called 'free range', but in those days, they were just 'eggs'. As I grew up I watched hill farming becoming increasingly more difficult. It was a shock when Billy, unable to make ends meet, hanged himself from a beam in the barn.

The other summertime event was the family holiday, when we would go off to the seaside. Being by the sea was always fun, though on my first holiday, not long after the war, I caused a bit of a scare. When my parents woke on the first morning at the guesthouse, my bed was empty. Unable to bear the excitement of seeing the sea for the first time, I had gone out and they couldn't find me – I was already far away exploring the beach. That got me into big trouble, just as disappearing on the school trip to London Zoo did a few years later …

In 1953 Queen Elizabeth II was crowned. I remember the headmaster calling everyone into the main hall and announcing in sombre tones, 'The King is dead, long live the Queen'. We had no TV to watch her coronation, but our next-door neighbours had one. Their front room was full as we and other neighbours crowded in to watch the event on their twelve-inch black and white screen, after which there was a street party to celebrate. What was more exciting for me was the simultaneous news that Everest had been climbed by Tenzing and Hillary. Strangely, I was also disappointed. Knowing it had been unclimbed, and despite having done little more than play around on our local boulders and moor-edge cliffs, the thought had already crossed my mind that it might stay that way until I was old enough to climb it. Happily, I later discovered it wasn't the only mountain waiting to be explored.

4

TEENAGE KICKS – PART ONE

I am glad I shall never be young without wild country to be young in.
Of what avail are forty freedoms without a blank spot on the map?
A Sand County Almanac, Aldo Leopold

The nearest I got to climbing in my pre-teens was playing around with my mates on the Wimberry boulders. Even in the 1940s there were lots of well-scratched routes there, marked by the nailed boots of climbers. Likewise when we eventually ventured on to our local crags of Dovestones and Alderman, we found nail marks in the easy gullies and chimneys we scrambled up.

But it was not until I went to Hulme Grammar in 1951 and met Alwyne 'Olly' Whitehead from the nearby village of Dobcross that I really began to explore the hills and cliffs. Over the following years, they became our playground. Any climbing books we could find such as Kirkus's *Let's Go Climbing!*, Shipton's *Upon that Mountain*, G.W. Young's *Mountain Craft*, Gaston Rébuffat's *Starlight and Storm* and Slingsby's *Norway: The Northern Playground*, were avidly read. Though I didn't know it at the time, Slingsby's book was to play a part in tempting me to Norway and the Lofoten Islands on my first 'expedition' in 1962.

It wasn't just climbing that attracted me to the hills, it was also about exploring our local moors and wild places, learning about wildlife. Seeing the white hares on the snow-swept winter moors; in spring, the first swallows arriving at the old moor-edge barns; lapwings rising from the meadows with the heavy flap of their wings, or watching a kestrel hovering above the moor edge then dropping like a stone on to prey. I once saw a merlin catch a finch; it was struggling in the predator's talons when, to my surprise, it escaped, flying in small, fast, crazy spirals towards the ground, outmanoeuvring the merlin at every twist and turn. They plunged together into some ferns, the merlin soon rising without its prey that had cleverly escaped in the undergrowth.

Another day while following a moorland stream Olly and I saw a trout in the shade of a projecting rock. I had heard about 'tickling trout' but this was my first opportunity. Amazingly it worked, and we gleefully sold it at the village fishmongers. I even managed a repeat performance the following year.

In 1954 we finally discovered real climbing. We were making our way up Greenfield Brook where Dovestones Reservoir is now, when we spotted some climbers high above on the cliffs of Alderman. We knew they were real climbers as we could see they were using a rope. Wanting to see what they were doing, we scrambled up through the pine forest and the long steep hillside above only to arrive after they had gone, but unwittingly they had left us a life-changer. There, on a rock at the bottom of the crag, was a small book. It was titled *Climbs on Gritstone, Volume 1, Laddow Area*. Flicking excitedly through its pages it described the cliffs of Chew Valley and *real* routes on them, which all had names and grades of difficulty – we had even done some of the easy ones. This was fantastic. Very few people climbed in those days; we hadn't even known that rock climbing guidebooks existed, but here was a book that described climbs on our hills. Life would never be the same again.

Next week, Olly turned up at our house with Barry Kershaw, a mate of his from Dobcross. Barry had 'found' a rope on the back of a wagon. It looked strong as it was about an inch thick, but we had no idea how to use it. We didn't have any slings for runners, but we didn't even know what a runner was. We had a rope and that's all we needed: we were going climbing. We set off for Dovestones Edge and soloed some 'Moderate' routes that were in the book, but which we had done previously, before taking it in turns to lead some Diffs and VDiffs then finishing with Swan Crack (a Severe). I can't remember if one of us led it or whether we simply top-roped it. Having climbed it out of curiosity while writing this book, I suspect it was the latter. It didn't matter; we were *climbers*!

Discovering what we were up to, my parents bought me a hawser-laid nylon rope, a waist-line, two slings, and two plain and one screw steel karabiners for my fifteenth birthday, 'before I killed myself'. Hemp ropes were still in common use but I chose nylon as it had been used on the successful ascent of Everest. At my request my parents also bought me a pair of boots with the new Vibram rubber soles for walking and climbing, rather than Tricouni and clinker nailed boots that, like hemp ropes, were being replaced by post-war technology.

One day, kitted out in our new gear, Olly and I walked over the moors to Lad's Leap, one of the more remote cliffs in our Laddow guide. There were only four climbs there and none harder than Severe, but we had a great day out. By the time we had walked the seven miles to the cliff and done the routes it was quite late. I had been asked by a guy called Tom Stephenson if I would operate the projector that evening for a slide show at Greenfield Methodists; he had just walked something he called the Pennine Way. We ran back the seven miles and arrived just in time, though Mum wasn't impressed by my clothes that were not up to standard for a 'do' at the Methodists.

The talk was a revelation. The Pennine Way, it turned out, had just been created by Tom, partly in an effort to open the moors to the public, as many were still private. It was hailed as Britain's first long-distance walk. On the second day, you make your way for about 260 miles from Edale in the newly created Peak District National Park, to the Scottish border, passing over the moors above Greenfield in the process. Excited, Olly and I came up with a plan: we would follow it as far as Ingleton then head west to Kendal and walk around the Lakes – a similar length. That way we would not only have a good long-distance walk, but also get to know the Lake District in readiness for future climbing trips. I rather suspected that if we didn't do it then, I would never do it; climbing was already an obsession, with frequent reprimands from teachers for doing pull-ups on the half-inch-thick wooden doorframes while waiting to go into class.

It was therefore fortuitous that we did our Pennine Way and Lake District walk when we did. We booked into youth hostels for the whole route. Both of us had already learnt rudimentary map reading in the school cadets, so despite some parental concern we set off happily on our three-week journey.

The first few days along the Pennine moors were straightforward and included our longest walk yet, almost thirty miles, as we headed north from Haworth to Malham. Some of it was over rough moorland; today's paved trail of gritstone slabs to protect the way from erosion hadn't been thought of back then. There were no Pennine Way signs either. In fact, there was sometimes no path at all as we must have been among the very first to walk the route. In Malham we spent a day exploring Gordale Scar and Malham Cove, the biggest and steepest cliffs we had ever seen. There were only two climbs in Gordale at the time, and none at Malham.

At Ingleton, we left the Pennine Way for Kendal. From there we walked to Windermere and our first experience of the hills of the Lake District, up past Troutbeck to a high pass where we had our sandwiches while gazing at the lakes and mountains spread out around us. We were in our element! On our way down the valley of Pasture Beck to Ullswater, we saw some trout in the stream and successfully tickled one, though we put it back as we already had dinner ordered at the Patterdale Hostel. The next day was our first-ever real mountain day, up Striding Edge to Helvellyn, our first 3,000-footer.

From the top we continued north along the ridge and down to Keswick – a long mountain day. Having walked south past Derwentwater the next day, we spent the night at Honister Pass, and it was to be the start of some bad weather. We briefly lost our way the following day in pouring rain on cloud-covered hills near the remote Black Sail Hostel in Ennerdale. The following day conditions were no better, so hoping for a nicer day to climb Scafell or Great Gable, we stayed another night at Black Sail and went up to the cloud-covered summit of Haystacks for some bouldering.

With the weather still the same the following day (we were learning about the Lakes …) we had no choice but to continue, struggling up to the top of Great Gable just for the hell of it before descending to Wasdale, disappointed to see nothing of either the Gable or Scafell cliffs. More rain spoilt our plan to climb Scafell the next day, leaving us to walk in our now permanently wet clothes – our so-called waterproofs were useless – through more low cloud over Walna Scar and beneath the mist-shrouded cliffs of Dow Crag to Coniston.

Coming down from the high hills the weather improved, cheering us up as we walked to Hawkshead, though disappointed that we had missed out on almost all the famous summits and cliffs that we had read so much about and been so eager to climb. Our trip almost over, we walked to Windermere the next day and went rowing on the lake before hitch-hiking home. We had learnt a lot and the knowledge we had gained of the Lake District stood me in good stead over the coming years. I had seen enough to know it wouldn't be long before I was back up there on climbing trips.

5

TEENAGE KICKS – PART TWO

Around this time we plucked up the courage to chat to another gang of lads, all much older than us, who we had seen in the village. They were obviously climbers – they had ropes and rucksacks – some even had nailed boots. Among them were Graham West, Mick Roberts, Jimmy Curtis, Stan Wroe and Roy Brown: the original Chew Valley Cragsmen, soon to become the well-known Manchester Gritstone Club.

Roy was particularly friendly and became a role model to me, living as he did in a converted hen hut not far from Wimberry Rocks. He was in his mid-twenties and I used to go up there whenever I had the chance, listening to tales of climbing on the local cliffs and elsewhere over constant brews of tea boiled up by the friendly roar of Roy's Primus. He had kitted out the hen house with a bunk and table and was living the life of his choice, working when necessary but otherwise out on the hills. As far as Roy was concerned, life was an adventure. He was an inspiration. He was someone who had broken the mould of the seemingly unquestioned normality of school then work and two weeks' summer holiday a year. He opened my eyes to other possible lifestyles.

That's not to say I wasn't enjoying school. Our chemistry teacher Frank Seale was a climber, and asked Olly and me if we would like to go to the Isle of Arran with him. Frank didn't climb hard, but he loved his mountains. On our first day we walked up the five miles of swamp called Glen Sannox, and gazed in awed admiration at the huge bulging slabs and overhangs of the then unclimbed lower north-east face of Cìr Mhòr. Frank thought it looked 'bloody awful' and I agreed – but I was impressed. It looked good to me; it was the biggest cliff I had seen. We did the classic Arran ridges including the A'Chir Ridge with its 'bad step' and exposed traverse where Frank got his rope out – probably quite rightly, though we found it easy and enjoyed the rough granite. We also looked across to the 335-metre VS route up the south ridge of the Rosa Pinnacle, first climbed in 1941. It's one of the longest rock climbs in Britain and was then described in our guidebook as 'one of the hardest expeditions of its kind in the country'. In years to come it joined the ranks of routes in Ken Wilson's celebrated book of 'Great British Rock Climbs', *Hard Rock*. It was far beyond Frank's climbing abilities, and ours, but it looked superb and went on our mental ticklist of climbs to do. We also enjoyed the superb scenery out across the Clyde and over towards the mountains and islands of Scotland's north-west. It all looked truly wild and wonderful.

The summer of 1956 we were up in north-west Scotland once again in Frank's old van, climbing Aonach Eagach, Quinag, Suilven and An Teallach. On the same trip we took the ferry over to Skye and the Cuillins. There, Frank thought the traverse of Sgùrr nan Gillean followed by the abseil descent of the Bhasteir Tooth was beyond him, so Olly and I went on alone, though with some apprehension. Frank also introduced us to the mountains of North Wales.

Still exploring our home crags, Barry and I biked over to Shining Clough one day. There were no fancy gears on bikes in those days, so cycling about fifteen miles each way plus a fairly long, steep walk to and from the crag in addition to getting four decent routes done was quite a day. The Chew however was still our stomping ground, with lots of new climbs and new cliffs to explore. Olly and I did our first new routes there in 1956.

Next year, with the experience of our Welsh, Lakes and Scottish trips behind us and some decent VS routes done, we ventured on to the walls of Dovestones Quarry – England's tallest gritstone cliff, touching forty-five metres. Vying in height with Dinas Cromlech in Llanberis, it is notoriously loose and not many people climbed there – almost no one these days. Eric Byne described it in his 1965 guidebook *Rock Climbs in the Peak* as, 'this tremendous crag of gritstone, one of the most formidable and exposed climbing grounds in Britain'. But fifty years on, when English crag climbing is predominantly clean and safe, it's now known as Death Quarry. I still enjoy it.

It was a blatant challenge, dominating the entrance to the valley, provocatively waiting to be explored, we had of course climbed George Bower's classic 1928 VDiff, *Waterfall Direct*, the only route in the quarry in the 1948

Laddow guide and its VS variations that were added in about 1930. It was water-washed and clean with no seriously loose rock to worry about, but perhaps because of its location and height it had something of a reputation. We had climbed it, but spotted a chance to do a new route. We had sports every Wednesday afternoon at school, so one fine July day we grasped the moment and escaped from a cricket match. Just over an hour later we were in Dovestones Quarry roping up for what turned out to be a forty-five-metre Hard Severe in the centre of the cliff, its crux at the end of an unprotected eight-metre second pitch. Both of us got a real buzz climbing up into the unknown, not knowing how hard it would be, or if we would be able to find a way to the top. We did more new routes in the quarry that year, before the guidebook *Further Developments in the Peak District* was published. That opened our eyes to other, far more serious climbs, that had already been done by the likes of Joe Brown, Wilf White, 'Nat' Allen and others from the Valkyrie Club and its successor, the famed Rock and Ice Club, as well as by Graham West and his friends from the recently formed Manchester Grit club.

This guide was soon followed by *Recent Developments on Peakland Gritstone* by R.G. Wilson, which also included climbs in Dovestones Quarry by Alpha Club lads Pete Bamfield, Richard McHardy, Al Parker and Dave Saunders. It even included some routes on Dovestones Edge that were first climbed by Olly, Barry and me, though none were credited to us as nobody knew us.

6

THE RIMMON

Olly and I were out on the local crags at every opportunity, and with some other local lads, we formed the Rimmon Mountaineering Club, named after a mythological shepherdess who loved the local mountains and over whom two local mountain giants, Alderman and Alphin, had fought. Among the original team, people who appear in this book – along with Olly and me – were Paul Seddon, Brian Hodgkinson, Tony 'Jonah' Jones, Brian 'Smiler' Woods and Jeff Sykes, who had a one-piece down flying suit instead of a sleeping bag and once tried to sleep on a roof beam in an old barn as the floor was covered in cow muck. Inevitably he fell off, much to our delight. On cold days Jeff would leave his down suit on and climb in it – he said it saved him getting out of bed!

We were soon joined by Alan Waterhouse, who together with me started Troll Climbing Equipment in 1965, later joined by Paul in 1970. Bruce Mills – aka 'Droop' due to his extremely relaxed attitude to life – was another regular, with his friend Barry Taylor. Barry we called 'Erg', short for 'Ergonomic': designed to minimise physical effort and maximise efficiency – as he was fond of explaining. Keith 'Cockney' Chadwick was a 'comer-in' from London, as was Alan Baker. Harold Heald – aka Harpic – was, like the advert for the toilet cleaner claimed, 'clean round the bend'. Last but not least was Mick 'Chipperfield', who had a big tent, and was always indispensable on trips away.

Others soon followed, including Rob Holt, Tony (Nick) Nicholls and Bill Tweedale – all destined to become members of the 1965 Troll Wall team, as were Maggie Woodcock, Jeff Heath and a later member, John Amatt. Wayne Garside, aka 'Owdham Roughyed', Adrian 'Aido' Garlick, Brian Roberts and his younger brother Speedy, and 'Dog' Holden – a dog team musher on the British Antarctic Survey – were also members, as was John 'Fred'

Finnigan who, with Rob Holt, made the third ascent of our *Rimmon Route* on the Troll Wall. Barry Kershaw still climbed with us occasionally, but was a bit of a loose cannon (a peculiarly apt phrase), vacillating between the Rimmon and the Grit as the fancy took him. Club dinners at venues such as Edale, Malham, Kilnsey and Wasdale Head were inevitably wild and memorable occasions rivalling those of the Manchester Grit.

Other climbers – including girls – also joined the club, escaping from parental control at weekends with a variety of excuses, in particular Vivien Nichols, Di Barlow – becoming Di Taylor when she married Ken – Barbara Platt who married Paul Seddon, and Phyllis Waterhouse, wife of Alan Waterhouse.

We eagerly ticked off the recently published routes both in Dovestones Quarry and over on Wimberry, though I was happy when Paul chose to lead *Blue Lights Crack*, a typically nasty route of Don Whillans's (a notoriously hard lad) with a bad landing if you came off. In the quarry, Smiler and I climbed the *White Slab*, which had already gathered a bit of a reputation and on which I almost lobbed off on loose holds in the 'sensationally exposed' final overhanging crack. Soon after, Jeff and I climbed Joe Brown's, Nat Allen's and Don Chapman's 150-metre *Girdle Traverse*, which was described provocatively as, 'One of the hardest expeditions on gritstone', throwing down an irresistible gauntlet even though it was the only expedition on gritstone.

It turned out to be something of an epic, unexpectedly involving three more of Joe Brown's routes, being rained-off three times and each time returning up a different route – a good effort on Jeff's part as only one of his boots had a sole. Next summer we returned and did the whole route in one glorious afternoon. It was worth it.

While 'Dovies' was always the big challenge, with a tip-off from Roy we were already exploring another local quarry, Den Lane. It was only minutes away from the village square in Uppermill where everyone – bikers, climbers, and other local lads and girls – met in one or other of the two cafes where the first jukebox had just arrived.

The shortest way from the square to the quarry was to scurry through a private mill yard, jump across the canal lock, cross the railway lines and there we were, adrenaline at the ready. We did thirty new climbs there in 1957, including our first new VS routes. Another cluster of quarries high up on the curiously named Pots and Pans hill provided more new routes. We also did ten climbs on yet another 'new' crag, Charnel Stones – a natural crag not far from Dovestones Quarry. We developed Standing Stones, which, it seemed, other climbers had rarely visited because of its 'quarry-like' appearance. How wrong they were! And what's wrong with quarries anyway? We climbed eight new routes there that year. Pule Hill Rocks was another 1957 discovery and easy to get to, just a quick hitch up the road. Some of the lorries going up were so slow you didn't need to hitch a lift. Barry Kershaw showed me the trick of jumping up on to the back and taking a free ride to the top, making sure you jumped off before the driver picked up speed on the other side. We did over fifty new routes there that year, often kipping in a cave. We also found Shooter's Nab, coincidentally at the same time as Graham (Gray) West and Mick Roberts discovered it. We even turned up there on the same day, and a number of good routes were done, Barry's *Cuticle Crack* being the hardest, now graded E2 5c. My school note-book was filling up – and not with schoolwork!

In 1958 Olly and I did our first peg route in Den Lane Quarry using home-made wooden wedges and pegs made from milk crates and railway sleeper ties. We didn't really have much idea what we were doing, but we had read about it and thought we should have a go. It did at least enable us to get up overhanging cracks that were usually choked with dirt and loose rock. Then we discovered that engineering nuts could be threaded on to slings and jammed into cracks to make runners, making these now-clean cracks climb-able by normal means. Our new climbs were creeping up the VS grade. Some of these 1950s Rimmon routes have been upgraded to HVS 5a and 5b, even the occasional E1.

Harnesses didn't exist. The rope was still fastened to the body by a waist-line and steel karabiner, or simply tied around the waist. The climbing mantra of the day was, 'the leader never falls'.

Other than falling off a solo attempt of *Cave Crack* at Laddow and break-ing a bone in my hand, 1958 was the year I had my first real fall when an overhang collapsed about ten metres up a new route in Den Lane Quarry. I had one runner, a jammed knot, about halfway up. We had always wondered if they would hold, or simply compress and pull out, but it held. Olly stopped my fall only inches from the ground. Normally we cleaned routes as we climbed them, but on this occasion we returned another day, abseiled down and pulled more obviously loose blocks off, before I led it. Olly named it *Tony's Terror* to my everlasting embarrassment.

Abseiling was still done the original Victorian way, by winding the rope between the legs then around the body, though it would soon be replaced by the much more comfortable method of passing the rope through a kara-biner in a 'sit-sling' looped round the legs, then up over a shoulder and round the back. It was, coincidentally, less damaging to clothing, but either way, most climbers' pullovers and anoraks of that time were worn through at the shoulder by rope abrasion from abseiling and belaying. Trousers didn't fare much better either. We were a tatty lot.

I left school that year and went up to Langdale after my exam results came through. I was really chuffed to pass all three of my A levels. School was over, I had no plans: I was going climbing. We kipped in the infamous Wall End Barn where the farmer, Ike Myers, came around every morning with the greeting, 'Out of yer pits, you sons of Satan, let's 'ave yer shillings'. There were some good bouldering problems on the gable end of the house and the old outdoor farm toilet was a cosy double-seater, which wasn't too unusual in those days. We had hitched up to the Lakes and were out on the crags every day and in the Old Dungeon Ghyll pub each night, as were most of the Langdale climbing crowd. It was a great scene, and good to be part of it.

We had a bonanza year in 1958 with over 200 new routes on our local crags, mostly climbed by Olly, Brian, Paul, Barry and me, with some routes by Jeff, Smiler and Jonah. I also first met Vivien Nichols at around this time at a Gritstone Club dinner. She had already been climbing with some lads from the Manchester Grit and joined us most weekends, even doing some new routes with me. The route *Womanless Wall* on Standing Stones tells a tale: it's a three-star VS described as being a great piece of gritstone … a big steep classic at the upper end of its grade. Nowadays there are runners, but back in 1958 there were none until near the end, and there are some committing moves halfway up a rising diagonal traverse. Viv wouldn't follow, and I didn't blame her though I still got a right earful because of the unprotected traverse. Generally she was up for anything though, a bit of a wild girl – as fiery as her hair. We had a great, if somewhat turbulent, three years together. Never a dull moment!

I was then to get an opportunity I couldn't refuse: my uncle Sid worked on Fleet Street and was involved with, among other things, a company called Chris-tian Salvesen which owned a fleet of Norwegian whalers. His son had been to the Antarctic with them the previous year and I was really envious. How exciting was that? With a head full of stories of Moby Dick, Scott and Shackle-ton, South Georgia and the Antarctic, I asked if he could get me a job. He said he could, and he did. I was over the moon, but my mum and dad weren't keen.

7

WHALING DAYS – SOUTH GEORGIA BOUND

The chief harpoonist, a Norwegian of massive build … recalled the
frustration of the storms they had had at the start of the season. It was
impossible to hunt in that sort of weather. You could never spot the
whale spouts because of the spindrift, and anyway the bow dipped too
violently to aim the harpoon gun. For long stretches they had to shelter
in the lee of an iceberg; a week once went by without a 'Blaast!' ('There
she blows!') He personally had bagged 323 whales this time and only
two of them were blues. He was pretty sure they were disappearing …

The Observer on a voyage of the *Southern Venturer* in 1962,
four years after my voyage

My dad had been to Hulme Grammar and left with good exam results.
He wanted to go on to university, but coming from a poor family he had to
work; there was no choice. Now here I was throwing my opportunity away.
I knew he had high hopes for me, and my going to university meant a lot
to him, but I had different aspirations. When I told my parents I wanted to
go whaling they weren't happy. That night I could hear them talking down-
stairs and Mum saved the day.

'If it's what he wants, we should let him go.'

'If we do, he'll never settle down,' my dad replied prophetically.

Back in 1958 we lived in blissful ignorance of environmental and wildlife
issues. In many ways this has continued until quite recently as was remarked
on in *State of the World 2015* by Katie Auth in a Worldwatch Institute press
release. She commented, 'Our sense of the oceans' power and omnipotence
– combined with scientific ignorance – contributed to an assumption that
nothing we did could ever possibly impact it.'

No one in the 1950s thought the seas might be fished out within fifty years.
No one thought whales were nearing extinction. The International Whaling

Commission was in charge. They decided the permissible catch: how many sperm whales, how many fin, humpback and blue. Not only that, but the ship's captain wasn't informed which species of whale could be hunted and how long for until the day before, so everything was OK – or so everyone thought. And yes, it was bloody and cruel, and on occasion the ocean ran red with blood, but for an eighteen-year-old lad fresh from school, it was life in the raw. But when Greenpeace began its campaign against whaling in 1975, I joined immediately: I had seen the slaughter.

So in 1958, ignorance was bliss. At the end of our final school term that summer, the headmaster lined us up in the main hall. 'And where do you intend to continue your studies,' he asked each boy as he walked down the row. 'Oxford, sir, reading history'; 'Cambridge, sir, reading physics.' Then it was my turn: 'The Antarctic, sir, going whaling.'

I boarded the *Southern Venturer* and had a medical check by the ship's doctor who was one of the few Englishmen aboard. We also had a brief chat and he asked about my exam results, though I thought nothing of it at the time.

I was bunking in a cabin with three lads of my age who had also signed on as mess boys. One of them, 'Ginger', was from Newcastle, and I went with him to his parents' house the day before we sailed. It was in a block of flats, a grim place and a totally alien concept to me. Going up the flights of stairs, it smelt of pee and somebody had crapped on one of the steps. Ginger didn't seem to notice but I realised for the first time how lucky I was to have been brought up in a village in the country.

We sailed to Norway to pick up most of the crew, and then we sailed south. The doctor asked if I would like to work with him and his assistant in the ship's hospital. This sounded better than serving food in the mess and washing pots. My exams had obviously done some good and I was sure my parents would be pleased. Most of the crew were Norwegian, many from the far north, including Lofoten and Vesterålen. There was also a fair scattering of Scots from the Shetlands, Orkneys and Hebrides. They were tough men but friendly and hard-working; for most, this was an annual trip to the southern whaling grounds to supplement their meagre crofting income.

Soon after crossing the equator we were accompanied by wandering albatrosses drifting tirelessly alongside our ship, just beyond arms' reach on their long motionless wings spanning over three metres. They even accompanied us through the wild winds of the roaring forties where the ship's rivets creaked and groaned in the heavy seas that slammed into its sides, often above our cabin porthole.

Chatting with the men, I discovered that there were impressive mountains in Norway's Arctic north, giving me the idea of a climbing trip up there, though I soon had my own little mountain adventure in South Georgia, where we docked for a few days. Just the mention of its name filled my mind with thoughts of an island lashed by storms and filled with majestic peaks of snow and ice. I knew the tales of Shackleton and his great survival adventure. It was an island fortress guarding the gateway to the Antarctic and the unknown. Now I was in the whaling station of Leith Harbour, surrounded by those very mountains and with a day free I was tempted. My equipment was poor, just an old anorak and sweater, a pair of fancy rather than functional trousers, and an old pair of 'klets' (lightweight climbing shoes) – hardly the gear for glacier travel. Indeed, I didn't intend to set foot on a glacier, just to *have a look.*

I set out for Glacier Peak and its surrounding glacier. This was the most prominent peak in the immediate vicinity of the bay, with a rock ridge circling northwards around the glacier to Corunda Peak above the harbour. Within half an hour I was at the foot of the glacier, feeling very small and apprehensive. It was my first glacier, yet the temptation to climb it and try to climb Glacier Peak by a ridge that – as far as I knew – was unclimbed, was irresistible.

I set off up the glacier, which rose pleasantly towards the summit ridge, then levelled off to an area of deep crevasses and ice séracs. Impressed, I sat down to ponder the situation. The view was superb. Across the valley a rock face rose steeply for about 450 metres, seamed with gullies that were rotting away on to the screes below. Above and beyond, thrusting like countless Excaliburs from a lake of clouds, were innumerable jagged peaks, their icy summits glistening and beckoning in the sunlight. I sat alone in the solitude of the mountains, until the cold of the glacier penetrated my trousers and I returned to the reality of my situation.

Inspired by my surroundings, I was in no mood for going down. I leapt nonchalantly across crevasses until suddenly *scrunch*; my foot went through the snow. With a sickening feeling in my stomach I crawled rapidly on to safer terrain and once more sat down. Behind me a hole led the eye down into pitch-blackness. This wasn't so good. Still, I reasoned, the day was yet young and with only another thirty metres or so of glacier and its final bergschrund to cross I could take my time and continue.

Beyond this last crevasse, the snow rose steeply; my rubber-soled klets didn't help at all. The snow was too hard for step kicking, and any attempt at jumping back across the bergschrund would almost certainly have ended in its green-blue depths. The only way out was to scrape holds into the icy snow with my fingernails. This was tricky, but I soon climbed high above its gaping mouth, with only a thirty metres of rock to reach the summit ridge. *This is more like it*, I thought. *It looks a bit loose, but at least it's rock.*

The rock wasn't 'a bit' loose, it was actually collapsing. Block after tottering block littered the wall, interspersed by crumbling bands of shale. I eased along from hold to hold hoping that no more than one would give way at the same time. Then, after what seemed hours of suspense, there I was at last, sitting astride the crumbling knife-edge ridge.

Thank God I'm up, I thought, exceedingly impressed by myself and my amazing location. Beneath my right foot a shattered chaos of slabs swept down for about 600 metres to a deep green sea, bubbling and foaming white on the rocks. To my left was the face I had just climbed, the black hole of the bergschrund gaping like the mouth of a whale. Ahead and behind snaked a fantastic, impossible ridge of crazy pinnacles leading to the summits of Glacier and Corunda peaks. The view and feeling of isolation were unforgettable. The only trouble was, how to get down? There was no way I was going on that face again.

My only option was to move cautiously along the ridge then descend steep scree, which disappeared into the jaws of the bergschrund. Nasty, I thought. Before I knew it, I was sliding helter-skelter, bottom-end down, straight towards the depths of who knows what. Those scree stones were sharp too. I remember thinking, *I'd better do something about this quick, or I'm a goner*. As I reached the mouth of the bergschrund I pushed my legs out to bridge the gap. They just reached the lip of the glacier on the other side and I jammed myself across the crevasse. Stones rattled on into the icy blackness. Then all was silent. Laughing with relief, I decided that if I ever got down I'd give climbing up immediately.

Carefully unjamming myself, I slowly reached across and pulled over on to the glacier where I sat down with a sigh of relief, but not for long. The backside of my trousers and the equivalent area of my bum had ceased to be. Instead there was a shredded mass of skin dripping blood on to the snow. This was disastrous. Not only did I have to descend the glacier and walk back down the valley with a torn backside, but I also had to get back on board ship without looking like the fool I was. With my anorak tied around my waist I was soon nonchalantly strolling up the gangplank trying my best to look like a hard mountaineer instead of an idiot.

The following morning the ship left for the Antarctic whaling grounds.

8

WHALING DAYS – ANTARCTIC ADVENTURES

We sailed south-east into the ice, and the whaling was non-stop with regular catches of sperm whale and fin, 295 humpbacks in three days, and awesome blue whales, the largest animal our planet has ever seen. There was also my work in the ship's hospital. We had patients most days, sometimes with headaches or stomach problems, often with cuts that needed cleaning and a stitch or two. More excitingly for me, I also helped with a couple of appendectomies, swabbing out the clinic first so it could be used as an operating theatre. Once the sheets were in place leaving only a small portion of the patient's skin exposed, it didn't seem so bad when the incision was made exposing the appendix and part of the intestines. A quick snip and a few stitches and the job was done.

The doctor's skills were really put to the test with one extremely serious operation. A lad of about my age, Peter Gillies, had fallen from the crow's nest of one of the catchers, the *Southern Archer*, and was unconscious and bleeding badly from internal injuries. I was called to the hospital and by the time he had been hoisted on board I had swabbed down and disinfected the surgery until it was spotless, which was hardly my forte. Meanwhile the doctor checked all his surgical instruments, explaining all the different names to me. 'Would I be okay during the op?' he asked. I reassured him I would and he emphasised that it would be my job to pass the instruments to him when requested and most importantly to check them in and out during the operation.

Peter had fallen on to the catcher's bulkhead and smashed some ribs, which had punctured his spleen. It was a long operation lasting nine hours, during which time the ship was stopped to reduce its roll. While the doctor operated I had to help mopping out Peter's chest and stomach cavity, which were awash with blood. Then his heart stopped and the doctor massaged it until it started again, saving him from dying on the operating table. It seemed to take ages. Meanwhile, I was very much aware of being in charge of the numerous clips, scalpels and other instruments, passing them to the doctor when needed and counting them in and out.

'Is that everything?' he said when we finished. What a question! 'Yes,' I said hesitantly, hoping I hadn't got it wrong. I then nursed Peter for three weeks until an oil tanker came down to take him back to the UK.

Finally the end of the season came and I was glad when the last whale was killed and we were able to start our return voyage back to the rocky shores of South Georgia. In another month the southern winter would be starting and the iceberg-scattered seas through which we were sailing would freeze. By now I was missing the crags and the camaraderie of the climbing scene as well as the girls. Back home it would soon be spring and there were routes to be done. I had itchy fingers.

Back in South Georgia there had been some snowfall. I managed to snatch a day off to wander along the coast of the island to the Norwegian whaling base of Stromness a few miles away, which Shackleton had reached on foot over the mountains with five of his men, making the first crossing of the unmapped interior of South Georgia's terra incognita. His polar quest had come to an end when his ship, *Endurance*, was crushed by the pack ice in October 1915. They then struggled to reach Elephant Island with three small boats, after which Shackleton and five other men sailed in one of the open boats to the southern coast of South Georgia. From there, they crossed the mountains to raise a rescue, which sailed from the nearby whaling station of Grytviken. Shackleton was buried there in 1922, having died from a heart attack on his subsequent Antarctic venture.

Beyond Stromness, whalebones littered the beach and penguins waddled clumsily down the rocks to drop as though suicidal into the crashing waves, and then disappear like speeding torpedoes out to sea. Further along the beach, gigantic sea elephants lay idly in our path. We threaded our way somewhat nervously between them, at times only a few feet away. If we came too near any of the calves, the mother would raise her head to emit a horrible gurgling sound. Later that day, we passed a small sleek calf on its own by the water's edge; it stared at us timidly with large round eyes before sliding into the water leaving only a swirling eddy in its wake.

On the way back up the Atlantic I had a lot of spare time so one day I went down below decks to where there was a rope-making machine. With a bit of instruction I soon got the hang of it. I unlaid a thick piece of nylon rope then, using the machine, retwisted the threads into a thin cord, then cut it into shorter lengths for knotted slings to use as runners when climbing. Quite accidentally I had made the rope far too stiff, but I quickly discovered that this meant the slings could be formed into 'cheating sticks' with an open eye at the top end that could be looped over spikes of rock for runners that were otherwise out of reach. The slings could also be formed into U-bends, which would make threading chockstones much easier. I wasn't the only one that liked them when I got back home; I should have patented the idea!

A chance encounter fifty-five years later in the Shetlands led to me meeting Peter Gillies again – the injured lad whom I tended. It was great to see him and I was very pleased that he was still alive after my amateur nursing all those years ago.

9
KEEP ON ROCKIN'

I met Alan Baker soon after my whaling trip; he was living under the Cromlech boulders in the Llanberis Pass. Nowadays, it wouldn't be possible to sleep under an overhang just a few feet from a road and leave all your camping gear there while you went climbing. Primus stove, pans, food, sleeping bag and any other gear not needed at the crag could be safely left. I moved in with him and we climbed together for a few days – the start of a lifelong friendship. Al was responsible for seriously pushing my grades. Having done a few climbs together, he pointed me up my first Extreme, *Gryphon*, (now HVS 5b) on Carreg Wastad. Next was one of Peter Harding's Extremes, *Kaisergebirge Wall* on Clogwyn y Grochan, now also 5b. The following day Al suggested I have a go at *Spectre*, one of only two routes in Peter Harding's 'Bumper Fun Guide' to Llanberis and Clogwyn Du'r Arddu to have the grade of Exceptionally Severe. That really put me off and I found it hard and scary with not much protection at the crux. Al obviously thought I managed okay as the day after he pointed me up *Ivy Sepulchre*, which was the other Exceptionally Severe, also a Harding route. It was my first route on Dinas Cromlech, the most imposing cliff in the pass, and had an even scarier reputation than *Spectre*, being described as 'a very serious and difficult climb'. In fact, for mere mortals like me, routes first done by Peter Harding, Joe Brown and other top climbers carried fearsome reputations, which were always a psychological barrier. The description went on to say that 'the crux involves some loose rock, vegetation, overhangs, a fight with a holly tree and delicate wall climbing'; enough to put anyone off. These days it's cleaner and safer and goes at E1 5b.

If it weren't for Alan, I wouldn't have gone near it. It was all right for him, I was at the pointy end. He didn't tell me until afterwards that he had already tried it and had vivid memories of trying to avoid putting too much weight on two bendy pegs. It was in fact *all* the book claimed, but once started – like all climbs – it was just a matter of focusing on the next moves while ignoring what was to come and what protection there may or may not be down below. In fact, not having many runners was the norm in those days and with my Dovestones Quarry apprenticeship I was already familiar with loose rock and vegetation. And anyway, when you are in your teens, you're invincible. I was really chuffed when I topped out. Even more so when Al arrived with a big grin to tell me that Joe Brown – of whom I was in awe – was at the bottom and had been watching.

I had bought a 250cc Enfield motorbike with some of my whaling money, which made it easier to get away at weekends. It didn't last much more than a year though. I crashed it a couple of times with Viv on the back, once into a wall going up Langdale and once into a roadside cliff on the way back from Llanberis. When it eventually needed some serious repairs I decided to sell it, save some money and go back to hitching. It was safer. We hitched every-where. Even getting the thirty miles or so to Stanage Edge was a weekend trip with half the time spent hitch-hiking. When one of the lads bought an old short-wheelbase Land Rover a couple of years later, twenty-two of us crushed in with all our gear to get to Stanage. We were stopped halfway there, on the Snake Pass, by the police. 'I think there's a few too many in there,' one of them said, eyeing the wheel arches scraping on the tyres and trying not to smile. 'Let's have half a dozen of you out.' He sent the rest on their way with a warning to drive carefully.

Climbing most days couldn't last forever while I lived with my parents. My dad came home from work one day and passed me the local paper.

'There's an advert for a job in the pathology labs at Oldham Hospital,' he said. 'It might suit you.'

There was no getting out of it. My ward rounds included what was locally called 'The Bottom Block', where mentally disturbed patients were treated. One of the female patients there had a crush on me, one day managing to lock me in a padded cell, which was an interesting experience. I also had to do my stint in the morgue, helping with post mortems – a strange job, especially as it was usually just before dinner. One day I was asked to go to the neighbouring hospital a mile or so up the road to bring a leg. It was well wrapped up, but even so I got some strange looks on the bus.

After two years, and to my parents' dismay, I jacked it in. To save them the embarrassment of me being at home and not working I found a cottage to rent at ten bob a week up on the moor edge, and I moved out.

After a trip to the Alps with Paul I soon found myself penniless and took on a number of manual jobs. When I was out of work – which was often – I was out climbing most days, often 'accidentally' turning up at my mates' at meal times.

Barry Kershaw was still on the scene. He was a powerful lad and a hard climber with an aggressive reputation on and off rock. My parents thought he was a really nice lad, and he could be a good mate, but being in his company was always dodgy, particularly if he had drunk a few pints. In 1957 I soloed one of his new routes, *Double Overhangs*, in Den Lane Quarry, then led it blindfold for a bet not long after his first ascent. Although it was a strenuous VS with two big overhangs, the holds were good, so if you knew where they were it wasn't hard. Barry took it personally. The following day he arrived with a sledgehammer and knocked off a key hold and was rumoured to be looking for me.

In later years Barry sometimes worked as a steeplejack, climbing mates helping him out if he needed a hand. On one of the mill chimney demolition jobs he did, he hired two Rimmon lads, 'Aido' Garlick and Brian Roberts. Arriving at the site they asked how they would get up the chimney – Barry had pegged it to the top and there was a rope hanging down tied to a bosun's chair. 'Sit in that,' he said, walking off to his van. They thought he had gone to get something, but he started up the engine and drove off. A rope that had been lying on the ground came tight and before they could jump off they were zooming up the chimney.

On another occasion, I was coming back from Ben Nevis one winter with Jonah and Smiler when we decided to stop off in the Lakes. We arrived at Barry's caravan at Wall End Barn quite late. His wife Sylvia was in, but Barry was out. Not good news. Barry coming in late from the pub could only mean trouble. When he finally arrived he had obviously had a skinful and was itching to smack someone.

''Oward,' he said, 'let's have an arm wrestle.' This wasn't a good start.

'Sorry Barry,' I said, 'but we were just off to kip in the barn. We'll see you in the morning … '

But he wasn't having that, and grabbed my arm. Within seconds it was a full-on scrap and I did the worst thing possible: I bust his nose. Blood was pouring down his face. Not a good plan! Sylvia saved the day, screaming at us to 'Get out,' which we did, fast, scurrying off through the night into Ike's barn and up the ladder into the hayloft. It was full of sleeping climbers, who we fell over in the dark, before hiding deep in our sleeping bags in the furthest, darkest corner.

Back in the caravan we could hear shouting, then moments later the barn door burst open to be followed by Barry coming up the stairs muttering 'I'll kill the bastards'. We shrank into the hay and held our breath. Stumbling across sleeping bodies, he continued his growling mantra about killing us, but despite flinging various sleeping climbers about in his search in the dark, he failed to find us and finally fell back down the stairs, still mumbling death threats. A few minutes later, with the coast finally clear, we did a runner and were soon out of the valley.

The only person I knew that ever sorted out Barry was Sylvia. Many years after the above event, Sylvia and Barry's two daughters were working at Troll. One day Barry came in – we already knew from the local gossip that he was in trouble with Sylvia. She stormed across the room, grabbed a metal dustbin lid and beat him over the head with it, simultaneously kicking him out of the door. Tough girl, Sylvia! From then on, whenever he was home he kipped in their garden shed. He continued his rough and tumble life of climbing, steeplejacking and working on pylons, but sadly died of leukaemia at the early age of forty-seven in 1987. A short life, but packed full of action.

Scrapping seemed to be part and parcel of our early years. We rarely managed to hold club dinners in the same pub twice. Wasdale Head Inn was probably the only place that never bothered about the wild goings on – all the climbing clubs' dinners were the same. At one of our dinners in an Edale pub, Harpic Harold drove into and round the room on a powered lawnmower, saying he'd come all the way from Blackpool and didn't know how to stop it. That got us banned not only from the pub, but from the village.

Our local police seemed to think we were some kind of 'Hole in the Wall' gang up to no good. They turned up at my cottage one winter's day accusing us of a local burglary. 'Why us?' we asked, perplexed. 'There were climbing boot footprints in the snow,' one of them said. As we all had evidence we had been elsewhere the previous night they let the matter drop, but we weren't impressed.

On another occasion I was even stopped in the village by the local bobby who said, 'If I ever catch you on your own at night, I'll beat the shit out of you'. What for, I don't know. They obviously weren't used to a bunch of lads living in a moor-edge cottage, frequently out of work, on the dole and shabbily dressed. They seemed to think we were up to no good and knocked on our door more than once. They had no idea we were simply rock junkies living the good life. As a similar bunch of climbers that hung out in Llanberis in the 1970s and 1980s, new routing in the Deiniolen quarries and also on the dole were to say, we were 'paid by the queen to explore the crags'.

But there were no police or grumbling neighbours up at Chew House, which was up on the moors by Chew Reservoir and three miles from the village. One summer, Harry Mumford, the waterman up there, asked me if I would stay there for a week to look after his hens while he and his wife had a holiday. I jumped at the opportunity. Weather permitting, we would be cragging right through the week. The otherwise remote Laddow was only a mile away, with Rob's Rocks and the gloomy Wilderness Rocks almost on the doorstep. On rainy days and evenings it was party time. The house was soon in a real mess, but we had a big tidy up before they got back.

When I turned twenty-one I had been climbing on Scafell with Paul Seddon and a Lake District mate of his, Pete Routledge. We left the crag late and ran back to Langdale where I was plied with beer and bet that I couldn't drink twenty-one pints. Who could? Two was my limit. By the time I'd had eight I was well out of it. Apparently I was then treated to various shorts, each qualifying as two pints. It was a wild night, most of which I don't remember.

As I kept puking up, I was dumped in Ike's farmyard where two of the Rimmon girls, Viv Nichols and Di Barlow, took pity on me and managed to get me into my pit. I don't think I slept. Instead, I spent most of the night being sick. I was surrounded by it, and it stunk. In the morning I could see double. I had never had such a terrible headache. High above, two Gimmer Crags drifted in and out of focus. The lads went climbing, which made me feel even worse. Then Barry kicked me and said he had a new route to do, how about it? No chance. The girls brewed up and cooked up a pan of beans for me. By midday I felt vaguely better. At least there was only one Gimmer Crag now.

Barry was soon back and growling, 'C'mon 'Oward, I've got this new route to do up on Blake Rigg'. There was no escape. Barry meant business. Friend or not, headache or not, there was no arguing with Dobber Kershaw. He had already acquired a reputation as a fighter.

So off we went up to Blea Tarn and across to the crag where he pointed me up the first mossy pitch to the foot of what was obviously going to be a typically steep Kershaw offwidth. He grunted his way up it and I followed, feeling slightly better now I was up and climbing instead of feeling sorry for myself in my pit surrounded by spew.

I wasn't working and I wasn't on the dole either. I was also down to my last two bob, and with no food in the house I was hungry. I had reached starvation point. I could either spend my last money on fish and chips, or, plan B – buy some air rifle pellets and shoot some rabbits, which would supply more than one meal. So I bought a tin of .22 pellets and went up on the moor at dawn with Roy's air rifle. There were plenty of rabbits, but hitting a rabbit darting about in high heather needs a shotgun, not an air rifle. I eventually gave up my rabbit hunt and now, both penniless and starving, I went for a job. Getting work was easy in those days if you didn't care what you did, as there were still plenty of woollen mills in Saddleworth.

Working in a weaving shed wasn't much fun. The rattle of the looms and shuttles was so loud that people had to communicate by sign language. The air was full of dust that coated everything. Billy, one of the men I worked with, used to make his first brew on a Monday morning by half filling his mug with tea leaves and sugar before topping it up with boiling water. The result looked like tar. The tea leaves and any remaining sugar were left in afterwards ready for the next brew, which saved him washing up. It would last him all week, then he would empty it out and start afresh the next Monday.

The mill wasn't far from Den Lane Quarry, so having discovered that most people clocked out at five and overtime was optional, I used to stay on every Thursday then, when most people had gone, climb out over the wall, run up to the quarry, grab an hour or so bouldering and be back to clock out at seven getting two hours of overtime which was three hours' pay, then off to the pub where we met that night to discuss our weekend's climbing plans.

One weekend the Rimmon organised a 'Laddow Guidebook Day': half a dozen of us walking almost thirty miles, round all the crags in the guide and doing a VS on each. It made for a good day out and was a fitness tester in preparation for a trip to the Lofoten Islands. The girls had a major feast ready for us when we got back after twelve hours on the hills. We didn't see anyone that day despite climbing on every crag in the guide. When compared to Derbyshire's popular gritstone cliffs, the northern Peak's remote moor-edge crags and quarries were seldom visited.

The Manchester Grit club had done a disappearing act. They had discovered Derbyshire limestone. When we met them on Sunday nights at Greenfield's Pennine Jazz Club, Graham West would grin at us from behind his beard and, eyes twinkling, he would ask where we had been all weekend. He knew full well the answer would be 'On the grit'. This always seemed to amuse him and his reply would inevitably be that it was high time we changed over to limestone for some decent climbing. Like Gray West I was on the British Mountaineering Council (BMC) Peak Guidebook Committee that met in Matlock under the leadership of that doyen of the Peak, Eric Byne, so he knew we were working on the proposed guidebook to Saddleworth and Chew Valley. Gray and the Grit lads, on the other hand, had already finished their section of the guide covering Wilderness Rocks and had moved on to Peak limestone, which offered a wealth of undiscovered rock. His guidebook *Rock Climbs on the Mountain Limestone of Derbyshire* was published in 1961 and opened everyone's eyes to this new world of Peak District climbing and to the possibilities the overhanging limestone walls offered for aid climbing, at that time considered an essential technique for anyone planning to climb the big walls in the Dolomites.

Raven Tor epitomised this new climbing scene. In an article entitled 'Raven Tor' on the subject of gritstone versus limestone, commissioned for *Mountain Craft* in 1965, I wrote about Gray's route *Mecca*, saying, '*Mecca* was the culmination of three years' efforts and ranks among the finest of the artificial climbs … The situations on it are almost incomparable. It is a tribute to the foresight, determination and skill of Graham West who, along with Barry Roberts, completed the first ascent in February 1960'.

In 1960 I was in Arran and headed off with Paul for the *South Ridge Direct* of Rosa Pinnacle, which I had first seen on my trip with Frank and Olly. By ten we were well up on the ridge on beautiful rock that more than lived up to our expectations. Paul led the S-crack – a great pitch for gritstoners – which gave me the higher and overhanging Y-crack. Above that some easier but enjoyable climbing brought us to an overhang thirty metres below the top. By now it was raining so we sheltered beneath the roof and spent a pleasant though chilly half-hour eating sandwiches and peering out at the cloud-shredded peaks beyond.

Eventually, it eased off and we crept out only to find that the only point at which the route passed the overhang was also the funnel that collected all the water falling on the expanse of slabs above. Within minutes we were soaked to the skin, which rather defeated our half hour of sheltering below, but soon we were out on the top of the pinnacle with the summit of Cìr Mhòr itself only five minutes away. We had really enjoyed it, but the weather had broken and as we walked back glimpsing the gloomy black walls of our other objective, the unclimbed north-east face that I had first seen when I was there with my chemistry teacher, it was obvious that we would have to wait another year before we attempted it.

We returned next summer and had terrible weather, but we climbed Rosa Pinnacle again, five of us reaching the easy upper slabs below the final pinnacle, but only Paul and Brian Hodgkinson topping out. The rest of us had already had enough and scurried off for a hot brew. Towards the end of the second week when the others were leaving, Roy arrived on the island and he and I went off with a pocketful of food and our sack full of gear to Glen Sannox. We were both pretty much penniless but the woman in the cafe gave us a couple of cold pies and by evening we were up the glen and bivouacked beneath the dark shadow of the north-east face. It was a splendid sunset with the jagged peaks of the Witch's Step silhouetted against a blood-red sky, while in the darkness of the high corrie the dim shadows of deer moved softly about. With luck it seemed like the next day would be the one good day of the fortnight.

We awoke at about six in the morning with a bitter cold wind blustering down to the sea and the black ridge of Cioch na h-Oighe etched against the golden glow of the rising sun. In the wan light the north-east face looked cold and grim so we curled up in our pits till the wind eased and the sun was higher, providing a somewhat doubtful warmth. With our last excuse to lie in gone, we breakfasted on our pies and a remarkably refreshing can of cold vegetable soup before crossing over to the bottom of the face which now looked disturbingly uninviting, its base being undercut by a metre-and-a-half-wide line of overhangs.

With a little anxiety and one or two false starts we eventually found a way through. At last we were at grips with the crag, the day was fine and we were in good form. A quick layback on small holds and the overhang was passed;

the armour was pierced. Above, a thin crack snaked up to end in a black bulge at fifteen metres. A line of holds then led us out to the right, then fortunately another crack started but finished abruptly under a roof fifteen metres above. I banged a peg in for a belay and poised myself on a tuft of grass to bring Roy up. The situation already looked dodgy – left was obviously out, above was a roof and to the right was a ten-metre slab of steep, smooth rock.

Roy tried the roof first, passed it, declared the upper slab impossible and came carefully back down. Next, he inched out to the right on minute holds till, balanced precariously on the opposite edge, he cleared a crack of its vegetation and climbed up it making for a large ledge beneath another even larger overhang. Another peg went in, slid in this time as the crack was too wide, but anyhow it was secure for a downward pull. I followed gingerly across wondering just what I was supposed to be standing on, but at least it was good to reach a ledge. Apart from that we seemed to have crossed from the frying pan into the fire. I peered out to see a nasty expanse of bulging rock above and retreated. Roy went up, stepping out on to the wall and came back. I went for a look on the right, and after a long traverse could still find no possible break, so returned wondering how we would escape from the ledge.

Roy decided on another go and once more managed to step out on to the wall. This time he saw a small spike above to the left. After five minutes of cursing and cowboy tactics he lassoed it with some line, clipped in, and with the protection of the runner tiptoed up out of sight. He led on up a groove for the full forty-five metres of rope before being forced to stop and put in a peg belay. My turn next, up past the jams and out on to the wall then on past Roy following the steep grooves for another rope's length to another peg belay. At one point I nearly leapt off, as I pulled up on a piece of grass that hissed at me. I let go in a cold sweat wondering if a snake could possibly lurk in such a desperate place. I tried again and once more it hissed at me, so some peculiar bridging moves ensued, before I hurried on to the belay.

Above this Roy led on again and brought me up on to the left arête of a gully mentioned in the guidebook as 'the unclimbed Gully A'. We followed its left rib for 120 metres of enjoyable Severe climbing. On the left, the face up which we had come dropped down for 150 metres into Glen Sannox, while to our right was the thirty-metre vertical black wall of the gully that descended from a small col high on the ridge of the mountain. Once there, another ridge rose across the upper edge of the face for a further ninety metres of carefree climbing, bringing us to a small grassy knoll just beneath the main peak of Cìr Mhòr. It had been a great day with thirty metres of climbing. We rested contentedly in the sunshine. Beneath us was the huge dome of the crag, split by the cavernous Gully A. Beyond were the calm waters of the sea, shadowed by the setting sun. We likened it to a place made famous by Coleridge, and called the route *Xanadu*.

I sent the route information to the Scottish Mountaineering Club only to be told that some Scottish climbers had done the lower wall and the ridge up the side of the gully the week before. Only the summit ridge was new. In total there was 380 metres of climbing. We didn't doubt a route had been done on the lower wall, but we did doubt it was the same as ours. We had both done enough new routes to know one when we saw one, especially one climbed the week before. No grass had been removed, no holds cleaned, no belay pegs placed and removed, no sign of anyone. Neither Roy nor I were ever convinced it was the same climb. I later discovered a climb had been done somewhere on the cliff, three weeks previously. Not that it mattered, I had first seen the cliff six years before and had looked forward to climbing it ever since. Roy and I had one of our best mountain days together, exploring over 300 metres of rock, and there're not many routes of that length in the UK – new or not. We were more than happy with our mountain adventure; it's surprising what you can do on a pork pie and half a can of cold soup.

10
WINTER WANDERINGS

On our first trip to Ben Nevis we started on the usual easier routes, which weren't necessarily that easy using long wooden-shafted axes, hinged ten-point crampons and no ice screws. When the first screws came on the market, they were great for pulling wine corks, but useless for anything else. Descending *Number Four Gully* with Alan Waterhouse – a Rimmon regular – after our first day out, we had a mini-epic when Alan fell the full length of the gully. He was too shaken up and bruised to climb the next couple of days, so I went up alone climbing the *West Gully* on to *Tower Ridge*, then down the other side, across the corrie and up *Slingsby's Chimney* on to the North East Buttress and down the lower pitches of that.

The conditions were good, so the following day I thought I would go 'just for a look' at *Gardyloo Gully*. It's only grade III these days but quite steep, and back then it still had a bit of a reputation, finishing as it does right on the summit. For me, going 'just for a look' is really a euphemism for going 'to have a go'. Once at the bottom I decided it looked climbable, so I ate my chocolate bar for the day, as I didn't want to lob off with it uneaten.

The following winter, I met up with Paul, Smiler and Jeff – all Rimmon lads – in the Cairngorms and we walked up to Jean's Hut, at that time a draughty bothy in Coire Cas close to where the ski cabin and lift is these days. We had three days of mediocre weather but good snow and ice climbing in Coire an t-Sneachda. There were some old sheets of chipboard in the hut, and a large can of diesel. Nights were spent trying to survive the bitter cold by soaking pieces of the chipboard in diesel, heaping them in a big frying pan and burning them. Not the best of plans. All that we achieved was to fill the hut with black diesel fumes to such an extent that we were dying of asphyxiation and had to open the door, thereby defeating the object. We tried variations of this each night but to no avail. Our sleeping bags were so useless that we spent our nights not just in them but in all our clothes, still damp from climbing.

On the fourth day we decided to head for *Hell's Lum Gully*. The snow was perfect, so it was crampons all the way, crossing the high plateau in glorious sunshine with Loch Morlich shimmering in the sunlight and ahead of us the long valley of the Lairig Ghru, and eventually Glen Avon, with its frozen loch over 600 metres above sea level and the impressive cliffs of Creagan a'Choire Etchachan and the Shelter Stone Crag, its boulder bivouac visible below.

Paul takes up the story in the *Rimmon Journal* from where we had descended to in the upper reaches of the glen:

Jeff and Smiler chose a route up the left side of Hell's Lum, Tony and myself going for the gully and all hopefully meeting at the top afterwards. Its left wall was curtained with icicles ten feet long and a foot thick. The gully itself seemed to have good snow with a short vertical ice pitch at fifty feet and an overhanging one at about a hundred feet, and no doubt a cornice, but that was out of sight. Tony got the first pitch which went without a problem over the vertical ice, leaving the overhanging ice to me, but I passed it with a few cut holds and found a dodgy belay.

When we reached the final pitch, the weather was changing rapidly. Dark, heavy clouds were sweeping in alarmingly and our once quiet gully was whistling and roaring as the wind swirled over the top covering us in spindrift. We topped out over the cornice into a complete white-out with a blizzard sweeping across the plateau. Smiler and Jeff were waiting, so we set off immediately, all roped up in zero vis. It wasn't long before we realised we were lost, but Tony had the compass. Well he thought he had, but he hadn't, but he did have the map. We tried keeping on the level, contouring round to the east then north into Coire Raibert, which would lead us to the upper edge of Coire Cas. It seemed a good idea but was hopeless. Still roped up, we thought heading into the blizzard might solve the problem as it seemed to be coming from the right direction, but it changed so frequently we gave up on that idea too.

We were lost. Furthermore we hadn't left a note in Jean's Hut and weren't expected home for two or three days, so no hope of rescue even if we wanted rescuing which we definitely didn't. It was three o'clock when we left Hell's Lum and now already four thirty. It would soon be dark. We needed to get off the hill. After another hour of erratic wandering and with darkness gathering and snow still falling we reached the top of a steep scree descending into eerie gloom with the possibility of hidden cliffs beyond. Having abandoned thoughts of going down the ominous-looking screes we continued ahead into the snow-filled night arriving at an unexpected uphill slope. Deciding we had no option, we went up and after a couple of miles of wandering reached the top of another scree. It was now totally dark, but down seemed to be the only choice.

I don't think we will ever forget that long descent. Down and down, still roped up, first on scree then on snow and finally on rock, slipping, sliding and cursing. It seemed an eternity. Then suddenly the cloud lifted briefly, it had also stopped snowing and we saw we were approaching an easy slope into an unidentifiable glen. It wasn't at all familiar. We wondered about bivvying but decided against it as we were too cold and wet, particularly me and Smiler, as we had fallen into a stream. As we began the long trudge down the valley we wondered if it might be the Lairig Ghru, which cuts completely through the Cairngorms. Having no idea by now which way we were walking without compass or stars, we didn't know if it would take us to Braemar or Aviemore, but either way it would be a fifteen-mile walk. Thinking back along our probable wanderings we guessed we were heading north to Aviemore, but weren't really sure.

We hadn't even had any breakfast, as we didn't want to waste any time because it was such a lovely day and we wanted to get going. But it had turned into a nightmare journey, tripping and stumbling through deep heather in the dark. Eventually we spotted our first tree proving we were at least getting lower but the going was now even harder, picking our way blindly through a forest of gorse. Then, in the distance we saw the lights of a village. We had no idea which village but who cared, it meant we were going somewhere. After another hour or so we finally reached a path. To celebrate, we ate our only food for the day, my two Mars bars and some biscuits. By ten o'clock, seven or eight miles later, we reached a dirt track, leading us to a memorable crossing of an extremely rotten bridge and soon after that, a tarmac road that we recognised: it was the Aviemore to Glenmore road. At least we were at the right end of the valley!

We finally plodded down the main street and into the Aviemore Hotel. We were so knackered we hadn't even bothered to unrope. We had no money with us, but when we finally collapsed into large chairs in a warm room we were served with hot sweet tea and ham sandwiches. Luxury! It was midnight. An Austrian guide had the temerity to ask if we had been climbing, while some British soldiers who were in the Cairngorms on a winter training exercise asked us with big grins if we could give them a chorus of *Mammy*, as sung by Al Jolson in his blackface make-up. It was only when we saw ourselves in the mirror that we realised just how black our faces were from burning diesel-soaked chipboard! Meanwhile, as well as organising the food, the lady at reception had told the local policeman about us. He was a veritable Sir Galahad, driving us as far as he could up the snow-filled track towards Jean's Hut in his new Triumph Herald. By one thirty in the morning, about sixteen hours since we had started, we finally collapsed into our cold and soggy pits. We had done our climb and walked almost twenty miles, most of it in the dark and in awful conditions. It had been one of those days!

On another trip to the Ben, after a few days of climbing in bad weather the rest of the lads decided to take it easy for a day but I went out in the afternoon with Erg (Barry Taylor) who hadn't done much winter climbing previously. He also wrote about it in the *Rimmon Journal*, from which I include an abridged version:

We made our way to the Little Brenva Face with no intentions of doing any serious climbing. We didn't even have crampons with us. Curtains of mist swallowed up the hut as we picked our way in solitude over boulders and across patches of snow that were becoming heartbreakingly sludgy due to the fine drizzle. Although we could only see seventy feet or so in any direction we finally took a chance, how big a chance we didn't yet know, to go for the summit.

Tony led the first pitch and I followed over a small crevasse and up a reasonably hard bit of rock to reach a sloping ice-covered stance and belay on a peg hammered in between rock and ice. As Tony led on into the mist, I realised that the drizzle was not only making conditions desperate, but water was finding its way down my neck, up my sleeves and in through my cheap ex-army duvet which was soaking up water like a sponge. While following Tony up the next pitch and trying to pass an off-balance move on some rock, there was a deep rumbling sound above. A distant 'plane maybe? Or thunder? Then 'Oward shouted down, 'Avalanche! Hurry up Erg'. Luckily it passed us by and I reached the belay which was a sling that kept falling off a rock knob, and an axe stuck in snow like porridge. Tony went up again over snow and a blue ice bulge into which he hammered a couple of rock pegs that fell out immediately after he moved up. Avalanches were still coming down but he said the next belay was in a safer place.

It was, so we had our bit of food and some brandy. The mist was clearing, so we made for a ridge on the left, crossing a snow chute beneath dodgy-looking cornices that were now in sight above. We reached the ridge in two pitches, a harsh freezing wind hitting us as we climbed on to the edge, moving together on wind-crusted ice where crampons would have halved our time, a nerve-wracking experience. Up on the top, while 'Oward was looking for his compass, I was fascinated by the noise made by the frozen surface of my duvet rattling in the wind. Descending, we found *Number Three Gully*, but it looked bad, so we moved on to *Number Four* which provided a splendid glissade, a bit different to Alan's monster fall down it the other year. What a fabulous feeling, shooting down through the mist between the black walls of the gully. It had been a good day out after all. We discovered later that we had probably climbed *Slalom*, one of Ian Clough's routes.

11

NORWAY – ARCTIC ADVENTURES

In the summer of 1962, the Rimmon organised its first 'expedition', going up to the Lofoten and Vesterålen islands in Arctic Norway, which the Norwegian lads on the whaler had told me about. Nowadays it wouldn't merit the term 'expedition', but back then it was considered remote. Five of us went: Jonah, 'Harpic' Harold, Mick 'Chipperfield' and his invaluable large tent, Big Jim Cooper from the Manchester Grit, and me.

Following up my whaling conversations, I had discovered Per Prag's inspirational paperback series, *Rock Climbs in Lofoten, Norway*, which was published in 1953 and was later to become part of his 1963 book *Mountain Holidays in Norway*. It was filled with pointers to unclimbed walls and even mentioned numerous unclimbed peaks. This extract is typically inspirational: 'The scenery is truly magnificent – the giant peaks, glistening glaciers, remote mountain valleys, thundering waterfalls, peaceful lakes and blue fjords cutting deep into the mountain ranges … Although most peaks have been climbed there is certainly scope for further exploring … there are walls and ridges which will yield good sport, but which have never been climbed. The scope for new climbs of all standards of difficulty, particularly in Arctic Norway, is still considerable and several problems of a high order of difficulty remain.' Who could ignore that?! With minimal information to go on, it was to be a great trip – adventurous and fun.

Our main objective was Reka, described as 'the most impressive peak in Arctic Norway'. Having sailed from Newcastle to Bergen with little money, we jumped the coastal ferry for 1,000 miles from Bergen to the island of Langøy where we climbed a new route on its north-west face on our first day. Its upper pitches were climbed in a blizzard and were unseasonably covered in ice and snow. The worst midsummer weather for years continued, but undeterred we climbed more new routes on nearby peaks before sailing over to the island of Hinnøya. There we rowed up two lakes in a borrowed boat, and Harpic and I did an unforgettable ascent of a great-looking arête that turned out to be atrociously loose, once again topping out in a white-out.

Jonah and I then made our way to Austvågøy on a milk boat. Now in much better weather, we did a traverse of the peaks of Trakta, Store Trolltind and the three Trolltindmuren, completing it in twelve hours with two lads from the Swiss Alpine Club. Almost fifty years later, I was told that it was the first one-day traverse of the peaks, and many Norwegian climbers still consider Trakta among the most difficult mountains in Norway.

Be that as it may, Jonah and I were then penniless. Getting home became an adventure in itself, jumping ferries, working for food in hotels and cafes and being taken in and fed by farmers as we slowly hitched our way south. We made sure we passed through Romsdal to get a look at the notorious Troll Wall, Europe's biggest sheer rock wall – then still unclimbed. Unfortunately it was concealed in mist and rain, which should have been a warning. It didn't occur to me then that in three years I would be climbing it.

12

JOBS ON THE ROCKS

I got my first climbing job at Plas y Brenin as a 'voluntary' instructor just prior to the Cuban Missile Crisis. For a few days everyone thought the end of the world was nigh with both Khrushchev and Kennedy threatening nuclear Armageddon. When it didn't happen, it made waking up every day to that inspiring and much-photographed view up Dyffryn Mymbyr to the Snowdon horseshoe more beautiful than ever. Additionally, my living costs were covered and I got a bit of cash as well so I was more than happy – as were my parents, who were once again able to hold their heads high in the village, telling people I was a climbing instructor in Wales. John Jackson, 'Jacko' – a highly respected mountaineer who was on the expedition in which George Band and Joe Brown made the first ascent of Kangchenjunga – was the director, and Rowland Edwards was the senior instructor, from both of whom I learnt a lot.

Roy Brown was also guiding and instructing in Wales at the time, based at the Mountaineering Association hut above Llanberis with Eric 'Spider' Penman, a well-known UK climber. It seemed there was a career to be made in climbing after all. I had a great time there, climbing almost every day in Ogwen, the Pass or at Tremadog, often taking groups together with Rusty Baillie, another instructor. We usually managed to get the best of our groups up to VS standard by the end of each week. Rusty and I also climbed together on my home crags, adding another new route in Dovestones Quarry, a fine HVS 5a arête called *Unicorn Direct* described in the 1988 guide as 'the best route of its standard in this quarry'.

When I finally left Plas y Brenin, I got a lift back to Manchester with another instructor, Dougie Baines, on his 600cc Norton Dominator.

'Haven't you got a helmet?' someone asked, seeing us about to leave.

'No, why?' I replied, as it was fairly normal in those days.

'Well, good luck then,' he said, adding, 'no one ever rides without a helmet with Dougie!'

I soon discovered why. His plan was to do Plas y Brenin to Manchester in an hour, which is over eighty miles and that was on A roads. He had a brand-new fairing when we started. It was already scraping the road on our first bend out of Capel Curig. From then on I shut my eyes and hung on tight at the first sign of a bend or any traffic ahead of us. He took all the bends so fast that the bottom of both sides of the fairing had worn completely away when we cruised into the centre of Manchester. He didn't do it in an hour, but it wasn't far off. I wished it had been two. Never again!

Now back home, I discovered that Viv had, understandably enough, done a runner and was going out with a rugby player. I wasn't happy, but I wasn't going to argue. And anyway it wasn't long before I was away again, this time instructing at the Outward Bound school at Ashburton in Devon. On my first day I was told, 'You'll be helping out with a canoeing course today'.

When I met the lad in charge I said, 'I'm not sure I'll be much use; I've never been in a canoe'.

'Don't worry,' he said, 'just do what I do; you'll be OK.'

Which I was, but in future years, accidents and new health and safety regulations made that kind of thing impossible.

Ashburton was a great place to work, climbing at the Dewerstone and Chudleigh, and up on Dartmoor. Returning home after a month or so I soon moved on to instruct at Rhowniar, the Outward Bound girls' school at Tywyn. It was there that I met Bob Orrell who was chief instructor and became another lifelong friend. Jonah also came down, enjoying the instructing and climbing. While there we discovered Craig yr Aderyn (Birds' Rock) and climbed a number of new routes, some together with Alan Waterhouse and other Rimmon lads along with Jim Perrin, a teenager from Manchester we used to meet up with occasionally in Chew Valley and Wales.

Bob, Jonah, me and a friend of Bob's, Dick Blackmore – an ex Royal Navy chief petty officer – also did what we were told was the first canoe crossing of Cardigan Bay, a distance of about thirty miles as we took a slightly curved route so that we were never more than ten miles from shore. Though quite how that was presumed safer, I'm not sure. Although it was reasonably calm when we set out from Tywyn, by halfway a big swell was running. We were in double canoes and frequently lost sight of each other, hidden by the increasingly large waves. As Bob said later, 'Dick had just finished two years of boozing in Hong Kong and weighed eighteen stone. He damn near sank our canoe!'

By the time we were approaching Abersoch we were paddling straight into big seas and struggling to make headway. We finally made it on to the beach feeling very pleased with our day's efforts. So much so that next time we went climbing at Barmouth I borrowed a canoe and paddled the twelve miles there.

The winter of 1962–1963 was a bad winter. It was known as the Big Freeze and was one of the coldest winters on record. We had been climbing in Wales and arriving back in Greenfield in the evening we expected to see others from the Rimmon and Grit in the usual pub, but it was empty.

'They've all gone up Chew Valley to Wilderness Gully,' the landlord said. 'There's been an avalanche. Graham West and Mick Roberts were in it. Everybody's gone up digging.'

We were horrified. We couldn't believe it. No one had heard of avalanches up Chew before, and what a disaster that people were in it, especially Gray and Mick, the most respected climbers in the area. It was dark and snowing, but we set off immediately following what remained of a trail of deep foot-steps up the narrowing snow-filled valley alongside the river. When we arrived, the gorge beneath the gully was full of figures digging in the snow.

Gray and Mick had been high up the gully when the avalanche came down. Two other younger lads were lower down. One had explained they:

> were in pairs with Graham and Mick in front. Everyone had ice axes except me, but we weren't roped. The snow in the gully was deep, but it was packed hard and the footholds were good. We were well on the way up when I saw a block of snow coming down at us. Then I heard someone shout 'Avalanche' and the next moment the gully was full of snow rushing down. I got to one side of it, but one of the other lads got caught. I couldn't see anything at first, but then I saw him half buried and helped him out. There was no sign of the other two.

They hurried down the valley and gave the alarm.

The search was called off around midnight due to the terrible conditions. By then Gray and Mick had been buried for eleven hours. When Gray was eventually found around midday the next day, he was under three metres of snow high up on the opposite side of the narrow ravine of Chew Brook, carried up by the force of the avalanche. Mick was about fifteen yards away.

The Saddleworth-Chew guide was published in 1965; Eric Byne dedicated it to:

> the memory of our late climbing guidebook companions, Graham West and Michael Roberts, who were so tragically overwhelmed by an avalanche of alpine proportions which swept down the East Gully of Wilderness in the Chew Valley on January 20th 1963. Both were 'hard men' of considerable climbing and mountaineering ability and with a reputation of toughness and indestructibility that was almost legendary.

They were the first climbing deaths in our community. We were all at the funeral, but why them? They had been like gods to us lesser mortals. However, being young, our own invincibility returned.

Not long after the tragedy, I was in Dovestones Quarry with Cockney, climbing a new winter route in great conditions. Soon after that I returned with Erg and climbed *Waterfall Direct*. Its V-chimney was heavily verglassed and capped by three cornices giving a great winter climb. Erg on the other hand was fed up of getting showered in ice and snow and told me to get on with it, so I hung a sling on the peg, stuck in the front spikes of a crampon and stood up. It held. Eventually I was able to cut holds in the cornice, the sun by now shining across the quarry and brightening up the gloom. Finally I cut a groove though the lip, got my axe in beyond and tried to pull over, but I slipped back as a snow foothold broke. A second try with my crampons on the iced walls was more successful, bringing a good crack into reach for a peg belay. Erg soon followed, complaining about me sending snow down his neck. He lead through, over the second and third cornices and up the higher glistening snow slopes to the windswept moor edge where I joined him after four hours of superb winter climbing.

It was this year that Alan Waterhouse had started to make alloy wedges and hexagons in the engineering factory he worked at. And as we were getting into aid climbing in Derbyshire, I knocked up a three-inch-wide leather waist belt made out of belting used in the local woollen mills to drive the machinery. It was riveted together by one of our local cobblers, Cyril Hesden, and included a built in 'cow's tail' loop for clipping into pegs. It also had gear loops all round it, simplifying the carrying and sorting of gear.

Prior to the arrival of nuts and pegs, all we carried were a few slings round our necks, so gear racks suddenly became important – not just for carrying gear, but for keeping it sorted and easily accessible. It was also possible to attach a figure-of-eight leg-loop to the waist belt, for use as a sit-sling, making climbing under roofs easier, and more comfortable. This also improved both abseiling and aid climbing, and was a forerunner of sit-harnesses. Initially unknown to me, 'Tanky' Stokes – a well-known Sheffield climber – also started making waist belts in his cobbler's shop at about the same time, though his design was narrower and without most of the various extras. He was a member of the Alpha Club and one of the leading lights in the Peak, so it was interesting to see we were both thinking along the same lines.

In later years, following our ascent of the Troll Wall, a version of my waist belt (it never had a name) became the Troll Mark 2 belt. A few years later that became the basis for the Mark 5, which incorporated leg loops and had a belay loop at the front. And that became the template for just about every climbing sit-harness ever since.

Back in 1963, 'Troll' didn't exist. Initially we just made the nuts and belts for ourselves and any of our mates who wanted them. Bob and Ellis Brigham who owned our local climbing shop in Manchester got to hear about them and started selling them in 1964. It wasn't until after our Troll Wall climb the following year that we stamped 'Troll' on them, and they took off as a brand.

13

DOLOMITE DAYS

In 1963 we had a Rimmon meet in the Dolomites. I hitched out there with Cockney, staying a night in a posh Paris suburb with one of the Rimmon girls. She was working there as an au pair, and sneaked us in for the night as the family were away. We arrived at the Sella Pass after four days on the road. Not bad, but it was a long walk up the pass with our sacks stuffed with heavy camping and climbing gear.

We camped at the pass, climbing on the Sella Towers and on Sassolungo where we almost soloed the *Pichl Route* on the north face. Though not particularly hard at around 4b, its reputation as being one of the largest faces of the Alps had attracted us, but being long, soloing seemed sensible. Even so, despite starting in reasonable weather, the cracks and chimneys approaching the summit still had snow and ice in them so we roped up, arriving on the complex summit ridge in cloud, with sleet turning into snow.

We eventually found the summit shelter in the mist and bivvied there. It turned out to be a tin box, its floor covered in ice. We weren't surprised when we were told later that it was the first ascent of the *Pichl Route* that year. Having survived the night we failed to find the correct descent as we made our way down through the cloud, with nothing to be seen until we were just one rope length above the screes with the final wall overhanging all the way. Unable to find anything to abseil from and with no desire to go back up, we eventually found a minute hole through the rock just big enough to poke through a couple of separately knotted loops made from our nylon bootlaces to abseil off. I can't remember who went first!

We then moved over to the Catinaccio Group, camping by the river below the east face. The 600-metre east wall of the Central Catinaccio looked steep but friendly enough. It would be our first grade VI and the weather was good so we went the next day. Our optimism was ill-founded. Though the climbing was going well, the weather had crept in, rumbling occasionally in the distance and suddenly worsening as clouds enveloped the wall. Flashes of lightning accompanied by a clap of thunder and a truly alarming rockfall from directly above followed. In its aftermath we were now disturbed only by the hiss of windblown hail on the wall and the last trickle of falling stones. The air reeked with the acrid smell of scorched dust and blasted limestone. In the gloom of the swirling cloud, the silence was awesome.

I leaned out from the meagre shelter of the dripping bulge under which I had crouched. A pebble ricocheted off my helmet and into the dampness of space.

'Cockney,' I shouted anxiously. No answer. Again I yelled down into the mist, my gaze searching down the line of the ropes that passed through the pegs and disappeared in the haze. His reply was reassuring – he was OK – and I relaxed into the comfort of my hollow.

The storm had been gathering steadily for the past hour. Then we ourselves were in the drizzle of the mist and soon the first flash of blue dazzling lightning had hit the face – apparently below us – accompanied by a great crack of thunder. Cockney had jerked with the force of the electrical impulse passing through his body, while I was halfway up a pitch and clustered with buzzing ironmongery, unhappily aware of my situation. The second flash came as I reached a small ledge and I shook involuntarily with the force of the electricity as the air reverberated around me with the deafening roar of thunder. It was followed immediately by the nerve-wracking crash of tons of falling rock and I shrank under the poor security of the bulge in a desperate endeavour to mould myself into the rock and disappear under my helmet. The boulders crashed and fell in black whirling, screaming, whining masses only inches from my face; the air stank and dripped and I wondered how Cockney was faring on the ledge below.

He commented later in his inimitable style in the *Rimmon Journal* that:

Lightning began to flash about. 'Hurry up,' shouted 'Oward. Flash bang! The lightning just missed my foot. Woosh, I went up like the clappers not bothering to look for holds. Crash! The lightning struck again and a ton of rocks came past. 'Guess what, that makes the route fifty foot shorter,' said 'Oward in his usual amused tone.

Such was our introduction to grade-VI rock climbing in the Dolomites. It was two days before we were once again on rock, attempting our next one. Dark clouds still blanketed the Marmolada but above us in the blue of the sky there were only a few lazy white puffs of cloud. Arching up and out into them for 300 metres was bulge upon bulge of yellow dazzling rock that formed the sun-drenched east wall of the Northern Catinaccio. Wavering up into the yellow and blue of our upward horizon was a dotted line of steel – an iron road of pegs engineered three years before by Bepi De Francesch and Quinto Romanin.

We scrambled up to the base of the first vertical corner that was taken in one rope length of forty-five metres. There were pegs in every couple of metres, some of which were quite good and consequently removed by us to supplement our meagre supply, while the use of an etrier sped things up. Another shorter pitch and we were up on the ledge beneath the main out-ward-leaning mass of the wall: we were suitably impressed. The dotted line of golos picked its way upwards and outwards undeterred by the overhangs; even if we could not 'tear along it' we hoped we would be able to follow it.

Now using both etriers, I worked my way up clipping the ropes in every third or fourth golo to save on karabiners, and gradually became more and more detached from the rock and surrounded by space. Higher up many golos were missing and it was increasingly worrying to note that many of the in situ ones were only held in place by bits of rolled-up fag packets. The roofs were also becoming more pronounced at this point. Looking down from the lip, the screes were way, way below, while Cockney was tucked under the red blob of his crash hat dangling off the belay.

I peered over the bulge above me. Six metres higher, the line of golos led towards a hollow in the wall. Reaching it I was surprised to find myself still hanging free. In this illusory world the hollow was merely a depression in the overhanging wall. Having run out a full rope length I had no option but to belay, hanging happily over the void.

Cockney began to climb up, disappearing immediately from sight under the roof as the ropes slithered up to pass around my back and hang in ever-growing loops five metres or so out from the wall. Arriving at the belay he tied himself on and we sat there savouring our position, yet our only contact with the rock was a couple of rusty golos. It was definitely food for thought and should have been quite disturbing, but we dangled there as innocently uncaring as a couple of kids on the park swings.

Then I was away again up the golos, until after ten metres I passed two that were bent and twisted. I reached a blank bulge of rock where one was missing – presumably someone had fallen here. If so, I had no intention of repeating the performance and yet I could see no way of passing the blank space. Then I saw a minute hole hidden between a couple of rock crystals about a foot above the golo I was in: if I could get a peg in it, it might just do the trick. Fortunately one of them fitted and I was just able to hook a fifi into the next golo by holding it upright at arm's length, between finger and thumb.

Between there and the next belay point where there was a stance for one foot; there was only one golo missing so we were soon together again looking out across the wall where the line of golos ran out to the right and up to a commodious ledge. It was a delightful traverse, no longer the ceaseless striving upwards but now a series of pleasant little pendulums. It finished with ten metres of free climbing up to the ledge and away from the security of the fixed gear, which emphasised our exposed position above 250 metres of empty space.

With only one more pitch of serious climbing to go, we rested on the ledge and looked down and across to the Vajolet hut in the valley where a large crowd had gathered to stare up at our progress. It wouldn't be long before we would be down there for a meal, before heading off to our camp by the river. Meanwhile the last few golos beckoned to us from the fringe of the final roof, which we reached by another fifteen metres of free climbing; then once more that swing into space till the angle eased and suddenly we were up on the crest above the plunging depths of the wall; only a scramble to the summit remained.

While we were having fun in the Dolomites, Paul and Brian were in Romsdal, where they climbed various summits with Arne Randers Heen, Norway's elder statesman of climbing; already sixty but still running around the mountains. On their way up Store Trolltind they stopped to look down the Troll Wall from a scary ledge on its lip. The view from there to the valley 1,500 metres below is enough to put anyone off. Jonah and I had seen nothing of the wall when we passed through the year before due to rain and low clouds; this was the first view of this already notorious wall by anyone we knew. They said it looked unclimbable, but before returning home they did the third ascent and first British ascent of the formidable 1,500-metre east face of Kongen, itself a route with a reputation and some complex route finding. With only a four-sentence route description to go on, they had had a lot of scope for adventure.

Back in the Peak District, I was once more on the dole, checking routes in Chew for the proposed new guide. The lady at the dole office already knew me.

She said, 'Are you out of work again?'

To which I replied, 'Well, yes, but I'm still writing that climbing book for the British Mountaineering Council. They don't pay, but it will be good for Saddleworth when it's done. It'll only take a few weeks more.'

So, being a nice lady, she signed me on once more.

We also began climbing more in Derbyshire, often camping by the river at the entrance to Chee Dale. On Saturday nights we went off to the pub in various vehicles after climbing. One day, Smiler and I were last to leave the crag on his motorbike and sidecar. Somehow he managed to miss the first bend, dumping the bike and us in the river. The bike was totally submerged. Smiler being Smiler he never stopped grinning, and we both thought *no worries, they'll be back when they notice we haven't arrived at the pub*. But they weren't. *Good mates we have*, we thought, as we struggled the rest of the evening to get the bike back out of the river and up the banking. Just as we triumphantly got it up on to the path the others arrived back. It was after closing time.

'We wondered why you never turned up,' they said. 'The food was really good!'

Back in our tents, we got out of our wet gear and into our pits. One of the Rimmon girls, Maggie Woodcock, took sympathy on us, brewed up and stayed talking with me for a while. It seemed she was no longer going out with Jonah who she had just been up to the Lofoten Islands with. He was still away, whereabouts unknown. We discovered later that, having left Norway, he was hitching round Europe trying to find Cockney and me. Penniless, he finally got back home after scamming a ferry ticket off the British consul in Calais.

Soon after that Maggie and I started going out together … and it wasn't just because she had a scooter to get to Derbyshire on! I found it all very embarrassing as Jonah was a good mate of mine, but he philosophically shrugged his shoulders – he was never short of girlfriends.

14

MOROCCAN MOUNTAINS

Doug Scott, a member of the Nottingham Climbing Club, was – like us – very active in the Peak at this time and we had met occasionally on the crags. He had been out to Morocco in 1962 and told me about climbing Jebel Toubkal, North Africa's highest mountain in the High Atlas Mountains at 4,167 metres. It sounded like an unusual and interesting place so I mentioned it to Jonah, Erg and Joe Broadbent – another Rimmon lad – over a bottle of rum on Christmas Eve. We reckoned we could each raise our train fare to Algeciras plus about £40 each, which might last us six weeks. It did … almost. We left four weeks later, hitch-hiking to London before catching the train. From Algeciras we got the ferry to Tangiers, the Moroccan authorities checking our passports before we disembarked. They took a dislike to us.

'What are you going to Morocco for?' they asked.

'We are going to climb Jebel Toubkal,' we replied, thinking that would please them, but no.

'How much money you have?' they asked.

'Almost £40 each,' we replied. Not a lot, we knew, but about a month's pay, so not bad.

'You are not allowed in Morocco,' they said. No discussion was permitted. 'You have to go back to Spain.'

It seemed our trip was over before it had begun, but disembarking back in Spain, we spotted another sign: 'Ferries, Algeciras to Ceuta'. Ceuta is a Spanish enclave on Morocco's Mediterranean coast. *Maybe we can get in that way,* we thought, so we bought more tickets, our funds rapidly dwindling.

We got into Ceuta okay. It's part of Spain, so no problem there. All we had to do now was cross the border into Morocco. At the border checkpoint there was such a crush that our passports were stamped without a question.

We were in and back on our way to Tangiers. On arrival, the bus station was heaving with people, some in Western dress, others in djellabas, some carrying swords or knives. Even the odd one with an old musket. We were out of Europe and in Africa for the first time. It was a whole new and exciting world. The evening was spent (and that is the correct word) being conned in the back streets where we stayed in a dingy hotel.

On we went to Casablanca where we bought three watches from a street vendor for a couple of quid as nobody had one. They looked expensive but a few days later the hands fell off one. Soon after that, another stopped working, then the third was stolen. At the ancient walled city of Marrakesh we found a cheap doss near the big square, the Djemaa el-Fna, the thousand-year-old 'Place of the Dead' where executions once took place. There was nothing dead about it when we got there and, unlike today, no tourists either, just a chaos of colour and sound, bustling with snake charmers, performing monkeys, Berber dancers down from the Atlas Mountains, Gnaoua drummers, water sellers, storytellers, medicine men, acrobats, jugglers, even a donkey smoking a cigarette; food stalls too, heaped with vegetables, spices, delicious oranges and irresistible freshly made sugary doughnuts. It was a strange new world and we loved it.

Behind the square, the bazaar's warren of alleyways were a great place to get lost in, full of shops and food stalls with the snow-capped Atlas mountains forming a glorious sunlit backdrop against a lapis sky. We left next day, after buying a large plastic bottle of paraffin for our Primus stove. Well, we watched him fill it up and it smelt like paraffin. We were told the bus left at eight for the village of Asni at the foot of the High Atlas. We loaded our gear on to the roof and by quarter to eight were ready to go. Strangely no one else seemed interested, but by half-past ten the bus was finally full. The driver, having apparently run out of conversation and drunk his morning's quota of mint tea, decided he might as well set off as there was nothing else to do.

The road to Asni was narrow. On the right was a vertical rock wall, on the left steep scree plunged 150 metres into a gorge. The driver's foot was down all the way, he cut every corner, threatened any approaching car with immediate destruction and completely satisfied our thirst for adventure. We arrived at Asni exhausted and eager to travel at mule speed, but a local mule-skinner refused to budge for less than a fiver despite prolonged bargaining. When he did set off the mules just about ran all the way, and when we arrived twelve miles and 1,800 metres later at Aremd, the last Berber village, we pitched camp and collapsed.

In the morning we were greeted by the headman who asked us up for a mint tea and to watch the dances. We spent the day as guests of honour, squatting on hand-woven straw mats on the roof of his hut watching the veiled, gaudily dressed dancers and listening to the drums. Almost fifty years later I was up at Aremd again. When I mentioned our previous visit, I was remembered, and we were once again treated to a meal.

Now on our own, the next day was 'the big lift' which was not too bad until we reached the snow line just above 2,400 metres. On just one bowl of porridge each – which was all our budget allowed – you can't carry 100-pound packs very far through deep snow. Stopping at 2,700 metres we staggered down towards the river, flattened out the snow and put the tents up, hoping for a good night's kip away from the frenzied all-night drumming at the Berber village. Instead, I had a dose of dysentery and spewed inside my tent. It was cold (and I mean *cold*). With cheap sleeping bags you don't get much sleep: you lie and dream of festering in the sun the next day.

Tomorrow came, the ice melted rapidly off the tents and we were actually going out to climb. We had neither a decent map nor a guidebook, but we climbed both Angueline and Bouguinoussene in a day, though the snow was worse than useless except for the last few hundred metres above the 4,000-metre mark. Nevertheless, what rock there was gave enjoyable climbing at about VDiff standard.

After basking in the sun on the summit, which turned Barry's face into an unsightly scab, we leapt off the top with intentions of glissading back to the camp. Instead, having dug ourselves out of the slush, we stumbled, slid, fell and cursed our way back down the thousand or so metres to the tents, declared the day a success, stewed up, brewed up and kipped down.

Once again we suffered a night of sub-zero temperatures, during which Barry grew some cold sores. Jonah and I spent the next day in sun worship, while Barry became the proud owner of a sore throat. That evening we decided we would get up at 3 a.m. to climb Toubkal. Fortunately, although we woke at three precisely, the moon disappeared, and this being our only source of light, we went back to sleep and forced ourselves out at seven when the sun came up, instantly melting the ice off our tents again and making the world more tempting. By eight we were away. Surely the snow would still be good? Joe wisely fitted his gaiters, ingeniously made from his pull-over-sleeves, over his boots and we cramponed up with great expectations.

But not for long. The snow was awful. It was soon above our knees. Still, not to worry, by ten we had found a nice long rock ridge heading in the right direction. Unfortunately when we reached the top we were not quite on Toubkal. We weren't far out though, and once across an icy col, 240 metres of – dare I say it – perfect snow led us to the rock-strewn Nevis-type summit. We feasted on our Enerzade drink to celebrate and fell asleep in the sunshine. Barry's nose became a shining crimson blob.

On the way down I had great success in getting us all lost on steep snow above a large face, but Jonah eventually found an escape route into a fantastic gully. We shot down amid clouds of snow in a gripping glissade of around 150 metres. Then once more the process of stumbling, sliding, falling and cursing through a never-ending wet flour bag to the tents ensued.

We spent another night in chaos while Barry cultivated a magnificent cough, then another day in the sun. When we tried to light the Primus in the morning, it was empty, so we filled it with our paraffin from Marrakesh and tried again. It still wouldn't light. We tried again, still no luck. We poured some of the paraffin on to a piece of paper and tried to light that. It went out. It smelt like paraffin, but it obviously wasn't. The man in Marrakesh had sneakily filled the bottle with water and poured a drop of paraffin on top. So that was that. We had been conned.

With no good reason to stay, we left for the palm trees and beaches of the blue Atlantic and then headed off to Tafraout further south. It was on the edge of the Sahara so we looked forward to the warmth and sunshine after the sub-zero nights in our camp. Our road map also showed it was on the southern tip of the Anti-Atlas Mountains so we wondered if there might be some rock, which there was. Tafraout was surrounded by rock, but what drew our immediate attention was the cattle market that was taking place on the sandy street just ahead of us. Bony cattle were lined up by the side of an almost non-existent stream which oozed slowly across the dusty road, already thick and red with blood. One of the cows was just having its throat slit, blood pumping into the slimy water, into which the cow collapsed, legs kicking in its death throes, flies everywhere. It was then beaten with sticks until the blood stopped pumping, before it was skinned and butchered, the legs and head cut off while the other cattle looked on. The meat was weighed and sold on the spot. A lady who was standing next to us bought the brains.

'Where are you staying?' she asked with a French accent.

'Well, nowhere yet, we only just arrived,' we said, sensing she was going to make us an offer, which she did.

She was French, she said, an artist living there and painting the exotic scenery. We could have a room for free in her house if we liked. It was obviously an offer too good to refuse so we settled in and she brewed us some mint tea then rolled a big spliff of marijuana. Dope hadn't hit the Saddleworth scene, and we knew nothing about drugs. The only stories we had heard were bad ones. Still, nothing ventured, nothing gained. The joint was passed around a few times and she rolled another while we all smiled like idiots. Then she served up the raw cow's brain in olive oil. We kipped down early that night and had strange dreams.

The next day we went climbing on huge hot granite boulders and the escarpments that crossed the hillside. In the hills behind, bigger cliffs looked tempting but we were almost out of money so decided to head for home. We took the bus to Agadir and were offered a lift on a ship that was going to England, but the Moroccan port officials wouldn't stamp our passports and escorted us off the docks. It would have solved our money problems and been a great trip home, but with no choice we set off by bus to Ceuta. Barry changed what was almost his last money on the black market in a back street, showing the man a fiver. The man went into a nearby house, came out with some notes, counted them from one hand to the other while we watched and agreed it was correct. He then folded them up, gave them to Barry and took the fiver, disappearing immediately back into the house. Barry unfolded the outer note to reveal pieces of newspaper folded inside. Sneaky sleight of hand! We dashed into the house but it was empty.

Soon after we were sat in a side street, eating some bread and commiserating with Barry, when a lad of about our age appeared looking wild-eyed and agitated, bouncing around from one foot to the other and flashing a knife around.

'Money,' he demanded. 'Give money!'

We laughed, as we didn't really have any money worth giving, but that really wound him up, stabbing the air and jumping about like a maniac.

'Go away,' we said, '*allez*,' which made him even worse.

Jonah said, 'C'mon, let's 'ave him, he's spoiling my dinner'. So the four of us got up and he wisely did a runner.

When we reached Gibraltar we kipped in a grubby dosshouse, but at least we could have a shower. After that, we split up. I jumped a train to Madrid and another from there to Paris. The ticket inspector was constantly moving up the train but I managed to keep ahead of him. At the border everyone had to get out and walk through a barrier where two officials inspected both the ticket and the passport. It should have been impossible to get past but I waited until they seemed distracted by someone and simply mingled with the crowd. Not easy for someone in tatty clothes with a huge rucksack just back from a month in Africa to *mingle* among clean and well-dressed people, but to my surprise I did it! I had crossed the border! I was in France and back on the train to Paris ... but so was the inspector. Eventually I had nowhere to go. I was in the last carriage and he was headed my way.

The toilet was vacant so I went in, locked the door, filled the washbasin and stripped off. There was a knock on the door.

'*Billett s'il vous plaît.*'

I lathered myself in soap and made some splashing noises.

Another knock. 'Pardon,' I said, 'I'm washing,' but he wasn't deterred.

A key was inserted in the door and I could hear a crowd gathering in the corridor hoping to see me arrested for not paying. The door opened. And there I was, naked, having a body wash.

'*Pardon monsieur,*' the inspector said, shutting the door hurriedly to giggles from the ladies. And then he left, seemingly embarrassed, moving away along the corridor. I never saw him again all the way to Paris, whereupon I casually crossed on to a local platform, jumped on to a train going a short way out of the city, left it at the first opportunity, then hitched to Calais and home.

We had climbed Toubkal, our highest mountain to date, had some great experiences and learnt a lot about the world beyond Europe. We had also discovered Tafraout's climbing potential, both the giant granite boulders and big quartzite cliffs of nearby Jebel el Kest.

Many years later, Dennis Gray got in touch with me. He was going to Morocco; could I suggest any climbing areas? I pointed him at Tafraout and he liked it so much he went again with Ron Fawcett, doing some bouldering and taking some pictures for *High* magazine. That attracted others, resulting in a guidebook. It's now one of the best and most accessible climbing areas in North Africa.

15

NORWAY – THE TROLL WALL
AND OTHER ESCAPADES

One of the greatest ever achievements by British rock climbers.

Joe Brown

I was in the Dolomites again in 1964, first with Stan Wroe then with Erg. We got some good routes in, and Stan and I wondered about having a go at the Old Man of Hoy the following year as it was still unclimbed, though by Christmas I had a better idea: the unclimbed Troll Wall. I discussed it with John Amatt – a new member of the Rimmon. Soon after, I qualified as a BMC Peak District guide, taking clients on both trad and aid routes, but the Troll Wall was becoming an obsession. I hadn't been back to Norway since 1962, but John had been the previous year and knew about the wall's reputation, and Paul and Brian had been in Romsdal in 1963, though their comments that it looked unclimbable hadn't been encouraging.

I was also aware that it was known as 'the Vertical Mile', and was described as 'the largest overhanging wall in Europe'. It was reputed to be smooth and holdless for 1,500 metres, and impossible without the aid of bolts and bivouac hammocks. Enquiries soon revealed that it had been rejected by some of Britain's best climbers, and just to add the finishing touch, it faced north and was as far north as Denali in Alaska. Surely it was beyond our capabilities? But you never know until you go.

The Rimmon funded a recce trip for Smiler and me and we went up there that winter on the assumption that if there were any ledges on the wall they would be obvious in the snow – which they were. As were two obvious lines: one sneaking its way through overhangs near the centre of the wall to reach the summit from the bottom right; the other also trending left to reach a big ledge halfway up Arne Randers Heen's Trollryggen Pillar, then up the extreme left edge of the wall. They both looked climbable, but we fancied the one up the wall itself. All that was needed was to get a team together from the Rimmon. I didn't fancy John's idea of asking some 'big names' along. If climbing's about anything, it's about being out on the hill with your mates, and having a good time together – success or failure.

Meanwhile, Jack Longland, the BMC president, stuck his neck out by offering to act as patron, giving much-needed credibility to our efforts to attract sponsors. At least someone believed in us; everyone else thought we had no chance.

The news of our attempt was out in Norway before we even got there. Top Norwegian climber, Ralph Høibakk, commented in Norway's *Aftenposten* newspaper that there were many Norwegians interested in the wall, but he didn't think there would 'be two groups on the wall at the same time'. Anders Oppdal, one of Norway's top climbers, said he and Ralph 'had talked about it for a few years but had no plans'. He also said he was an opponent of prior publicity. I agree with him there, not my scene at all and never was, but the word was out. We had needed gear sponsorship as well as local information from Norway and it seemed Romsdal's best-known climber, Arne Randers Heen with whom I had been corresponding had unsurprisingly let the cat out of the bag. Even so, Anders said, 'I can guarantee that no Norwegian climbers will approach Trollveggen (the Troll Wall) before the English have either achieved the goal or given up,' but he hedged his bets by adding, 'there are possibly other Norwegian climbers who have more definite plans than us. When the English give it a try, it's quite possible that this could speed up plans on the Norwegian side.' He wasn't wrong!

Suffice it to say, it was the last and biggest of Europe's great north walls to be climbed, and despite everyone's doubts, we – a group of unknown climbers – did it, as did a team of four Norwegians who topped out a day before us via the other line we had seen on our recce. I wrote the full story of the climb immediately after the ascent then shelved it as everyone was making far too much fuss about it and I didn't like being in the limelight. Then, in 2011, when Dave Durkan, a friend of mine in the Norwegian Alpine Club, asked if I had anything unpublished on my Romsdal climbs in the 1960s, I remembered the manuscript and sent it to Ed Douglas to see if he thought it might be of interest. Ed recommended it to Vertebrate Publishing and they miraculously slotted it into their schedule. Doug Scott very kindly wrote the foreword and *Troll Wall: The untold story of the British first ascent of Europe's tallest rock face* was published that year. It received the Special Award at the Romsdal Mountain Festival in Norway followed by an invite to Trento in the foothills of the Dolomites where it received the Premier ITAS Award at their mountain festival, and to my surprise another award the next year, once again in Italy, in Tolmezzo.

It had indeed been a truly epic climb on which we almost died on our first attempt due to the atrocious weather, the exposed position of our second bivouac, and our eventual forced retreat through icy waterfalls – all in our totally inadequate 1960s bivouac gear and clothing. When we finally completed the ascent it was after five and a half days of perfect weather. We met the rest of our team and the Norwegian team as the skies were darkening for another onslaught of rain, snow and thunder that lasted for days. How lucky we were! It was reported in the Norwegian press that the Norwegian climbers thought our achievement put theirs in the shade, which was over-kind of them and far too modest.

Upon our success, one very well known British climber who was very familiar with Norway and who had provided information for us found it so incredible that he actually wrote to J.E.B. Wright, the editor of *Mountain Craft*, implying that we must have found a way to sneak up the back without being noticed! Wright gave me a chance to reply, but in the end the letter was never published. Conversely, Joe Brown said 'the ascent must rank as one of the greatest ever achievements by British rock climbers,' which blew me away, as did Aslak Aastorp's description of our route as 'a masterpiece of route finding at the highest free and aid standards of the day'. I felt his grade comments were over enthusiastic, but I liked the route finding bit, as finding what was acknowledged as the best natural line up the wall was something I was always pleased about.

Fifty years later in 2015 on the anniversary of the climb, Arne Larsen wrote in the Norwegian magazine *Klatring* about the leader of the Norwegian team, Leif-Norman Patterson. His article, which was later translated into English by Anders I. Ourom, says Leif 'was, by far, the most experienced of the four man team and … without Leif-Norman Patterson's initiative there probably wouldn't be a Norwegian Route on the Troll Wall, and the British team would not have had to share with others the honour of the first ascent of North Europe's highest and steepest mountain wall.'

This overlooks the undoubted ability and commitment of the rest of the team who, I'm sure, were quite capable of overcoming any obstacle met on their route even without the new American gear and Leif's undoubtedly inspirational leadership. None of us had expected the fame created fifty years ago by the press in their portrayal of *Climbers Compete on the Troll Wall*, so the fiftieth anniversary was a perfect opportunity for us to jointly dispel the myth, with members of both 1965 teams on stage. It never was a competition.

Back home after the climb, I thought I had better turn my scribbled diary into something more legible, so over the next couple of months I wrote the story and had it typed. During this time I was also lecturing on the climb and what with that and the articles that had been in the press nationwide, I was becoming increasingly well known and being recognised on the crags and in the pubs. It wasn't my scene, so I stuck the story away on a shelf and decided not to publish it.

The success of the climb also meant that the gear we had used was suddenly in demand, so Alan Waterhouse and I had orders for our alloy wedge nuts, as well as hexagons, waist belts and rolls of climbing tape (tape being another newcomer to the climbing market); we even got orders for bivvy tents, despite the fact that we had almost died of hypothermia and suffocation in ours. We put the name 'Troll' on the gear and we had a business. We spent ninety quid on a bench drill and other bits of engineering equipment necessary to make nuts, and set it up in my cottage bedroom. The waist belts were made in a local leatherworks and that was it. I wasn't getting rich – far from it – but I was working as and when I wanted, and climbing the rest of the time.

At the same time, Paul Seddon was also setting up a nice little sideline in climbing gear known as Parba. He was working for a greenhouse construction company and had access to aluminium bars, giving him the idea of making H-section chocks of various sizes. They were lightweight and two-directional, the largest fitting both two- and three-inch cracks. So, with our chocks ranging from less than a quarter inch up to one inch, and Paul's fitting even larger cracks, climbing would never be the same again.

Then two things happened almost simultaneously.

Maggie, with whom I had very much enjoyed the last three years, including our Troll Wall trip, decided our relationship was going nowhere. We remained friends, but shortly after, my mate Bob from the Outward

Bound school invited me to help crew a ketch he had been asked to skipper from Majorca back to England so I jumped at the chance. Life with Bob was always good value and I had never been yachting, so it would be a new experience.

While crossing the Med, with reports of 'severe gales' off Portugal and in the Bay of Biscay, Bob decided to take the shortcut via the Canal du Midi and the Canal de Garonne from Sète near Montpellier to Bordeaux, a distance of about 300 miles, then another fifty miles down the Gironde estuary to reach the Bay of Biscay. The sail across the Med was a real pleasure and the cruise through the canals was luxury. Shaded with plane trees and passing idyllic French countryside and medieval castellated cities such as Carcassonne, it was good to take turns on the locks to get a bit of exercise ready for meals of fresh food bought in the villages and washed down by local wines every day.

Once out into Biscay we met the bad weather and had a swift, but choppy, passage northwards under sail, Bob navigating us into the lovely harbour on Belle Île where we moored up. The next day he had a bad stomach and went to see a doctor. He couldn't speak much French and the doctor's English was no better, but he was given a prescription and went to the chemist. A young girl handed him a large box.

'What do I do with the medicine?' Bob asked, but she just blushed. 'Can anyone help me?'

Bob asked some other customers, who started giggling. Then an old man led him out of the shop. '*Monsieur,*' he said, with a grin, 'zee instructions are simple.'

Producing a pear-shaped tablet from the box, he bent over and left Bob in no doubt when he said, 'You stick zem up your ass.'

Sadly, Belle Île was as far as we got. With worsening weather heading our way, we were paid off with enough money to get us home.

Back home I kept myself busy making and selling Troll nuts and belts and, as we were selling rolls of tape to climbing shops, ready to be cut up and knotted into slings, I had the idea of making sewn slings in four-foot and eight-foot lengths which have now become the norm of 120 centimetres and 240 centimetres. They were less likely to tangle than knotted slings when carried over the shoulder, and were stronger – the knot being a weak point. Their lengths were the right size for me, but have become ubiquitous. When we tested the first trial slings on the test rig of a wire rope factory just down the road, either the sewing broke or the sling broke at the edge of the sewing at a similar strength to a knotted sling.

Next we designed a block of sewing that was so strong the tape broke over the karabiner, making it stronger than a knotted sling, which always broke at the knot. Despite this, very few people trusted the sewing and they weren't selling well. Then I hit on the idea of using two blocks of sewing placed close together, which was completely unnecessary but for some reason made them acceptable.

If the karabiner was placed round the area of double tape between the sewing blocks, the karabiner broke when tested. The sling remained intact. The test rig we were using had no safety screen and the first karabiner that we broke hurtled past close to my head, punched a bullet-sized hole in a pane of glass and dinted the wall on the far side of the next room where other people were working. It was quite a few years before Wild Country began to make tape slings with just one block of sewing, but by then sewn tape equipment was commonplace and accepted, and Troll too reverted to the same.

I was also still guiding and instructing in the Peak while completing the Rimmon guide to *Selected Climbs in the Romsdal and Isterdal Area of Central Norway*, which we had promised our Norwegian Troll Wall clothing and food sponsors. In it was our own Troll Wall info and that of the Norwegian team, plus other notes of theirs and info from Paul and Brian who had climbed there in 1963. The bulk of it was collated from other, older notes, in particular Per Prag's inspirational *Mountain Holidays in Norway* series. Arne Randers Heen was my mentor, vetting everything and adding his own notes on routes of his such as the superb *East Pillar* of Trollryggen, his famous grade VI that forms the almost 1,800-metre-long left edge of the Troll Wall and was climbed by Arne and Ralph Høibakk in 1958. Also *Fiva Route*, similarly long though easier at grade IV and just beyond the extreme right edge of the wall, first climbed by Arne and E. Heen back in 1931.

Tom Patey and friends had tried *Fiva* in winter without success, and three Scandinavians were killed on it in the winter of 1966. Following the publication of our Rimmon Club guide, UK pioneers Joe Brown and Geoff Birtles climbed it in eleven hours (the guide said eight to twelve, which were Arne Randers Heen's figures). When I finally got round to climbing it in 1968 we did it in about ten hours, benefiting considerably from our knowledge of the area. If Arne did it in eight, he was a fast mover!

I mention this as the brevity of the original four-sentence description of the route in the Rimmon guide almost led to another disaster when British climber Gordon Stainforth and his twin brother chose it for their first big wall climb and had an epic on it. I'm happy to say that following our ascent the route description in my 1970 guide doubled in length. Remarkably that book continues to sell to this day despite having had almost no updates other than excellent photos contributed for the latest edition by my Romsdal friends.

16

LIFE ON THE OCEAN WAVE

*… going to the right place, at the right time, with
the right people is all that really matters …*

Colin Kirkus

In the autumn of 1966, Rob and I flew out to Reykjavik with three other Rimmon lads, Jeff Heath (one of the Troll Wall team), Wayne Garside and Rex Fleming. An English girl who was on the flight worked at the British Embassy and found us a place to doss for the first night; then, as we were all more or less penniless, we signed in at the Salvation Army hostel the next day.

A few days later the *Jon Thorlakson*, the trawler that Rob had been working on with Rimmon lad Bruce Mills the previous winter, came into the harbour. As usual the crew had taken their pay, signed off and mostly headed for the nearest bars. The skipper, who remembered Rob, signed the five of us on.

We sailed a couple of days later. Other than the skipper and first mate, the rest of the crew including the ship's cook were drunk and in their bunks, but the cook had thrown a bucketful of sheep's heads into a cauldron, clamped it tight on the stove and left it on slow cook. That was our food for the first couple of days and it was simmering away nicely. In fact the food wasn't bad: lots of fish of course, and always plenty to eat, but it didn't suit Wayne who was constipated for the first two weeks at sea. Then one day he was late for 'Heave up' – the call to bring the nets in. He had gone to the loo. Not a nice place – to be avoided or visited only in extremis, which Wayne was finally doing. When he eventually emerged with a beaming smile, the skipper gave him a triumphal blast on the ship's horn that exceeded even Wayne's own rectal explosion.

The *Jon Thorlakson* was named after an Icelandic poet, but was called

The Submarine by Rob as in bad weather he said it spent much of its time underwater. He wasn't wrong. Working on deck up for'ard, we were frequently thigh deep in the sea, having been warned by whoever was up on the bridge shouting 'Wave!' – which meant grab something and hold tight, or be sucked through the scuppers and out to sea. Fishing was carried out up to – and sometimes including – gale force eight conditions. In the worst weather, the sea used to come rushing down the ship's decks and woe betide you if you weren't hanging on. It sometimes even burst into the mess, filling it almost to tabletop level so that you were sure the ship was going down, then just as suddenly, it rushed out as the ship heaved herself up again. Meanwhile, plates, cutlery and food were all over the place, but nothing flustered the Icelandic crew; it was all in a day's work. Rob and Bruce had even fished in a 'severe gale,' force nine. And to make matters worse, in sub-zero conditions the decks and rigging could become festooned in ice, making the ship top heavy and threatening a rollover in big seas.

Regardless of conditions, the work was always hard and the hours were long: six hours on, six hours off, two shifts a day, though compared to an English trawler it was 'easy street'. The daily working hours of Icelandic crews were limited by law, hence the need for two watches, whereas the English boats had only half the crew and sometimes worked around the clock if the fish were there to be had. Additionally their reward was pitiful and a fraction of what an Icelandic crew could expect on sale of the catch. The English profit was weighted massively towards the trawler's owners, but in Iceland, reflecting the prevailing communist political ethos of those times, the crew's divvy was far more equal, the skipper not getting that much more than the humble 'deckie'. So on board the *Jon Thorlakson*, we were among the lucky ones.

Still, it wasn't easy. Meals were eaten in the six hours off, so there wasn't much chance of getting a good kip, particularly in rough weather. The deckhand's bunks were in the bows, which rolled and rose and fell massively. Sometimes in the darkness you had the feeling the ship had gone so far underwater it would never rise again, until rise it did, shuddering and shaking itself like a wet dog as it emerged from the sea. It was on days like that that the sea could come rushing into the mess as we were having a meal, as always making me think the ship was going down.

Trawling off south-east Iceland as we sometimes did, the night sky was lit by the glow of the new volcanic island of Surtsey, which had erupted on the sea bed from between the North Atlantic tectonic plates in 1963 and had now risen above the surface, belching ash and steam into the skies. Off shift, and once in our bunks, the only way to sleep securely was to jam one foot against the footboard, wedging the other leg sideways, knee to toe across it, with one hand against the headboard and the other forearm jammed between bunk and roof. That way you were wedged in and somehow slept if you were lucky, until someone entered the cabin, oilskins dripping wet, shouting 'Heave up!' This meant they were going off shift but the nets were coming in, so it was up and out on to rain- or snow-lashed decks and no lingering.

On one heave-up, the net burst in the sea, threatening the loss of the catch after hours of trawling. One of the Icelandic crew climbed down the cable on to the net, mending it while thigh deep in the sea, which was rising and falling and threatening to sweep him off to certain death at any moment. Like the rest of the Icelandic crew, he had Viking blood and was seemingly oblivious to the danger, as was the guy who unceremoniously pushed me out of the way when I couldn't chain the 'back gate' to the ship. These 'gates', which are made of huge timbers bound in steel, keep the net mouth open when trawling. They are tremendously heavy but as they are hauled up someone has to pass a large chain through a steel eye in the gate. I was back-gate man. In big seas, it can be lethal. Twice I missed my opportunity before being pushed away as another deckhand leant out over the sea, passed the chain through and hooked it fast as the gate swung back. Had he taken a second longer, he would have been crushed.

We sold our first catch in Bremerhaven, in Germany, whereupon everyone except us and the skipper got drunk on the bonus, leaving us to take the ship back out to sea. We had better things to do with our money. By mid December, after another trip, we had enough cash in our pockets to move on. Wayne and I got a job on a Danish cargo boat sailing out of Reykjavik to Denmark and on to England, which was perfect; it got us home while earning money. While it was being loaded with fishmeal we watched the sea slowly rise above the Plimsoll line. I had always thought that ships sank at that point, but it didn't. When they finally stopped loading, it was so low in the water that its well deck was covered. Though still in the harbour we needed our sea boots on to get from the bridge to the bows and to batten the hatches down to make the ship watertight!

There were only five of us on board: the skipper, the mate, the cook and us. Out at sea, the weather was atrocious. The North Sea is notorious for its steep breaking waves. On watch, taking my turn at the wheel with the skipper while the others slept, there was a severe storm – force eleven. The unwelcoming cliffs of the Norwegian coast were occasionally visible not far away. There was no definition between the sea and the sky. Spray was everywhere. Waves were breaking over the bows and slamming against the bridge, threatening to smash the windows. The ship was virtually underwater. It looked wild to me, but the skipper looked unconcerned. *So why should I worry?* I thought, trying to be optimistic.

But then the steering broke. I had been steering into the storm, but suddenly the wheel was spinning loosely in my hands. The ship was impossible to steer. We would soon either be rolled or pushed sideways towards the cliffs. It needed no words from me. The skipper took one look and vanished down to the engine room as the boat started swinging sideways across the waves.

'Hold the wheel. I fix it,' he said, as he dashed down the ladder.

Minutes later his head popped up. 'OK?' he asked. It wasn't.

He vanished again and reappeared almost immediately. Still no good. We were now being pushed in towards the cliffs. Down he went again. Then I felt the pressure of the sea on the wheel. We were back in business. The skipper's head appeared through the hatch. Now he looked really worried.

'OK now?' he asked, urgently.

'OK,' I grinned.

Wayne and the others slept through it.

We had planned to leave the ship on arrival in England, but the skipper told us his next port of call would be Norway and he was short of crew so as the pay was good we decided to stay with him then sign off in Norway. With a couple of days to spare in the UK we went home, collected our climbing gear and set off across the North Sea. Suddenly, and unexpectedly, we had a plan.

17
NORWAY – THE ROMSDAL YEARS

*You don't have to be a fantastic hero to do certain things – to compete.
You can be just an ordinary chap, sufficiently motivated.*
Sir Edmund Hillary

We ended up in Oslo at Christmas hoping to find a party, but it was dead, until we met a long-haired hippie who asked us back to his pad. He put some good music on, opened a whisky bottle and rustled up some food, commiserating with us, and telling us that Oslo was a ghost town over Christmas.

'Nothing happening, man, but we can have our own party.'

He was a member of the Public Enemies, a leading Oslo R&B band that had recently been voted the most popular band in Norway. I don't know how many whisky bottles he opened that night, but it didn't do me any good. I spent most of the next morning being sick.

We then called in to see Jon Teigland – one of the Norwegian Troll Wall team – who put us up for a few nights. The temperature was way below zero but he slept with his windows wide open 'for training'. His bed must have been warmer than our sleeping bags – we were freezing. Or more likely he was just tougher. One day we went to do a winter climb that Jon had had his eye on, but with the permanent sub-zero temperatures the snow had never consolidated, so after stumbling around in birch woods, waist deep in powder snow, we eventually gave up. We never even saw the crag.

Later that year we made an attempt on a direct route up the 450-metre north face of Blåstolen in Romsdal with him, but again had no success.

We left Jon's and arrived in Åndalsnes in time for the New Year celebrations with Arne Randers Heen. Odd Meringdal, the tourism director for the area, fixed us up with accommodation in a flat above the house of the family who ran the youth hostel in the neighbouring village of Veblungsnes. And very helpful they were too, though they didn't know what they had let themselves in for. For that matter, neither did we. More and more friends arrived and squashed into the room. Rob arrived first, then Bill Tweedale, soon followed by two more Rimmon lads, Tony Martin and Jim Rothwell, armed with a very welcome wooden crate of tea. It wasn't long before others turned up, including Cockney and my old mate Roy Brown from the Manchester Grit. True to form, Roy knocked a cabin up for himself in the woods further up the valley. None of us had any particular plans but we were destined to have some great times there both on and off the rock.

Romsdal is Norway's answer to Yosemite, though rarely so hot and with considerably less reliable weather, being only about 400 miles from the Arctic Circle. I was in my element: having grown up in Chew Valley, I had developed a lifelong taste for new routes. As Doug Scott wrote about his own early new climbs – also done in the late 1950s and early 1960s – in the first part of his autobiography, *Up and About*:

> They weren't the hardest routes in the Peak District but we had good fun and always climbed from ground up, without practising them first. Although many of these routes seemed piddling little climbs they were new and therefore intrinsically more significant than climbing something old; pioneering is naturally at the essence of rock climbing and mountaineering.

With a bit of self-belief the world was full of potential climbing adventures; you didn't need to be an ace climber. Now here I was with my mates surrounded by a seemingly infinite supply of unclimbed cliffs, anything from 100 metres to over 1,500. When we had topped out on the Troll Wall I had lain in the sun and wondered what I would do next. Now, I knew.

Rob, Wayne and I had a decent stash of money off the trawlers, but to keep it coming in we did odd jobs for anyone, including building log cabins, tree felling, gardening for the owner of the Grand Hotel and unloading ships in the fjord. Once, we were hired to dig out a souvenir shop that had been avalanched at the head of the Trollstigen pass. We were kept on as additional staff as an American cruise ship was coming. The passengers hadn't a clue about money and not only assumed the krone prices were dollar prices, but having been on a North Sea cruise they also had pockets full of francs, Deutschmarks and Danish kroner, which they poured on to the desk saying,

'Is that enough?' We didn't know either but it looked more than enough so on the shopkeeper's suggestion we accepted it anyway.

Having been lent a canoe, Rob and I once canoed across the fjord, humped sacks of cement down a ship's gangplank all day and canoed back again. We canoed across again soon after and scrambled up through the woods to a cliff we had seen, climbing a couple of routes there. Six of us – Roy, Bill, Rob, Wayne, Cockney and me – formed the Romsdal Corps of Guides. Roy had been a Mountaineering Association guide and instructor and I had my own guiding and instructing experience and BMC qualification. Romsdalshorn, Bispen and the Trolltindan summits, with the awesome view down the Troll Wall from the Bruraskaret gap, were the most popular climbs. The only other person guiding in the area was Arne Randers Heen. None of us ever had any accidents, though I once saw Arne, who was then in his sixties but still extremely fit and knew the mountains better than anyone, guiding four clients down off the very exposed summit of Romsdalshorn, all moving together. Arne was behind with two ropes in each hand, one to each client!

That year was a bumper year for new climbs, starting in the winter and lasting all the way through to October. Winter snows were not only on the hills until spring, but all the way down to the valley and in irresistibly good condition. So much so that one day I cramponed up right from our front door on to Setnesfjellet's north-east ridge. Halfway up, where the ridge steepened slightly and narrowed, I broke through the frozen crust and was caught in a windslab avalanche, luckily stopping myself before I was swept down the face. Changing plan, I contoured out on to the steeper east ridge, summiting on a spectacular blue-sky day and making it back down without problem.

Following our canoeing and climbing day and with snow still low on the mountains, Rob and I next found a nice, if somewhat icy, 450-metre VS to the summit of Nesaksla, just above Åndalsnes. Then, a little further up the valley, and above a large boulder popular with climbers, we found Mjølva cliff, 400 metres high and studded by large pines rising from good, conveniently spaced ledges. It had no routes on it but it was below the snow line and caught the sun with the snows of Setnesfjellet gleaming white across the valley. It was a fun place to climb, exploring multi-pitch routes and it had easy abseil descents from the trees.

Further up Romsdal a more serious objective also caught our attention. Not far from the dominant truncated rock tower of Romsdalshornet, the 1,000-metre west face of the less conspicuous peak of Holstind rises directly from the valley. Most of the snow had gone from the wall and the temptation was too much for Bill and me. Much of it turned out to be relatively easy, though it had its moments including an HVS crux and an exposed yet enjoyable icy traverse high on the wall. We climbed it in just over ten hours, topping out before dark to bivouac in Vengedalen, below Romsdalshorn.

By this time the walls of the Trolltindan massif that rise out of the bitter cold of Romsdal's sunless midwinter depths were thawing out. They offered three miles of mostly unclimbed rock rising from close to sea level, to around 1,700 metres.

Wayne and I made an early visit and a bad choice, finding frighteningly loose rock in the lower half of our chosen route which didn't please Wayne as he was belayed directly below me on the worst pitch, but we were rewarded by a fast finish up 300 metres of excellent snow and ice, glistening in the afternoon sun. More importantly we saw some immaculately clean glaciated bulging slabs over to our right. I went back with Rob, finding a brilliant little route up the south-east spur of Norafjellet, beyond the north end of the Trolltindan peaks. I say 'little', but it involved 600 metres of climbing, but we were becoming so used to big routes that anything around 500 or 600 metres felt small. The crux was 100 metres of perfect, bald, bulging rock, polished smooth and round by the glaciers of the last ice age.

After a false start we found a way up the centre by what had initially seemed an unlikely line. Some pegs in a hairline crack got us started, followed by some delightful tension traverses across hopeles-looking bulges, then up and back by an unexpected but perfectly placed little ledge to reach the exit groove. We were to find more of these features on our other rock explorations, seemingly impossible at first sight, but always passable with a bit of cunning.

We were of course also climbing the classics, initially just for our own pleasure. Routes like the North Wall of Romsdalshorn, an excellent 300-metre grade III (Severe) climb with huge exposure, starting almost vertically above the valley floor, an alarming 1,000 metres below. Or the similarly enjoyable and exposed 300-metre grade III east ridge of Bispen. Plus the classic traverse of the highest Trolltindan peak: Store Trolltind, at 1,788 metres, which crosses the gap of Bruraskaret with its instant and awesome view down the overhanging Troll Wall to the Rauma river 1,500 metres below. Increasingly we were being asked to guide visiting climbers, so together with our search for new routes and doing odd jobs in the village we were kept busy.

The valley was also becoming busy with visiting climbers, not just from Norway, but from the UK and around Europe. The Rimmon Club's little guidebook that we had promised our Troll Wall Norwegian sponsors was paying off. Joe Brown and Tom Patey arrived, adding their own new climbs both in the Trolltindan massif and further afield in neighbouring Eikesdal where they made the first ascent of the superb west face of Goksøyra via the 1,500 metre grade VI north-west rib. A steady stream of UK climbers, notably Jim Duff, Tony Wilmott, Ed Ward-Drummond, Ben Campbell-Kelly, Geoff Birtles and Doug Scott, also turned up in the valley in the late 1960s, climbing our Troll Wall route and making their own new routes. Pete Livesey and John Stanger had grabbed the second ascent of our *Rimmon Route*, climbing it in 1967 in just two and a half days now the pegs were in place.

I'm pleased to say the third ascent was by two Rimmon lads: John 'Fred' Finnigan and, very deservedly, Rob, who had been a key member of our support team when he helped to get our gear up to the first bivvy in 1965 and off again afterwards, despite awful weather.

Fred wrote about their ascent, saying:

> Our first go was a disaster starting with stumbling through the forest below the scree slope with Rex helping carry some gear. At one point he fell down a hole leaving his glasses dangling on a branch six feet above him. Then we made a continuous push which saw us trapped just as it went dark on the little ledge at the end of the left traverse that finishes the Great Wall. Our packs were dangling 150 feet below at the end of the sack-hauling line with all our gear in them but as we tried to pull them up they jammed under overhangs. Then it started to rain, then to sleet. I recall a very miserable few hours waiting for the light, wondering how the hell we could reverse the Great Wall if we had to.
>
> Surprisingly, we were racked by thirst as most of the water was falling metres out in space; thankfully, or we would have been soaked. In the morning, Rob did a 120-foot free rap and jumared up as I hauled the sacs so he could guide them around the overhangs. We carried on another pitch but we could see the Exit Cracks above

the Narrow Slab had turned into waterfalls so we headed down. We had spent over forty hours with a few hours falling on to slings on the bivvy ledge as our legs cramped up. When we went back two weeks later we made a leisurely approach in the light, bivouacked in the good 'first bivvy' above the first steep pitch then again above the Exit Cracks and topped out around 5 p.m. It was a doddle compared to the first time.

A French team was also on the wall that year, climbing a direct route over twenty-one days placing 600 pegs and fixing 800 metres of rope, in so doing bringing even more international attention to the area which, until 1965, had been almost ignored outside of Norway other than by Slingsby and his companions in the 1880s.

In fact, 1967 was a busy year in Romsdal. Perhaps its busiest ever. Not content with his Troll Wall ascent, John Stanger then went on to make the first ascent of the formidable 1,200-metre South Wall of Mongejura over a period of three days with Brian Thompson and Dave Walsh. The same trio together with Jon Teigland also grabbed one of the area's last great problems: the East Face Direct on Kongen – which has an impressive twenty-one-metre roof two thirds of the way up the 1,400-metre face.

Rob, Wayne, Bill and I had tried it earlier in the year with Wayne manfully jumaring the lower half of the route; a huge expanse of glaciated slabs swept ever more steeply up from the birch-forested floor of Isterdalen. It was a long haul up to a good bivvy ledge with all our aid gear for the big roof plus bivvy gear and food for three days, but Wayne, priding himself in his strength, offered to hump all the gear, so none of us objected. The weather was warm and it was good the next day too – maybe too good.

We had barely climbed a couple of pitches in the early morning when water started to drip on us from the big roof. It wasn't raining. The winter snows up on the summit were melting in the morning sun. The decision on whether or not or not to continue was resolved when the drips rapidly became an icy cascade. We had no choice; we abseiled off as fast as we could and retreated to our bivvy – fortunately just outside the waterfall – to dry out and to follow Roy's dictum, 'When in doubt, brew up'.

As our proposed line over the big roof was now out of the question, we opted to exit up left, finding another good bivouac site a few hundred metres higher, below a huge diedre in the south-east face. It was now possible to escape the mountain with ease by heading for the low col between Kongen and its neighbour, Bispen. This option rather spoilt the integrity of the route, but the big yellow diedre above us looked impressive and would take us back on to the east face above the overhangs, so we continued up it the next day despite the weather having clouded in rather ominously. It wasn't easy but it was good climbing on steep and sometimes interestingly loose rock. As we gained height we met the lowering clouds and by the time we had finished the final overhanging chimney on to the east face it was snowing heavily. We bivouacked and hoped for better weather, but it worsened in the night. Now cold and wet we climbed on and up into the mist, snow and increasingly strong winds, simply heading for the top and wondering if we would be able to find the way down through what was now a blizzard; none of us had been on the summit previously and visibility was virtually zero.

We needn't have worried. We knew we had reached the top as the terrain suddenly levelled out, but we were surprised and happy to hear voices and see our good friend Halvor Sødahl appear from the mist together with Herbert Grüner, one of Romsdal's great mountain pioneers, and his son Torleif.

Despite the atrocious weather, Halvor dutifully took the requisite summit photos before we thankfully and blindly followed them down a complexity of snow-filled couloirs to the south ridge and the snow-and ice-covered lake of Bispevatnet, which we crossed before descending to the road.

Halvor had become a great friend. We knew him from 1965 and had met him again soon after our arrival. He and his parents had a photography shop in Åndalsnes and had taken us under their wing, making us welcome. Coffee and snacks were always available and Halvor also came up with a little money earner: if I had an interesting climb planned he provided some film, developed the photos and sold them to the press sharing payment fifty-fifty, which we were both happy with. Then he announced he had bought a small house in the village of Veblungsnes not far from the hostel we were staying in, just across the river from Åndalsnes. It was ours to use and the rent was minimal. We had a home, and it rapidly filled with climbers from the Rimmon.

Soon after our Kongen climb, the four of us set out for another big new route, the central of Romsdal's three pillars, the East Pillar of Semletind, or Søndre Trolltind as it was called on our old maps. Like its neighbours the East Pillar of Breitind and the Trollryggen Pillar, it snakes up from almost sea level to over 1,600 metres. Arne Randers Heen and two other

Norwegians had climbed the upper half by a long approach from the right four years previously, but the whole pillar had never been climbed in its entirety. It was now midsummer and light enough to climb through the night. It was also a full moon, so based on our theory that the weather was always better at that time of the month we left in the very early morning having been out partying through the night. We had grown familiar with Romsdal's mountains and wanted to make a fast ascent, so we cut our gear to the minimum. We knew the way off the Troll peaks like the back of our hand – or so we thought – so the map and compass were dumped along with spare food and most of our bivvy gear, and off we went. After all, it never goes dark in the 'Land of the Midnight Sun', and according to our theory the weather was settled, so we figured we could just keep going until we got back down again.

Surprised to find a good way through the birch forest we kicked our way up a massive snow slope, a relic of springtime avalanches that had been sweeping down the huge couloir between our summit and Breitind. We crossed the bergschrund exactly as planned into a line of grooves writhing like a snake up otherwise smooth glaciated slabs and bulges on to the nose of the pillar, roping up in two ropes of two to follow a perfect crack and chimney line twisting up and out on to the crest of the ridge. We passed a large overhang by walking through an unexpected and quite surprising hole. Further obstacles were passed first by a tension traverse and then by tricky bridging between the wet walls of a chimney. We were going well and halfway up the route moving together on the easier ground, when it started to snow. Where did that come from? Unnoticed, the weather had clouded in. When we looked up our summit and the headwall, somewhere high above, were already concealed in cloud. So much for our full moon theory.

Too late now to think of retreat we knew where we were going and soldiered on to reach a big ledge below the headwall. With no shelter or good bivvy gear we needed to top out despite the foul weather. We hurried on into increasingly heavy snow, now following the general line of Arne's route as it wound around on to the north side of the final 300-metre ridge. By now the descending clouds had swallowed us. Thunder rumbled overhead. A full-on winter storm in midsummer was not on our agenda. Neither was a major rockfall. Lightning hit the cliff high above us, sending rocks like jagged cannonballs out of the clouds to explode around us with the smell of cordite. Bill took a direct hit on his helmet, which was smashed. He hung limply and silently on the rope, unconscious. His face, which was streaming with blood from a gash in his head, was a ghastly shade of white. For a horrible moment we thought he was dead. We suggested bivouacking until he recovered, but Bill, who always thrived in adversity, would have none of it. So we continued into the storm, finally emerging triumphantly, our first ascent in the bag, over the cornice into the blizzard and white-out.

Reasonably confident in our knowledge of the descent route, we formed a roped-up line and set off into the whiteness, tossing snowballs a metre or so ahead to mark the snow just in case it wasn't there and we were about to walk into space over a cornice. Remarkably we were on route and descended easily until, still in zero visibility, we found ourselves going up again, which was odd since we *should* have been continuing down … or so we thought. We backtracked a little and tried again to the right, just in case we were returning up a shoulder of the hillside we had just come down – but the slope still went up. We repeated the manoeuvre a few more times but always without success. Having made a full circle of failed attempts we found ourselves back in our own tracks. All very mysterious!

We retraced our steps to a large boulder and curled up for the night on damp rocks beneath the partial shelter of its dripping roof. Next morning the cloud had gone. We looked out to see a large, shallow snow basin along the far upper edge of which we had walked numerous times in the past. Now, a line of footprints was still just visible in the snow, descending into it then coming up repeatedly almost to its upper edge, but always returning to the bottom. If we had continued a few steps more on our first attempt we would have been out and on our way down. As it was, the sun was now shining and the now snow-capped summits looked splendid under the clear blue sky.

The remaining unclimbed pillar, the East Pillar of Breitind, Bill and I climbed. The weather was settled and the few drifting clouds were coming from inland rather than the sea, which is always a good sign, so when we came out of the local cinema one evening we made a snap decision and set off – it was summer and light enough to climb around the clock.

The lower half of the pillar is split by an impressive twisting chimney, offering the only way up the truncated spur. The first 200 metres were easy, so we climbed unroped until a couple of tricky pitches brought us up to an ominous-looking roof which, to our relief, we discovered had a hole behind it. Problem solved! But out of the frying pan and into the fire: above us was a smooth wall capped by a dripping overhang. We passed it with some tricky climbing and a long diagonal tension traverse off a dodgy spike. Eventually on easier terrain we unroped and followed the pillar up to the headwall. The weather was still good. The Semletind Pillar where Bill had so nearly been killed rose alongside us from the valley, now 1,300 metres below. Down there, surrounded by the green of the trees, an exquisite turquoise pool glinted in the sunlight. The river, white with rapids, was some distance away from it. The pool looked extremely tempting, but could we find it? We decided to go and have a look at the next opportunity, though right now we still had 300 metres to go. We were in luck; no epics for us this time. A snow ramp led us up to the right where we roped up again for a series of nice pitches up the headwall, arriving on the top in the sun after ten hours.

Soon after, a gang of us went to look for what became known as the 'Green Pool', for a party, and as luck would have it, we found a suspension foot-bridge across the river. There was a sign on it saying 'Dangerous. No Entry', or words to that effect, but that was the least of our worries. It was immediately above some rapids and it was ancient. Many of the foot-planks were missing and the tension had gone from one of the hand-wires, so the whole thing leant to one side and wobbled alarmingly, which simply added to the fun. We crossed precariously with our food, beer, cassette player and sleeping bags, left them on a perfect beach by the river and searched the birch woods for the Green Pool. That too was perfect: deep, crystal clear and glacial green, but not ice cold, having seeped in slowly through the forest. We plunged in, joining the trout swimming in its sun-dappled depths. Then back to our beach for the night. It was a great place, seemingly unknown to others and perfect for a party with plenty of driftwood for a fire.

But it wasn't all good times. Three other English lads, Ken and Rob Stannard and Derek Little, had been living in the valley and had become good friends. They were also into the new route scene and had gone with Wayne to climb a route on the east face of Bispen high above the famous Stigfoss, a waterfall that plunges dramatically down the cliffs closing the end of the Isterdal valley. Sadly Ken had fallen and been killed. I was out climbing that day but all those that could make it were at the rescue and his funeral in the little church in Veblungsnes was packed with climbers. We all knew it could have been us, but life goes on. The summer turned into autumn, there was a scattering of early winter snow on the tops and it was time to think about home. I had been away for over a year.

I had some catching up to do at Troll. Our nuts and belts were selling well around the country and Alan and I moved the business out of my cottage bedroom into a large old shed in the village that had been a wartime doctor's surgery. At least there was no swarf in the bed any more. I also got to know Denny Moorhouse and Shirley Smith of Clogwyn Climbing Gear (Clog). They had an impressive set-up and they were obviously going to be successful. Despite being competitors we got on well; Troll was always more about harnesses and tape gear rather than engineering.

By the mid 1970s, both Troll and Clog had become world-famous brands and design and market leaders, but in the mid to late 1960s it was all pretty low-key stuff. We survived but weren't making much money and with winter almost over I was keen to get back to Romsdal. Rob and I stopped off on the way, working for a couple of weeks in a fish factory on a small island just off the coast. We were liver-pickers: all we had to do was stand at a conveyor belt and as the gutted fish came past and flick the livers into a bucket to be turned into cod liver oil. Not the best job in the world, but it paid well.

Our guiding had already built up a good reputation and we were kept busy enough with Romsdal guiding, though it was frustrating when we knew our friends were out doing new climbs as we too also had other objectives. Luckily, Per Harvold, a friend of ours from Åndalsnes, enabled Bill and me to kill two birds with one stone by hiring us to guide him up the 1,600-metre Trollryggen East Pillar. It was one of the routes we wanted to do. We had now done the first ascents of the east pillars of Semletind and Breitind, the other two of Romsdal's three pillars, so climbing this highly reputed classic first done by Arne Randers Heen and Ralph Høibakk would complete the trilogy.

The pillar forms the left edge of the Troll Wall and was first climbed in 1958 but had had few subsequent ascents. Ralph was only twenty-one and Arne fifty-three when they made their ascent, which was Arne's sixth attempt. Per Harvold had also tried it and even crashed a small plane trying to get a closer look. We jumped at the chance of going with Per and had a great two days with him, finding our way unerringly through the complexities of the overlapping slabs that make up the lower half of the pillar and which had foiled a number of other attempts. Our bivvy halfway up the left edge of the Troll Wall was a real pleasure; the weather was perfect and we made good time to the top the next day.

18

THE TIMES THEY ARE A-CHANGING

My life was to change.

In 1968 I met Mille, a receptionist at the Åndalsnes Grand Hotel. She wasn't into climbing but we immediately hit it off and she came over to England to join me in the winter.

The following February we were married, and had a reception at a pub on the moors, having to walk home afterwards in a blizzard as the road was blocked by snow. Alan Waterhouse, my partner at Troll, paid the registrar, as I had no money. I had actually just earned forty quid building Norwegian log cabins with Smiler for an English company, but that went on the reception. A couple of days later we were off again building cabins. Mille was with us, though I'm sure she never imagined she would be spending her honeymoon with two lads in a grubby run-down 'hotel' in Wolverhampton.

The next job was better. We stayed in a caravan near Cromer on the east coast while building a large Norwegian log house for Rolling Stones guitarist Bill Wyman in the grounds of his Elizabethan mansion, where black swans swam in the moat. An unusual start to married life.

Once back at Troll, it was ticking over nicely and becoming increasingly well known so that Mille and I were just about making ends meet in my ten-bob-a-week, moor-edge cottage, though it was a wild winter and unless we barricaded the kitchen and living room doors with rugs, snow used to blow all the way into the house. Of course, if we were out the snow simply blew in under the door anyway, forming a small drift across the floor. Not quite what a Norwegian girl was used to coming from a centrally heated home, especially as she was expecting a baby that summer.

By April we were back in Halvor's house in Romsdal with the rest of the Rimmon regulars. We were guiding again, but I never got any new routes done that season. I fancied a route up an unclimbed wall just left of the 1,500-metre east face of Dronninga, and set off with Cockney despite lacking the usual anticipation. We were well up the lower part of the route when I told Cockney I wasn't into it – something I had never done before. The upper wall was obviously going to be hard and I just didn't have the commitment. I felt really bad about it and hated letting Cockney down, though I guess he understood. The baby was due any time soon. *What am I doing up here sticking my neck out on a big and serious unclimbed wall?*

A few days later Mille and I left for the south to her parents', and a couple of weeks later our daughter, Tannith, was born. It wasn't an easy birth. We had gone to the local maternity hospital where Mille went into a seemingly endless labour. Finally an ambulance was called and we were rushed across town, lights flashing, bells ringing, to the main hospital. I went in with Mille but was told, 'Sorry, fathers aren't allowed at the birth in Norway'.

'Well,' I said, 'you'll have to throw me out as I'm not going.' They could see I wasn't going to leave so I was allowed to stay.

A couple of weeks after Tannith was born we were back home in England where I resumed work more or less full-time at Troll with extra money earned working for a security company some evenings. I was also climbing regularly with my mates including Bill Birch from the Black and Tans club who was now married to Maggie and living locally. Mostly we went out just for the day rather than the weekend, as there was now family life to think about.

Among other things, Bill and I created a 300-metre traverse in Dovestones Quarry, which was still one of my happy hunting grounds, taking a line across the lower half of the face and returning across the upper wall on the original Rock and Ice route. We were also climbing in Derbyshire, working on Paul Nunn's guide *The Northern Limestone Area* which was published that year, too late to add some more new routes at Great Rocks Dale that Bill and I had done.

Two old friends of mine from the Rimmon, Ken and Di Taylor, lived just over the fields from our cottage. Di had helped me out years ago, finding a place for Roy and me to camp when we left my first hillside cottage, then helping me to move all my gear to my next cottage on her horses. She had married Ken a few years ago and they now had two children and were expecting a third. We called in often and Mille and Di became close friends with kids of a similar age. Ken worked in Oldham while Di looked after their kids and ran the farm with its ever-changing menagerie of dogs, cats, hens, ducks, occasional geese, pigs, goats or turkeys, and a Jersey cow that Di milked every day, which also meant having a calf or two around. Also there were always a couple of horses for riding. It was the hippy dream, 'the good life', homely and friendly with a log fire in the living room and an Aga cooker heating the beamed kitchen.

Everybody envied their lifestyle, as indeed did a part of me. I was ready for a change from Romsdal and with a wife and daughter I needed to do more than scrape a living at Troll, but domesticity was never my dream. For years I had wondered about the Yukon. I knew that good money could be made there and I had read Robert Service's inspirational poetry. He got it right when he wrote 'The Call of the Wild'.

Maybe this was the time …

19

ON THE ROAD AGAIN

My 1970 guide *Walks and Climbs in Romsdal* was one of the first guidebooks to be published by Walt Unsworth at Cicerone Press. Also that spring, momentously for British and world climbing as well as for Troll, Don Whillans called in at our shed in Greenfield, sticking his head through the door and saying, 'So this is where it all 'appens!'

He was arranging the equipment for the proposed 1970 Annapurna South Face expedition, which had an all-star line up led by Chris Bonington. It was going to involve a lot of fixed rope work on steep terrain and Don wanted a harness that they could sit in while jumaring with heavy sacks. He had made a mock-up that looked more like a nappy than a harness, but it was a start. Based on that, we made a modified prototype that wasn't much better, but we stuck with it and it kept improving. Eventually we had the basics of a web harness; it just needed refinement. With that more or less sorted, and the wild still calling, Mille, Tannith and I were ready to go to the Yukon, maybe for a year.

That meant leaving Troll again. It wasn't quite profitable enough to pay a good living wage, but it was definitely going places. Alan had a well-paid engineering job so couldn't afford to leave that, but there was a possible solution.

Paul Seddon with whom I was climbing a lot at that time also had a full-time day job while making climbing gear in the evenings. I asked him if he would be interested in joining Troll. That weekend Paul and I went to Great Rocks Dale and climbed a new route we called *The Merger*. Paul took the Whillans Harness project on and together with Alan refined it further and improved the buckle. It was to be the world's first climbing sit harness.

I set off for the Yukon and Mille and Tannith took the ferry to Norway to live with her parents until I found a job. Having waved them goodbye,

I spent sixty of my last eighty quid on a flight to New York – the cheapest way to cross the Atlantic. With only twenty quid left I had intended to kip in Central Park, but an American I was sat next to on the plane warned me strongly against it, saying it was full of drug addicts and criminals. I took his advice and went directly to Canada by bus. This left me with a fiver in my pocket when I got to Toronto. Having walked out of town on to the Trans-Canada Highway, I slept in a snowdrift in temperatures way below zero at the side of the road, being woken at dawn by the sound of an air horn and hissing airbrakes. I had a lift – and what a lift! – all the way across the country to Edmonton.

The driver offered me a bed in a motel room the first night, which I refused, saying I would kip in the cab. But he wouldn't have it, so I joined him for a meal, also at his expense, and then discovered there was only one bed, a double.

He wouldn't listen to any talk of me sleeping on the floor, so I climbed warily in with him. He cracked a couple of beers, turned on the TV and slotted some coins into the bed, which to my surprise began rocking. Things were turning strange.

My concerns were unfounded; he was a great guy. A French–Canadian and grandson of one of the Hudson's Bay Company 'voyageurs' who used to travel the country by canoe, trading and collecting furs. I travelled with him for a week, helping to offload his truck at stops along the way, eating and sleeping with him and being paid at the end of the journey. It was a good start.

In Edmonton I got a doss at the Salvation Army hostel and a week later had found myself a job in an opencast mine on the Yukon/British Columbia border. It hadn't been easy, queuing up most of each day only to be told no, and no time to explain my circumstances, having a wife and daughter and no money. Finally, I waited outside the door one night until I saw the guy leaving, stopped him and had a chat.

'Come back tomorrow, and I'll fix a job for you,' he said. Six weeks later I had enough money to buy a trailer home to live in and fly Mille and Tannith over. Mille soon got a job as a waitress in the camp canteen and with both of us working we were earning around £400 a week instead of the £20 I was getting back home.

20

CANADA – YUKON YARNS

On the greenly phosphorescent snows, herald of the dawning, glows
The witch light of the hidden sun. Then blushing pink to swiftly run
The gauntlet of the clutching night, pale peaks reflect the morning light.
Deep down, darkly, hollows nestle in the gloom where bull moose wrestle,
And unknown, languid, ice-fringed lakes await
the dropping dawn that makes
Inverted mirrors of their deeps, ring-banished when the grayling leaps.
But still the mountains in their glory conceal
below, frost-gripped and hoary,
Dungeon valleys where the nascent day yearns
for the sun's first cleaving ray
To cut them from their pine-locked womb that
holds the darkness like a tomb.
Then, from the chalice of the dazzling peaks the
morning light pours forth and seeks
The lingering refugees of night, last shadows shrinking out of sight
Till over all the sun holds sway, creator of the newborn day.
'Ode in a Mountaintop Dump-shack',
written while on nightshift, winter 1970–1971

… Well, you have to do something while sitting alone in a freezing dump-shack all night!

The winter, as always in the Yukon, was bitterly cold and long. Temperatures on the mountaintop where I had started work in an opencast mine as a lowly 'dump man' were regularly down to anywhere from −10 to −40 °F, and sometimes as low as −60. That's −23 to −50 °C. Being a dump man is a crazy job, but it does leave plenty of spare time to read and write – even poetry. It was one of the easiest jobs I've ever had – all that was required was to sit in a sentry box high on the mountain above a scree slope of quarry waste and wait until a truck arrived. Sometimes they were frequent, sometimes maybe only a few times each shift. All I had to do then was put down my book, step outside, make sure the truck didn't reverse over the edge before it dumped its load of rock, then nip smartly back in and settle down in front of my stove again. In winter, the upside was watching the Northern Lights, which burned with red and green fire over the dark pine forests. The downside was that the fuel in the small gas stove usually froze at around twenty below, just when you needed it, so it could be decidedly chilly. The same used to happen in our trailer home.

The job didn't last. Within a few months I had been promoted via 'shovel-oiler' (terrible job) to 'driller's mate', which paid even more money than did sitting in a dump shack. Unless we had a breakdown, it was also much warmer, though we had some memorably cold shifts. One night the temperature was −60 °F. In addition, a fierce wind was blowing, the wind chill bringing the effective temperature down to −120 °F, or −80 °C. We were dispatched to the summit of the mountain to bring the drill down. In those conditions, drill steels can break like twigs. Pee seemed to freeze before it hit the ground, that's if, like me, you were daft enough to experiment, but we thawed the engine out with blowtorches and got the job done.

On days off, I sometimes hitched out to see friends. 'The Quartz Creek Gang' lived in some log cabins in the bush a few miles down the track that ran from the mining camp to the Alaska Highway, 100 miles away. Beyond that, the nearest town was Whitehorse, another 250 miles further up the dirt road – snow-covered for much of the year. Being the early 1970s it was the hippy era. The Quartz Creek Gang were living the life. Marijuana bloomed in the ambient warmth of the log-burning stoves and high-voltage psychedelic rock boomed from the sound systems. Like many of the others working up at the mine, those of them that went to work were often stoned, driving fifty-tonne dump trucks and other heavy machinery while high on pot or LSD, or whatever high was available that week. Perhaps it was just as well that dump men were up there to ensure they didn't reverse over the edge of the mountain.

There was a company bar in the mining camp, but I didn't frequent it much, heavy drinking not being my scene. I wasn't keen on the barman either, or on the white supremacy ethos of some of the miners. The last time I went, one of the Native American guys who lived on the edge of town was asleep, head on his table, obviously drunk. The barman shouted over to him, 'Hey, you, are you going to spend any more money in here?' There was no answer. He then pulled a baseball bat out from under the bar, obviously there for this purpose, and muttering loudly about 'drunken Indians,' walked across, hit him hard across his back, knocking him to the floor, then dragged him to the door and threw him in the street. A few people grinned. Nobody cared. It definitely wasn't my scene. I had a feeling that any comment from a 'goddam hippy' would have met with the same response, so I drank up and left. The guy I was bunked up with when I first arrived was typical: he had a battered four-by-four and when it broke down for the umpteenth time on the Alaska Highway he simply shot it, then hitched back to camp.

On a night out with the Quartz Creek lads, I was talked into trying some mescalin, a drug extracted from peyote cactus seeds, and used by the Apache, Comanche and other southern states and Mexican tribes. I found myself floating up through the roof and watched, alarmed, as the building, the forested valley and the mountains receded below me as I drifted into outer space. Not only was I soon millions of miles out of my comfort zone and mingling with the Milky Way, but I didn't know the way back. I wasn't even sure there was one. *Bloody hell*, I thought, this being my first out-of-body experience, *I've really done it this time!* I was definitely worried. Quartz Creek lad Big Joe knew what was going on in my head – he was an expert. He had been there himself and knew all there was to know about Carlos Castaneda and his weird tales of peyote-inspired adventures with an astral-travelling Native American shaman. Noticing my faraway look, he talked me back down, bringing me back into my chair with a rush.

'Let's go for a walk,' he said, which was exactly what I needed. Once outside, he said, 'Watch this,' flicking his hand forwards and sending flashes of lightning streaking from his finger ends!

Sometimes I would go off alone for the sheer pleasure of enjoying the winter solitude, snowshoeing through the pine forest to an abandoned trapper's cabin I had found not far from the Dease River. On other solo trips into the hills I camped under a tarp slung between pines.

Everyone said I should have a gun in bear country, so I got myself a Winchester – 'the gun that won the west', though I was happy I never needed to use it.

In the long winter nights, green phosphorescent undulating curtains of light floated across the black backdrop of the sky as the aurora borealis unfurled its eerie shimmering glow. In the surrounding silence, pine trees sometimes exploded as the sap froze at forty degrees below zero – a true wilderness thermometer. In the mornings I would stay wrapped deep in my sleeping bag, huddled close to a reluctant fire, clutching a hot drink while cooking breakfast. More often than not, an egg cracked into the frying pan would break into two frozen halves before slowly melting, indicating temperatures below −23 °C.

After the break up of the winter ice on the rivers, I sometimes went down to the cabin with Ernst Renner, a friend from the mine. Ernst was a Swiss guide, but was working there as a carpenter. One day we borrowed a couple of gold pans and having slept at the cabin walked though the pines to Chinaman's Gulch, which had been worked by the Chinese in 1884, extracting £200,000 of gold. It also looked like it might be our lucky day. After a morning's work we had found a few minute grains that we put to one side in a folded cloth while we continued panning. Some minutes later there was a noise behind us; we looked around and, unbelievably, a squirrel was making off up a tree with the results of our morning's efforts!

That winter, Ernst and I decided we needed to climb. The previous autumn we had walked up a lonely valley, surprising ourselves with the discovery of a small but classically pointed peak hidden away in its recesses – a mini-Matterhorn. It was time to climb it! Not that we had any climbing gear – we both had a pair of good mountain boots, but no crampons. We also had harnesses and I had a rope, and that was my contribution. For his part, Ernst, being a carpenter, was able to make some wooden wedges, drilling them so we could thread some thick cord through to make slings. We also made some longer knotted slings – and that was it.

We arranged a lift out along a forest track and, with an early start, were soon on our mountain. Not being over-optimistic, we picked the easiest line up a long corner that caught what little there was of the morning sun. It was littered here and there with snow and ice, but was mostly rock and it appeared climbable. The climbing was also traditional: deep cracks and chimneys, or bridging across steep corners while struggling to hammer in a wedge, pass a sling round a chockstone or drape it over an icy spike before tying it round the rope, all useless of course. We reached the top just in time to find a concealed and fortunately easy way down as the short, subarctic day started its swift return to darkness.

Night had fallen before we reached and crunched our way jubilantly down the moonlit snow-filled valley to the frozen track. We were unsure where we would sleep in the biting cold, but reaching the track, we found a sheltered snow cave under a roadside cornice and settled into our sleeping bags for the night. We were more than satisfied with our day and ready to continue our walk out at first light.

We had hardly settled in when the noise of an approaching vehicle broke the silence. Then headlights pierced the night. We tumbled out of our sub-zero snow cave still in our sleeping bags. The pickup driver nearly skidded off the icy road in shock. He turned out to be a Native American friend of ours who had been up in the hills looking for moose, so we swapped stories of high adventures as he drove home through the endless pines and before too long we were back in camp enjoying hot brews and T-bone steaks with the night shift. The itchy-fingered rock junkies had got their fixes!

21

CANADA – 'THE TRAIL OF '98'

One of the few lads at the mining camp who was anxious to see more of the Yukon, rather than to blow the results of their work on booze and women in Mexico or Hawaii as many of them did, was a tousle-haired Canadian called Ken Minchin. I suppose it was inevitable that we would get together to follow one of the routes of the 1897-1898 Klondike Gold Rush.

In the aftermath of the 1896 gold strike at Bonanza Creek in the Yukon, the Klondike Gold Rush was at its peak. Those who could afford it chose to wait and take the easy way by boat up the coast of British Columbia and Alaska to Nome, then on to Dawson by paddle steamer up the Yukon River. Most tried to reach the gold fields by the dreaded Chilkoot Trail from Skagway in the south-eastern corner of Alaska, over the pass to Bennett Lake then down the Yukon River to Whitehorse and Dawson after the break up of the winter ice, the subject of Robert Service's *Trail of Ninety-Eight*.

We were well aware of the Chilkoot Trail but Ken knew of a less well-known gold rush route of ill repute, the last part of which followed river systems for almost 1,000 miles. It goes from the Mackenzie Delta on the edge of the Barren Lands in Canada's Northwest Territory, over the Continental Divide, the mountain barrier running the length of the Americas, and on through the Yukon Territory to Alaska, then up the Yukon River to Dawson City, the gold rush boom-town. We had minimal information and no experience of serious canoeing other than my crossing of Cardigan Bay in Wales, but both of us felt it was time to escape work and have an adventure. Being in the Yukon, what better choice than to follow a Klondike trail – especially a notorious one.

The would-be miners had started much further south from the Great Slave Lake, then boated north for 1,000 miles down the Mackenzie River.

Ken had already rafted that the previous summer, but it was the next part that was infamous: from the Mackenzie Delta, the way on crossed the Great Divide by following the most difficult section of the 'freshwater north-west passage', up the Rat and down the Porcupine rivers, finally meeting the Yukon River in Alaska, not far from Dawson City.

Few of the would-be miners had made it up the Rat River, but it sounded like fun, so in the summer of 1971 we resolved to have a go ourselves. We bought a sleek 'Indian style' canvas and cedar canoe that would slip quietly through the water without disturbing wildlife, unlike the noisy – though more robust, and therefore safer – fibreglass or aluminium ones, and flew with it from Whitehorse to Inuvik.

Apart from the crew, on board the plane there were just a couple of Inuit and ourselves, and flying out across 600 miles of unpopulated forests, mountains, lakes and rivers was a sobering experience for two lads on their first real canoe trip!

Inuvik, 'The Place of Man', is a small town of wooden houses built on stilts in 1961 above 300 metres of permafrost by the eastern shore of the innumerable intertwining rivers that make up the 5,000 square miles of the Mackenzie Delta. In 1971, there was no way in except by river or air or with dog teams over the mountains by a route on which 'The Lost Patrol' of Mounties (Canadian Mounted Police) had vanished in the winter of 1910. Nowadays, this lonely 400-mile route is taken by the Dempster Highway, opened in 1979 from Dawson City to Inuvik, thereby robbing this part of the Arctic wilderness of some of its magic and mystery.

To the east of Inuvik the wild Barren Lands extend for over 1,000 miles to Hudson Bay, while to the west, stunted forests rise up towards the Richardson Mountains that form the northern limit of the Continental Divide.

We should have slept at Inuvik, but we couldn't wait – it was almost midnight on midsummer's night, and the sun's glow was reflected on the water as we pushed our canoe out into the river trying to look like experts though it was the first time we had been in it. A small group of Inuit waved us goodbye as we paddled off up the blood-red river and into the unknown.

It was tricky stuff, crossing the hundred miles of the delta, and it took us a few days. The river was in full flood and the steep banks of the innumerable ever-changing islands were crumbling, bringing soil and pine trees crashing into the river with ominous roars: taking the easiest paddling line close in to the side could be dangerous. One day we passed a pair of lynx staring at us from the riverbank; another day, we passed an Arctic fox sitting forlornly on a rapidly shrinking island. The ever-present buzz of mosquitoes filled the air, though we managed to avoid the worst of them by keeping out in midstream whenever the opposing flow of water permitted.

Navigation was a challenge, as not only is the network of rivers in the delta tremendously complex, but the constantly collapsing banks change the detail of the land. To confuse matters further, despite the flatness of the delta, the maps are covered in what at first glance seem to be contour lines – but they're not: they are lines of magnetic variation. So what with a maze of twisting rivers, disappearing islands, the moveable compass direction and the endless forest, finding one little river that leads out of the delta and goes up into the distant hills was far from straightforward. (On our return, we were told of a couple that tried to navigate the same route but gave up in despair. They simply headed towards the evening sun in a straight line, dragging their canoes up and down the riverbanks and through the woods until they got on rising ground and could see where they were – not much fun!)

On the fourth day, we made it through to the south-western reaches of the delta where the Peel River slides quietly into it after a tumultuous journey north from the Yukon. There was a fishing camp there occupied by a few Gwich'in people tending the smoke cabins where the summer's fish catch was being preserved, while whittling away at new snowshoe staves for the coming winter. Some younger lads were out in the river with nets. The rest of their group were upriver fishing for grayling. We stopped and chatted about life in the Arctic and our next objective, the Rat River, the site of the would-be gold miners' Destruction City and the location of the shoot-out with the 'Mad Trapper of Rat River'. This had taken place only forty years previously – in their lifetime – and was well remembered.

Leaving their camp, we turned north again – or should I say seawards, as north by the compass was anywhere but north! Paddling up a side stream of the delta known as the Husky Channel we passed the first of many trappers' cabins we were to see on our journey. Inside, mukluks, snowshoes and a rifle hung on the wall, on which old photos were pinned. Tins of food and ancient blackened pots and pans decorated the shelves. In the corner, a pot-bellied stove and a bunk huddled together for warmth. Like all northern backwoods cabins it had that primal homely smell of caribou hide and wood smoke.

Paddling on, the narrow entrance to the Rat River nearly slipped by us. Almost concealed by the encroaching pinewoods and thickets of willows was a small stream. *Could this really be it?* We puzzled over our map expecting something bigger for the exit of a fifty-mile-long river, but it seemed we were in the right place and we turned up into it finding faster-flowing waters. As we left the delta, now heading upstream, the river widened, becoming shallower, rocky and impossible to paddle. Time to practise our 'lining' skills learnt from a book a few days earlier. It had also informed us that 'The Rat should only be attempted by experienced canoeists with a guide,' and that 'ideally four people are required to line each canoe'.

Ah well, we thought, *here goes …*

To successfully line a canoe upriver requires a degree of skill only learnt through experience. It involves walking on the riverbank or, more likely, in the river, both people on the same side, each with a rope to the canoe, one to the bow and one the stern. You then pull the canoe up the river. To avoid boulders or shallow water it's frequently necessary to let the canoe out to the far side or reel it in to the near side. This is achieved using the lines: slacken the front line and pull in the stern and the canoe is pushed out across the river by the force of the water. Tightening the front line causes the reverse to happen. Which all sounds fine until you get it wrong, when the canoe immediately swings sideways and capsizes. As we quickly learnt it's all a matter of teamwork and fast reactions. We only capsized it once, but despite careful packing, the invading river damaged our best camera, soaked much of our gear and destroyed some of our food. *Only another 700 miles to go*, we thought ruefully, wondering not for the first time if our plans weren't a bit too optimistic for beginners.

It was some compensation to know that the would-be Klondike miners of 1898 had met similar problems. Having successfully boated down the wide, placid waters of the Mackenzie, they had endeavoured to get their boats up the Rat, only to lose most of them in these lower rapids, together with their supplies. From the remnants, they made a camp they called Destruction City and what remains of that is now used as a caribou hunting camp by the Gwich'in Indians. Most of the miners never got much beyond here though a hardy few continued to pack their gear upriver.

For us, things were easier. We still had our canoe and equipment and most of our food, though the latter was not a problem; it was midsummer, the rivers were rich with fish and wildfowl were everywhere. We caught fish for supper and plundered a few ducks' nests for half a dozen eggs for breakfast, making sure to leave three or four carefully untouched eggs in each nest. I have to say we had a shock when we cracked the first egg next morning and found a half-formed duckling inside, but it was too late then and we didn't want to waste them so we cracked them open, mashed them up and had duckling omelette. Very good it was too!

Another day of walking in the ice-cold waters of the river followed, building up our canoe-lining expertise until we flattered ourselves we were getting quite proficient and capable of letting the canoe out, when necessary, through the boulders to the far side of the river and deeper water. It was hard work, demanding total concentration, but extremely satisfying, our toil getting us another five miles upstream.

This second day on the Rat brought us to the location of the 1932 gunfight at the Mad Trapper's cabin. He had become famous, this lone trapper whose name was Albert Johnson, seeking the snowy solitude of the 'Far North'. William Nerysoo, a Gwich'in trapper, had reported him to the Mounties for stealing animals from their traps; this may have been unfounded, though he was undoubtedly intruding on their land. The Indians and Mounties then sledged in up the frozen river to his cabin where he refused to come out to talk, so they tried to dynamite him out, but to no avail. A fifteen-hour gun battle ensued in which he shot and killed one of the Mounties. Not a good plan, but I guess being dynamited had made him a *tad* grumpy.

According to the Gwich'in no one had crossed the mountains so far north in midwinter. The snow was deep and powdery and the temperature was down to minus forty with few animals around for food. But when the Mounties returned a few days later, Johnson had gone. With their Gwich'in guides and dog teams, they tracked him upstream into the mountains where he killed his second Mountie. They then lost him as he crossed the Divide heading in the direction of Alaska and freedom, 400 miles away. He would have made it were it not for Canada's first ever manhunt by plane. As a result, he was spotted a few days later still snowshoeing determinedly westwards. When they shot him down in a final gunfight he had been alone in the wilderness in midwinter for over five weeks, catching his food as he travelled. He still had plenty of ammunition left as well as a couple of dead squirrels in his pocket.

Having spent the previous winter in our dump-shacks with the temperatures frequently down to forty below and now seven days out from Inuvik up this remote and lonely river, for Ken and me his achievement seemed superhuman. It's a pity he killed the Mounties – he deserved to make it.

It took us another five days of hard work lining the canoe up the icy waters, still checking the map carefully at every twist and turn as we had one more tributary to find before we could reach the Divide and Summit Lake. The river was becoming shallower as we splashed upstream, by now accustomed to and thoroughly enjoying our labours of the day, almost two weeks from civilisation and totally committed to our own resources. But where was the final creek known as the Little Bell? The mountains were close and we felt sure it was imminent. By now, the banks were covered by matted willows and dwarf spruce and we were beginning to wonder if somehow we'd missed this final but crucial stream, until, listening carefully, we heard over the continual rushing of the river the different tone of a small waterfall. Looking closely through the tangled bush we found a small cascade falling over some rocks – it was hardly wider than the canoe. Could this be it?

Without hearing it, we would never have seen it – it was so well hidden in the undergrowth, but we had a good feeling about it that paid off. Having prised apart the branches and hoisted our canoe up into this small rivulet deep in its own gully, we abruptly emerged above the treeline. Scrambling out and up the bank we could finally see ahead up a gently rising valley striking west into the mountains towards Summit Lake. Eureka! The few remaining struggling would-be miners must have felt the same elation.

We were at last able to get back in the canoe and slip through the lazy waters of this little stream, the banks so close we sometimes had to lift it round the frequent meandering bends as we worked our tortuous way up the mountain valley. Rounding one bluff, we came face to face with a cow moose and her calf, which is not a good thing to do. She lifted her massive head – dripping with water – snorted, stared us in the eyes, then pushed her calf out on to the bank and, much to our relief, lumbered out after it. Half a ton of moose in the canoe would not have been welcome!

The stream slowly diminished in size until we were pushing our canoe beneath an arch of interwoven willow. The next day the stream disappeared altogether forcing us to 'portage' the last mile over the tundra, the air so thick with mosquitoes it was almost impossible to breathe. Downriver, we had managed to avoid the worst of these Arctic nasties, either being *in* the river during the day when they seemed far fewer, or escaping into our tent at night. Up here, we had no choice but to rapidly search for our mosquito nets or go insane.

We spent a lazy day at Summit Lake, swimming, enjoying the Arctic sun and fishing. The stream feeding the lake seemed to be more fish than water; we hung a net across the mouth and beat downstream towards it with our paddles, bringing out handfuls of grayling and a massive pike. We were hungry lads and we ate the lot! From here it was going to be a cruise: downhill all the way for 600 miles to the Yukon River.

We paddled out across the lake in the early dawn, serenaded by the eerie and lonely call of the loon. We were really into it now, over the McDougall Pass into the Yukon Territory and heading west down to the junction of the Bell Creek with the Porcupine River – it may well have been 1898. We shared the euphoria of the few miners that had made it over the pass. They must literally have been on their last legs, but now they could at last build a raft and head for the gold fields where they dreamed of untold riches. Exhilarated by crossing the pass and happy to be going downriver, we shot our first rapids like experts and drifted on sideways or backwards as we took advantage of the river's flow while reclining at our ease and eating bannocks made earlier in the day.

Wildlife was still abundant. One evening, a fully grown black bear drifted downriver past our camp. The only gun we had with us was a .22 for rabbits, having decided against everyone's advice that we really didn't want to shoot any large game however dire the situation – silly, really. There was nothing we could have done, but we had surmised that in a season of abundant food, unless we posed a threat, then any bears would be likely to leave us alone. In fact, as the bear passed us by, he appeared to smile at us, re-enforcing our somewhat dubious theory before floating on downstream obviously enjoying the ride.

The following night we heard heavy feet treading the pebbly beach outside our tent, followed by heavy breathing. *Had we caught up with the bear?* Something large tripped over the guy lines. *What to do?* We peered cautiously out in time to see a bull moose with a massive spread of antlers ambling unconcerned into the river. Haunted by the bear, we didn't sleep much more that night.

Other days were equally memorable. Once, silently drifting along downstream, stark naked in the sun as was our custom, we came around a bend to see a wolf, its back to us, digging in the riverbank. We could hear young birds chirping in a hidden nest. Ken, sitting behind me, quietly slipped his paddle into the water and steered us towards it. Just before the bows touched the bank, I reached out with my paddle and slapped the wolf on its bum. I swear it leapt vertically in the air and, while still airborne, spun round, saw these naked apparitions and took off, cartoon-like, into the woods without ever touching the ground! We collapsed in the canoe and laughed the rest of the day.

Another day we heard a banshee-like screech coming from downstream, enough to make our hair stand on end. Was it a Sasquatch, the yeti of the American wilderness? Again we slipped into stealth mode and paddled on cautiously, paddles never leaving the water, to see a lynx on a sandbank, totally preoccupied, playing cat and mouse with a gopher. As we quietly drew nearer, we could see it let the gopher go, turn its back on it and walk away ten yards or so to a position on the riverbank high above. The gopher lay trembling on the beach. Was it free to go? It took a cautious step. Its tormentor ignored it studiously. It took another step nearer to freedom – nothing happened. Then it set off fast, making for the undergrowth by the water's edge. The lynx leapt through the air, raced down the beach, with another blood-curdling scream caught it with one large paw and threw it high in the air. By this time, we had touched shore. The lynx was still unaware of our presence, so intense was its concentration on its prey. Once again in nature's glory, we stepped out of the canoe armed with our paddles, knights to the rescue. We had nothing to worry about; one look at these alien life forms and the lynx forgot the gopher and made a dash for the forest. The small animal lay quivering, wondering what new nightmare was about to befall it. We carried it into the undergrowth where it lay as though dead. By the time we'd had lunch it had gone, our second good deed in two days, though sadly counterbalanced by the fine, fat rabbit we shot and ate that night (though we did share the scraps with a red fox who sat on the edge of our campfire glow, eyeing us with curiosity). Such is life!

Halfway down the Porcupine we arrived, earlier than expected, at Old Crow, the only village on the whole of our journey and built close to the trail of the annual caribou migration. As elsewhere, the Gwich'in residents still lived by hunting, fishing and trapping, pretty much untainted by 'modern' life, as they have for thousands of years. They refer to themselves as 'caribou people', as their life and culture are intertwined with the fate of the caribou. When I wrote this in 2016, for the previous thirty years they had been fighting proposed oil extraction projects in the Arctic National Wildlife Refuge. To them, its pristine coastal plain where the caribou calve their young is 'the Sacred Place Where Life Begins'. President Obama had recommended that the refuge and its coastal plain be designated as wilderness, but now, in 2018, the futures of the reserve and the Gwich'in people hang in the balance: the Trump administration has made clear its intention to open the refuge.

We got our first unexpected glimpse of the village as we came round a bend in the river, drifting along in our usually relaxed mode, though fortunately dressed. We saw a cluster of cabins on the high riverbank some fifteen metres above us. A group of old men were sat on a bench, grinning. There was something in that grin I didn't like – they knew something we didn't. Then we felt the tug of speeding water and heard the sudden noise of shallow rapids as the river abruptly changed course, turning across itself and sweeping sideways down a gravel shoal. A few yards further and we would be grounded in midstream. This was going to have to be good or we would capsize our canoe in full view of the village thereby providing the day's entertainment. Full reverse right on the bows while simultaneously pulling the stern hard left; shoot out right through the rapids, reverse the procedure to fly out downriver in the fast-flowing narrow channel directly under our audience; then hang a hard right again to spin the bows upstream and come to a screeching halt at the small landing platform. We did it! We were so impressed we half expected applause, but the locals looked on inscrutably – they probably did it every day.

A couple of dozen sled dogs howled mournfully as we entered the village. All we had left for food was a bag of flour, so we bought a few items – though all were expensive, having had to be flown in.

Having chatted with the locals, we headed off downstream where we soon crossed unannounced into Alaska and the USA, passing the abandoned cabins of Cadzow's trading and customs post. Beyond was the worrying hundred miles of Rampart Canyon, cliffs rising sheer on both sides of the river. Our concerns proved unfounded. We shot through in a memorable day, arriving unexpectedly at a prospector's camp just in time for a mountainous meal. And then we were down in the flatlands, sliding once more through a wide, winding river in the dark forests below the lonely mountains of the Brooks Range. The last days down this final stretch of the river past the abandoned Indian settlements of Burnt Paw and Howling Dog were among the most beautiful of the trip. Canoeing towards the evening sun, a glowing orb impaled on the black lances of the pines, we slipped silently through a placid river of gold, the only sounds the drip of water from the paddles, the occasional call of a moose or the primordial spine-tingling howl of a wolf.

On our last day, we emerged into the fast-flowing mile-wide waters of the Yukon River, our journey over this little-known gold rush trail completed. Dawson City, that Mecca of the miners, was a simple boat's journey upstream, but our six-week break was over. We flew out in a small plane to Fairbanks and so back to the Yukon. The puzzled American passport inspector asked why we had no entry stamp. 'We came in down the Porcupine,' we said, not without some pride in our journey. 'No stamp in means no stamp out,' he replied, sending us on our way, no one any the wiser.

Just over forty years later while at the annual dinner of the Black and Tans Climbing Club in February 2013 – the year after the above story was published in my ebook, *Adventures in the Northlands*, Christine Birch, wife of Eddie Birch, an old climbing friend of mine, gave me a biography of Robert Service, *Vagabond of Verse* by James A. Mackay. As a lover of Service's poetry, I was both surprised and pleased to find that he had done the same canoe trip as us, intending to 'pack and track like the pioneers'.

Mackay wondered if perhaps 'Robert's motive in undertaking such a hazardous venture was to prove himself. He was acutely aware that although he had chronicled the Yukon in verse and prose, he was something of a fraud. He had not actually been on the Trail of Ninety-Eight and the gold rush that inspired him had been almost over by the time he got there. On hearing of his plans, the Indian agent at Fort McMurray said, "Young man, you're going to your doom".'

22
HOMEWARD BOUND

A few weeks after we had flown back from Alaska, our canoe came upriver on a barge to Whitehorse, from where it was transported by truck back to our mining camp. Having paid Ken out for his share in it, I swapped it for a VW Beetle just before the snows came.

By late spring of 1972 I had done exactly two years at the mining camp. That was a year longer than intended but we had money in the bank and we were ready to move. We sold our trailer home, dug our VW Beetle out of the snowdrift that had covered it for about six months, surprised that it still started, and had a party. It was a good party too, and a nice day with some of us enjoying the sun, sitting on the trailer roof with plenty of beer and other substances – as was the norm in those days. That's when the Mounties arrived. Rumour had it they were paid by the mining company and always tried to bust people leaving so they could be fined heavily and as a consequence have to stay on for another year. Whatever the truth of that, they were definitely looking for drugs and should have hit the jackpot, but despite the search, to my amazement they found nothing.

We left the Yukon and started our American road trip. At Yosemite we camped at Glacier Point high above the huge sweep of the Apron slabs with a spectacular view of Half Dome and the winding Merced River far below. We were woken before dawn by a bear trampling on our little VW trying to get at food inside. It eventually gave up and wandered off but we felt vulnerable and were happier when we moved down to Camp 4. It was Tannith's fourth birthday for which we had bought a large cake, consequently having to chase off another bear that wanted to join the party. I wandered off up Half Dome the next day returning to find Mille talking to a climber. He was working in the valley and fancied climbing *Royal Arches*. I only had my mountain boots but it sounded good to me – and it was. After two years off rock I was surprised I climbed reasonably well.

Leaving Yosemite, we drove past the beautiful climbing area of Tuolumne Meadows before descending through the snow-capped and forested High Sierra to Death Valley. It was hot. Too hot at 120 °F (touching 50 °C). Even a dip in the visitor centre pool didn't cool us off. Our ageing Beetle didn't like it either. It had been using a lot of oil lately and I had bought a gallon of it a few days previously. The engine drank it all before it finally crawled, smoking and coughing at walking speed, over the last pass to escape the valley.

It was a relief to freewheel most of the way down into the next little town, which seemed deserted. We were still uncomfortably hot, so seeing what we hoped was an empty house we leapt into the garden pool for a swim before heading out to find a campsite. Then it was on through Las Vegas and past the Hoover Dam to Arizona and Nevada and the awesome Grand Canyon before crossing the Painted Desert into Hopi and Navajo country.

We walked up to the thousand-year-old Hopi 'sacred village' of Oraibi high on a mesa, but a scrawled sign outside said 'No white men'. I couldn't blame them. Then on to Window Rock, the Navajo capital, before heading south across New Mexico to El Paso. There we crossed into Mexico, driving almost a thousand miles across a high plateau of poor land and poor people, still camping wherever our day ended despite thunderstorms and heavy rain most nights.

Eventually our little Beetle struggled over the 3,000-metre pass that guards the northern entrance to Mexico City where we stayed a few days, doing what tourists do. The backdrop of Popocatépetl, a snow-capped, almost 5,500-metre-high volcano to the south, reminded me of poetry in my English class at school where I had read but only dimly remembered a few lines about 'Shining Popocatépetl/The dusty streets did rule', from W.J. Turner's poem *Romance*. Its 'shining summit' wasn't something I ever expected to see, but it certainly looked tempting.

Instead, thoughts of the Pacific coast drew us west through Toluca to Acapulco where we camped on the beach, swimming and going to see the La Quebrada Cliff Divers plunging impressively for over thirty metres into a narrow zawn. Then south through Oaxaca with its brightly dressed indigenous people and verdant countryside with thatched villages and ox carts to Guatemala where our car embarrassingly died at the border. When my passport was stamped as we entered the country, I noticed they had stamped a picture of a car in it. Apparently having arrived in a car I was obliged to take it out on departure or pay a fine to the value of the car, as new. With fingers crossed, we pushed it through the border post which, luckily, was at the top of a hill, and it obligingly started again as we rolled down the other side before driving on to a campsite near Guatemala City.

Leaving our things in the tent, we set off next day to visit the market in Chichicastenango, an ancient Mayan town. Then the inevitable happened: the car died again on the way, this time for ever. We were stuck in a jungle valley between two high passes not far from the village. *What to do?* I had got the car in exchange for my canoe in the Yukon and didn't fancy paying the authorities the price of a new car, but it was definitely dead. We walked up to Chichicastenango and gave the car's papers to the local police, telling them they could have the car for which they signed the necessary documents. Later, having enjoyed our day in the village we caught a bus back to our campsite and next day I went to the customs office in the city to explain the situation. They weren't happy.

'You have to give the car to us,' they said.

'But it's no good.' I said. 'The police own it now. The engine is finished. It's just scrap, *terminado*, *caput*. It's not worth bringing it here, and anyway, I can't, it's not mine any more, it belongs to the police.'

They still wanted the car. 'You have to give it to our department, not the police,' they said.

And there was the matter of the fine. I was told that if I didn't take the car out of the country, I not only had to give them the car but also pay the value of a new one as a fine. I was definitely not happy.

'OK,' I said, 'I'll be back,' sincerely hoping I wouldn't be, while wondering how to get out of the country and into El Salvador with the picture of a car in my passport.

Looking at the roadmap, I noticed much of the southern border followed a river. Maybe Mille and Tannith could catch a bus and I could swim across? But that would create the problem of me being in El Salvador without an entry stamp, which was probably not a good plan. Though maybe it was better than being in Guatemala and owing them a few thousand of my hard-earned dollars? While asking around for other ideas, a local said it was a bad plan anyway as the river was full of crocodiles. Maybe crossing over the mountains was a better idea? But no, there were armed patrols up there. It wasn't looking good. Then a family on the campsite who had their own car said they were leaving for El Salvador the next day, and we could join them. We jumped at the offer, though I hadn't a clue how I would get across without being arrested. As we approached the border I finally had an idea: I creased my passport continually so that it automatically fell open at a blank page. The driver gave all the passports together to the passport officer, who studied the driver's, stamped it, flicked the rest open, including mine, stamped them all and waived us on. I was out!

From El Salvador we caught the bus to Honduras where Mille was made welcome being Norwegian, but I was told I couldn't enter as I was British and Britain had stolen a part of his country.

'You only had logging rights,' he said, 'but you claimed it and called it British Honduras.'

'But I have to be with my wife and daughter,' I pleaded.

In the end, he relented and stamped me in, but he wasn't a happy man. (The following year, despite Guatemala's claims, British Honduras was renamed Belize, finally becoming independent of Britain in 1983.)

From there, still travelling by local transport, we entered Nicaragua, and on to Costa Rica where we took a train through the jungle to enjoy the Caribbean coast for a few days. The little hotel was a real dosshouse. The blanket over the bed was red, but disturbed by movement in the night I switched the light on and it was black. Then the blackness moved: it was totally covered in cockroaches, which scuttled away at speed into every crack in the walls and floor. It wasn't easy to sleep again, but we found another place to stay next day before returning to San José and catching the bus to Panama.

Having found a reasonable place to stay we were told a cruise ship was leaving for Rome in a few days, but old habits die hard and I rather liked the idea of working my passage back home on a cargo ship with Mille and Tannith as passengers. I asked around for a couple of days at the Panama Canal docks and finally found a job as a deckhand on a Norwegian ship, but no passengers allowed – not even Norwegian ones – so Mille and Tannith booked their cruise ship and I signed on to the cargo ship.

23

BACK HOME

Back in England, I called in at Ken and Di's farm. Di was outside in her dungarees and wellies wheeling a barrow full of cow muck from the shippon.

'Aren't you going to say hello?' I asked. I got a big welcoming grin.

'Oh it's you!' she said. 'I didn't know you were home. Where're Mille and Tannith?'

We were back in my hillside cottage. Troll was now in an old mill further up the valley – it was doing well. So well in fact, that both Alan and Paul were working full-time with occasional help from Rimmon lads. They even had enough work to put me on the payroll. If I hadn't gone to Canada, Paul wouldn't have been at Troll, but they were understandably a bit miffed about my prolonged absence, so suggested that I start on the wage I was earning when I'd left two and a half years previously. That was fine by me; I was just happy to be back with them at Troll.

Working there was never about money; I worked there because I enjoyed it. It was great to wake up in the morning looking forward to going to work, although I called it 'going to Troll'. As the saying goes: 'Choose a job you love, and you will never have to work a day in your life.' It was like that for over twenty years until the climbing business began to change due to commercial pressures and increasing competition, but in the 1970s and 1980s it was fun.

Troll soon moved again into larger premises in Uppermill, Saddleworth's main village, and with our savings from the Yukon, Mille and I bought a second-hand Austin van and a house further up the valley. It was the first place I had lived in England since leaving my parents that not only had water on tap, but a bathroom and inside toilet – though like the others, the water was from a spring on the moor. The house also had a phone and we bought a TV, both were the first I had ever had. We also bought a coffee shop in Uppermill that Mille ran together with Di. It had two rooms, in one of which Mille opened a shop we called Bizarre, though it was known locally as 'the hippy shop', selling clothing, incense, jewellery and trinkets from places like Morocco, India and Afghanistan.

Climbing equipment hadn't altered too much in my absence, although the Whillans Harness – which had had a cautious reception when it was launched in the shops after the 1970 Annapurna expedition – was increasingly popular. One doubtful reviewer in *Mountain* magazine had written: 'If you want to be trussed in tape, this is the thing for you.' Well, people obviously did; we couldn't make them quick enough. Apart from its obvious safety advantages in a fall when compared with a rope around the waist or a simple belt, the Whillans also made it possible to carry a rack of gear with ease and order. We were also still making the Troll Mark 2 belt, plus a range of Troll slings, etriers, bandoliers, hammer holsters, the occasional hammock and bivvy tent plus other oddments.

However, the Whillans Harness wasn't accepted by all. By 1974, despite – or perhaps because of – its increasing demand in Europe (where the design was swiftly emulated by Petzl), the doyens of the UIAA Safety Commission were becoming concerned about the safety of sit harnesses in general. At that time, Paul had just become involved with UIAA standards via the BMC Technical Committee headed by George Steele.

Almost all continental climbers still used chest harnesses, although I had seen a climber wearing one fall off the first overhang of a Dolomite route. By the time he had been lowered to the ground, he was unconscious, only reviving after friends resuscitated him. However, Pit Schubert – technical expert at a meeting Paul and Alan went to – gave a talk on how dodgy sit harnesses were, but we were promoting the Whillans.

On his return, Paul told me, meticulous in detail as always, 'We did some drop tests with dummies off a cliff at Montserrat. I offered to jump off in the Whillans but Pit Schubert wouldn't allow it. His main concern was ending up upside down. In fact, that isn't the problem, but it is possible to smack your head against the rock as you can be thrown backwards in the arrest of a fall, particularly if you aren't holding the rope. There is also the unlikely possibility of slipping out of a waist harness if it is not correctly tightened.'

Even so, the popularity of the Whillans won the day and it was soon almost ubiquitous, paving the way for future sit-harnesses. In fact, it wasn't until 1993, over twenty years after the Whillans, that after promoting the use of full-body harnesses as a safer option, a UIAA Safety Commission update stated that: 'Recent developments in research concerning sit-harnesses have led the UIAA Safety Commission to reconsider its previous position … that [they] do not represent a safe way of tying in.' The report went on to say that graphic high-speed video images of falls in body harnesses resulting in whiplash and head injuries 'caused Pit Schubert to reverse his previous adamant stand against sit-harnesses and to admit that the question needed more study', although by then sit-harnesses had long been the norm, with Troll's designs at the forefront.

Meanwhile, not long after returning from Canada in 1972, I had met Mick Shaw. My Austin van was in the village garage for a service and the young long-haired lad who was working on it said enviously that he had read my Yukon canoeing story in the newspaper. He was younger than me and had just started climbing with some local Manchester Grit lads – Slim Jim and Bill the Drill. He was keen to do more, and we were soon away most weekends, often down in Wales where we got to know Denny and Shirley of Clog well, so in addition to having all the Troll kit we also had anything we needed from Clog.

It was good to be climbing with someone new to the game, introducing Mick to crags in the Peak District and the Lakes, but Wales was our favourite venue. We always looked forward to Gogarth and Cloggy, at which we had many memorable days. Three of the best being in August 1983 when we camped at Cloggy by the lake for a couple of nights, and what a cracking long weekend it was. In no hurry, nothing to prove, just enjoying being there alone on the cliff, on both the East and West buttresses: the interesting rope moves of *Llithrig* followed by the ever-greater exposure of *Sheaf*; the powerful *Shrike* and the delicate pleasures of *Bow-Shaped Slab*; the in-your-face verticality of *Vember* and the inquisitive, ever-searching, tentative probing of *Slanting Slab*. Then by night, we sat by the tent near the lake watching Perseid meteor showers streak across the clear night sky.

By now, Troll had numerous expedition orders. 1976–1977 was typical, supplying gear for around twenty expeditions, including two winter ascents of the Troll Wall by Czechs and Poles, plus the ill-fated British Ogre expedition on which Chris Bonington cracked some ribs and Doug Scott broke both his legs. Our reputation was spreading and we were now making harnesses for caving, hang-gliding and industrial use by steeplejacks and

North Sea oil workers.

Around that time, 'Friends' came on the market in sets of four sizes, designed by Ray Jardine and marketed in cooperation with Mark Vallance of Wild Country, who gave me a set to try. Mick and I were down at Gogarth the next weekend, that most 'Friendly' of crags, but Mick wouldn't use them, his argument being that all the routes had originally been climbed without, so using them would reduce the chance of big falls, thereby reducing the 'fear factor', and psychologically downgrading the routes.

'Well,' I said, 'the same applies with nuts. There were lots of hard routes climbed without them in the 1950s, but we all use them now and think nothing of it, so just think of them as big nuts.'

It wasn't long before he succumbed; the temptation was too great. Like other new climbing inventions, they were double-edged: for the elite they made previously unthinkable first ascents possible, while for the rest of us they made previously poorly protected routes safer and therefore easier. So Mick was right: it's cheating really.

A rumour was also going round that Wild Country were designing a harness with Pat Littlejohn, which was rather worrying, as we had the harness game to ourselves. The Whillans Harness had taken over from the Mark 2 and held centre stage worldwide. It was time for a rethink. I started off by playing around with our Mark 2 waist belt, the one we had used on the Troll Wall. It could be attached to a sit sling to make a crude sit harness, a bit like the American Forrest harness that was also made at Troll. My objective was to combine the separate waist and leg loops into a one-piece sit harness. It wasn't working. The sitting position was uncomfortable, whereas the Whillans – despite rumours to the contrary – was very comfortable.

Why did the Whillans work? I climbed in it all the time and frequently had hanging belays, but to check, I hung in it from our harness-testing beam in the mill to remind myself what was going on. The answer was immediately obvious: it worked because the crotch strap we had designed with Don for the Annapurna climb took the load first, pulling up and away from the body, and lifting the leg loops to take the bulk of load on the thighs before sharing it with the waist belt. The problem was simple: how could I repeat that without copying the Whillans crotch design?

Sitting in the Whillans, suspended from the beam, I had one of those 'Eureka!' moments: a small loop (or 'belay loop' as it became known) would do exactly what the upper half of the Whillans' crotch did. All it needed was a different shape of leg loops to go with it. The Troll machinists quickly made the first sample. The world's first 'belay loop harness' was born; we called it the Troll Mark 5.

We exhibited it at the shows in England and Germany at the same time as Wild Country's Littlejohn harness came out. Within a year the Mark 5 principle was copied by the world's harness manufacturers and rapidly became the template for almost all climbing harnesses. Even today, over twenty years since we sold Troll, out of the dozens of harness designs now available most use the Mark 5 concept.

I used to say I never had a holiday. Even when I was away from Troll, I was still working 'testing gear', which was indeed true, as where better to design and test gear than on the crags … though I can't say that Alan and Paul were overjoyed by my frequent absences.

That said, another trip soon loomed on the horizon. Bill Tweedale had been climbing in Romsdal with some Danes while I was in the Yukon and had been invited to go on an expedition to Greenland to attempt the 2,000-metre unclimbed south face of Ingolfs Fjeld. Was I interested? I was! Dolfi Rotovnik was one of Troll's export customers in Denmark and the leader of our rather grandly titled Anglo-Danish Expedition, which included Niels Ole 'No' Coops Olsen, Kaj Olsen and Pete Christensen on the climbing team, with four others and Dolfi forming the support team, with plans to explore nearby peaks in this little-known area.

1 Me and my sister Kathryn, 1946.
2 My mum and dad, seaside holiday, late 1940s.
3 With Kathryn in the very early 1950s.

4 On the first ascent of *Rimmon Wall*, Ravenstones, in the Peak District, 1963.
5 In the Peak District, winter, 1963.
6 Whale catcher, coming to the factory ship, 1958.

7 Bob Orrell, me, Dick Blackmore and Tony (Jonah) Jones, posing for
the press after our canoe crossing of Cardigan Bay, Wales, 1963.
8 Di on the *Fehrmann Route*, Campanile Basso, Dolomites, 1984.

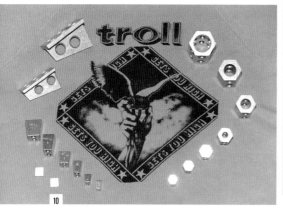

9 Troll Mark 5 prototype harness, 1978.
10 'Troll gets you high' T-shirt and chocks.
11 The three directors of Troll: Alan Waterhouse, me and Paul Seddon.
12 The three pillars of Breitind, Semletind and Trollryggen with the Troll Wall in shadow below the latter, and the highest peak, Store Trolltind, on the far right. Romsdal, Norway.
13 The Norwegian and British teams celebrating after the Troll Wall climb, Norway, 1965.

13

14

15

16

17

14 On the first ascent of the south-east spur of Norafjellet,
   Romsdal, Norway, 1967.
15 Me in the early 1970s.
16 On the top of a new route in southern Norway, 1975.
17 Crossing the Mackenzie Delta, Arctic Canada, 1971.

18 Unloading our equipment on our Ingolfs Fjeld expedition in East Greenland, 1973.
19 Carrying gear to Ingolfs Fjeld. East Greenland, 1973.
20 On a new route, *Forbidden Fruits*, at Great Rocks in Chee Dale, Peak District, 1977. The crag is now buried in quarry waste.

21 On our way to the Karun River: Ernst Renner, Mille (above), Tannith (below) and Mick Shaw. Iran, 1976.
22 The south face of Iharen. Our chosen route, the *Kohlmann-Dufourmantelle Direct*, climbs the columns directly
    below the summit. Hoggar Mountains, Algeria, 1979.
23 Mick Shaw carrying water from the guelta in his goatskin. Hoggar Mountains, Algeria, 1979.

24 Tannith in the Taghia Canyon, with Jebel Oujdad in the background. Morocco, 1980.
25 The then unclimbed face of the Cathedral (Imsfrane) on the way to Taghia. Morocco, 1980.

26 The M'goun Canyon – Mark and Tannith on the mule, and Mick and Di behind. Morocco, 1980.
27 A committing crossing of the M'goun River. Morocco, 1980.
28 Tannith and Mark with Muhammad, our guide. Morocco, 1980.

29

30

31

32

29 Di on the rope, crossing the sea to the Old Man of Stoer. Scotland, 1984.
30 Di thirstily devouring a melon after we returned dehydrated from climbing Jebel Kassala – water was in short supply.
31 Mick and Di on the summit of Jebel Kassala. Sudan, 1983.
32 Taking a break during the five-day train journey to Nyala, western Sudan, 1983.
33 Sheikh Atieq, the head of the family that welcomed us to Wadi Rum and encouraged our explorations. Jordan, 1984.
34 Isolated Bedouin camp in the south of Wadi Rum.

35 Di on the first pitch of *The Beauty*, Jebel um Ejil, Wadi Rum, late 1980s.

24
GREENLAND

In the summer of 1973, we flew to Kangerlussuaq in western Greenland, where reindeer grazed by the runway. From there we took a smaller plane across the ice cap to the landing strip on Ammassalik Island before going by helicopter to the Inuit village now called Tasiilaq, just south of the Arctic circle, and then north on a small whale and seal catcher to Kangerlussuatsiaq Fjord. It cost quite a lot of money and took nine months' planning, all to get nine men to the foot of a remote mountain and, hopefully, at least two of us on top. Reaching our chosen objective was not merely a matter of adhering to plans and schedules; finally we were dependent on two imponderables: the whim of the Inuit and the state of the ice. Both move in their own time and neither pay heed to the strange unnecessary urgencies of people with obscure missions such as climbing mountains.

We left Tasiilaq a couple of days late which was quite reasonable really, but this lessened the time available for climbing which, as it turned out, was not at all reasonable. Even at Tasiilaq the ice was thick. By the time we reached the isolated cluster of cabins known as Sermiligaaq to pick up our Inuit pilot, we had already been squeezing between 'bergs only a metre either side of the boat and everyone was decidedly impressed.

After Sermiligaaq, with the stink of seal meat and the howling of the dogs filling the night air, we came into real ice and that, I would have said, was that. The Inuit crew obviously knew better and directions were passed from the crow's nest down to the man at the bows then back to the bridge as we crunched through narrow leads or ground our way through floes of ice. Winding through the maze, the boat went deviously north following or forcing an irretraceable path, only to find after an hour or so the way was impossible, then back by other cracks and crannies to explore the shoreline, in and out, round and about.

I had given up all hope of reaching the mountains and wondered if the Greenlanders were doing it because they were paid by the hour, or for the occasional seal they bagged to supplement the strips of dried seal blubber they were chewing on: difficult to chew, and strangely inedible, but no doubt good for you. I was wrong of course; as the night wore on and with thanks to their persistence we were greeted with our first view of Ingolfs Fjeld.

Then the mouth of the fjord blocked solidly with ice. Up in the crow's nest, oblivious to the sub-zero temperature, even the Inuit skipper didn't seem too optimistic as we wound slowly north crossing the whole mouth of the fjord to find only one small entrance. In we went, twisting and turning, creeping and crunching through the ice, but with little more than fifteen miles to go, out we came again – no chance. So back we sailed; back across the mouth of the fjord, back to the southern cliff-rimmed shore and, if we hadn't missed something the first time around, back home.

Months of work and planning would have been wasted if they hadn't spotted one last possibility: between towering 'bergs drifting seaward from the Glacier de France at the head of the fjord. This time we were lucky; as one lead ended, another opened as we twisted our way through the barrier into the inner waters of the fjord.

The boat was unloaded without problems and chugged back into the echoing tunnels of the ice-filled distance. Fjord Camp was established and the first carry began jovially through springy heather and with roaring waterfalls to please the eye and ear. Higher, we continued with somewhat less pleasure through stumpy hummocks of bog-concealing grass, disturbing ever increasing swarms of mosquitoes. Finally, we staggered sweat-ridden up a mind-blowing, mile-high ascent of loose boulder moraine that rose steeply into the glacier-filled cwm below the wall.

The south face was a breathtaking sight – worth all the hassle of the past months, even the toil of the past hours, and it dominated everything around us; huge, even frightening, in its immensity. We entered the cwm and pitched camp like insects trapped in the web of a large and evil spider. The more we looked, the larger and more ominous it became. It was time to get to grips with it before we were mentally demolished.

The next day, after another carry from the fjord, Kaj and I made a quick reconnaissance of the route to be greeted with the rumble of avalanches down hidden couloirs and the nasty hiss of falling stones. Summer was starting late, but a way was visible. Our proposed route straight up the central pillar was a definite possibility, and an obvious 300-metre chimney splitting the lower slabs and overhangs seemed to give access to it. The morning after, we began.

Bill hammered the first peg into the vertical edge of a waterfall cascading down this section of the face. Off to a wet start, but the first blow had been struck and we were away. This initial pitch alongside the waterfall and across a hanging snow sérac gave access to the chimneys. Following these we ran out our first 240 metres of fixed rope on unexpectedly easy climbing with only occasional harder sections.

Thinking it was too good to be true, we left our gear and descended to base in the cwm, while Kaj and No took over with some extra rope and equipment to establish a bivouac. The first obstacle had been passed with surprising ease. It only remained to haul the gear up for a bivvy before attempting the next section, which would be a traverse of the huge rock amphitheatre to gain the central pillar.

The second day of the climb found Bill, Pete and me cursing and sweating as we worked our way painstakingly up the lower pitches with the haul bags. Five people and 1,800 metres of unclimbed rock equals a lot of gear, especially when the descent of the only known route takes two days. We weren't even sure the planned descent could be found in bad weather, as we had no knowledge of the other side of the peak. For this reason we were carrying sufficient pegs and slings for a descent of our own route. After a day of hard effort we reached a point a couple of rope lengths from the bivvy and Pete, preferring life at base to the dubious pleasures of bivvying, abseiled back down. Bill and I jumared up to the bivvy into which I collapsed with relief, leaving Bill to brew up.

The next morning, with clouds creeping in from the coast, we went back down to the haul bags and refilled our climbing sacks with essential ropes and ironmongery and returned to the bivvy to have a go at the slabs above. Meanwhile, three black Danish dots left base to continue with sack hauling and carrying – a job I didn't envy in the slightest. The route ahead – if we could cross the danger zone – looked superb. A long pillar of rock thrust its way up the centre of the face between two couloirs providing a classic direct line to the summit. Each tower of the ridge would present its own unique problem. True to form, the uppermost was also the longest and looked the most difficult. Beyond, easier-angled rocks led to the summit.

Gazing upwards, our minds climbing ahead of us to the top (wouldn't the view be superb!), we were abruptly brought back to the reality of our ledge as a huge tower at the top of the central pillar a hundred metres to our left detached itself from the summit, followed by a torrent of house-sized boulders.

We watched in awe as the rocks fell, seemingly in slow motion. They were so far above us and to one side that we had no sense of imminent danger as they crashed down the opposite side of the amphitheatre and smashed against the wall, still half a mile above us. There, they exploded in a cloud of smoke, a thousand pieces of screaming shrapnel heading out across the wall in our direction. Suddenly, supremely aware of a sky filled with black death-dealing missiles, we watched, now in fear, intending to duck or dodge as each one whirled past. Increasing in size as they rushed downwards, it soon became only too obvious that there was nothing to do but curl up and wait.

Decision made, we put our sacks – still full of gear – over our heads as the first rocks ricocheted off the walls above and around us. The air filled with dust and cordite. There were thuds and thumps as boulders and stones crashed on our ledge, jabs of pain on partly unprotected hunched shoulders and legs, then a receding rumble and the hiss of an avalanche in the couloir below, and it was over. The avalanche continued for half a mile out on to the glacier, but stopped just before reaching our camp. The sky was thick with dust that settled slowly over the face and, from the wall below, only silence.

Was anybody hurt? We should have been dead. My leg throbbed from a bad bruise but otherwise I seemed unbelievably intact. Bill peered out from under his rucksack, still with a brew in his hand – the sack was in shreds, but he was in one piece. What of the others down below in the chimneys? Shouts were drifting up, all completely indecipherable. We got the walkie-talkie out and managed to contact Dolfi down on the glacier some distance away. The news came back: 'Everyone okay.'

The mountain had made its point; without a drop in temperature it would be a very dodgy business crossing the amphitheatre. Not only that, but the first bivouac, despite its seemingly safe position on the edge of the basin, was just as exposed to rockfall as the actual bed of the couloir. The first job was to move into a safer shelter. This took up the rest of the day as Bill and I explored various possibilities above and below, before at last discovering a shallow cave partially protected by a leaning tower into which we moved the gear. By now, Kaj, No and Pete had joined us and we were all five together on the face for the first time.

Kaj and No decided to continue that evening and have another look at crossing the slabs. They left us in our sleeping bags to ponder the advisability of it all, and for the next few hours the occasional ring of a peg, not to mention the all too familiar hum of falling stones, punctuated the light Arctic night until we slept.

We were awoken at four. Kaj and No had returned after crossing the slabs by some difficult grade VI climbing with tension traverses and pendulums. Ropes had been fixed almost to the central snow couloir and it was our turn to go. The weather still held but looked doubtful as Bill and I set off up the diagonal prusik on our third morning. Frequent anxious glances at the scarred surface of the slab above us were a constant reminder of the hell that could erupt at any second. We climbed on to the end of the fixed ropes and moved out beyond to view the snow couloir. It was peppered with rocks. Jagged pieces littered the ledge around us. On the other side, a further 150 metres of slabs had to be crossed before we could expect any adequate protection from rockfall.

This whole exposed section of the route had to be crossed at least once, probably twice, by each of the five of us in order to provide sufficient food and gear for the ascent of the pillar. There was also the question of descent, which would more than likely be in bad conditions. *How then would we cross the couloir, and how would the ropes fare in the meantime?* We pondered the chances of five people crossing two or three times in safety and decided in the present conditions the odds against us were too great. Virgil wrote in the Aeneid, 'Fortune favours the bold', but this was a disaster waiting to happen.

All was not lost, for across to our right, curving up into the clouds hanging on the summit, was another pillar forming the right-hand rim of the basin. If we could follow this we were still in with a fighting chance for the top. With a positive course of action open to us rather than the ignominy of retreat, we returned down the ropes for a talk with the other three. An hour later, new plans agreed, we had traversed back into the entry chimneys and Bill was moving off up a superb 45-metre diedre. A truly enjoyable pitch of jamming and bridging, it brought us to ledges beneath a sweep of slabs split by beautiful curving cracks and overlaps.

As the first snow began to fall we put on our jackets and Bill grabbed the lead again, jamming and laybacking up another pitch of perfect rock.

My lead next, and above us lay another bulge. Loving every minute of it and oblivious to the snow I moved up to the lip and, just where it should have been, another crack appeared and snaked off up the next slab. A long traverse to the right brought nothing, but a peg in the crack and a tension traverse left revealed another perfect crack. We had been able to fix 150 metres of rope and the way ahead looked clear, at least to the base of the mist. Not only that, we had enjoyed an excellent day's climbing after the frustrating retreat from our original choice of route. Back at the bivvy we changed roles again with Kaj and No, who retrieved the ropes they had placed the previous night before resuming with our new line of ascent. Pete, feeling there was little he could contribute at this stage, abseiled back to base while Bill and I ate and slept contentedly in our familiar surroundings.

The fourth day dawned and it was snowing gently as we packed the gear and set off up the ropes making two arduous trips each with heavy sacks where we had climbed swiftly and without effort the previous day. The snow fell thicker and the wind increased as we went slowly upwards. Eventually we decided to continue with one sack each and return later for the others. It was early afternoon when we arrived at the small ledge where No and Kaj had bivvied, now almost 900 metres up the face. Visibility was down to one rope length and the rocks were plastered with snow. We crawled into the tent, wet but happy, and were soon clutching hot brews in our numbed hands. But not for long. There were still two other sacks to be brought up, and the sooner we went for them the better.

That was an unpleasant trip: 180 metres back down the face on snow-crusted ropes, then all the way back up, wet and cursing. We cursed even more when the time came to retrieve the sodden, heavy mass of ninety-metres of rope to fix tomorrow or the day after on whatever lay above – if the weather cleared. The weather, however, remained the same with only a few brief bright patches thrown in for contrast. The gear was covered in snow, and ice hung from the ropes. As afternoon came around and the snowfall continued unabated we set off down the wall to join the others at base.

The face remained plastered in snow for three days with the summit towers sheathed in ice, until finally the constant flow of avalanches swept it clean. Eventually the weather cleared. After a sun-drenched day of cloudless, impeccable blue skies we resumed our attempt with high hopes of success. Kaj, No and Pete went first in the evening. As they moved out of the chimneys on to the upper slabs beyond the first bivvy, Bill and I followed.

By midnight we were on the wall again. The fixed ropes were a little worse for wear. To the south-east a few clouds were visible again on the coast. By 2 a.m. a blizzard was sweeping once more across the face – strange to think that only twelve hours before we had been basking naked in the sun. Caught by the totally unexpected storm we were forced to stop at the first bivouac, struggling miserably into a wet tent. Conditions worsened rapidly throughout the night and within a few hours the whole of the face was once again coated in heavy, wet snow. We radioed our position back to Dolfi and a few hours later, with the storm still raging, started our descent through the waterfalls of the lower chimneys. The others, who had spent the morning in the upper bivouac, were bitterly frustrated at being forced to descend yet again without the weather having given us a chance to attempt the steep upper walls, but mountains will be mountains.

On the lower summits, the weather was better. Tom Rishøj and Peter Søndergaard made a first ascent of a fine alpine ridge just across the valley. Bill and I did a quick climb up the eastern couloir and ridge of an outlying tower above base, naming it Angdan Tower after our expedition name. Then the gear had to be carried back to the fjord, where the throb of a returning boat's engines heralded the end of our stay. We had failed in our attempt on Ingolfs Fjeld, but we were happy to be alive and had experienced a wild three weeks in Greenland's mountains in good company, which can't be bad. Before leaving the fjord we sailed further up, disembarking to collect some huge plants like wild rhubarb with an astringent taste. The Inuit loved this Greenland delicacy, and it was fun to spend time with them gathering the crop.

The south face was climbed two years later. Tony Mercer had attempted it in 1971. He returned in 1975 with a team of eight including Keith Myhill and Jim Davenport, gaining direct access from the glacier to the central pillar and grading the climb 6,200 feet (1,890 metres), ED 6+.

A couple of years later I was back in Greenland with Mick and some Danes, climbing a recently discovered set of peaks called the Organ Pipes. It was a fun trip climbing two new summits and doing some canoe exploration. Paddling up the middle of Tasiilaq Fjord, stripped to the waist enjoying the sun, Mick and I saw a white-crested wave of water approaching in the distance. At first we were unsure what it was. As it neared, we noticed with some anxiety the windswept spray and rough water behind the initial wave – and suddenly we were in it: a mini tsunami driven by a strong katabatic wind sweeping down off the ice cap. We were instantly soaked with ice water, with no time to put our clothes on. If we continued we would soon be dead of hypothermia even if we didn't capsize.

But luck was on our side. Though most of the shore was rocky or cliff lined, we just happened to be level with a small shingle beach. It was the only one we had seen, and our only hope. Turning the canoe sideways against the waves was not a good plan but had to be done.

'Okay?' I asked.

'Go for it,' Mick replied.

We cranked it round, taking on water, and paddled hard for the shore over a quarter of a mile away. Grounding on the beach, we leapt out only to see the canoe lifted by the wind and slammed into the cliff. We dragged it down and held on to it until the wind dropped as suddenly as it had started. The rest of the way back to camp was an anticlimax, but once again I'd had three great weeks in Greenland.

25

LIFE AT TROLL

Though Troll's initial aim had been to commercially produce chocks and waist belts, by the 1970s we were best known for webbing equipment. Clog had the reputation for metal gear, chocks and karabiners. Pete Hutchinson and Pete Merron who had started Mountain Equipment (initially with Pete Crew) in 1964 were already famous for their quality down equipment. Bill Wilkins did Ultimate Equipment tents. We all knew each other and at the Harrogate show we usually ended up kipping on the floor of Denny Moorhouse's mother. She was a very respectable and nice Harrogate lady who never batted an eyelid when her house was invaded. She used to say, 'You're not smoking those funny cigarettes again are you, Denny?' 'No mother,' he would reply, with a twinkle in his eye.

At the actual shows, we would be exhibiting new gear which, in later years, also included the new colour schemes as climbing was becoming increasingly fashionable and trendy. You got the colour wrong at your peril. Di Taylor had by then started working at Troll and we even used to visit ski shows to check out the latest clothing trends as climbing gear colours were always a year behind those of the skiing trade. By the 1990s it was all getting very competitive; everybody was selling everything, and competing with everybody else. Additionally, new British safety standards for climbing gear made innovation increasingly difficult.

But back then it was a good scene and a real pleasure to be part of it, with people calling in at Troll for a chat or for expedition gear. Doug Scott, who I had known since climbing in the Peak in my late teens, was an annual visitor.

'I could do with a few of those slings, youth, and half a dozen of your Whillans Alpinist harnesses – it's the best mountain harness there is, and do you still make those bivvy tents? We need a couple of them, and some etriers would be handy.'

Once, when my old mate Alan Baker was helping out at Troll, Doug and Alex MacIntyre were also in, having a look at how things were made – all three of them looking disreputable.

'It's Tony's scruffy mates again,' someone said.

'On the scrounge again,' came the laughing response.

Maybe they were, but Alan was doing some repping in London for us and Doug and Alex were off to the Himalaya on different trips. In fact, Alan was an accountant, Doug had been a teacher, while Alex was the BMC national officer, planning his Changabang West Face trip – one of the most serious and difficult Himalayan expeditions to date. Troll was supplying harnesses and slings plus our recently developed single-point hammocks. Doug had recently summited Everest and Alex, together with Nick Colton, had just made the first ascent of what became known as the *Colton-MacIntyre* route; a notoriously difficult climb on the north face of the Grandes Jorasses, destined to be an Alpine classic. Who *wouldn't* supply them with gear?

Doug Scott and Chris Bonington were both infallible on following up on their promises of photos and gear reviews on their return, such as Chris's quote after the successful 1975 Everest climb that, 'We thought the Troll harnesses were the best in the world'.

Choe Brooks was another regular visitor to Troll. He was doing some great routes at that time, including the first winter ascent of the *Swedish Route* on the Troll Wall with Hans Christian Doseth and Steve Bancroft. He used to call in asking if we had any free offcuts of material he could use to make chalk bags to sell directly to climbers. It never seemed to occur to him that we also made chalk bags that were of course sold in the climbing shops. He would consequently be undercutting us and the shops, but I always found him some anyway. He was a local lad with a permanently cheeky grin and he needed money to climb, so I couldn't resist.

The other good thing about Troll was that it was almost always possible to escape from work whenever the weather looked good, like grabbing a winter morning to dash over to the frozen waterfall at Kinder Downfall or a spur-of-the-moment decision to go down to Wales for a day's ice climbing or, in summer, nipping out on the local crags if friends called in unexpectedly. Providing I had completed the new catalogue and finished work on any new designs, costings and adverts ready for next year's autumn exhibitions, I could also head off on a long trip abroad without affecting production.

Having been away I always came back with new ideas; getting into the mountains and away from the daily routine always cleared my head. It also suited my lifestyle and, as a consequence, Troll was always understanding if any of the other employees wanted an extended holiday or time off. It was, in fact, a great place to work.

Once people started to work at Troll they almost never left: it was a good place to be, with a friendly village atmosphere. Years later, after we sold Troll, it was always a pleasure to be told at chance meetings with ex-Troll girls in the village what a nice place it was to work.

26
PERSIAN PERAMBULATIONS

Following my two Greenland trips and a winter trip to the Kabylie Mountains in Algeria that was more rain than sun, I fancied some hot rock and wondered about Persia – now called Iran – then under the rule of the Shah of Persia, an empire founded 2,500 years ago by Cyrus the Great. Don Whillans was dismissive of the country's climbing potential. He had driven through Iran on his motorbike on his way back to England after an expedition in Pakistan. ''Eaps o' mud,' he said.

I already knew about Alam-Kuh up in the north. It was high at 4,848 metres but reputedly very loose, and it seemed Iran's highest mountain Damavand, 5,671 metres, was just a slog. Undeterred, I had a feeling there might be some big walls in the Zagros Mountains, a little-known range of limestone peaks over 4,000 metres high and stretching a thousand miles from the Persian Gulf to the Elburz Mountains just south of the Caspian Sea. *Surely there was something hidden there?*

I asked the Alpine Club librarian, Margaret Ecclestone, if she had any info. Delving through old journals offered real hope for optimism: Sawyer wrote in 1894 of 'sheer precipices of 4,000 to 5,000 feet' near Borujerd, which is in the eastern Zagros not far from Kermanshah, and Tilman who passed through Iranian Kurdistan in 1942 mentioned a long pinnacled ridge with thousand-foot cliffs dropping down to the road near Kermanshah. My *Encyclopaedia of Mountaineering* also seemed to indicate possibilities; a report from Iran talked of cliffs of more than 1,500 metres. N.L. Falcon, reporting in his geological survey of 1932, claimed that 'precipices a mile high are not uncommon and often the smooth limestone slabs of the gentler slope rear upwards for a similar distance at an angle of 70°'. Describing the Karun Gorge he said it is 'grander than the Grand Canyon', and quotes his colleague J.V. Harrison, who says it is 'walled by 8,000-foot cliffs on the north, and 7,000 feet rock slopes on the south'. He also mentioned other cliffs of 900 metres. Dennis Gray, general secretary of the BMC, assured us that while passing through the area near Shiraz they had noticed a number of interesting peaks. Dennis gave me a letter introducing me 'to whom it may concern' at the Iran Mountaineering Federation and elsewhere, saying that he had 'no hesitation in asking that you give them every assistance'. Chatting with Clint, one of the Manchester Grit lads, I also discovered his brother was working as a driller based at an Italian pipeline construction camp near the head of the Karun river, a strange coincidence and possibly a useful contact.

You never know until you go, and it all sounded increasingly worth a look. I gave Ernst a call and he was keen, as was Mick. So I bought an old electricity board van and kitted it out with a bed and stove. Mille and Tannith came along too, which I really enjoyed, being together on the road again, and off we went with Mick, picking Ernst up in Andermatt and heading east through Venice into what was then Yugoslavia, camping on the empty beaches of what is now Croatia. Then on increasingly poor roads we passed through the very impressive Tara River Canyon – the longest in Europe, now in Montenegro. One day, rattling down cobbles, a spring broke, which Mick, our 'expedition mechanic', mended with strips of old carpet. It lasted the whole trip and Mick was renamed Magic Mick by Tannith.

Then on through Turkey to beautiful Istanbul with an essential stop for news of the route further east at the well-known Pudding Shop where the 'Magic Bus' stopped on its way to and from Afghanistan on 'the hippy trail'. Just across the road the domes and slender minarets of the Hagia Sophia and Blue Mosque formed a magical skyline above the Bosphorus, across which was Asia. Having invested in a Turkish bath where the masseur almost broke Ernst's back, we went back to the van on the outskirts of town. A guy even bigger than Ernst's masseur arrived and wanted money but as we were parked on some rough ground and there were no parking signs we ignored him. He bent down and attempted to let down a tyre, so I kicked him up the arse. Not surprisingly he went berserk, but Ernst and Mick dragged him off me and we quickly jumped in the van and sped off down the road.

The almost 1,000-mile journey on through eastern Turkey was uneventful but increasingly interesting the further east we went, with ox carts on the road, villagers working in the fields manually harvesting and threshing their crops, and occasional groups of nomads. In a village near Mount Ararat, we were invited to spend the night with the local miller who proudly showed us his water-driven stone mill in action. Then we entered Iran and three days later drove into Tehran. Tannith, who was eight, wrote in her diary, 'All the drivers are crazy and one of them bumped into the van and made a hole in the side.' Having found the post office we endeavoured to pick up some expected mail at the poste restante – something that was always guaranteed to be next to impossible. Having ascertained your surname initial, the clerk would hand over a grubby bundle of letters to sift through. Some would have the correct initial, some not. Some were ancient. It was a rare and happy moment if one of us actually received a letter, as this was our only connection with home.

We also visited the Iran Mountaineering Federation (the IMF). I had previously bombarded them with letters to various elusive addresses finally receiving a reply to a couple with answers that were only remarkable for their lack of information. When we tracked them down in Tehran, we were greeted with a similar lack of enthusiasm. However we eventually extracted a few relevant details. Firstly, that there were some climbs on a 400-metre face near Yezd, of which they had a photo. Secondly, they did not know of any walls at all in the Central Zagros. The one place they really enthused about was the south face of Kuh-e Bisotun, a mountain peak near Kermanshah; presumably the one mentioned by Tilman and perhaps by Sawyer, which they told us was 1,000 metres high and had had three ascents: one Iranian-German and two Polish. All routes, they said, were difficult, and they felt sure the region was destined to be one of international fame. Nevertheless, they had no route descriptions and we weren't sure if they were talking of three ascents of one route, or three different routes. On the subject of weather, they told us we should have come in the spring, despite the fact that one of their letters had recommended October!

Armed with this wealth of conflicting and confusing information we headed south past Damavand into the desert following the eastern edge of the Zagros where it and its rivers disappear into the Dasht-e Kavir, the Great Salt Desert. We were made welcome in an oasis, but there was nothing of climbing interest until just after Yezd where the cliffs steepened and heightened to around 150 metres or so. We spent a couple of days in this area where one particular gorge or 'tang' had very dramatic rock scenery. Trucking around the area the following day brought us a view of Shir Kuh (4,055 metres) which we presumed was the peak the Iran Mountaineering Federation had shown us a photo of, but the day was hot and we were not impressed.

On we went through the Dasht-e Lut, claimed to be the hottest place on earth, where the sand surface in summer reaches 70 °C, then to the south-east end of the Zagros range where it merges with the Makran Mountains between the Persian Gulf and the Great Salt Desert. Westwards then, through rivers and along rattling roads of corrugated mud and rock – our broken spring performing perfectly – and straight through the centre of the southern Zagros, home of the colourful Qashqai people. It was so hot we used to sit in the fast-flowing irrigation channels to cool down. The water had usually come miles though tunnels from the mountains, with shafts of anything from twenty to 200 metres deep dug from the surface every fifty metres or so during their construction. These 'qanats' date back over 2,000 years, and create a reliable year-round water supply for desert villages, making crops possible in otherwise hot and arid terrain. It was fascinating country, but still no climbing, so we journeyed on to Shiraz and its crowded bazaars and carpet sellers. Nearby, the magnificent carvings, columns and arches of Persepolis, a location chosen by Cyrus the Great but built by Darius the Great around 500 BC, told their silent tales of past glories.

From Persepolis, we headed northwards through regions of interesting but small cliffs and towers with Mick once again taking his turn at the wheel. We passed a bus on a long, straight stretch of road, then, looking back, Mick noticed it was speeding up. Before long it was alongside us. The driver slowed to our speed and eased in ever closer, forcing Mick towards the edge of the road, beyond which the hillside fell steeply to a gorge. The bus driver obviously wasn't pleased about being overtaken and was fully intent on pushing us over the edge. Then we saw a narrow bridge coming up with room for only one vehicle. With both vehicles almost touching and our inside wheels skimming the edge of the drop, Mick masterfully managed to stop within a few feet of the bridge, which the other driver sped across. He had almost succeeded in killing us. We lingered awhile to recover and allow the bus to disappear before continuing to Isfahan.

Like Istanbul, it is a stunningly beautiful city with exquisite blue faience-tiled mosques, their cusped arches decorated with stalactite pendentives, perhaps the finest being the Shah Mosque constructed in the early seventeenth century and now a World Heritage Site. We also wandered through other buildings and courtyards; its old bazaars were big enough to lose ourselves in, the cries of the muezzin echoing down the alleys where shaded caravanserais, tea houses and cafes had cool, splashing fountains of water – that most rare of desert sounds – with oranges floating in the pools below. What could be more welcoming after a hot desert journey?

From there, our quest into the unknown took us west towards the heart of the central Zagros and the great Karun river, home of the Bakhtiari tribe, accessible only by dirt roads and potholed tracks, and barred by river crossings and hills supposedly unpassable without four-wheel drive, which we didn't have. We churned on regardless through choking dust, being towed out of a stream by a passing Land Rover before arriving at the village of Do Polan (Two Bridges) with the back bumper hanging off but otherwise little worse for wear. The local military (each village had a soldier or two) were totally incapable of understanding why we were there and obviously wouldn't be happy until we left.

But we hadn't come all this way for nothing. According to Falcon's report there were cliffs up to 2,400 metres high just twelve miles further down the canyon. We needed to check them out, and climb them if they looked good. The next day, before setting off to follow the river downstream for a recce, Ernst, Mick and I arranged with Mille to be back in three or four days. Not enough, but it was the best we could do. Mille and Tannith stayed with the van with directions to drive up to the Italian prospectors' camp just upriver where Clint's brother worked if they had any problems. When the soldiers found only the two of them at our campsite by the river they weren't happy. 'Not safe,' they said, 'tigers, wolves, bears.' They were definitely wrong about tigers, but they didn't mention people: the local shepherd boys across the river who had apparently tired of their midday game of throwing goats off the high river bank into the rapids to watch them struggle out downstream had already smashed one of the van windows with a large stone thrown a huge distance with a sling. The soldiers told Mille we had to leave as soon as we got back.

Meanwhile, we were heading down the canyon following intricate trails between cliffs and overhangs and across dangerous slopes 100 metres above the river, until at the end of the first day we arrived opposite a beautifully situated village. A wire spanning the fifty-metre-wide river was the only means of crossing it and before long a small group of people arrived on the opposite bank. One man tied himself to a pulley and, suspended from the wire, pulled himself hand over hand to our side. One at a time he then roped each of us to him and pulled us back across the river where we were invited to stay the night. We had heard beforehand of the hospitality of the Bakht-iari people and were not surprised to find carpets laid out on the ground outside the headman's house at the top of the village. The teapot was ready on the charcoal burner and dark-eyed, dark-haired girls in rich costumes were preparing a meal, grinding rice between stones, pounding it in a hollow log and winnowing out the chaff in gleaming metal trays.

Sitting on the rugs we were treated to tea and salted pomegranate with unleavened bread, after which we said we should leave as we intended to camp a little further downstream. The headman however insisted we stay and stressed the dangers of wildlife in the area. When he served up heaped bowls of rice and fresh ibex we were finally convinced.

Next morning we were greeted with bread, eggs and cheese before setting off downstream again. We reckoned we had already come the twelve miles mentioned by Falcon, but despite the fact we were in the bottom of a beauti-ful canyon with occasional cliffs high above us there was no sign of the promised 2,400-metre wall; a major problem as we couldn't leave Mille and Tannith too long. A couple of miles further on brought a view down the canyon to the point where it changed direction to the west, and still no cliffs in view. Since Falcon explicitly stated the cliffs were north–south faces, it was obvious even from our outdated map that if they existed at all they would be at least another day's walk downstream. We had to turn back and decided to visit the pipeline construction camp for a chat with their pilots and perhaps a look at better maps than ours, which were of little use.

Back at our camp, Tannith said she had made a paddling pool but a snake had come in, and Mille told us of her hassles with the local militia who had given us one day to move out. We spent it at the construction camp where a glimpse of up-to-date but officially unobtainable maps showed us much to our surprise that Zardeh-Kuh was not the highest peak in the Zagros as we had always thought and which the IMF had indicated. Instead, another summit some eighty miles south rises to a height of almost 4,570 metres and, judging by the contours, has a very steep 1,500-metre face to the west. The pilot we were talking to however had no knowledge of that area but had flown in the Zardeh-Kuh region and thought that no big walls existed there (despite Sawyer's and Falcon's reports). It also seemed from the maps that the Karun Canyon walls (if they existed at all) must have been further downstream than Falcon's estimate, where the contours indicated extremely steep sides of around 1,500 metres.

Replenished with wine and information but disappointed at not being able to travel further down the canyon, we headed out the next day moving northwards and passing numerous small groups of nomadic Bakhtiari on their annual way south from the high mountain valleys where snow would soon be starting to fall. Some forty miles from Zardeh-Kuh we were forced to a halt by the abysmal state of the dirt roads where ruts, especially in the villages, were deeper than even our high undercarriage could pass. Since by this time the body and chassis joints had snapped at the front end, we decided it was time we looked elsewhere. Our last chance was the wall of Bisotun first reported by Tilman just outside Kermanshah, north of the Zagros and near the well-known cave system of Ghar Parau, which had been explored by Pete Livesey and friends. With Livesey having been in the area we weren't optimistic. Surely he would have climbed it or at least commented on it if it was any good.

Back on the main road, we passed Oshtoran-Kuh, a peak mentioned by the IMF, but saw nothing to attract our attention and the map showed no indication of better prospects on the other side. Fresh snow on the summit and sweeping rain clouds (the first of the trip) reinforced our decision to press on as rapidly as possible into Iranian Kurdistan before the weather broke completely.

Arriving at Bisotun in the late afternoon, we were at last greeted by a big wall – not only big but very accessible: 1,000 metres of rock towering directly up from the side of the old 'Royal Road', the Silk Road from China to Baghdad; a site of sacred springs above which are rock carvings dating back 2,500 years to the reign of Darius the Great. Described in a tourist leaflet as the 'Mountain of God', the wall extends two miles along the road and is characterised by numerous pillars of what would prove to be painfully tenacious limestone.

At the request of the local police, we camped near their police post at the foot of the cliffs where we picked out a line up the most central pillar. It showed no indications of previous ascents but looked as though it would give two or three days' climbing of a reasonable difficulty. This was quite enough considering the state of the weather, which had deteriorated to daily thunderstorms and savage onslaughts of rain.

We went up next evening to bivvy some 150 metres up the face, where the serious climbing began at the foot of the pillar. The next day, despite their steepness we were surprised to find that the initial pitches were rarely more than mild VS. Due to the unbelievable friction – like climbing up vertical hedgehogs – jamming was something to avoid! At 300 metres we passed a metre-and-a-half overhang with a peg for aid, and more steep cracks and chimneys brought us to the first of the terraces that cut across the wall.

The next 150 metres proved more difficult. With the weather still holding for the first time in a week we decided to press on, though no bivouac sites were visible above. An easy pitch brought us back into verticality and landed Ernst in the lead; this proved to be the nasty one. My turn was fortunately easier; I moved up in increasing darkness to the ropes' end – a ledge six feet by two, and our home for the night.

By the time the bivvy tent was suspended on to the ledge it was pitch black, but the weather was kind and we were inside, sleeping bags dangling over the drop and hot potatoes and soup inside us before the first fierce winds blasted torrents of water at the tent and threatened to tear us from our perch. Fabrics had improved considerably since my first polyurethane version made for the Troll Wall climb, and Troll was now using Ventile for the outer tent face. Not a drop penetrated the wind-battered tent as thunder and lightning flashed between the towers and lit the walls around us. Sitting on our ledge, the night passed with the occasional moment of sleep punctuated by more thunder or the sharp reminder of spiky limestone jabbing into the body. Eventually the skies quietened and in the half light of dawn the rain stopped and we dug out the stove for a brew. Mille and Tannith had had a better evening, having been invited for dinner with a local family near the spring of Taq-e Bostan with its 1,300-year-old carvings of horses, elephants and wild boars.

Little the worse for wear and with the rock already dry again, we began the next day pleasantly across slabs into an open couloir. Hidden away at the end of the first pitch there was (as always!) a perfect bivvy spot with room for all three to stretch out in comfort. Above, more chimneys and steep enjoyable slabs brought us to the third terrace where the wall deteriorated into a tangle of summit towers and gullies. We chose the central one and were rewarded with steep enjoyable climbing with few difficulties. Beyond, a short chimney brought us out on to the summit plateau – some 1,200 metres of climbing behind us. It was barely midday as we lay out in the sun, surprised by the lack of difficulties on the route and the consequent speed with which we had completed it. With another day's food and water in the sack, we fed well before descending the intricate but easy-angled slabs and gullies of the north face. By late afternoon we were back in camp with hands and boot soles almost worn away, but what better excuse to share our last can of beer!

After Bisotun, we journeyed on passing through Rezaiyeh where Tannith was impressed by the events in the market, writing, 'a little girl held a big snake that was alive and a man let the snake bite him in the arm and it bled. Then another man came and broke a stone with his hand and balanced a sword on a little knife. Then another man tied three chains round his chest and broke them all in one go.'

The next day we crossed back into Turkish Kurdistan, passing nomads with huge camels, their big snarling dogs with nails sticking out of their collars attacking our tyres. Once across the Euphrates we were happy to reach the tempting Mediterranean coast, at that time unmarred by tourist resorts, delighting in the greenness of its pine forests and the sparkling blue waters of the sea. Such a contrast after the long brown dusty miles of Iran. Then came ancient Troy before crossing the Dardanelles strait to western Turkey and back to Greece.

The trip was almost over. Though climbing was always the excuse, like most of my trips it was also about exploration and the journey itself, being on the road with friends, every day a new experience, meeting and learning from people of other cultures with other lifestyles. We had found one big wall, done an enjoyable new 1,000-metre climb, and had a good adventure – though still leaving some unanswered questions.

There are now over forty climbs on the Bisotun cliff but the mystery of the Karun river cliffs remains to tempt others with a nose for adventure. Undoubtedly, the best way to find out about them would be to descend this fast and beautiful river in a raft – which is what Tom Allen and Leon McCarron did in spring 2014. Tom emailed me recently to say, 'From Do Polan down to Ma'dan there was some utterly stunning terrain. I'm no climber but I imagine you could pick any number of spots. The descriptions about towering cliffs on the north-east side and rock slopes on the south-west side of the valley are correct. Also, there are more true canyons upstream of Do Polan than downstream, while from Ma'dan onwards the water is backed up behind a series of dams.'

By a strange coincidence, while I was writing this, I met and spent a few days trekking with Leon in Jordan. He was doing a long-distance walk in the

Middle East including most of what had been a project of ours, the 650-kilometre Jordan Trail. He told me there were what looked like 1,200-metre cliffs in the Karun Gorge, around eighteen to twenty-five miles downstream of Do Polan where the river takes an abrupt turn to the west, saying 'They were huge – real towering cliffs'. In a further coincidence, while researching trail funding following our completion of the Jordan Trail, who should pop up on the web but Tom, who was creating his own long-distance, 932-mile, Transcaucasian Trail from the Black Sea to the Caspian Sea. Funny old world.

Most people we met in Iran had been very welcoming, a few had been a bit offhand, most particularly the bus driver who seemed hell-bent on killing us. There was certainly something in the air and we weren't surprised when demonstrations against the increasingly brutal, corrupt, and openly extravagant regime of the Shah of Persia – who was supported by the USA and UK – commenced soon after our return home. Five years prior to our trip, the shah had celebrated the 2,500th anniversary of the founding of the Persian Empire in Persepolis at an astronomical cost of around $20 million – that's over a hundred million dollars in today's money, making it the most lavish banquet in modern history. This obscene extravagance inevitably invited criticism not only in the Western press but also by many in Iran, and contributed to the shah's downfall in 1979. He made his ignominious exit to the USA and then Egypt, to be replaced by Ayatollah Khomeini, who became the supreme leader of the Islamic Republic of Iran. It wouldn't be the last time that political upheavals followed in our footsteps, or in some cases overtook us.

Ernst was tragically killed on New Year's Day 1979. A huge and unprecedented avalanche from high up on the Pazolastock near his home in Andermatt killed him and his friend, Michael de Pret-Roose – vice president of the Ski Club of Great Britain – and two members of Michael's family.

27

AND THEN THERE WERE TWO

In 1978 Paul (Tut) Braithwaite was married in our local church, three years after he had played a major role on the successful Everest South-West Face Expedition. It was a top-hat-and-tails job. Doug Scott was best man, Chris Bonington was there too, and Al Rouse in his topper and open-toed sandals. Ken Taylor and I were ushers, so also in topper and tails. Richard McHardy was there with his wife, Babs, plus lots of others from the climbing fraternity. Many of them kipped at Ken and Di's, and Doug entertained us the following morning trying not very successfully to ride Di's horse bareback.

It was a much less happy and more traumatic year for me: Mille left me. Living with a rock-obsessed climber obviously wasn't the life she had hoped for. I was awarded custody of Tannith who was now nine years old. She saw her mum at her coffee house every afternoon after school and stayed with her at weekends, which meant I could still get away climbing. For me, having grown up in a happy family home, I felt I had failed Tannith by not giving her the same, though in time things settled down into a new routine and frequent visits to Ken and Di's home offered a feeling of normality for Tannith who was always happy there with their three kids – plus of course she had other friends living nearby.

With my regular climbing partner Mick away in Canada over the summer, Tannith and I went down to Cornwall for a couple of weeks with Ken and Di and their kids. Ken wasn't climbing much but Di and I did some decent routes together on a couple of days. She hadn't climbed since the Rimmon years; unlike me she had given it up for her family, but she was still keen and very capable.

One day, having had a full day on Chair Ladder, the tide was coming in but it had been such a good day on the warm granite with seals lying on their backs in the sea watching us, that we couldn't resist one more route. Scrambling quickly down to the bottom of the cliff, we saw that the start of our chosen climb was already under water so I boulder-hopped between waves to a rock a few feet from the crag. Di joined me then I jumped for the cliff, jammed swiftly up a crack, took a quick belay and just as she leapt off the rock, the next wave swept in and covered it. An hour later we were up and on our way back to the camp. Neither of us realised it, but not many years would pass before we were spending more time together – and not just on rock. The rest of the year I immersed myself in Troll and home life with Tannith, but as always, my mind frequently wandered to places afar.

28
ATAKOR ADVENTURES

By the start of 1979, Mick and I were both ready for another desert trip. After cancelling a trip to the Hoggar in 1977 because of a problem with my back, it was still on our ticklist. Sadly Alan Baker, who would have been with us originally, couldn't join us this time, so we had to leave without him on our 3,500-mile journey south.

The Sahara stretches for 3,000 miles across North Africa, and has long presented a tantalising mystery and a challenge to European travellers, explorers and mountaineers. Concealed within the desert, remote mountains provided a refuge for various tribal peoples who undoubtedly reached some of the tops on hunting trips. Early travellers and Victorian adventurers also climbed a few remote summits, but it was not until the 1930s that mountaineers and cartographers began to climb and document ascents of North Africa's numerous and varied peaks, from the frequently snow-capped mountains of the High Atlas in Morocco and the Simiens in Ethiopia to the barren volcanic plugs and craters of the Hoggar and the Tibesti in Algeria and Chad. The great theme linking these early European ascents had always been adventure and exploration. Our journeys had a similar ethos: we went with no other purpose than adventure and exploratory climbing for the fun of it, preferably in little-known mountains 'far from the madding crowds' and among people of a different culture than ours.

In the late 1970s travel still had its problems and information was difficult to get. The Hoggar Mountains in the Atakor region of the Algerian Sahara looked particularly interesting and it seemed there were still plenty of new climbs to be discovered. I had read in the *Alpine Journal* about the second British expedition to the Hoggar by Paul Luckock and friends who went in the winter of 1976–1977, a couple of years earlier and coincidentally the year that we had originally planned to go. I also managed to get some climbing information as well as some maps from Bernard Domenech, a member of the Groupe de Haute Montagne, and from the Italian Alpine Club. They showed the Trans-Sahara Highway didn't quite reach Tamanrasset and the Hoggar, but hopefully we would sort that problem out when we came to it. There were no roads in the Hoggar anyway, so Mick knocked up some sand ladders from pieces of scrap metal in Troll's workshop. Permit applications were unnecessary; just jump in Troll's VW van and go!

Mick's girlfriend Elaine, who worked at Troll, came with us, and with Mille gone, Tannith also came along. She had permission for time off school from her teacher, Jane – the wife of Tut Braithwaite. It wasn't a problem in those days.

After five days we were in Morocco for the first time since 1974, having taken the ferry to Ceuta – this time without any hassle. From there we headed east into the Rif Mountains, notorious for cannabis farms, with kids running into the road and trying to stop the van while waving what were obviously large blocks of hashish. Late in the day we stopped to fill up with fuel and a local wandered across to us and started chatting. He offered us a place to stay on his farm, which he said was nearby.

A farm in the Rif Mountains sounded dodgy, but it was also intriguing. We agreed and followed him down a track through forested hills towards the coast, eventually emerging at his farm in a remote valley surrounded by cannabis crops. Having sat by the fire and been offered mint tea, he showed us around. In one building was a press for making hash blocks, in another a still for making hash oil. He told us that he took it down to the coast at night on donkeys to meet yachts from France and Italy. Meanwhile his wife was preparing what turned out to be a delicious tagine dinner flavoured with local herbs – and we knew what those were – followed by a few joints which were passed around as the evening progressed. In the dim light of the fire, a few cattle could be seen contentedly chewing their cud in a recessed corner of the kitchen. *Were they also on marijuana?*

'I can strip the bodywork of your van and fill it with hash,' he offered. 'We will respray it afterwards and no one will know.'

'Thanks,' we said, 'but we are going into Algeria. We definitely don't want to be caught by their customs people.'

Finally he agreed it would be a bad idea and directed us to his barn for a night of sweet dreams on bales of marijuana. When we woke, bread was being made outside on the fire and we were greeted with mint tea and doughnuts – and there's nothing better than a sugary Moroccan doughnut! We left soon after, having thanked the family while wondering uneasily if he had stuffed some hash blocks under the van for his mates to collect over the Algerian border.

It was just as well he hadn't; the customs were a keen lot. They knew we had just come through the Rif.

'You have hashish?' they asked.

Fingers crossed, we said no, but we had to totally empty the van, which was a major job. Having checked everything and been asked about the climbing gear which was a total mystery to them, they wanted to peel off the fleece lining that was glued to the inside of the van's bodywork, but luckily abandoned that idea when one of them who was inspecting our food supply found some soup powder. They opened the poly bag, sniffed it, poked at it and tasted it.

'Maybe hashish?' they asked, as if they'd hit the jackpot.

'No,' we said. 'It's soup powder.' Then one of them had a great idea.

'Maybe you hide drugs here?' he said, jabbing at my arse with his finger and grinning at the thought. 'Maybe we have look?'

This was getting out of hand. I hoped he was joking.

'Sorry, my friend,' I said, 'we have no drugs. Nothing. We are visiting your country to see the Sahara and climb in your mountains. We don't use drugs.'

Finally they gave up and we drove off to make a much-needed brew, only to be followed by soldiers who moved us on. It was a relief when we left Algeria's northern hills at the end of the day and, having had our first view of the Sahara, descended to camp in the sands. Heading south the next day, our first stop was the oasis of Laghouat. Tannith wrote in her diary, 'The ladies were covered in white cloth except for one eye peeping out and the children wore djellabas and looked like Jawa men from Star Wars.' The kids were jolly enough, but it wasn't a particularly friendly place and they were obviously not used to strangers.

We moved on to Ghardaïa, a much larger fortified hilltop town built almost a thousand years ago, its white, pink and red houses overlooked by an ancient mosque. It was an interesting place to explore, getting lost in the warren of alleyways and enjoying the large oasis of date palms and gardens, contrasting with the encroaching Sahara. From there, the deteriorating road took us on past the edge of one of the Sahara's biggest regions of sand dunes to our next camp outside the oasis of El Goléa, another Berber town and said to have almost 200,000 date palms – the gateway to the southern Sahara.

With the road almost gone we headed south again the next day, one of the few passing trucks sending a stone spinning up through our windscreen, smashing it so badly we couldn't see, so we had to take it out. We stopped further on at the oasis of In Salah where a huge creeping dune covered the western side of the town. There was no chance of replacing the windscreen, but a cafe owner donated a sheet of polythene and we found a few bits of wood so we could cover the hole when we left it parked up anywhere, or when it was too dusty to travel with no window in, which meant peering through a hole in the polythene – though luckily that was a rare event. Otherwise we just carried on without a window and soon got used to the idea; it was getting hot, so the breeze helped! We could have been robbed any time we left the van in the desert or at an oasis, but we never were.

Now, 600 miles into the Sahara and over halfway to the Hoggar, we ventured off the well-travelled piste to look at some rock towers. But as Tannith wrote, 'We got stuck in the sand because on top it's hard and once you get through that you start sinking. We used Mick's sand ladders, but one of them broke and the other kind of went crooked.'

They got us out though, and we gave a couple of locals a lift to Arak before continuing to camp in the desert, reaching Tamanrasset (also known as Tam) the next day. Situated on the edge of the Hoggar, Tam is a Tuareg oasis at the centre of an ancient network of camel-caravan trading routes. Additionally, the Trans-Sahara Highway, which was completed a few years after our trip, reaches it from the north from where tracks head south to Niger and Mali. With water coming from springs in the Hoggar, despite extreme summer temperatures, fruit, dates, nuts and cereals are grown successfully.

While wandering around the busy market we met a young Tuareg lad called Moktar who asked us to his house for tea and became a good friend. As there was a campsite in town we slept there and Mick and I went off the next day for a swift climb on nearby Jebel Adrien. We then picked up Tannith and Elaine and headed out across the sand to camp at the foot of Iharen, an impressive volcanic plug of basalt columns reminiscent of Wyoming's Devil's Tower, rising around 400 metres from the desert to 1,563 metres.

We were up and out early next morning trying to beat the heat, and climb the *Kohlmann-Dufourmantelle Direct* on the south face. Graded TD+/ED, it was, as far as we knew, the hardest free climb on Iharen and as hard as anything in the Hoggar. From what bit of information we had, it had something of a reputation, but it was an obvious and attractive line. Paul Luckock and his team had had an epic on it two years before. Being unsure they were on route, they finally abandoned their attempt due to dangerously loose rock. Their ropes then jammed on an abseil over an overhang into the unknown and they only escaped after tying all their slings to the end of the abseil ropes to reach easier ground. On escapades into remote mountains it was rare that anyone knew where we were. Any problems or accidents had to be dealt with; no one was coming to the rescue.

The route looked good and was oozing with cracks. Initially the angle was easy but the basalt columns soon swept up into the vertical. We made our way up what sometimes turned out to be worryingly loose crack lines between the columns. Even some of the belays were dodgy, and being a south face it was increasingly hot – there wasn't even a desert breeze. By the time we topped out it was roasting. A great summit though, and in a spectacular location with other dramatic peaks rising from the desert – as was the sound of AC/DC drifting up from the van. We didn't linger. The descent was problem free, chopping sun-bleached remnants of old abseil slings and replacing them with new ones. It was reassuring to know we were on route, and we saw no sign of Paul Luckock's final dodgy abseil. We were back by mid-afternoon and surprised to find the beers which were stashed deep in the back of the van were still amazingly cool.

In Tam the next day we looked for a replacement VW window, but it was a vain hope. Instead Mick and I each bought a Tuareg cheche (the traditional Tuareg headdress) to keep the sun and sand off our faces, which was particularly useful when driving without a window! As we were going deeper into the Hoggar, Mick also bought a goatskin water bag to carry additional water from any springs or wells, after which we drove out for eighteen miles on sandy tracks to the foot of Jebel Adouada.

This time our route was on a north-west face; it was an easier route and barely half the height of Iharen. Out of the sun, we stayed cool and cruised it. Perhaps we were acclimatising to the heat. It was time to go further into the Atakor, driving the stony desert tracks between rock towers to the 'guelta' or spring where we topped up our water bottles and Mick's goatskin after a group of Tuareg ladies had filled their goatskins and gone off into the desert with their donkeys. Before leaving we grabbed the chance of a good wash further downstream and found some mint to make a brew of mint tea.

Another fifteen miles further on, after breaking a shock absorber, we finally camped at the foot of the Hoggar's most impressive peaks, the Tezoulags. We were interested in the west face climb of the South Tezoulag, a 350-metre TD with a long, good-looking diedre. It was an excellent route on the best rock we had climbed on this trip. Rhythmic climbing with few difficulties, our now tanned, dust-dry hands moved quickly on the warm, rough rock; movement flowed, conversation was sparse, skies were blue, a landscape as lonely as the moon. We basked in a breezy hollow on the throne-like top, a vulture wheeling effortlessly over the heat-hazed void. The climb had gone so quickly we decided to head over to the North Tezoulag and climb its slightly harder *South Ridge Direct*, which also went with ease – two routes for the price of one – finishing on one of the Hoggar's highest summits at 2,760 metres.

We spent the next day looking around the area and visiting the hermitage of Charles de Foucauld, a French Catholic missionary who lived among the Tuareg people in the early 1900s – a truly wild and remote place to live with stunning views across the towers of the Tezoulags. We noticed a small caravan of camels coming up the track, the people pitching camp just above ours. One of them looked familiar – it was Reinhold Messner. It was less than a year since he and Peter Habeler had climbed Everest without oxygen – he wasn't hanging around. Before long he was on the cliff and soloing the route Mick and I had done the morning before. Except he left the big upper diedre to follow a parallel crack line to its left. Mick had also gone wandering off to explore some crags behind us, so when Reinhold got back I went over to his camp with a bit of a tongue-in-cheek question to throw into the conversation.

'You seemed to be off line on the upper part of the route,' I said.

Just at that moment, Mick arrived, but hadn't heard what I had said.

'Were you lost up there, Reinhold?' he asked, rather more pointedly.

It was bad timing. One of us asking was bad enough, but two of us coming out with the same impertinent question must have been really annoying.

'I do not know any route. I do not have a guidebook. I make my own way,' he replied. Sorry, Reinhold, just an English wind-up.

The following day an icy wind blew at our camp, which was up at around 2,000 metres, so we picked a route on the smaller neighbouring summit of Le Clocher du Tezoulag. The crack system had ice in the back but we shivered our way up it successfully before dashing back to camp for a hot meal followed by a panful of steaming rice pudding. No cold beers needed that day. It was still cold the following day, but with the wind dropping the four of us went for a walk around a nearby mountain and had an early night: we had plans.

Dawn found us heading for a new route up a hanging diedre halfway up the left side of South Tezoulag's west face. The rock was poor and nuts pulled through the sandy crack. In the end, I placed a peg to pass the overhang and belayed over the lip on a giant thread. The first 200 metres were already fanned out below us; ribs of rock among gullies of aromatic herbs. The warm, scented smell of the desert drifted up. The next 200 metres were equally obvious: an inescapable, slowly widening corner crack. At half height it was blocked by a three-metre roof, fortunately with a retaining wall formed by one side of the corner, a knee-width nasty that Mick overcame with admirable determination and considerable cursing. Above, the crack continued to widen remorselessly, a body-width struggle, then a back-and-foot sweat, and finally a speleo trip winding incredibly between ever-larger chockstones. Suddenly we reached a fanged ridge through a gap in its teeth, greeting the sun and laughing in the wind: another day, another top.

We were on the move again, heading north through the dramatic Rhoufi Gorge and a high pass in the mountains of Aurès, into Berber country. Tannith wrote, 'It was cold and windy in the front of the van without a windscreen and lots of insects blew in'. We reached Constantine, a remarkable city split by a 300-metre-deep gorge with narrow suspension bridges above the Rhumel River. In its ancient markets along Rahbat al-Jammal, we were somewhat bemused by groups of heavily made-up girls in gossamer dresses, sitting in stone cells behind barred doors along the alleyways and beckoning me and Mick in. Whoever they were, and whatever their business, one lot fancied Mick and chased him down the passageway. The only time I ever saw him run away from girls!

We camped that night on a Mediterranean beach before driving into Tunisia where we camped in a Roman harbour at ancient Carthage – Tannith being pleased to discover her name was derived from that of the Carthaginian moon goddess.

A couple of days later we sailed to Palermo in Sicily, once again being the subject of a futile hashish search. By now, getting a window for the van was becoming a priority. In Messina we found a supplier. He was a jovial and very well-groomed Italian who invited us into his office for coffee while the window was fitted, the walls were hung with photos of him with Louis Armstrong, Marilyn Monroe, Bob Hope and Nat King Cole. Like many other Sicilians he obviously enjoyed good connections in the States!

Driving back home, our windscreen wipers squished away at Sheffield's grimy drizzle as we peered out at the landscape of chimneys and the austere, grey cooling towers sweeping ever more steeply skywards, reminding us of the soaring volcanic towers of the Hoggar. Westwards a dim sun sank disconsolately into the murk while 3,500 miles to the south the same sun would be casting a warm glow across the desert.

29
MEANWHILE, BACK AT WORK ...

Back at home I was still climbing at weekends with Mick and as always was involved with the next year's new designs for Troll. It was around this time that the use of chalk was becoming commonplace. Although it was originally used in the mid-1950s by American climber John Gill it wasn't really until the 1970s that its use became commonplace in the UK, perhaps popularised by Pete Livesey, Ron Fawcett and Chris Gibb after a climbing trip to Yosemite in 1973. They brought some back and continued to use it, though its use didn't become widespread for some time.

Notable south-west climber Rowland Edwards remembers someone using a stick of chalk to mark holds and around the same time his son Mark was using a sock filled with chalk with a safety pin holding it in place ... perhaps the first chalk ball? But not everyone was happy about chalk, most notably Pat Littlejohn and the Clean Hand Gang continued to climb clean and leave no trace. Ken Wilson too campaigned strongly against it, referring to its users as the 'powder puff kids', but even Ken gave up in the end.

I also had – and still have – my reservations. While I realise I am on dangerous ground here in an age when a climber isn't a climber without a chalk bag, I have to say I have never used chalk, that creator of dotted lines and defiler of a cliff's natural beauty, whose only *raison d'être* is to allow the user to climb harder. If chalk had only contributed to making the previously impossible possible, I could understand it, but what an unsightly penalty we paid when everyone got the habit. Even Diffs have become marked by chalk. The passage of a climber up a cliff should no more leave a trail than a walker in the untrodden wilderness. The way should be left for others to find without following a dotted line. Having said that, those dots of chalk on impossible gritstone walls never fail to impress, though as Ken said,

Stanage soon started to look 'like a school blackboard'.

Once, when climbing in Wadi Rum where route finding is a necessary skill, I made the second ascent of a climb done by some French lads the previous year. It was a steep and fairly blank-looking face with no obvious line, just a crack to head for a few hundred metres up. With little rain, chalk marks can linger in Rum. Arriving at the cliff, finding the start was easy as it was marked by chalked holds. Higher, where we had expected to need our expertise in searching for the best way, linking unseen but hoped-for natural thread runners, we simply followed the chalk, ignoring the false leads where we could see the first climbers had initially erred. We were able to climb almost without thinking up and across the face to the distant beckoning crack. In doing so the climb had lost its essence.

It wasn't long before commercial obligations at Troll outweighed my morals. Initially people were making their own chalk bags, but they were just up Troll's street. We already had the raw materials and the expertise. Our first design was the '6a Chalk Bag', named by me to justify its inclusion in our range. If I could climb up to 6a without chalk, then anyone could, and anyway the first ascents of most UK climbs at that time had been done without chalk. It simply wasn't necessary for the vast majority of climbers. Inside each chalk bag we put a small note to the effect that 'This 6a Chalk Bag is filled with invisible chalk. Use it with discretion and keep the crags clean.' No one took any notice but I felt better about making them.

But back in the 1970s, partly due to indoor climbing walls, chalk and a more serious approach to climbing – more training and less beer, climbing standards were soaring. We signed Ron Fawcett on at Troll, our first 'sponsored climber'. He and his wife Gill used to call in, arriving in Ron's Reliant Robin. Ron was always good to chat with and an inspirational climber. There couldn't have been a better name for Troll to be linked with, but a few years later, while I was away on a trip, Trevor Jones who was involved with Troll's marketing, and therefore with Ron, delayed some of his payments and tried to deduct some money for his use of Climbers' Club huts. The result was that by the time I was back, Ron had left and I never got to know the reason why until I saw him much later. I didn't blame him, but by then it was too late: Ron had moved on, and quite right too.

Our connection with Doug and Chris continued throughout all of my years at Troll, which was great for our mountain products. We were also joined at various times by other climbers, including Adam Wainwright,

Ian Vickers, Jibé Tribout, Keith Sharples, Gary Gibson and Rowland and Mark Edwards. In addition to testing gear, Mark also did some great T-shirt designs for us. They were also doing a lot of new routes down in Cornwall at the time, and using Troll gear and clothing, which was always good free publicity in the magazines. Keith and Gary were also avid new-routers. Gary seemed to be constantly cleaning the crags for climbs, and as most of the grit and soil seemed to get into his harness, he was the perfect gear tester, wearing harnesses out quicker than anyone. Mark Leach was also on the Troll team. He made the first free ascent of the aid route crossing the main overhang at Kilnsey, naming it *Mandela* as everyone said, 'It would never go free'. Pete Gomersall and Bonny Masson who were also actively developing Yorkshire limestone crags became a regular part of our design team and were great to work with. My favourite harness, the 'Black Master', came out of that partnership, as did the '9a Harness', which was one of Pete's ideas and was then the lightest harness in the world at 200 grams.

On the clothing side, Troll's lightweight and quick-drying multipurpose 'Omni Trousers' – which were almost indestructible – were a big seller for many years and came from a suggestion by Bonny. I still wear Omnis and use a Black Master harness, though I no longer wear stripy Troll tights, which sold like hot cakes in the late 1980s. Actually there's nothing better to climb in! Graham 'Streaky' Desroy also became part of the team and was a great frontman for Troll and our sales rep for many years. He worked at Troll with Frank Bennett, another valuable team member who had been in the climbing business as long as anyone, and seemed to know everyone and everything about the outdoor trade.

Andy Perkins was another full-time 'troll'. Using CASE funding (Co-operative Awards in Science and Engineering), we sponsored his Leeds University research into the development of a drop-test rig and a shock-absorbing lanyard. The project also included work on abrasion resistance and harness comfort and resulted in a PhD in textile engineering. Andy then joined Troll in 1988 working with me in research and development before taking over from me when we sold up. I had been keen to sell for a while, which is why I had looked for someone to work with me; a climbing company without a designer wouldn't last long.

In fact, I had always hoped to sell up when I was fifty, in 1990, but I was actually fifty-five when we found a buyer. We had done our first million pounds annual turnover in the 1980s; there were thirty of us then, a nice size and all from local villages – like a large friendly family. But we couldn't stay that way: the rule of the business world is that you have to expand to survive as well as becoming more competitive. As Edward Abbey said, 'Growth for the sake of growth is the ideology of the cancer cell'. It's death or glory out there in the commercial world, but we have finite resources on our little planet and despite only being a small company I was increasingly uneasy about gobbling them up at an ever-increasing rate just to keep ahead of the others, especially as nylon is a byproduct of oil, an increasingly dirty word. As Worldwatch said in 2015, 'Economic growth drives most environmental problems, and it has produced a world in which human activities have grown too large for the planet to accommodate them sustainably'. Sometimes, like Kerouac, I felt guilty for being a member of the human race. Running a business is being stuck in a trap: beat the competition or fail. We were growing too big and I wanted out.

Troll had become Britain's leading harness designer and manufacturer, exporting around the world, and had a wide range of other climbing and industrial safety gear to complement it, as well as a rope-access training team, all originating with the Mark 2 waist belt and the nuts and other homemade gear used on the Troll Wall in 1965. The camaraderie of the early years was going. As far as I was concerned, it was becoming more about making money than making climbing gear. Gone were the days when Troll made web gear, Denny Moorhouse of Clog made metal gear, Pete Hutchinson and Pete Merron of Mountain Equipment made down gear and we all kipped on the floor at Denny's mum's house for the Harrogate trade show.

By the early 1990s our annual turnover topped two million and we had around fifty employees. By now it seemed every climbing company made or sold every product. Fashion and colour were becoming more important than function and design. Business was simply about profit margins and growth and keeping the accountants and bank manager happy. Sitting in interminable meetings I found my mind wandering the hills and dreaming of my next trip rather than concentrating on boring accounts. Designing and making climbing gear had always been my motivation for working at Troll. For me, money was secondary. Ironically, new health and safety regulations – which, thanks to Paul, Troll had been in the vanguard of along with DMM – inhibited innovation, which was where my main interests lay. It was time to go, away from balance sheets and back to the real world of rock and wild places.

Denny had known how I felt for a long time and phoned me one day to say he had found a possible buyer, who I phoned after discussing it with Paul and Alan. He came to see us and made us a good offer, no negotiation needed. You might think the rest would be easy, but it wasn't. Once the accountants and solicitors got their hands on it, the final meeting was ludicrous.

We drove down to an expensive-looking office in Birmingham early one morning expecting to be back at Troll by five, as it was just a matter of signing the deal. They began with the expected amicable chat of businessmen's pleasantries and platitudes. My mind was already drifting to Morocco's bazaars and carpet salesmen serving up mint tea while chatting with their customers to establish friendship before pushing for the highest price possible. As the Bedouin say, 'Even if the wolves are friendly you can't be sure you will succeed', so I wasn't surprised when we eventually got down to business and they attempted to nibble away at the deal, coming up with reasons why the offer should be reduced. We weren't budging. We had already shaken hands on the deal: if they didn't want to honour it, they could forget it.

Lunchtime came and went. Documents were laboriously and meticulously discussed. Tea and coffee followed. At about 5 p.m. we said we'd had enough, we were going home. Instead they phoned out for pizzas and more coffee. 'Just a couple of hours more,' they said, knowing full well they were lying.

We talked into the evening. I told them they were wasting their time: they were talking to climbers and this was just another big wall. If we needed to bivvy we would do, but we weren't altering the deal. Alan had had enough anyway and went to sleep on a table in the next room. Good plan! They thought they would tire us out and we would succumb, but Paul and I hung on in there through the night. At dawn the next day they accepted we weren't going to budge and agreed to pay the original offer. What a waste of time that had been. A huge document was prepared for signing: Alan first, then me, then Paul. But, Paul being Paul, he said he never signed anything without reading it first, and who could argue with that? We had been there for twenty-four hours and there was enough reading in there to take up another day. Finally he relented and signed.

There was just one more job to be done: for the last few years we had employed a managing director and he had to go as part of the deal. I said

I would give him the bad news. When I arrived at Troll in the afternoon, straight from Birmingham, he was at his desk, waiting. I had no idea how I would tell him but fortuitously I noticed that the day's cryptic message on his desktop calendar read, 'The web of our life is a mingled yarn, good and ill together'. And so it was.

'Good news?' he asked hopefully.

'Well, yes and no,' I replied. 'It's as your calendar says, "good and ill together"; we sold, but I'm afraid they need your resignation.'

I felt terrible about it and agreed he should discuss it with the new owners. He managed to negotiate a few more weeks, but that was it. I still have the calendar page, Thursday 1 June 1995. I had wondered how I would feel after thirty years, but I never regretted it for a minute. I was free again with no work obligations. With Troll now owned by non-climbers the climbing side of the business was almost destined to fail, but I think I can safely say that the Troll equipment designed before and after the Troll Wall climb was revolutionary and has had an ongoing beneficial impact on climbing safety and therefore on climbing standards to this day.

The new owners, who had been financed by venture capitalists and really didn't know what they were doing in the climbing world, were forced to sell to a French company. Soon after that, they merged with an American company. They didn't advertise and they didn't know what to do with it. Hugh Banner paid a pittance for what was left of the climbing side, and it later re-emerged as a small climbing company in Yorkshire. Frank Bennett who headed up our sales team became the key man at Lyon Equipment. Graham 'Streaky' Desroy – well known for his climbing, especially in Yorkshire, and also for his notorious choice of highly colourful Hawaiian shirts – had been a great frontman for Troll, and also left, rightly being grabbed by DMM, while Bill Vinton, another climber and outdoor enthusiast in sales, emigrated to enjoy the great outdoors of Vancouver Island's superb west coast. Mark Carr, a keen climber, alpinist and paraglider who lived in the Wye Valley and looked after our sales down south, moved to the Shetland Islands to a remote west-coast croft with his soon-to-be wife, Christine. Andy Perkins achieved his ambition by becoming a guide in Chamonix. In 2004, he and Neil McNab were presented with the Denali Pro Award by the Denali National Park and Preserve and Pigeon Mountain Industries (PMI) for their 'exemplary contributions to the Denali climbing community with regard to safety, self-sufficiency, and assistance to other mountaineers' in recognition of their selfless and exceedingly strenuous efforts to help in two technical mountaineering rescues. In 2016, Andy received an honorary doctorate of science from the University of Nottingham for 'outstanding success and distinction' in climbing-related activities, including his work at Troll, plus work for the RSPB on a Moroccan sea cliff.

Troll's climbing team weren't the only ones to make successful careers for themselves. Three lads from Troll's rope-access training side started their own rope-access company, TAG, and employed other 'trolls', including our secretary, Tracy, who had basically run Troll in our last years. They did so well that they too sold up a few years later and the company continues to be successful, still employing ex-trolls. Barry Kershaw's daughter, Hillary, one of Troll's top machinists and our specialist sample maker, started her own heavy-duty sewing company, Red Road, employing other Troll machinists, and it continues to do well. Alan retired to what we euphemistically called 'his ranch' for his love of horses. Paul, who had been deeply involved since 1974 with writing what had become obligatory European health and safety standards for climbing and industrial safety harnesses and equipment, so enjoyed the task that he stuck with it and was eventually awarded the OBE for his efforts. He continues to enjoy the outdoor world and still spends his winters skiing.

Me? I still had the climbing bug. Di and I lingered at Troll long enough to introduce the next year's new designs. We had no fixed hours, coming and going as we pleased, eventually going out to Jordan where we were looking for unexplored treks, canyons, climbs and caves for a new guidebook covering the whole country. Wadi Rum was by then becoming popular with both climbers and trekkers. It was soon to be acclaimed as 'one of the world's best desert climbing areas,' and listed in *The Telegraph* as one of the '50 greatest adventures to try in your lifetime,' but the rest of Jordan's mountains were a blank on the map, and as far as we knew we had it to ourselves.

30
SPANISH ROCK

I have digressed. The sale of Troll was at this point far in the future. To go back and continue with my tale, I was still in my late thirties and hoping to sell when I was fifty. I was enjoying life and happy with my biannual big trips away.

In the summer of 1979 I had an invite from one of the old Rimmon lads, Aido Garlick, to come out to the Picos de Europa to climb the 700-metre *Rabadá-Navarro* route on the west face of Naranjo de Bulnes. I drove out with Tannith, Ken and Di and their kids, stopping off for a look round the Cirque de Gavarnie in the French Pyrenees before heading for Aido's. When we arrived he was sitting with his wife Gill on their patio, overlooking the red pantiled roofs of the old hillside village of Asiego in northern Spain. In one hand he had the inevitable freshly opened can of cold beer. With the other he was stroking one of his pet ducks. It sat contentedly on his lap until disturbed by our arrival, which prompted it to leap off and waddle away across the yard, squirting copious amounts of green fluid from its bum.

Aido gestured around him. 'What do you think?' he said.

Beyond the rooftops, the flower-filled meadows plunged steeply down towards the chasm of Cares Canyon, from which the arrogantly thrusting tower of Naranjo de Bulnes rose to 2,529 metres. Though not the highest mountain around, it nevertheless dominated the other snow-capped peaks. The vertical west wall was staring us in the face. It was reputedly the best rock face on Spain's best mountain, and according to Aido, the *Rabadá-Navarro* route not only ranked among the finest Extremes in Spain, but had never had a British ascent.

We all walked up to camp near the almost abandoned village of Bulnes. Nowadays, European development grants have brought an underground funicular from Cares to Bulnes, attracting huge numbers of tourists, but back in the 1970s it was a hard slog up the old packhorse trail from the canyon; the village was only accessible on foot and had very few residents in a cluster of decaying houses. When we arrived, it rained. And it didn't stop. Naranjo and the Picos vanished in the descending clouds. Fortunately for us, one of the few remaining residents eked out a meagre living by running a bar. We spent all next day in it.

On the third day, it was still raining and we still hadn't seen Naranjo, so we packed up our wet tents and retreated to the beach – less than an hour's drive from the canyon and as spectacular as anything in Cornwall. Next day Aido and Ken went off for 'a quick drink,' but one pub led to another and it was two days before they got back. By then the sun had been shining for a day and I was chomping at the bit. The weather looked settled though cloud still hid Naranjo from view. It remained hidden as Aido and I stumbled up through the mist on a scree-covered slope above Bulnes, then, miraculously, the clouds parted. We were gobsmacked. A sea of cloud billowed beneath us. Ahead, the huge grey west wall burst through it like a breaching whale. Above was a blue, cloudless sky. It was going to be good!

We kipped in a small hut near the base of the wall. It was full of Spanish climbers who asked in broken English what we were planning to do. Afterwards, they chatted among themselves in Spanish about the likelihood of our success. With his fluency in Spanish, Aido understood the whole conversation, much of which was mocking our chances of climbing the route. Just before we kipped down he spoke to them in the local dialect and embarrassed them as they realised he knew exactly what they had been saying.

Next day we were on the wall. With a night-time temperature inversion, the sea of white cloud still filled the valley almost up to the hut, but above us the blue sky beckoned. At that time the route was still mixed free and aid at A1 5b, almost all the aid being in the initial pitches. Aido launched off up the main aid pitch doing most of it free and we were on our way: the rock was immaculate. Wonderful pocketed limestone led us on and up into the blue on our own private pinnacle of rock while the cloud-sea lingered beneath us, now concealing the hut and the world from view. It was a magical day. Halfway up the face, the route breaks out left to traverse the great central shield of rock. We were told that most parties escape to the right at this point but the true continuation involved a committing traverse left for about a hundred metres – very reminiscent of *Beeston Eliminate* in the

Peak District – but with protection from tied-off bolts. It was my lead and the climbing was delightful: tip-toeing out to the horizon and beyond, holds never initially apparent but always there, tentatively clipping what was in fact tat and not daring to think of the consequences.

Then came the abseil, short but overhanging above 250 metres of space, to a narrow ledge. We pulled the ropes and there was no easy way back: the only way out was up. A couple more traverses took us to the bivvy ledge. It was around mid-afternoon but the weather was settled so we relaxed and instead of dashing for the top, we enjoyed our room-with-a-view, our cheese butties and oranges. I should point out here that ever since, Aido has claimed there were no oranges left; he swears I peeled them in my pocket with one hand while belaying him with the other, then ate them while he was climbing. It's a good story, and who am I to spoil it …

Oranges or not, we had a good night and the weather was still fine in the morning. We soldiered on up the route, by now winding our way up steep cracks and chimneys on the cold north ridge. Just as we topped out, some Spanish lads were arriving up the popular south face armed with copious amounts of bread, sausages, cheese and wine – perfect timing! We made a slightly inebriated laughing descent of the south face abseils and were back down on the beach by evening.

31

MOROCCO – HERE COMES THE SUN

Morocco is Africa's colourful and multifaceted answer to Nepal, and one of my favourite countries. Quick and easy to get to, in the same time zone as the UK and full of superb climbing and trekking areas. At the start of the 1980s it was still little changed from our early 1960s trip. For most British climbers Morocco was about snow plods and easy rock scrambles. There were some stories about sport climbs on the dramatic roadside cliffs of the Todra Gorge, but that wasn't my scene. I had heard tales of big limestone cliffs in the Central Atlas, north of Marrakesh, and a big river gorge that led from there into the Sahara.

As with our Algerian trip, Bernard Domenech sent me some information. Taghia Canyon had been discovered by French climbers four years previously. Some good routes from 300 to 1,000 metres had been done on impressive limestone peaks, but no Brits had climbed there. There were also some French routes from the 1950s not far away on Jebel Aioui, and over on the eastern side of the massif, the M'goun Gorge, which was the only access to remote Berber villages other than crossing high mountain passes, offered some unique trekking. It all seemed perfect.

Mick and I drove out through France and Spain in Troll's VW van with Elaine and Tannith. Di came out later, joining us for the M'goun trek with her son Mark, who was almost ten years old, like Tannith. On the fifth day we took the ferry from Spain to Ceuta. A couple of days later, having run the gauntlet of kids leaping into the road in an effort to sell blocks of hashish and now on increasingly poor roads, we already had a cracked window. Tannith wrote, 'We stopped the night on a 6,000-foot pass. On the way up we went over a bridge with a great big hole which we nearly fell down.'

From there a tortuous road with deep muddy ruts, rocky riverbeds, more bridges with gaping holes and narrow tracks above precipitous slopes made for an interesting drive. Being May there was still some snow around, but it was just about passable in our van. On the opposite side of the river, reached by roughly cut log bridges, villagers waived cheerfully from scattered Berber villages, the last one being Zawyat Ahancal, a place through which Wilfred Thesiger, one of my desert heroes, had passed in 1955. Beyond there a mule track continued east up the main river gorge to Taghia. High above we could see the edge of the castellated north face of Jebel Aioui, our first objective. We drove up the track and parked opposite the cliff, disappointed to find a deep valley dividing us from the foot of the crag.

There were around forty routes to choose from on Aioui, all in the region of 500 to 800 metres and all grades – some of them aid routes. We chose what was recommended as the classic of the wall, the 750 metre *Eperon des Ihanesalene*, graded TD+, sixteen pegs. It was a grim walk-in, having to descend into the valley then scramble steeply up the other side to reach the cliff, knowing there would also be a long descent from the summit after the climb before having to scramble back up to reach the van. Despite the grade and the mention of pegs, we climbed it free. To our surprise it was never more than VS, although it was very unusual in that it followed a spectacular ridge so narrow it was often only inches wide, much of it quite loose; the situations were fun. When the rock was good however, it was excellent, and at the end of the day our hands and PA soles looked as though they'd been through a shredder.

We topped out in the late afternoon and were heading down when we found a decent bivvy site. It didn't look like we would make it back before dark and we had told the girls we might not be back that day, so we decided to kip down and make another early start as soon as it became light. As the darkness drew in, we noticed two pairs of large green eyes silently stalking around us. We had heard there were leopards up there; it was useless trying to sleep. We repacked our bags and, armed with peg hammers, set off down the hill, still being followed alarmingly closely by the glowing eyes, the reflected green of each leopard's *tapetum lucidum* cells behind its retinas contributing to this night-hunter's vision. Nearing the valley floor and still in the dark, we spotted the glow of a fire in a cave from which a dozen dogs that were guarding a Berber shepherd's camp dashed out into the blackness, barking savagely up the hill towards us. They sounded worse than the leopards. We rapidly retreated up the hillside towards the green eyes and climbed on to a huge boulder, where we sat until the sun rose and the shepherds called their dogs. Later, at a campsite in the foothills, we heard a howling in the night and asked the campsite manager what it was. 'Leopards,' he said, 'we hear them often.'

We spent the rest of the day down by the river and looking around Zawyat Ahancal then shuttled our gear and food on foot part way up the valley towards Taghia, stopping early to camp and swim, and explore a side canyon full of climbing potential. The next day we pitched camp below the village of Taghia with big cliffs blocking the end of the valley, surprised to find French and Swiss climbers up there.

Taghia was a beautiful remote village only used in summer when the local Berbers moved up the valley from Ahancal to graze their livestock. As Tannith noted in her diary, 'The Berber women wear lovely clothes, made from gold shimmering material and ornaments'. As always it was good to be among friendly mountain people, but as we were soon heading off to meet Di and Mark we only had time for one route. One of the French lads, Wilf Colonna, suggested the 750-metre south pillar of Jebel Oujdad, first climbed four years previously in 1977 and graded TD+, twenty pegs. With a fairly long walk in, it meant another early start to have any chance of getting back in the day.

We started at first light in thick mist, expecting it to lift in the heat of the day. The approach followed a shepherds' track constructed diagonally across the lower walls of the west face, eventually curving around under the south wall, but with the cloud still down visibility was close to zero. We couldn't find the climb. It was midday when the mist abruptly cleared, first a glimpse of blue above, then suddenly the white wall towering steeply above us. We had a problem. Tannith and Elaine were expecting us back that day, but if we started now there was no chance we would make it. On the other hand, if we returned all the way back to camp we would have to walk up again tomorrow. You know what we decided, don't you?

We reckoned we could be back soon after first light next day, so roped up and climbed as fast as we could only using a couple of pegs, but even so it was a totally different prospect to the climb on Aioui. Almost vertical throughout, sometimes overhanging and rarely relenting much below VS with a few sections of 5a. It was good climbing on generally perfect rock. I was in the lead on the last pitch which ended fortuitously in a shallow cave just under the summit as the sun set. We bivvied there, sharing some water, an orange and some bread and cheese before curling up together for the night then rising at first light.

It was early morning when we got back to camp. The girls had been invited for breakfast with the French lads and were worrying about us, so Wilf had set off to see where we were, and missed us coming down the back. Although we never got chance to climb together on this trip, he became a lifelong friend. We have since visited him often in his home in the Alps to ski and climb, and he came over to England on a climbing road trip with some of the other French lads. We also invited him out to Wadi Rum on our second visit in 1985 and, like us, he has been an annual visitor ever since and now runs a horse safari and guiding business there.

The next day we went off exploring another side canyon with huge cliffs rising straight from the river. The next day it was time for us to leave, and we woke to hear rain on our tents. Looking out, two local boys had lit a fire and were making bread, which they shared with us for breakfast, a nice send-off for our last morning. Having walked back to Ahancal we set off in the van driving on terrible roads before kipping the night in the foothills near an irrigation channel full of croaking frogs. We had just got into our sleeping bags when a boy tapped on the window and gave us a tray of mint tea, bread, olive oil, home-made yoghourt and boiled eggs, epitomising the generosity we frequently met from local people on our travels.

Di and Mark arrived the next afternoon at Casablanca airport and we were off on our next trip, driving east through Rabat to Meknes, buying some groceries and a couple of large straw hats for Mark and Tannith. Then on to Fez with its warren of alleyways, donkeys squeezing past us loaded with goods, visiting the numerous craft shops and markets and, of course, the famous ancient dye works … which Mark fell into!

Having crossed a pass to the eastern side of the massif the next day we were once again invited into a Berber home for lunch on our way to Midelt, the following day driving along the edge of the Sahara to the Ziz Gorges with their river, oasis and palms. Beyond was the source of the Bleu de Meski; there were few visitors then, we more or less had Morocco to ourselves. We were treated to mint tea, and Mark and Tannith's straw hats were filled with apricots for them. Further down the road at Erfoud we spent an hour or so swimming in a pool before sleeping outside the van in the sand. Then on to Todra.

We camped in the oasis at Todra and tried our luck at tickling trout in the stream with no success, though we all went swimming further up the gorge beyond the very impressive climbing area, sleeping out a second night in the oasis where Tannith saw 'millions and millions of stars and shooting stars'. There's nothing quite so beautiful as a night in the desert.

We crossed the desert hills to Bou Thagrar where to our dismay we had a wide river to cross before reaching the start of our proposed trek. I waded through. It was about knee deep and soft underfoot. I wasn't sure we could get through in the van and getting it stuck in the river miles from anywhere definitely wouldn't be good, but we had come a long way and the trek sounded good, so nothing ventured, nothing gained. I waived them over. The van momentarily disappeared under a bow wave but emerged and rose out shedding water. We were over and drove up as far as we could towards the first 2,000-metre mountain pass we had to cross on what turned out to be a six-day trek.

Having left the van we were soon stopped for another free lunch before reaching the village of Amajgag, then on up a deep, narrow canyon, crossing the river frequently to reach the village of Imeskar. The next day would take us over the 2,990-metre pass of Tizi n'Ait Hamed and down to the M'goun Gorge. No one I had contacted in the UK had heard of it, though now it's known as 'the most remarkable gorge in the Atlas Mountains' and is on every trekking company's itinerary. When we were there we met no one other than the locals and they were surprised to see us, so it was all rather committing and fun.

We started early for the pass. It was a big climb and already a hot day, and we all had heavy packs with our camping gear, food and water in – even Mark and Tannith. Elaine wasn't feeling well and as we passed by some women working in the fields, an old lady stopped her, muttering charms and waiving her hands over her, seeming to repeatedly drag something out of her head and throw it away. Then, with what we could only assume to be some kind of a blessing, she patted her and waived us on our way. All very mysterious: how did she know Elaine wasn't feeling so good? But the magic, if such it was, worked. We had some lunch a bit further on in the shadow of a rock before setting off again on the long zigzag trail up to Tizi n'Ait Hamed, the first and highest pass. Then down and up again over a 2,400-metre pass before finally descending to the river after fifteen miles. The first of the villages was across the river but there was a big cave on our side that had obviously been used by travellers, so we called it a day, brewed up, cooked a meal and kipped down.

We woke to a view of green fields and a clear, fast-flowing river, a delightful change after yesterday's dry, dusty mountains. We were also surprised to find children gathered around us, guaranteeing us a warm welcome when we crossed the river into the village opposite. There, the women in their colourful clothes with necklaces and rings of amber and silver were spreading crops to dry on their flat rooftops or sitting in the shade hand-carding and spinning wool. We were invited for a breakfast of dates and locally made butter on bread that was cooked under the fire while we sipped our mint teas. As they only spoke Berber, they used sign language to explain that it would be difficult for children to descend the canyon as it was spring, so the river was fast and deep and the water would come over their heads. They said we could only reach the village of Tarzout, which was worrying.

After more invites for tea as we continued down the valley we finally found a place to sleep by the river. We hadn't brought tents so just slept under the stars. Beyond was the first of the gorges, rich with the smell of desert herbs. A woman who was also walking downriver asked us to join her. As we were now walking in the river, often knee deep, she carried Mark's sack and I carried Tannith's as far as Tarzout. Here she introduced us to Muhammad who had a mule, as by then it was obvious that this would be the only possible way for us to continue. We stayed the night there being treated to a tagine and negotiating a deal. Difficult with no common language, but we established with a sketch map and drawings of suns and moons that it would take another three days to descend the gorges. He was going anyway and we could travel with him, with Mark and Tannith riding with him on the mule.

As soon as we left the next day, the walls of the river closed in, overhanging cliffs trapping the fast-flowing water so that the mule was often belly deep. High above, broken wooden walkways hung from the cliffs, the remains of alternative routes used when the gorges were flooded and impassable. Tannith and Mark loved it, as indeed did Muhammad who was on the mule, singing happily with them throughout the journey. Nor were we the only ones using the watery highway; there were families on mules, a farmer with a heavy wooden plough on his shoulder, people going about their daily lives and finding nothing unusual about the journey in the river that, rising among snowy summits, descended through otherwise dry mountains, bringing life to villages, orchards, ancient kasbahs and vast palmeries before forming a great reservoir on the western fringe of the Sahara.

We slept each night in the villages, enjoying local food and hospitality, often eating during the day with locals, sometimes in riverside caves, their floors deep with years of goat droppings, or in the shade of ancient walnut trees or oleanders, their pink flowers in full bloom. Everywhere people were busy in the orchards. Arriving in one village, a man was just plunging one of his fingers into a fire to cauterise it, having accidentally cut the end off with his knife; he asked for a bandage and ointment, which we were happy to supply, there being no doctors to attend to mishaps in this hidden idyllic valley. On the sixth day, we emerged from the canyon into more open terrain. When we finally said goodbye to Muhammad it was a sad parting for everyone, but particularly for him and the kids as they had had a great time together, but having paid him and given him a well-earned tip we shouldered our sacks again and set off over the hill to find our van.

We had no decent maps but we found the dirt track without a problem and assumed the van was up the road to our right; but we couldn't find it. This was looking like a disaster: *had it been stolen? But maybe we were wrong. Was it in the other direction?* Mick and I ran off down the road and before long we found it, only to discover someone had punctured two tyres. This could also have been a disaster as we were nowhere near a garage, but luckily we had two spares. The following day we drove back out through the river to Bou Thagrar then on to Kalaat M'gouna where we bought fresh food and gave a lift to a lad called Moulay who was going to the lake beyond Ouarzazate into which the river flowed. After a swim and a meal, someone put a Pink Floyd tape on in the van and Moulay rolled a giant spliff. Our journey almost over, we slept by the lake, dreaming under the upturned bowl of stars.

We passed through Marrakesh again on the way back, Tannith writing, 'We saw a snake charmer with a scorpion on his nose and he let us stroke the snake. Another man pretended to shoot a donkey with a toy gun and it fell on the floor as though it was dead.' Another cigarette-smoking donkey was there too, also the storytellers and the Joujouka drummers, some of whom had made a record with Brian Jones of the Rolling Stones in 1971. We slept outside town on the edge of a field, Tannith waking in the morning to find a scorpion in her pillow of clothes. On our way though the next village they were preparing the day's market, someone pumping up a display of cow's heads with a bicycle pump, presumably to make them look fatter.

We reached the coast near Casablanca the next day, celebrating with a couple of bottles of wine before sleeping on the beach only to be disturbed by some bloke trying to get into Di's sleeping bag with her, which didn't go down well. She flew back to England the next day with Mark, while the four of us drove home over the next six days.

I called in at my sister's first, only to be told my mum had died two weeks ago when we were in the M'goun canyons. It was the worst possible homecoming. She had been a bit poorly when I left, but was up and about as always and gave no impression there was anything to worry about. Di had also called in to see my parents before she flew out to join us and told me my mum had seemed fine then. I guess she had bravely hidden her illness from both of us, but I wish she hadn't. Being away when my mum died was too much of a price to pay for what had otherwise been a great trip.

Soon after, my dad went to live with my sister, Kathryn, but a few years later he also passed away. I was glad I had some time with him before he died to share memories of family life and walk the moors together. I was also proud to be one of his coffin bearers. I knew I had disappointed him when I didn't go to university and again when I left my job in the hospital, but both he and Mum had always supported me even when I was frequently an out-of-work climber. Happily I had fulfilled their dreams by becoming a company director while they were still alive.

32

ALPINE ADVENTURES

As Mick was away, I began climbing a lot with John Smith, another local climber, soon to become a good friend. In addition to climbing regularly in the UK, we had two good summers in the Alps and the Dolomites.

On our second Alpine trip, a couple of miles before the German border (yes, European countries had borders back then!), we picked up three German lads who were hitch-hiking. Just before the checkpoint, one of them said, 'We'll get out and walk through and meet you on the other side'. We thought nothing of it. The customs officers searched the van quite rigorously, but there was nothing to be found, then as agreed we picked the lads up when we drove out into Germany. Soon after, when looking through the rear-view mirror, I noticed one of them was trying to get the fleece-lined panel off the side of the van.

'What are you doing?' I asked.

'I hid our dope behind the panel,' he said. What a dirty trick that was. If it had been found at the border it would have been John and me that would have been charged. You just can't trust potheads!

'Sorry,' I said, 'the panel won't come off,' so they had to leave it. Actually the panels were easily removed, and the grass provided some relaxing evenings.

Our first stop in my *Extreme Alpine Rock* book was Austria's Kaisergebirge, where we were tempted by the 300-metre, grade VI A1, *South-East Diedre* of the Fleischbank. It was a two-hour walk in, but the climb was on perfect limestone. We were robbed of the last remaining hard pitch by a surprise storm with marble-sized hailstones stinging our faces, piling up on ledges and rapidly covering any holds. We were soon soaked to the skin and freezing cold, but luckily there was an escape ledge at that point which we gladly took advantage of.

From there we continued south to Italy and the Sella Pass, waking next day to find four inches of snow on the ground and more still falling steadily. It snowed all the next day, and Smithy – never one for sitting around – was getting impatient. We drove down towards Cortina where the weather improved, nipped up the *South Face Direct* of the Cinque Torri on the way, then next day the nice 300-metre, grade V *South Arête* of the Punta Fiames which, according to our book, 'when viewed from one of Cortina's cafes … is so unmistakably an "edge" rising above the velvet carpet of the meadows that you know you must climb it', and so we did.

We followed that climb with the classic 500-metre grade VI, south-east face of the Tofana's di Pilastro Rozes. We were into climbing light on that trip, cutting things to a minimum with a small daysack made specially by Troll for our trip and later marketed as the 'Tofana', and sold alongside our 'Trolltind' and an even lighter 'Marathon' sack. I'm still using all three thirty years on; like all Troll gear they were built to last. I'm still using my slings and harness too. Today's health and safety bureaucrats wouldn't approve, even though Hillary Kershaw – once Troll's sample machinist but now with her own company – replaced my harness belay loop for me following a terrible accident in Yosemite in 2006 when renowned climber Todd Skinner was killed when his old and badly worn belay loop broke during an abseil.

Anyway, all we had in our Tofana sack was a small bottle of water and a couple of biscuits. We wore our rock shoes, harnesses and gear on the walk to the crag in just our Helly Hansen Lifas, which were of course designed to be underwear. I thought we were cutting it fine, but Smithy was happy, he liked cutting things fine.

The climb was excellent. I particularly remember a huge overhanging chimney at half height with tremendous exposure, projecting about eight metres out into space. We whizzed up the route quickly enough but were slowed down by changing weather as we approached the summit, now shrouded in cloud making route finding tricky. The descent down the north face which should have been straightforward was in almost zero visibility and surprisingly wintery, slowing us down even more and causing us some consternation with night imminent and us wearing only our underwear. Crossing steep ice-covered slopes in our rock shoes didn't help, having to put runners in the cliff to tension traverse across, but we made it down safely.

We then moved over to the Alps, planning to climb the classic *Cassin Route* on the Piz Badile, but it was plastered in snow, so on an invite from Tut Braithwaite we called in at a party in Pontresina. The Zinnemann film, *Five Days One Summer*, was being shot there and lots of the lads we knew were involved: Paul Nunn (Sean Connery's double), Martin Boysen, Rab Carrington, Joe Brown, Mo Anthoine, Eric Jones, Leo Dickinson, Tut, Hamish MacInnes. Ian Nicolson, who was one of the few we didn't know, later took over the role of Sean Connery after Paul had an accident. The spread was first class, with mountains of food including pig's heads with apples in their mouths, and endless drinks so it was a good evening.

Arriving in Chamonix we trekked up to the start of the *Frendo Spur*. The weather hadn't been good in our absence and someone told us a climber had had to be rescued the day before as he had been hit in the face in a rockfall, the stones of which were evident on the snowfield around the start of the climb. We decided to bivvy higher on the route to get an early start the next day while it was still frozen. To minimise the chance of being hit by rockfall that evening we began by a more overhanging start and bivvied in a safe-looking spot on the ridge, though someone lower down was hit by more falling rock and had to be choppered off, and one of our ropes was also slightly damaged.

Next morning we were on the move bright and early, using head torches while everything was still frozen. We were also keen to beat the expected crowd, but except for people gazing down from the Midi téléphérique, the only people we saw were some Italians higher up the route who shunted a load of snow on to me as I was climbing. There was also a constant sliding of snow coming off the face both left and right of us. The long, superbly positioned, exposed ice ridge that is the essence of the route was wonderful, and a joy to lead. Above, a short mixed ice and rock headwall brought us abruptly to the crest of the Aiguille du Midi, not far from the téléphérique station, so the descent back to Chamonix couldn't have been easier. Elsewhere that day, two climbers had been swept off another route and seven others were missing, more storms were forecast. We had been lucky.

We decided to escape the dodgy conditions and head back to Switzerland to try the west ridge of Salbitschijen, which we had seen the previous year from the south ridge and had been impressed by its dragon's back of spines that Tolkien's Smaug would be proud of. It's graded ED, and it's not only 1,000 metres long, but also complex, with most pitches VS and above, climbing up and abseiling off five towers before reaching the summit.

It's also described as 'the most beautiful, longest and hardest rock ridge in the Alps, on perfect granite'. It's given twelve hours, which doesn't leave much time for the descent.

Slightly concerned by the hyperbole, we decided on an early start and walked up to the bivouac box at its foot in the evening. There was some food there that we presumed someone had abandoned, so as we didn't have much with us, we ate most of it before discovering there was also some climbing gear in the hut. We then wondered if someone else would be turning up, but luckily we had the hut to ourselves all night.

We were off to an early start next morning, soon leaving the lower vege-tated rock behind for the immaculate granite of the ridge itself. Roping off one of the towers, I was dangling in space halfway down a free-hanging abseil, my descendeur exactly at the point where the rope sheath had been damaged in the *Frendo* rockfall, when there was a huge boom. I thought the ropes had bust or the tower had collapsed. John, who was on a ledge below, looked horrified, but to our surprise I was still there, gripping tight on the ropes. A Swiss military jet had broken the sound barrier just above us.

'I thought you were a goner!' Smithy said, grinning.

There were also lots of pegs. Most we just clipped and climbed past, but some were obviously for aid. As far as I was concerned the route was too long to mess about avoiding the odd pull on them here and there, but John did his best until finally stopped by a tricky move.

'C'mon, John,' I said. 'It's not Stanage, there's another thousand feet to go yet!' He didn't like pulling on the peg, but he got the point. When we reached the fifteen-metre aid crack just under the summit, he pointed me up it – straightforward stuff, and the summit needle not far above to pose on.

Having topped out, we were on the way down when we reached the edge of a big fan of snow narrowing steeply down into a hidden couloir. As on our other climbs, we only had our rock shoes on, so I was climbing down care-fully to see what the snow was like, but with time pressing, John threw caution to the wind and jumped past me expecting to sink in a few inches – but he didn't. Under a thin covering of snow it was ice, and he shot off down the slope, heading for the unseen couloir. The last I saw of him, having failed to dig his fingers and toes in, he was trying to force his elbows in as brakes, but nothing was working. He simply shot over the edge and disappeared. Then nothing. I shouted down but the mountain remained silent. I didn't merely think he was a goner, I was sure he was dead.

There was no way I was stepping on to the snow after that, so I moved back up and climbed cautiously down the rock ridge alongside until I could see into the couloir and shout, but still nothing, no reply, just the snow couloir curling steeply out of sight. I continued down, dreading what I was sure I was about to find. Then there he was: sitting up, grinning on some rocks, just beyond the bottom edge of the snow.

'Where've you been?' he said. 'I've been here ages!'

33

ALL CHANGE ...

Immediately prior to my 1982 summer Alpine trip, a friend of Di's had told her about a late-seventeenth-century farmhouse that was for sale up on the moor edge close to where I had lived previously. The old farm needed a lot of work doing on it, but as soon as we got back I jumped at the chance, sold up and bought it. Tannith and I moved in with Ken and Di for almost a year while it was being repaired, with me working there most evenings after Troll.

It was also around this time that I got another opportunity to go sailing, this time with Stan Wroe, who I had climbed the *Solleder Route* with on the Civetta. Like Bob, Stan also had his skipper's papers. He was doing some trips for the Ocean Youth Club. Another of the Manchester Grit lads, Bernard the Butcher, was first mate and I was signed on as second mate. We were sailing from Ardrossan on the Clyde across the Irish Sea to Douglas on the Isle of Man, then back over to Holyhead on Anglesey with a crew of youngsters in a sleek seventy-foot ketch. It was bright and breezy when we put to sea, spray flying, a joy to be alive, but as we left the Firth of Clyde the wind picked up and long before reaching Douglas we were slamming into big seas with a westerly force eight blowing.

We reached the harbour mouth, but even with the sails lowered and the engine on full it was impossible to make headway into the gale. After repeated attempts, Stan said, 'We're not going to get in, we'll have to run for Holyhead'. With night falling we turned tail, hoisted sail and sped through the heaving Irish Sea. Most of the youngsters were in their bunks feeling – or being – sick, while Stan, Bernard and I manned the wheel, the seas hissing threateningly alongside in the darkness. I cooked up a big stew. There weren't many takers but I was starving as it was our first real meal. We sailed into Holyhead's sheltered harbour the following morning. Stan had done a great job and as before I had really enjoyed being at sea under sail: there's something primordial about seas and mountains that stirs the blood.

Not many months later Ken and Di split, which was a huge surprise to everyone. They had been together almost twenty years and seemed to have a perfect marriage, each enjoying their own activities as well as time together at home and with friends, but things are sometimes not what they seem. They were still living together, but Ken had met someone else. He told me one day that Di was keen to do more climbing, and he didn't mind if she came away at weekends with John and me. It was also around this time that Mille sold her coffee house so Di was out of work and before long started working at Troll, soon getting involved on the design side. She was also doing good routes with John and me at Gogarth and elsewhere, sharing leads with me on *A Dream of White Horses* when Ken and the kids were also down there, watching from the promontory opposite.

Di also climbed on Cloggy with me, though it was never her favourite crag. 'Too gloomy,' she always said, perhaps because one of the earliest routes we climbed together was *Shrike*, one of the gloomiest on the cliff. Not a good choice by me but it's a brilliant climb. I also did *Great Slab* with Di, or I should say I did the first pitch: the weather had been overcast when we walked up. I had just got across and started the long groove above when it started to rain heavily. The rock immediately became slippery. I only clipped one rope into the runners in the hope that I could make a belay above the start to protect Di with the other, but it wasn't possible. Having removed my first runner just above the overhanging start she slipped off the wet and downwards-sloping traverse, doing a big pendulum and ending up hanging free in space. As the hillside drops rapidly beneath that part of the cliff I wasn't sure there was enough rope to lower her to the ground, but with the rain pouring down I didn't relish the idea of rigging a pulley system to get her back up on to the crag, so I lowered her, hoping for the best. To our relief the rope reached and I abseiled off. A memorable morning, and it was all my fault really; it had looked like rain before we started up the hill.

We made up for it on another day, climbing *Boomerang*. It was one of those glorious winter days: blue skies, glittering, firm snow, spring on the way and the early morning sun catching the obviously dry rock of Cloggy's Far Far East Buttress. It was our first rock route of the year and asking to be climbed. We kicked steps in the firm snow to the foot of the crag where a delightful corner leads up to the first belay. Above, some devious route finding through now snow-capped overlaps brought us out on to a perfect snow arête. I had never been to the summit of Snowdon after climbing Cloggy, but that day it was irresistible.

It is strange how things work out. I had known Ken and Di since our teenage years in the Rimmon. They had remained friends of mine, and had been together for almost all the time I had known them. Di had climbed with John and me a few times but suddenly our relationship was unexpectedly changing into something more. Though she stayed good friends with Ken – as did I – he eventually moved out of their house. I could have sold mine and moved in with Di and the kids who were now teenagers, but that didn't feel right; I felt I would be intruding on their family home, so I stayed at my moor-edge home with Tannith, but saw Di at Troll and some evenings and weekends though she lived with her children until they were older.

About three years later, having finished school, Tannith worked for a while in Norway not far from her grandparents. Then, perhaps inspired by her travels in some of the poorer parts of the world, she applied to work with the Ockenden Venture, a charity originally established to help refugees in Sudan, Pakistan, Cambodia and Algeria, but perhaps best known for its major role in the resettlement in Britain of Vietnamese refugees, which is what she was mainly involved in. Di and I drove her down to Dorset, discovering on arrival that Ockenden was near to Moreton, the location of St Nicholas' Church and the grave of T.E. Lawrence, or Lawrence of Arabia. The cottage of Clouds Hill where he had lived was also nearby and close to the place where he was killed on his motorbike in 1935. Curiously our visit there coincided with our discovery of the mountains of Wadi Rum in Jordan about which Lawrence had written so evocatively in his classic *Seven Pillars of Wisdom*. A serendipitous event.

Leaving Tannith down there on her own was rather traumatic, but it wasn't too long before she moved up to their Barmouth branch on the Welsh coast, easy for me to call in on when climbing in North Wales. Eventually she was transferred to Yorkshire, back in home territory, where she now works as a housing officer.

34
HARD ROCK DAYS

Glancing through my guidebooks I see that John, Mick, Di and I seemed to have a purge on the routes in Ken Wilson's superb *Hard Rock* book in the early 1980s. I don't think we climbed them because they were in the book, certainly not the ones in England and Wales, it just happened that way as we were away most weekends climbing starred routes, from *Coronation Street* in Cheddar Gorge to routes like *Extol* in the Lakes, *The Needle* in the Cairngorms and most of the Welsh ones. Then Di, Mick and I embarked on a Scottish trip.

The Cairngorms were our first stop. After a six-mile walk-in, we camped at the head of Loch Muick, enjoying the wildness of the place and climbing the 290-metre *King Rat* and its lesser neighbour, *Goliath*, in perfect weather. Then north again to the giant, slender sea stack, or rather tottering tower, of the Old Man of Hoy, which you pass when sailing to the Orkney Islands on the ferry from the Scottish mainland. It wasn't until 1819 that maps showed a stack separated from the mainland. Soon after that, a storm left it much as it is today. Nine years after we climbed it, a forty-metre crack appeared in its south face leaving a large dodgy-looking overhanging section that will inevitably collapse. It's definitely a dramatic piece of rock and Di was already a bit worried about it as she had just finished reading Al Harris and Lucy Rees's book, *Take it to the Limit*. In one of its gripping tales, two lads and a girl have an epic on the Old Man and we, two lads and a girl, were about to climb it.

Once on the main island of Orkney, we hired a local fisherman to ferry us over to the island of Hoy, then we walked in over to the far coast where there's a superbly located lonely bothy on an idyllic beach at Rackwick Bay. We went over to have a look at the Old Man that evening, which made Di even more concerned. Early the next day we set off to climb the classic 140-metre E1 *East Face Route* which was the subject of the 1967 live TV extravaganza. It's described in *Hard Rock* by Chris Bonington, who was on the first ascent, as 'Britain's finest sea stack … and probably most rewarding summit'. What a plum new route Stan and I had missed in 1965.

Anyway, all went well, remembering to leave the essential spare back-rope to facilitate a diagonal abseil down the overhangs. The final pitch involved climbing past a rusting steel cable that seemed to be holding the summit blocks in place – not very reassuring. Once up there, Mick took a photo of me and Di, but as he was unable to see anything other than us perched on the top, it looked like we were sat on the moors at home. With the spare rope in place for the overhanging last abseil, the descent was easy-peasy and we had a leisurely evening at the bothy before walking and sailing back the next day, then off we went on our *Hard Rock* trip to Wester Ross and Carnmore Crag, 'one of the remotest crags in mainland Britain'.

On the seven-mile walk-in we surprised a couple of salmon poachers who were extremely relieved to see we were climbers and not gamekeepers, after which we walked round Fionn Loch to the bothy beneath the crag. The impressive looking routes of *Dragon* – 'one of the finest routes in Scotland' – and *Gob* – 'a mind blower packed with gusto and excitement,' or so it said in *Hard Rock* – loomed above us amidst the overhangs, and gave us something to worry about until the morning.

Once again, we cruised them. I say this with no sense of bravado; we were all three simply going well and in no hurry. The weather was good and we did a route each day for the next two days, simply enjoying being there, during which time – as elsewhere on this Scottish trip – we saw no one. Except for the poachers on the walk-in, and a ghillie on our way back. We had just set off when he arrived in a small four-by-four rough terrain vehicle. He offered us a lift out which we gladly accepted, surprised when he headed straight for the loch … and into it. It was an amphibious vehicle! Once across we soon reached the road where the gamekeeper was waiting for him. He gave the ghillie a right earful.

'What the hell are you doing giving those guys a lift?' he shouted. 'You can get out and walk the rest,' he said, pointing at us.

Miserable sod. We felt really sorry for the ghillie and thanked him profusely while hoping the poachers had got away with their bags full of salmon.

Heading south for Ben Nevis, we discovered *Ardverikie Wall* was in our *Classic Rock* book, so diverted to climb this delightful 170-metre Severe. As the book says, 'It's the ideal place to break a journey in either direction between bigger and harder expeditions … four long pitches of delight over slabs, ribs, cracks and grooves with considerable exposure all the way.' *Rock Climbing in Scotland* even goes so far as to say it's 'one of the best routes in the country'. The next day as we walked up to the Ben, the clouds came in and for the first time on the trip the weather was threatening. We camped on a small rise with the cliff of Carn Dearg glowering darkly above us, clouds gripping its top. We were hoping to climb *Centurion* the following day, but it wasn't looking good.

The storm hit in the middle of the night. With the three of us squashed into a small two-man tent well past its sell-by date, we were soon getting damp. Then a stream started to come in at the door. We volunteered Mick to go out into the dark and the deluge to see what was happening. He poked his head back in to say that the small rise we had camped on now had a stream on either side and our island was about to be flooded. Time to up sticks and go. We squelched down the three miles of the Allt a'Mhuilinn and headed for home.

We returned to climb *Centurion* with Alan Baker and then the Old Man of Stoer, a seventy-metre, three-star Hard Severe sea stack. We were expecting to have to swim to reach the stack, so were more than happy to find an old rope fixed across to it a few feet above the sea. Mick got the short straw and went across first to test it, then Di went over, Alan and Mick taking great pleasure in getting the rope swinging so her feet were dunked in the sea.

Once across, the route was problem free, though once again Di gave us some laughs when she became the target of an angry fulmar that puked evil-smelling half-digested fish on her as she pulled on to its ledge. The top was a great place to enjoy the wildness of the coast with seabirds wheeling around us and the sea crashing and sucking on the rocks below.

A couple of abseils took us back down: time to remember and pay our respects to Tom Patey who was on the first ascent in 1966, but was tragically killed in 1970 when abseiling from the Maiden, another sea stack further north on the Sutherland coast.

35

SUDAN SAGA – KASSALA MOUNTAINS

Something hidden. Go and find it. Go and look behind the Ranges –
Something lost behind the Ranges. Lost and waiting for you. Go!
***The Explorer*, Rudyard Kipling**

Delving through my travel books in the winter of 1982–1983 I spotted some pictures of what appeared to be superb granite domes in Sudan. They looked well worth a trip. Di was keen, as were Mick and his girlfriend Elaine, who worked at Troll. We got our visas and tickets and I contacted the Alpine Club on the off-chance someone may have climbed there. Bingo!

Robin Hodgkin had been in Khartoum in 1939 and done a route with L.W. Brown to the main summit, Jebel Kassala, near the Ethiopian border. It looked to be a wacky place with interesting people, and the 550-metre climb was described as 'one of the finest climbs in Africa'. From his sketch it looked like there were other presumably unclimbed domes nearby. We had our objectives. Even if the mountains weren't as good as we hoped, my exploratory climbing – and in later years, trekking trips – were also about the journey and the people and their different cultures. The mountains were simply the lure that tempted us into little-known places, and the more wild and remote, the better.

By early March we were on our way. Arriving at Khartoum at five in the morning was a bit of a culture shock. It wasn't helped by the fact that the four of us had spent most of the last sixteen hours cramped on a Balkan Airlines flight. The only relief had been a few hours in the transit lounge of Sofia where sad-faced soldiers patrolled in the gloom and large grumpy ladies served bad coffee and stale sandwiches. It seemed the Soviet states in 1983 were not a happy place. Our first night in Khartoum didn't lift our despondency. Desert dust and litter were everywhere. Cavernous open drains full of garbage waited for the rains or the unwary to fall into them.

The smell of urine filled the air. We staggered with big sacks, tired from our journey, from one dingy-looking hotel to another. All were full (or so they said). *Was it us?*

Arriving in Souq Arabi we went up the steps of yet another dead-looking hotel. After a brief discussion we were accepted into a six-bed room with two Sudanese. Nice people. One changed beds so we could have four together before we left our gear on trust and set off for the Blue Nile – not so blue with wind sweeping dust out of the dawn. Donkey carts, horses, people and cars bustled about on the dirt roads. The day was getting hot and we couldn't find anything to drink.

Our first objective was the Aliens office (a welcoming name!) where we had to obtain permits to leave the city. We queued for an hour then, just as we were about to collect the permits, the official said, 'Come back at two o'clock,' and closed the shutter on his window. We weren't surprised; it was typical of life on the road. Someone else in the queue advised us to come back at one, as the office shut at two. That didn't surprise us either.

Back outside it was now really hot. We found a food stall and had some fried beans and meat with bread, sitting on the footpath. Still nothing to drink. Eventually we found some fruit in the market. Back at the Aliens office we finally collected our papers to allow us to travel east to the Ethiopian border. Just as importantly, we found a chai tea stall before going back to the hotel. At six that evening as the muezzin called the faithful to prayer, his cry echoing over the city, the sun setting red, we went back out for a meal and discovered a Hilton Hotel by the Nile, so went in for a look around, meeting a Saudi Arabian businessman who invited us to his room for some large gin and tonics.

He said he was going out for dinner to a nightclub called Happy Land and asked if we would like to join him. It sounded different and was a promise of good food, so why not? He called a taxi, opened the door for Di and me to get in the front, then sat in the back between Mick and Elaine. It wasn't long before he tried to grope Elaine in the darkness. She quickly pushed him off, but to Mick's surprise he then had a go at him, unsurprisingly meeting with an equally firm refusal. Regardless, with a meal in the offing we stayed with him and ate well before the music started and an exotic scantily dressed dancing girl appeared. Our host, who by then was completely drunk, spent the rest of the evening stuffing dollar notes in her underwear. It was late when we got back to our room, but we had eaten well and experienced the other side of life in Khartoum.

Next day we woke again to the call of the muezzin. Khartoum was already busy, people praying on the mat outside our door. By seven we were out in the dust of Souq Arabi having breakfast: the inevitable beans and tomatoes, no cutlery, just fingers and bread. A cup of sweet tea from a chai shop washed it down before we set off on a long, bouncy, squashed journey by bus for 250 miles across eastern Sudan to Gadaref, near the Ethiopian border. Villages of typical African straw houses called tukuls dotted the country-side, as we crossed bleached plains with the remains of sorgum grass and the occasional dead donkey or camel.

By midday we were over the Blue Nile before reaching Gedaref at the end of the bus route, but the driver took us on another eighty miles or so towards Kassala for free before dropping us off outside a few tea shacks as the skies turned red in the west. Black silhouettes of tall, lean, fuzzy-haired men with long swords strode jauntily by in the dust as we sat by the roadside. African music drifted out of the tea shacks. Life was beginning to feel good! Only three days from home and England was already far away in space and time.

Later that evening a market wagon came out of the dark, headlights visible for miles across the blackness of the desert; we jumped aboard amidst a crush of bodies and everyone smiled at our large sacks overloaded with climbing gear. Arriving in Kassala an hour later we were immediately befriended by a young student from Juba who took us along to the local cafe for the usual meal of beans. Smoke from the cooking fires filled the air, and as we wiped our bowl dry with crusts of bread we were given more, embar-rassing us with the generosity of people who had nothing. Afterwards we walked through town to the centre for students where we finally found a place to sleep below a mango tree; the bright stars of Africa such as we never see in England, shining overhead. It was good to be out of Khartoum.

We awoke to find the great grey-blue domes of Jebel Kassala towering 500 metres above the oasis, and very impressive peaks they were too, with almost featureless walls and slabs, just the occasional ribbon of a crack line and hot as hell! We had a terrible feeling that even early March was too late in the year, which had always been a possibility, but the trip couldn't be arranged any earlier – December and January would be the time to come really. Even climbing at Christmas, Robin Hodgkin had said the rock was uncomfort-ably hot, even in the morning. So hot in fact he felt the heat and thirst con-tributed to an accident on the descent in which he broke his wrist when a brittle hold failed – and, as we were to discover, there are plenty of those!

The village of Khatmiya, its thatched tukuls clustered together behind barricades of thorns or walls of clay at the foot of the cliffs, epitomised our vision of Africa. Eagles circled above and a few children gathered around, intrigued by these unexpected strangers with their fair hair and pale, anaemic skin. We had hoped to use a tukul as a climbing base but this seemed impossible, nor could we find a place to camp, so our only option was to return to Kassala where we met a couple of young English teachers who said we could camp in their backyard. They were teaching there for a year and were due to leave soon; written on their courtyard wall was a line from Pink Floyd's track 'Time', about waiting in quiet desperation being a very English thing.

Over the coming weeks we began to understand what they meant, but Kassala was a fascinating place. The local Bedouin tribes are predominantly Beni-Amir, Hadendowa and Rashaida, the latter famed for breeding racing camels which they sell in Saudi Arabia in exchange for goods which are smuggled back into Sudan. Most of them had three tribal scars on each cheek and dreadlocks or matted fuzzy hair, proud descendants of Kipling's dreaded 'Fuzzy-Wuzzy, at your 'ome in the Soudan; You're a pore benighted 'eathen but a first-class fightin' man'. Tall and impressive, they strutted their stuff around the dusty streets in swirling white djellabas with swords protruding from metal-studded leather sheaths slung over their shoulders and daggers strapped to their arms. One strolled through the market with horns in his turban, a sword on one shoulder and a huge spear on the other. When we asked what they used the weapons for, we were told, 'fighting and killing'. Swordsmiths were still making them in the market area, the preferred steel being Land Rover springs.

Next day Di, Mick and I returned to Khatmiya on the local bus to try Robin Hodgkin's route on the east face, then the only route on the massif, although according to Robin, the locals had made serious but unsuccessful efforts to reach the top, as the tree visible on the summit was 'The Tree of Life'. Anyone who could reach it and eat a leaf would live forever. The Italians had also tried when they occupied the region at the end of the nineteenth century, also without success. Hopefully we would fare better than them: what greater incentive do you need than a tree of life!

Leaving town we passed close to the mountains where olive baboons with their greenish hair were sitting on the boulders, grimacing and showing their teeth. The locals warned us not to get too close as they throw rocks at you! In fact they were quite big and we wondered about sleeping out with baboons for companions. As we worked our way slowly up the dried-out wadi leading from the village to the mountain pass, the jebels were already shimmering in the heat of the sun with massive Rüppell's vultures circling lazily overhead. Our sacks were heavy with climbing and bivouac gear and food – beans, bread, nuts, grapefruit, bananas and nine litres of water. Up on the pass a welcome breeze was blowing in from the east across the arid desert of Eritrea.

As we continued up through thorn scrub, cactus and boulders to the start of the route, we spotted what looked to be a bivouac site a hundred metres up the cliff. On arrival we found it was perfect, big enough for the three of us, and right at the start of the serious climbing. By the time we had things sorted and ready for the next day it was dark. The usual sunset glow was concealed by a red haze of dust that extended out across the desert, even concealing the hills of Eritrea to the east. We tucked into our food, enjoying both it and our position: it was good to be in the mountains again.

To our relief we weren't invaded by marauding baboons, but a strong wind blew through the night filling the air with dust, twigs and thorns, so we buried ourselves in our sleeping bags. Even so, the dust filtered in, though by the early hours the wind eased and at five, with a red dawn tinting the sky, we were awake and breakfasting on grapefruit and bananas. Taking Robin's advice, we were up and on the rock before the sun, though the sky was clouded over which was lucky for us; we didn't want the sun today.

Mick led up a wide crack system leftwards into a huge corner a rope length away. Di and I followed, climbing together: as a group of three it was the quickest way to go. To our surprise a few heavy drops of unseasonal rain fell (it shouldn't rain until May or June). The brief shower stopped almost immediately but Mick was already having problems on the next pitch where Robin said he 'climbed first on to Brown's head then used his outstretched hands as footholds'. Surprised at the difficulty of the moves we decided to employ the same tactics to save time, and with a bit of help from me, Mick was soon over the problem and on to the delicate slab above. This was also harder than we had expected, and the badly exfoliating skin of rock was creaking terribly – the first ascensionists were obviously handy lads, though they too had commented on the 'peeling skin' of the rock.

At about fifteen metres Mick passed a hand-made peg obviously dating back to Robin's 1939 ascent and forged by a local swordsmith. Above was a bulge in the corner but this was passed without problem, then another thirty metres took Mick out on to the slabs again almost to the base of the 'hanging garden' below the summit dome. Di followed with a bit of help from the rope, while I found a slightly easier way to the left as I'd had time to have a good look round. The rock, in fact, was not good, exfoliating badly due to great extremes of temperature.

Reunited, we moved together through the 'hanging gardens', a large area of boulders and trees with small, beautifully made weaver birds' nests high in the thorn branches. The vultures and kites we had seen the previous day must have still been sleeping as we made our way up on to the slabs that sweep up to form the summit dome.

Di came up after me, obviously remembering her recent big swing off the first pitch of *Great Slab* on Cloggy in the rain, and consequently a little nervous on the almost holdless slabs with thirty metres of rope hanging horizontally between us, but the friction was excellent on the rough granite and she soon padded across what Robin had called 'an extremely delicate bit'. I could sense her relief as the length of the rope between us and the consequent prospect of swinging off down the slab became less. Once at the belay she continued, now smiling, sensing the summit was near, moving on into the lead up a groove snaking up to the right and out of sight. This left me handling two ropes, Di's out and Mick's in, as he followed across the long traverse. As he reached my belay, Di called down happily that she was up and Mick and I followed together, laughing on to the top.

The sky was still overcast, a gentle breeze was blowing and a few drops of rain greeted us. We dumped the gear to look for the Tree of Life. Sure enough, there it was: it was a fig tree. Like the first ascent team we each chewed a leaf; it tasted awful, so we decided to forgo eternal life rather than eat any more. We had an hour on the top then, having finished our water, started down. It was getting hot and the huge vultures were circling on the thermals, wind rushing audibly through their curled-up pinions as they soared just above us, heads hunched back into their shoulders then occasionally stretching out their long, bald snake-like necks to peer down at our intrusion – a wonderful if scary sight.

Once down in the wadi, we decided to walk out to the desert where vehicles seemed to be regularly heading for Kassala. The heat was tremendous – like a baker's oven, as the saying goes. We moved from shade to shade along the sandy bed, passing a small herd of goats and a lone man kneeling in prayer. He was so absorbed that he appeared not to notice three oddly dressed strangers as we passed close by.

Eventually we scrambled down dried-up waterfalls of polished rock and entered the desert near a cluster of tukuls behind a stockade. The faces of women and children peered out, shouting greetings. We wondered what they must think of us emerging from the mountains and walking out into the desert, each with a large sack in the shimmering heat of mid-afternoon.

Once out in the sands, we found the tyre marks of the track between the distant village of Wadsharefy and Kassala, and followed them north around the mountain in the direction of town. It was overpoweringly hot but eventually a bus appeared across the sands from the south, the noise of its engine almost drowned by the singing of the passengers. As usual it was full to overflowing so it didn't stop. Next time perhaps, we hoped optimistically.

More buses and vehicles passed, but all further out in the desert, some seemingly coming from Eritrea. Eventually we reached an outcrop of rock and found some shade. The day continued, hot and slow. More vehicles crossed the desert in the distance and caravans of camels moved slowly through the mirage, merging with Eritrea's blue-hazed hills. The shadows lengthened a little. Our water gone, Di was getting worried, though if necessary we could have walked out the ten miles or so in the evening, but we were already thirsty and it wouldn't have been fun.

Eventually we heard another vehicle approaching. Di wasn't going to let it pass; she walked out from the shade, at first waving casually. The occupants of the pickup didn't seem to notice, so, seemingly convinced she was about to die in the desert – or so it appeared to us – she started to run, both arms waving like a windmill, shouting 'STOP! STOP!' It was a classic desert cartoon sequence and Mick and I curled up with laughter, but we were relieved when it stopped.

Back in town we gulped down fresh grapefruit drinks whisked up in stalls in the souk. We bought a watermelon and some oranges, which equally rapidly disappeared down our dry throats, then we headed for our camp. Happiness is fruit and a shower: how we take water for granted!

We had planned to do some new routes on these remote and beautiful domes but as we wandered among the jebels visiting the desert camps of the Bedouin tribes over the next few days, it became increasingly apparent that something was badly wrong: the battered vehicles we had tried to stop for a lift after our climb, and the people struggling in, sometimes on camels past the jebels, were coming from Ethiopia, and were dying of starvation.

I had been warned in a letter from one of my heroes, the great desert explorer Wilfred Thesiger, that Ethiopia 'is dominated by a set of blood-stained thugs and filled with Russian advisors and Cuban mercenaries'. There had been twenty years of war throughout Ethiopia including its northern province of Eritrea, with indiscriminate violence against civilians by the Ethiopian military. Unknown to us, the war against the Ethiopian Marxist regime, headed by Mengistu, combined with a drought of unprecedented proportions that the outside world had also yet to become aware of, was taking its toll and famine was rife. People were desperately seeking sanctuary, in Kassala, many dying on the way. It was no place for the frivolity of climbing, and having called at the small Red Cross clinic there was nothing we could do to help, so we caught the bus back to Khartoum.

It wasn't the last we were to hear of this tragedy. A year later in 1984, BBC reporter Michael Buerk and cameraman Mohamed Amin brought the plight of millions of starving Ethiopians to British television screens. In what has been called 'one of the most famous TV reports of the late twentieth century', Buerk described it as 'a famine of biblical proportions'. It was partially created by Mengistu himself who, it was said, had smothered Emperor Haile Selassie while he was sleeping. While an estimated 10,000 people were dying every week, Mengistu was spending large amounts of money celebrating the tenth anniversary of his revolution. He was also blocking delivery of grain to areas he thought hostile in Tigray and Eritrea. Bob Geldof was so distressed by what he saw and heard that he created Live Aid, vociferously persuading people around the world to part with their money to help the starving. We were among the millions of contributors.

36

SUDAN SAGA – TICKET TO RIDE

The Khartoum hotel we had previously stayed in was full, so we had a meal in the souk and walked out of town to camp in the Sunt Forest where the Blue and White Niles meet. Bloodthirsty mosquitoes hummed outside our tent and dogs barked through the night. Next day, in an effort to combat the heat, Di and Elaine bought full-length cotton dresses while Mick and I 'went native' in white cotton aragi tops with matching voluminous trousers. Finally we went to the Aliens office for permits to visit the Nuba Mountains.

The Nuba is a farming community with a rich cultural heritage, often painting and scarring their bodies and famed for wrestling and club- or spear-fighting contests. As always on our trips, we were as intrigued by meeting and living among people of a different culture as we were by the thought of exploring new mountains. Sadly it wasn't to be. All requests for permits to Nuba had apparently been refused since the publication of Leni Riefenstahl's book, *The Last of the Nuba*. Though she is best known for her 1935 award-winning propaganda film, *Triumph of the Will*, in support of the Nazi Party, her stunning photographs of the Nuba are a wonderful record of a disappearing way of life. However, her portrayal of the naked human form in what she saw as its primal splendour was contentious. It was alleged that she paid the Nuba to undress for fighting and scarification. We were told that the Arab government under President Nimeiry thought the photography was indecent in an Islamic country and portrayed Sudan as primitive and uncivilised.

We had another option, Jebel Marra, a remote extinct volcano on the southern edge of the Sahara and 800 miles to the south-west. Could there be climbing there? I had managed to source an article about the area from

British colonial days in which J.A. Gillan wrote that he believed he and Captain Hobbs were the first Europeans to reach the summit in 1918. The whole range extended thirty-five miles and was largely home to the Fur people who lived in palisaded villages in case of attack (from who or what Gillan didn't say). It seemed donkeys were essential to reach the crater rim and descend to the two Deriba lakes within. Interestingly he said the intervening cliffs reached a height of 210 metres. Gillan was told by the locals that, 'If the waters took a dislike to us, they would rise and overwhelm us.' And with the arrogance and disdain for Africans so typical of many in the colonial era, he commented that the Fur people, 'though not at present fit to be classed among the world's workers they are considerably in advance of their brothers and the Arabs on the plain … given better transport and experience of the value of money there is no reason why they should not in time become an important agricultural asset to Sudan.'

We arranged train tickets for the journey to Nyala, the end of the line, not far from the borders of Chad and the Central African Republic and close to the foothills of Jebel Marra. It's the journey as much as the climbing that attracts the desert mountain enthusiast. Given sufficient time, one might continue on from Nyala to the almost unvisited Ennedi towers in Chad, or travel north by the ancient thousand-mile slave-trade route of the Darb el Arbain, the 'forty-day road', to Cairo, following the intermittent camel trail still visible in Egypt's Western Desert past the lonely summit of Jebel Uweinat, which marks the meeting point of Egypt's border with Libya, Chad and the Sudan. We were happy simply to be heading west to Nyala and the mysterious Jebel Marra.

A couple of days later, we arrived at the station at 9 a.m. We thought we were early, but the train was already bursting at the seams. It was supposed to leave at 10.30 a.m., but despite the fact it was more than full, we doubted it's punctuality. Having found our names on a compartment door, we squashed ourselves and our sacks into an eight-seater compartment with the other six occupants and their mountains of gear. Sudanese never travel light. When the train left at midday it was virtually impossible to move anywhere. Not only were the carriages full, but the corridors were packed with bodies and luggage: old men, babies and women lying on the floor. We wondered about the next five days of the journey.

By evening the train had chugged its way slowly south alongside the Nile, stopping at every little village where crowds of people jostled at the windows selling food and drink. The train was so full it seemed impossible to fit a single person more on, yet still more arrived at every stop, climbing up between the carriages and on to the roof, pulling their bags up after them. Uncoiling their turbans, they lowered bottles down into the crowd to be filled with chai or water. Indeed, travelling on the roof seemed preferable to the hot, airless crush of the carriage. Leaving all our gear in our compartment and doing our best to avoid trampling on the tangle of bodies in the corridor, we climbed up to join those on top, but by nine at night it was too cold for comfort so we climbed down at one of many stops and went into the buffet car.

The cutlery was emblazoned with VR: Victoria Regina. Was it a relic of General Kitchener's time? It was the only cutlery we saw in the Sudan, everywhere else we ate with our fingers or by dipping bread into a communal bowl. Our meal was cooked on a partially open log fire; the food was good though quite dear at the equivalent of 60p each instead of the usual 15p. As a consequence of the price the carriage was empty but we were soon evicted as it closed for the night. As we were not at a station at that point, we had to return to our cabin down the corridor, inadvertently treading on sleeping children and women as we strode over hunched bodies (or bundles of rags – who could tell in the dim light?). No one complained; it was normal. Back in our cabin where our sacks were untouched, we squashed into our seats for a long hot night among a jumble of bodies all of whom obligingly squeezed over with no complaints. It passed slowly.

Dawn arrived with an attempted stretching of cramped limbs and at the next stop we stumbled out over the masses in the passage to seek the sanctuary of the buffet car. Simple comforts meant everything. After chai we went back on to the roof and rattled our way through the day, crossing the White Nile at Kosti, the last town before the swamps and floodlands of southern Sudan. At this point, our train turned west, heading out towards Nyala across 600 miles of the Sahel. 'Hel' is definitely the important part of this word. The scenery was bleak. The trees looked dead. Everywhere the land was flat. Dust filled the air; it pervaded everything. The sky was pale yellow; dry dusty villages came and went, their parched farmland waiting for the rains. Skeletons and rotting bodies of camels and donkeys littered the sides of the tracks. The train stopped five times a day for prayer and stops at villages were frequent, always with crowds of people waiting. Everyone seemed happy – strange in such an inhospitable land. We don't know how lucky we are.

We ate in the evening, delaying our return to our cabin until the last possible moment. Somehow this second night passed more easily – perhaps we were getting used to it? We slept in fits and starts and eventually the train stopped. It was still motionless at dawn so we went out to stretch and shake off the dust. In the buffet car we discovered that another train was derailed further up the line, something which happened fairly frequently as the lines were laid on drifting sand. No one knew if we would be there for an hour, a day – or maybe a week. That's life in the Sudan. We were past caring.

Midday came and went, shadows shrinking to nothing then slowly lengthening again. Nothing moved. People sat, chatting under the shade of the carriages. Time passed in its slow African way, nobody bothered. *Perhaps we really will be here for a week*, we thought. We lay quietly in the shade watching kites circle in the shimmering heat. In the mid-afternoon Di and I ventured out to the village with its clustered groups of people squatting round kettles. We chatted to them under the shade of a tree, where they shared their chai and a few nuts with us. Evening came, the sky reddening, the glow of numerous fires lighting the scene: the dark faces and the laughing eyes. We were invited to eat, and given a bowl of asida, which we hadn't had before: a large, gluey, flour dumpling in some sauce, and some kisra, an extremely thin tasteless pancake. The taste of the asida was okay, quite spicy, but it had the consistency of that green sticky slime that kids play with. The more we dipped in the bowl the less we enjoyed it.

Eventually Mick and Elaine arrived – they too had been wandering around the village. They joined us for another chai as the sky darkened and the stars came out. Suddenly a whistle blew. Action! People scurried through the dust jostling for a place on the roof of the train, or in the carriages and corridors. We were on the move again into the cold, empty night.

The train lumbered on at about ten miles an hour, swaying on badly laid tracks. Old broken rails could be seen in the moonlight, cast aside in the sand. Here and there upturned carriages lay rusting on their side. Before midnight we climbed down off the roof, it was impossible to cling to our swaying, sloping perch on its edge any longer; the people on the apex of the roof had tied themselves to the protruding air vents with their turbans.

Morning came – relentlessly westwards into the scrubland. Mile after mile of scorched earth with the bare grey blasted skeletons of tortured trees rising from the arid lands. The telegraph poles alongside the track had rotted or been eaten away by termites. The decaying remains of the upper sections of some of the poles swung in space like crucifixes suspended by the wires from the sagging and tottering poles on either side.

Around midday we reached Barbanousa, a major junction. Our line continued west and a branch line went south to Wau, where the jungles of the tropics begin. By mid-afternoon we were away again with a feeling of optimism; about 600 to 700 miles down and 200 or so to go; we should be there tomorrow morning, we hoped. Later, we went up on the roof, riding into another blood-red sunset and watching the world go by. The country, though still very dry, was becoming a little greener. Beautiful coloured sunbirds on the remnants of the telegraph wires flashed turquoise bodies as we rattled past and fires glowed in the dusk as we passed remote villages. At one, the sound of singing and drums filled the night and everyone on the train roof joined in.

It was still dark when the train stopped. Suddenly, after four and a half days, the air was full of urgency. Everyone wanted to get off at once. We sat tight and waited for our compartment to empty and the crush of bodies in the corridor to move. It was about 4 a.m. and we had arrived at Nyala. Half an hour later we staggered out half-asleep and re-established ourselves in the sand outside the train to sleep horizontally for a couple of hours. Luxury.

When we awoke most of the crowd had gone and we walked into town. The plan was to stay a couple of days, wash and clean up (we hadn't seen water now for five days other than in a drinking glass). Unlike the Sudanese who somehow remained immaculate, we were covered in dust and our hair and clothes were filthy, but our dreams of cleanliness were dashed as we couldn't find anywhere to stay. The only 'hotel' in town was full (it would be with 1,000 people arriving on the train), though eventually we did find a good cafe for breakfast. Outside, there was a fifty-gallon drum of water, where we managed to splash off the dust. With full stomachs and hands and faces vaguely clean we felt better. It was time to move on.

Nyala was a bustling market town – the best place we'd seen since Kassala. I managed to buy a 'heram' (the white turban made from twenty feet of cotton to keep out the heat and dust). In this and my aragi I was beginning to feel in place. Behind the market we found a lorry heading out to Niertiti up in the foothills of Jebel Marra. It would be leaving soon, or so we were told, so we climbed on board and sat there in the midday heat. The metal of the truck back was impossible to touch. We and it continued to melt until eventually we set off only to stop ten minutes later in another market where everyone got out. We wondered: *are we going to be here for five minutes, or an hour, or the rest of the day?*

We wandered around the market, eating oranges and soaking in the day. No rush. A horn hooted and everyone climbed back in the wagon. After quarter of an hour everyone got out to sit in the shade again. Two young girls with beautiful slim faces and high arched eyebrows sat in the dust breastfeeding their babies, unconcerned by a multitude of flies clustering around them. A couple of hours later we did a repeat performance then finally another wagon arrived and everyone changed vehicles. Action: we were on the road heading west again through villages of tukuls and out on to a good road leading to the orchards of Zalingei near the frontier with Chad. We wondered how easy it would be to reach the remote desert towers of Ennedi from there – I had never heard of anyone visiting them, but we were content to be on our way to Jebel Marra. That was just as mysterious.

The land was still dry with huge baobab trees sprouting from the sands, trunks three metres thick unexpectedly spreading into tangled root-like branches. After sunset we pulled into a cluster of shacks. Fires glowed at chai and food stalls and we wallowed in the happy atmosphere of a cool African night, eating eggs and doughnuts and drinking black coffee and chai. It was good to be away from the crowded train though the feeling wasn't to last long: when we moved on again the lorry was so full I spent most of the next hour stood on one leg with no space to put the other foot down.

A cool breeze blew and the stars shone brightly. We eventually stopped at a small village for another tea. In the dark night, drums beat and singing came out of the distance as we sat on straw mats among dimly seen but friendly faces, lit by the fire. Back again in the lorry we rose higher still into the hills, the vegetation becoming denser until narrow sandy tracks wound between palisades of woven straw, fencing in the village of Niertiti. Behind the straw walls, the roofs of conical thatched tukuls could be seen. It was after midnight. It had been a long day since we left the train and once again it felt like we were on another planet. We crawled under a shelter and into our sleeping bags for the first good night's sleep in a week; to lie down straight for a whole night was a forgotten sensation!

We woke leisurely to the noises of an African village. Next to us was a chai shop so we moved into its cool shade. Afterwards we went for a walk around the village – it was a paradise of cool shady pathways leading out between woven-straw walls, each sheltering courtyards and thatched houses, to gardens of greenery, with mango, orange and palm trees. A huge baobab tree almost six metres thick stood aloof on its own. People were laughing and smiling, welcoming us, shouting greetings and waving.

A dried-up wadi passed by the village square, the occasional pool or trickle between rocks showing signs of its abundance in the rainy season which was expected to start in a couple of months. Now, towards the end of March, holes were dug in the riverbed for water and boys and girls with donkeys filled up their water bags for the day. Just down the wadi the rocks of the riverbed stopped abruptly, dropping fifteen metres into a cool dark pool now almost stagnant – but what a sparkling sight it must be in the rains. A crowd of young boys were swimming and playing – many of them naked. It looked tempting but we decided against it, as most of the population has bilharzia, which is caught from worms in slow-moving water penetrating the skin. Even so, we risked the luxury of our first good wash for a week. Pigeons, ouzels, gold and red fire finches and other incredibly coloured birds darted among the trees and rushes. Black kites circled the skies. Women walked past with zias (large earthenware water jars) on their heads, or sat breastfeeding their children in the shade.

Next day was market day and by mid-morning the quiet village was bustling with activity as people from the surrounding Fur villages came in. Skins from slaughtered cattle were stretched out in the dust and fresh meat hung in the stalls. Small boys sold fruit drinks, and all the chai shops were full. Woman with tightly platted hair, nose rings and double earrings sold leatherwork. While all this was going on we found someone who would take us up to Quaila, the next village higher up the mountain. We packed quickly, bought what we could – tea, sugar, lemon and nuts – and were ready to go. There were no shops further up the trail but our guide said he could arrange for food. We hoped so!

Having strapped our four sacks on to his donkey, he then climbed on top himself – he wasn't a small man, but the donkey seemed unconcerned and we set off at a brisk trot. It was still very hot, but we had no choice but to leave, walking briskly out of the shade of the trees and into gently rising scrubland. Nearing sunset, we were still rising into the hills though the heat of the day had fortunately passed. The pace had also eased and we were able to enjoy the remoteness of our surroundings as the trail wound up over ridges and across dry wadis, twisting around small hills, but always rising up towards the crater rim. Behind us the sun was setting, the skies a deep pink and purple over Chad in the far distance. Ahead, a full moon rose over Jebel Marra, which glistened silver in the night. All around small fires could be seen in otherwise hidden villages until suddenly we turned through a stockade of thorns to arrive at our stop for the night amidst moonlit tukuls. We tumbled into our sleeping bags, hungry but happy.

We awoke feeling parched with dry throats, but managed to gather some twigs to brew a welcome cup of lemon tea. As we had no food other than peanuts we then had to wait for Abdulai, our guide, to bring breakfast as arranged, so we sat in the shade and waited … and waited. Things moved slowly. People came and went: half-naked women, all carrying babies; young girls of six or seven, also carrying babies; women with huge zias full of water on their heads. Camels, donkeys and horses passed by, and brightly coloured birds called to each other in the trees … but we remained hungry.

At midday Abdulai arrived with a large bowl of asida. As before, it had the consistency of uncooked dumplings – and tasted similar. Luckily it was surrounded by a spicy gravy with a few bits of onion and meat. Elaine didn't like it and Di was feeling weak with dysentery, so Mick and I dipped in and ate it all except for a particularly unpalatable mound of 'dumpling' in the middle which we surreptitiously saved for later when it went down well with a bit of sugar. By evening Di was feeling a bit better, but one eye was very red, perhaps due to the dust blowing everywhere. We went down to the river which rose from hot springs higher up the mountain, for a wash. A small waterfall provided a welcome haven and we sat under it relishing the cool splashing water. Finally we felt clean. Later that evening, we made another brew, but there was no further sign of Abdulai – it looked like one meal a day was all we were going to get. After a second brew we watched the sunset and listened to the sounds of the village coming to life; a mixture of laughing, talking, chanting and singing, filling the night air, while frogs whistled and croaked in the background. The full moon cast a silver glow over the scene as we crawled into our sleeping bags – still hungry but otherwise fine.

The plan the next day was to set off for the Deriba lakes in the crater of Jebel Marra, but as we half expected, it didn't work out that way. We awoke still hungry. Di had also had a bad night with her eye. There was no sign of Abdulai so Mick and I went to try to buy some food in the village and returned with dates, rice and sesame paste, the dates and a brew of lemon tea sufficing for breakfast. Eventually Abdulai arrived and after a long chat a decision was made to leave the following afternoon after the village's weekly market. This would avoid the heat of the day and allow Abdulai to do his business at the market. We also arranged for another meal and fixed the total price for the five days' food and three days' walk at the equivalent of £4 each. This seemed to please Abdulai so much he returned shortly with more asida dumplings. Mick and I tucked in. Elaine once more did without. Di managed to eat some but her eye was now really troubling her and I was getting quite worried about it. It was bloodshot and painful and I hoped it wasn't serious, as our eye ointment didn't seem to be achieving anything. Anyway, back to the asida! Once again we saved the big lump in the middle and Mick and I ate it later, this time with squashed lemon and sugar, imagining it was a pancake.

We made our way to the river further upstream, finding a beautiful spot surrounded by cactus trees with a fifteen-metre waterfall cascading down bright green moss into a pool. We sat beneath it feeling the warm water splash over us. Ecstasy! The river also had a lot of sulphur in it, which definitely helped Di's eye. Back in the village a woman with a gallon bowl of home-brewed marissa beer arrived. Mick and I drank some but weren't impressed: it had the consistency and colour of thick mushroom soup and the taste of sour fermenting yeast. We turned in for an early night finding a couple of scorpions hiding among the straw matting before dozing to the sound of singing and chanting which went on into the middle of the night and merged with our dreams.

Next morning we had our regular lemon tea for breakfast. Di's eye was undoubtedly getting better, but I had an attack of the runs – probably the beer! Later we cooked up some rice with sugar and lemon, then Abdulai arrived with his donkey – time to go. The trail wound up into a long desolate valley. Below, scattered areas of green marked the presence of water and hot springs. Around and above was a dusty multicoloured landscape of lava and volcanic ash, with rock outcrops of pink and grey, rust-red and ochre. We passed through an area of giant cactus, before entering a labyrinth of gullies and canyons cut deep into the ash. Route finding without a guide would be a nightmare in this maze of narrow ravines intertwining their ways up the hillside.

As the sun sank behind us we met a group of girls coming down the trail, bowls balanced on their heads. The formalities of greeting among the Fur tribe were gone through – the women bowing, curtsying, or kneeling on the ground and replying in a sing-song chant to Abdulai. After half a dozen greetings, backwards and forwards, normal conversation could then begin. It was a fascinating ritual, made even more unusual in the solitude of the mountains. The women passed on chattering and laughing among themselves down into the valley, leaving us to emerge in growing darkness from the maze of gullies on to the upper slopes of the dormant volcano.

By the time we reached the rim of the crater it was pitch black. The moon that had lit our way the previous night was nowhere to be seen. With a couple of hours still ahead of us, we continued into the night. Somehow the donkey picked out a route among the rocks and stones though the donkey itself was invisible in the darkness. Only the sound of its hooves and the dimly seen white turban of Abdulai bobbing up and down marked the way. If they got more than six metres ahead of us we had to shout as we could no longer see them.

Stumbling along the uneven terrain on the rim of the crater we were relieved when, an hour later, a glow on the horizon heralded the rising moon and the trail re-emerged. It wound down into the crater, passing through more narrow ravines, the donkey's sacks scraping on both walls, sometimes having to be pushed through. Dimly seen chasms appeared in the moonlight, plunging into the darkness beneath us. In the bottom of the crater, moonlight reflected from two lakes.

We emerged on to the crater floor by a salt lake, its white banks gleaming in the night. As we reached the shore, Abdulai stopped by a small muddy pool full of animal footprints and droppings where a freshwater inlet trickled into the otherwise undrinkable lake. We managed to get a bottle full of disgustingly dirty water before moving up the hillside a little to sleep under a huge tree growing almost parallel to the ground, its massive branches intertwined grotesquely in the moonlight. Abdulai lit a fire and we had some chai but nothing to eat before settling down for the night. He, on the other hand, knew something we didn't and obviously intended to sit there all night and keep the fire in, which was perhaps as well.

Everything was still and silent in the crater. We were half asleep when the drumming of hooves sounded occasionally, echoing in the distance. Suddenly it came louder. There was a crashing of vegetation above us, and we sat up alarmed. A herd of horses careered wildly down the hillside appearing suddenly through the bracken a few metres away, wide-eyed and nostrils flaring. Abdulai jumped up, shouting and brandishing a blazing stick and the horses veered off at the very last moment, narrowly missing us in our sleeping bags. At the edge of the fire glow, dog-like shapes moved noiselessly through the tall bracken – obviously the reason for the horses' alarm.

We awoke to birdsong in the tree just over our heads; Abdulai was dozing by the fire, which still glowed red. Colourful birds perched on tall grasses, storks and sandpipers walked around the water's edge. Horses were grazing in scattered groups around the lake. Di and I went to fetch water while Abdulai boiled up some meat and onions, which were hungrily devoured. Obviously enjoying his new role in life, Abdulai concocted his usual huge bowl of asida. Hungry as we still were, we couldn't eat it. Luckily we managed to dump most of the brain-sized 'dumpling' down the hillside without him noticing this insult to his culinary skills, though I'm sure he wondered about the vultures that flew in when we left.

There were a few cliffs around the crater rim, but nothing to climb, just volcanic ash, and anyway, Abdulai was moving on. It was afternoon when we crested the far side of the crater, looking forward to an easy three-hours walk downhill through a gap in the rim, once again just wide enough to squeeze the donkey through with its load. An hour later, small irrigated fields could be seen a hundred metres below us in the canyon, but our hopes of an easy day quickly vanished as we turned abruptly up the hillside, leaving what appeared to be the obvious way and winding tortuously back upwards. This went on for an hour until we reached the top of a high plateau. The gap we had come through in the crater rim was clearly visible, probably only a mile away – such is the complexity of the area.

Dusk caught us again as we made our way across the plateau and it began to look like another struggle in the blackness until Abdulai pointed out a group of tall trees in a hollow not far away. It was Taratonga, the 'House of the Wolves', our destination. We arrived at nightfall to the sound of a breeze in unexpected pine trees, and once through the village, we made our way along stone-walled paths to a building tucked among them. Despite the trees we couldn't find wood for a fire, so there was no brew that night, or meal either.

I awoke early with an annoying cough that seemed to be creeping up on all of us – it must have been due to the dust that was everywhere, everyday. Now in the daylight, we found some wood to make a fire for our life-giving lemon tea, but there was no food in the village, so no breakfast. The villagers, however, happy and friendly as ever, told us there should be a lorry passing on the track to the next village in half an hour, which would get us back to Nyala. We should have known better.

We walked right through the heat of midday, down a track ankle-deep in dust, eventually reaching Gorlangbang, the next village – but no sign of a lorry. 'There should be one tomorrow,' we were told, but we'd heard that one before. Our first objective was to find some food but as usual there was none; surviving on Jebel Marra seemed marginal to say the least. Although its inhabitants seemed healthy enough, we couldn't even get a brew. Finally we managed to revive someone's charcoal fire and, scratching up bits of wood from the village square, we rustled up a longed-for cup of tea. This done, things were livening up a little: some horses, their riders perched high on sheep's-wool saddles, harnesses with gleaming brassware, whips cracking over their heads, raced down the street. Later, camel riders rode in, resplendent on saddles of colourful rugs, piled high like thrones. Someone gave us a bowl of the dreaded asida.

The next day the promised wagon arrived, and we rattled our way down off the mountain to Nyala. The train was due in a couple of days, but then it was three days late. We managed to get beds in the town's only hotel – a truly dilapidated place. There was no water. The toilet doors were broken and where there should have been holes in the toilet floor there were, to put it bluntly, mounds of shit that oozed over the rest of the floor. Standing in there it was impossible to keep your feet clean, and when you peed, thumb-sized white maggots rose out of the mess. I was glad I was constipated.

The large communal bedroom was a terrible place, so we decided to put our tent up on the balcony. It was cramped but we thought it would get the four of us out of the room. However, the owner, for reasons known only to him, pulled the tent down and nailed boards across the balcony door.

When the train did arrive, three armed Sudanese soldiers of the Dinka tribe, all well over six feet tall, tried to throw us and the six Sudanese occupants out of our compartment, to claim it for themselves, throwing the belongings of the Sudanese out on to the tracks. They, like us, had waited three days or more, but after a brief argument they climbed back down on to the platform – in another week or so the train would be back. We, on the other hand, hung grimly on to our sacks and refused to go, worried that we were overstepping the mark, arguing with armed men; nobody was going to help us here, but the soldiers backed off and satisfied themselves with evicting us into the corridor, the three of them taking over the now empty compartment, spreading themselves over the seats.

The following morning the door slid open and they gestured to Di indicating she could sit down with them. She was reluctant, but I said, 'Go on, why not?', so she went in and the door slid shut behind her. A few minutes later there was the noise of a scuffle, the door burst open and Di came out; they had tried to molest her! Then there was some shouting along the corridor and a boy came running along as best he could over the crowds of people who were all shouting 'Thief!' The soldiers dragged him into their compartment, stood on him and beat him badly, despite his denials. The next day the soldiers left and the rest of the journey passed as before.

After five days we arrived back in Khartoum. We had some days to spare, but we came up with a plan and changed our flight departure from Khartoum to Cairo. We then visited Omdurman where we joined the crowd among the dervish in their multicoloured djellabas, who were performing outside the tomb of Sheikh Hamed al-Nil, rhythmically chanting 'La ilaha illallah' – 'There is no god but God', as they whirled around. Eighty-five years previously in 1898, 10,000 dervishes had been massacred there and 12,000 wounded by the army of General Kitchener with its superior weapons, as Kitchener sought revenge for the killing of General Gordon in Khartoum in 1885.

The following day we bought train tickets to Wadi Halfa, the Sudanese terminal 600 miles to the north on the Aswan dam, but with no seats reserved, we slept the night at the station and when the train arrived the next morning we joined the rush for seats. Managing to be among the first to get in, I threw myself across four seats with a Sudanese lad landing immediately on top of me having climbed through the window. A full-on fist battle ensued, sorted out by Mick who was close behind. We had claimed our seats! The journey was fine, trundling north across the Sahara and the Batn el-Haggar, the 'Belly of Rocks', and following the Nile for three days to Halfa and the shore of the Aswan dam where three barges were waiting roped together to take us north to Egypt and Aswan.

As with all transport we travelled on, the barges were seriously overloaded, but the journey passed uneventfully, although a week later, the whole contraption set on fire killing 317 people. The fire originated with a gas cylinder exploding in the kitchen. Within minutes all three boats were burning, helped by drums of petrol the Sudanese were smuggling into their country where fuel shortages are common. It was reported that while most drowned, many passengers tried to swim to shore but were eaten by crocodiles; more reportedly died from scorpion and snake bites.

Entering Egypt, another small group of English travellers was just ahead of us in the queue. The lad in front of me passed his passport over to be checked and I noticed his name seemed to be Viscount Emlyn.

'Is that your name or your title?' I asked, somewhat bemused – he looked more like a hippy than a viscount.

'It's my title,' he said with a grin. He was travelling through Africa and was an interesting lad who shared the rest of our journey through Egypt with us on his way home to Cawdor Castle in Scotland, which is linked erroneously with Macbeth in Shakespeare's tragedy.

The following year while on a climbing trip through Scotland, Mick, Di and I called in, and knocked on the castle door. 'Is Colin in?' I asked.

'Sorry sir,' the butler said, unfazed by our appearance, 'he's not here, he's at his other residence in England.'

Egypt seemed like paradise after the Sudan. We ate copious amounts of ice cream; we visited Luxor and the Valley of the Kings and hired a felucca to take us lazily down the Nile towards Cairo. We were so happy to see water that we even swam in the Nile, ignoring the risk of bilharzia.

A final sad note on the Sudan: despite their abject poverty, the Fur people of Jebel Marra had given us every possible welcome, but since then, total destruction has been brought to their villages and lives by the Sudanese government-backed Janjaweed fighters – desert Arabs known as the 'devils on horseback'. According to Cultural Survival, 50,000 people died, thousands more were raped and more than a million displaced. Supplied with weapons by Sudanese military intelligence, the highly mobile Janjaweed forces conducted what was described by international observers as an ethnic cleansing of the Fur, Masalit, and Zaghawa peoples. Following attacks by the Sudanese Air Force, the Janjaweed would sweep through on their horses, killing, mutilating, raping and kidnapping, before burning fields and houses, poisoning wells, and seizing anything of value. Their campaign was called genocide by US Secretary of State Colin Powell, but the Sudanese President, Omar al-Bashir denied any connection with it.

37

EXPLORING JORDAN – WADI RUM DISCOVERY

All men dream, but not equally. Those who dream by night in the dusty recesses of their minds, wake in the day to find that it was vanity: but the dreamers of the day are dangerous men, for they may act on their dreams with open eyes, to make them possible.

***Seven Pillars of Wisdom**, T.E. Lawrence*

'Welcome to Wadi Rum,' said Anthony Quinn in the persona of Auda Abu Tayi. It was Christmas 1983 and I was at Ken and Di's watching David Lean's epic film, *Lawrence of Arabia*. It was a pivotal moment in my life: great cliffs and desert canyons opened out before me as I saw for the first time the awesome valley of Rum and its surrounding mountains. There were more mountains than a climber could dream of and I had a suspicion they were unknown to the world's climbing community. I couldn't get them out of my mind. I had followed desert climbing developments over the past twenty years and never heard of anyone climbing in Jordan. I didn't even know if people were permitted into the desert so near the Saudi border. All I knew was that Brian Hodgkinson, one of the Rimmon lads, had worked in Jordan in the late 1970s but had never said anything about Wadi Rum, and Joe Brown had been in Petra in 1962 climbing to otherwise inaccessible places on its ancient tombs and temples for the archaeologists. He had never mentioned it either. Maybe the mountains were no good for climbing? They didn't look that way to me. You never know until you go.

I wrote to the Jordanian ambassador in London for contacts that might be able to give me information on Wadi Rum and permission to go there to climb, if it was needed. By early February there was still no response, so a spring trip was going to be out of the question, but I persevered, also writing to King Hussein. No response there either, but having contacted the ambassador again, I got the actual name of the tourism director and wrote again.

And again. I persisted with my letter writing to any person or department that might be able to help with my increasing Wadi Rum obsession.

It was summer before I finally got a reply – and a good one. I was at my desk at Troll when the fax machine whirred into life. I looked around, wondering if it might be an order for some gear, but no, it was headed 'Ministry of Tourism and Antiquities, Jordan'. It read, 'We are commencing a five-year plan to develop tourism in south Jordan and would like to invite you and your team to explore Wadi Rum for climbing.' We were in! And so began the 'golden years' of rock climbing in Wadi Rum. Mick Shaw and Di were both keen, and I rang Alan Baker to see if he was interested (silly question).

In late September, we went out to Jordan and hit the jackpot, discovering the climbing potential of the mountains of Wadi Rum, described by T.E. Lawrence as 'Rumm the magnificent … vast, echoing and godlike'. He wasn't wrong. The music of Frankie Goes to Hollywood was also in the charts at this time, their *Welcome to the Pleasuredome* forming a backing track to my subsequent slide show of climbing in Rum.

Like Shipton, in our discovery of the mountains of Jordan, we found 'a random harvest of delight', just as he did with his infinitely greater explorations described in his autobiography, *That Untravelled World*. They were to give us years of adventure among some of the world's most hospitable people. We have been in Rum every year since, having established a close friendship with the local Zalabieh Bedouin, something that has been of inestimable value to us and other climbers. They themselves proved to be great climbers and knew the mountains intimately, having passed down knowledge of their hunting routes through the generations.

Though initially suspicious of our reasons for wanting to climb there, they have a climber's pride in their routes; they pointed us towards them, giving only enough information to get us started, and were there to meet us on our return, grinning mischievously if we had been lost in the bizarre maze of these sandstone mountains. We liked their climber's sense of humour and thanks to them we learned to think like Bedouin hunters, who have learned to think like ibex. In so doing we discovered a wealth of unique Bedouin climbs, some of them ascending miles of rock to reach remote summits. It has been said that for their grade, they rank among the best rock adventures in the world.

Our expedition was a kaleidoscope of experiences. Courtesy of the tourism ministry, we commenced with a tour of Jordan: views of the Israeli-occupied Golan Heights to the north from the Greco-Roman ruins of Um Qais; grim Islamic and crusader castles hunched on barren heights to the south, reminders of past struggles in the name of religion; the black basalt ruins of the ancient caravanserai of Umm el-Jimal in the east, its gaunt walls standing like a scene of nuclear destruction out in the dry, flat stony desert near the Syrian border. Its three-storey buildings supported by black basalt beams had heavy stone doors still opening on their stone pivots; the abandoned castle of Azraq far out in the eastern desert where Lawrence plotted his northern raids; Roman cities, standing neatly with their well-defined streets, pillars, squares and temples; and, most awe-inspiring of all, the once-lost Nabataean city of Petra, the 'rose-red city half as old as time', which we entered through the 'siq', a narrow natural canyon winding through the heart of the mountains to reveal grandiose tombs carved into the rock walls of the valley beyond. Back then, Bedouin still inhabited its tombs and temples, earning a living from guiding tourists on horse, donkey or camel around this most magnificent and unique of ancient cities. We spent two days exploring its multi-hued sandstone ruins, while wondering about the rock and hoping it would be better in Rum not far away to the south.

We saw most of Jordan: the wooded hills of the north; the bare expanses of the eastern desert with its lonely castles and isolated but lush oasis of Azraq; the sub-sea-level Jordan Rift Valley, fertile in the north and arid in the south; the Dead Sea, the lowest point on earth with its salt-encrusted shores – a visit to which must be an all-time low for a mountaineering expedition; also the Red Sea with its coral reefs. Finally, for us the *pièce de résistance*, the desert and mountains of Wadi Rum: the reason for our journey to this ancient land; a place, to the best of our knowledge, previously unknown to mountaineers, though we were soon to discover that Tom Longstaff had been there before us.

We had a chauffeur-driven tourism ministry four-wheel drive, and had been told by the director that the only possible way to contact the Bedouin was via a diving-tour operator in Aqaba who occasionally took his guests on a drive through Wadi Rum using Bedouin guides. We made a token search for him, but didn't believe it was necessary. We were quite happy to introduce ourselves, so after camping a night on a mosquito-infested beach, we left the next day, our driver asking, 'Why do you want to go to Wadi Rum? There is nothing there, it's just sand, mountains and Bedouin'. *Exactly!*

The first thing that struck us when driving towards Wadi Rum down the potholed single-track road was the vastness and complexity of the mountains: a slowly encroaching profusion of towers, peaks and domes thrust skywards on all sides, their cliffs seeming to be melting like candles as we approached the actual entrance to the Rum valley. Nowadays a visitor centre distracts the eye at this point, but back in 1984 and until quite recently, the entrance was through a narrow defile between Jebel Rum and a rocky hill that hid the view ahead. We sensed something even more dramatic would come into view, but despite Lawrence's exuberant prose we were unprepared for its sudden grandeur and the superlative desert scenery, with massive red, wind-weathered, weirdly shaped cliffs jutting up from the orange sands beneath an incomparably blue sky. The valley runs for more than six miles between the towering walls of Jebel Rum (then thought to be Jordan's highest mountain at 1,754 metres) and Jebel Um Ishrin (only one metre lower, or so the old maps say) and was described by Lawrence as 'A processional way greater than imagination!' A note in my diary is less erudite. It reads, 'We were gobsmacked'.

Once in Rum itself, the purple-hued mountains reveal tawny multi-coloured hues of sandstone ridges and walls that rise abruptly for 500 metres from the desert floor, topped with frost-white domes worn smooth by millennia of caressing winds and rare winter rains. Overhead the sky is relentlessly blue; underfoot the sand is yellow, orange, rust and purple. All around there is emptiness, silence and space so immense that standing below the walls you feel dwarfed to insignificance.

Later in the day the valley possesses an ethereal quality, especially in the red glow of the setting sun or the eerie light of the moon. The scenery is unsurpassed in the Middle East. It is the result of a geological upheaval that shattered mammoth pieces of granite and sandstone, thrusting them upwards into towering cliff-bound islands rising from what was once the prehistoric Lake Disi, but is now the desert sands.

Man has inhabited these awesome valleys and mountains for at least 30,000 years. Squares of Neolithic stones of unknown purpose edge the valley. Thamudic cave drawings of camels, birds, leopards, oryx, ibex and other more indecipherable creatures abound on rock walls, particularly in the entrances to the numerous large ravines or 'siqs'. Ruins and ancient hewn stairways up canyon walls are also found, relics of Nabataean times, though the inhabitants of today are the Bedouin, with characters as colourful as the rock that rises abruptly above the village in an ever-changing kaleidoscope of grandeur. In 1984, most were still living the semi-nomadic life of their forbears, though thirty-odd years on, the majority now live in a village in the heart of the valley. When we arrived however, the village was predominantly a cluster of black goat-hair *beit esh-sha'ar* – Bedouin tents near the Beau Geste-style fort, located on what was a few years previously the border with Saudi Arabia, the border having been moved south in a land swap with Saudi Arabia to allow Jordan more coastal access to the Red Sea in which to build a port.

The inhabitants are mostly members of the Zalabieh tribe, a faction of the Huweitat confederation, shepherds and camel breeders – the *aaiil* – the aristocrats of the desert who arrived in the area in the early 1800s, migrating north from the Hijaz Mountains. Some continued around the head of the Gulf into western Sinai, pushing the Ma'aza Bedouin into Egypt's Red Sea Mountains, though the Ma'aza say they were already moving there as it was a better place. Others stayed in the mountains of Rum where perennial springs of clear water trickled from the fern-fronded interface between the sandstone towers and their granite plinth. Richard Burton, in his 1879 book *The Land of Midian*, says that the Huweitat are 'the aggressive element in the Midianite family of Bedawin' and that their genealogy derives from 'some of the noblest of Bedawi blood.' According to G.W. Murray in his book, *The Sons of Ishmael*, the Huweitat say, 'The human race was divided at the beginning into three classes; the tent-makers, the agriculturalists and the Haweitat.' Murray suspects that they considered 'the first two classes were created exclusively for the support of the third'.

Of those that stayed in and around the Rum area, the Zuweida faction based their camps around the springs of Disi to the north-east, near the foot of the great plateau which rises to the Sharra Mountains above Petra. The Zalabieh families settled in Rum itself, in the proximity of the springs around Jebel Rum and the other great mountains. They rediscovered the old Thamudic hunting ways and made new routes of their own for hunting ibex, becoming masters of their mountain and desert environment – but the area still remained remote. Only the occasional traveller such as Richard Burton passed through the area, commenting that 'The fountains flow in winter, in summer the wells are never dry; the people, especially the Huwaytat, are kind and hospitable'. This continuing traditional life was disturbed briefly in 1917 when the Arab Revolt recruited fighters from among the Huweitat, most famously, Auda Abu Tayi, described by T.E. Lawrence in his *Seven Pillars of Wisdom* as 'The greatest fighting man in northern Arabia'. From Rum, they harried the Turkish railway from Saudi Arabia and took their fortress in Aqaba.

Talking of Lawrence, I should mention here that although a few of the oldest Bedouin we met in Rum that year claimed to remember him, their memories had not been passed on. Géraldine Chatelard, a social anthropologist who knows the Bedouin well and who we met in Rum a few years later, told us that 'Lawrence was to all intents unknown before "the foreigners", as they called the film crew, came to make the film about him in the 1960s. King Hussein's presence during the filming is recalled as much more significant. But they remembered Emir Faisal and the sheikh of the Huweitat, Auda Abu Tayi, who their fathers had fought alongside, saying "It is well known Lawrence was a liar".'

They also told Géraldine that, 'Tourists always ask the same questions so we give them the answers they want, sometimes laughing at the their credulity, and making fun of each others' pretenses,' which is something we saw for ourselves. On one such occasion, when the village was still a tent village, we were sat with Bedouin friends. A tour group had arrived and some of them walked unannounced into their tent, put a camera tripod up and started taking photos. The Bedouin pulled their knives around to the fronts of their belts so they would be visible as they know that's what tourists like, then smiled obligingly. When the tourists had gone, everyone laughed, but we were embarrassed at the crassness of our culture. When this began to happen too often and a tourist pointed his camera impolitely into Defallah Atieq's tent, he quite rightly said, 'We are people, not ruins'.

The Huweitat also fought in World War Two in Glubb Pasha's Arab Legion. A number of the tribe led by Sheikh Zaal bin Mutluq, who had fought with Auda Abu Tayi in the Great War, joined the fighting as irregulars. On one occasion, while most of them sought cover in the trenches with the regular troops, Zaal stood on a hilltop in the open firing at Vichy French aircraft that were strafing them. He complained afterwards that war was not as good as it had been in the old days. This typically bold, relaxed and highly confident approach is today mirrored in the attitude of many locals towards climbing, enabling them to become familiar with every detail of their mountains during their hunting exploits.

When we arrived in Rum, they were – and still are to this day – proudly independent with a cautious distrust of strangers and central government, which is often inconsiderate and disparaging of them. They simultaneously have strong beliefs in their customs that generations of experience in these once-remote desert mountains have determined for them, particularly of hospitality, honour and bravery. They also highly value their freedom and are determined to retain it.

It was in Wadi Rum among these people that we found a new home for five fascinating weeks. They made us welcome in their camps, driving us around the mountains and pointing out their hidden water sources and ancient Bedouin hunting routes, including climbs up sticks jammed in overhanging cracks to get honey from bees' nests. We spent numerous nights in their tents and were invited as guests to their wedding feasts, where in the dark of the desert night to the sound of spine-tingling chants from the men, formless figures shrouded in black robes seemed to rise from the sands under the eaves of the women's tent to dance under the stars.

Lawrence had also camped close to Jebel Rum, near where the village is now, bathing at the foot of the mountain's east face in the spring of Ain Shelaali on 11 September 1917. When we arrived in 1984, there seemed to be no awareness among the Bedouin or anyone in Jordan that the spring was connected with Lawrence and could consequently be of benefit to tourism, but as I was reading through *Seven Pillars of Wisdom* one evening in camp it became obvious from Lawrence's description that the spring in the mountains behind us was in fact the place he had used. He wrote 'The sun had sunk behind the western wall leaving the pit in shadow; but its dying glare flooded with startling red the wings each side of the entry ... On the rock-bulge above were clear-cut Nabathaean inscriptions, and a sunk panel incised with a monogram or symbol ... but my attention was only for the splashing of water under the shadow of the overhanging rock.' Thanks to our identification, the spring is now known as Lawrence's Spring. The inscriptions are still there today though more pocked with bullet holes than they were in 1984. It was still the only source of water for the village camp when we arrived, though a few years later the government brought piped water miles across the desert to the rest house which is only a hundred metres from the village. When the locals asked if it could be continued to the village as they only had a small pipe bringing water down from Ain Shelaali they were refused. Their answer was simple: 'If you don't, we will blow the pipeline up.' They got their water!

Thirty years after Lawrence, three members of a British mission to Saudi Arabia travelling with the protection of Glubb Pasha passed through Wadi Rum. Inspired by the mountains they set off to make the first non-Bedouin ascent of Jebel Rum from the vicinity of Ain Shelaali. One of the trio, St John Armitage, stopped before the summit. The other two, Major Henry Coombe-Tennant and a lance corporal with the marvellous nickname of 'Havabash' Butler, made it to the top, or more likely to the southern summit. It was the first non-Bedouin ascent of any of Rum's mountains. A couple of years later a British survey team arrived, a few of whom made it to the top guided by Sheikh Hamdan Amad, a Zalabieh Bedouin from Wadi Rum. Despite these intrusions, when another British party arrived in 1952, the Zalabieh were still the only ones with an intimate knowledge of their mountains.

This British group included Tom Longstaff, then seventy-seven, but one of the greatest of the early Himalayan explorers. With him were his wife, Charmian, his daughter Sylvia and her husband John, who was in Glubb's Arab Legion. The previous year, Sylvia and John had been halfway up Jebel Rum, hunting ibex with a young Bedouin. John said 'It had been hair raising … poised between heaven and hell … never again would he set foot upon those ghastly cliffs'. Consequently, when Sylvia and Charmian decided to try again, they took Sheikh Hamdan as their guide. Like the earlier Thamudic hunters, he chose to climb via the west face, by the route up which he had taken the survey team, most of whom had turned back. The route ascended a huge rift that we later named the Great Siq, having discovered it completely splits the mountain. John went off hunting ibex on another mountain with Sheikh Atieq, the man who was to welcome us to Wadi Rum thirty-two years later.

Climbing the canyon's southern wall, Sheikh Hamdan's party reached a series of ledges, separated by difficult steps, then a steep chimney with a crevasse directly beneath and a 200-metre drop to one side. Finally, they reached the domes of the high plateau, through the maze of which Sheikh Hamdan led them to the summit. 'Hamdan climbed with bare feet as surely as a mountain goat,' Charmian Longstaff wrote in the Ladies' Alpine Club's yearbook. He was obviously also impressed by his two companions, 'You English women,' he said, 'are as strong as men'. They were certainly competent, as they climbed the canyon in two hours, taking 'another hour up and down the complication of white domes to reach the summit'; a good time that is still rarely bettered.

These three ascents of Jebel Rum remained the only known non-Bedouin ascents of any of Rum's mountains until we came. Although Tom Stobart, who had filmed the 1953 British Everest expedition for *The Conquest of Everest*, was in Rum in 1962 making an adventure film for BBC television, but he didn't do any climbing. When we arrived in 1984, Sheikh Hamdan was then an old man, but one of his sons, Hammad Hamdan, who had been a paratrooper in the Jordanian army, was still occasionally employed by them as a guide and became one of our closest friends and mentors. The young man that had been hunting with the Longstaffs was now Sheikh Atieq, father of five sons including Defallah Atieq. They were the people who welcomed us to Rum.

38
EXPLORING JORDAN – RUM ROCK

When we arrived at the disused government rest house close to the village and began putting our tents up, a young man walked across to us. He had classical Bedouin features, with long wild black hair, equally wild dark eyes and a flashing smile. He was Defallah Atieq. He asked why we were in Wadi Rum and what we planned to do. We said we hoped to climb, and showed him our ropes and other climbing gear.

'Why do you need all that?' he asked. 'We climb everywhere and need nothing, just a gun to shoot the ibex. I will take you to meet my father; he is the sheikh. You can explain to him why you are here.' Then he added what I have since learned is an Arabic saying, 'Remember that if you are hard with us we will break you, if you are soft with us we will squeeze you, but if you respect us we will be your friends'.

With our tents up, Defallah drove us into the desert, out across the orange sands and round the end of Jebel Um Ishrin – we were surprised to see yet more mountains which had been previously hidden from view, their domes of white sandstone rising like petrified cumulus clouds from the orange sands. Finally topping a dune we descended into a concealed sandy hollow ringed by cliffs, then over another dune to arrive abruptly at the hidden camp. Two of his brothers were there, Mazied, on leave from the army, and Eid, the youngest, still asleep in the tent. His father, then in his eighties but still strong and agile, was wrestling a camel to the ground to treat a wound. Defallah welcomed us to his tent, where his sword hung from a pole, and invited us to sit while he prepared coffee – a time-honoured ritual show of hospitality when welcoming guests that was very much a part of Bedouin life. He slowly heated the beans in a special skillet over the fire, then ground them with cardamom pods in a large brass pestle and mortar, chiming it like a bell to welcome guests. The coffee was then put into in a brass beak-mouthed coffee pot and hot water added. Then he tasted and approved it before Defallah offered three symbolic cups to each of us in turn: tradition-ally, the first is the welcoming 'guest cup', then the 'sword cup' is served to honour the guest and to show there are no disputes, and finally the 'pleas-ure cup' for shared enjoyment. Ceremony over, we were offered tea over which we explained why we were there.

'We hope to climb your mountains,' we said, 'and if the climbing is good, as Defallah says it is, we can write about them and maybe more climbers will come. If you are not happy with that then we can leave, but we hope it might be beneficial for you.'

After talking with his father, Defallah replied, 'My father thinks it is a good idea. We know many climbs, so we will be happy to help you. We are making dinner for you. You are welcome to stay tonight.'

It was the first of many wonderful days with people who were to become the closest of friends, and as luck would have it we soon discovered that their *dira* or traditional tribal area included all the best mountains and trek-king areas. At this point I should also add that for the Bedouin, Rum is not a true desert, though I continue to use the word as it's commonly accepted and used in promotional tourism brochures and by city-living Jordanians. As Géraldine Chatelard says, 'From the Bedouin viewpoint, Wadi Rum and surrounds are *badia*, a semi-arid steppe where annual rainfall, usually light but sometimes enough for dramatic flooding, allows for animal husbandry. It is not considered to be *sahra* "desert". Nor is it empty, each and every individual knows the names of the smallest canyon, valley, sand dune or crack in the mountains. Individual or collective memories are attached to such places which often derive their names from stories that happened to a member of the tribe.'

A good example of this is the little canyon of M'Khera Said (the shitting place of Said), named after Said who ate too many of the wild figs that grow there before falling asleep then being 'taken short', a story which they told us with a great deal of laughter while we were sat around a fire in a Bedouin camp – a place which Lawrence rightly called 'the university of the desert'. In fact, the mountains and ravines are so complex that without our new-found friends freely imparting their wealth of knowledge we would never have achieved so much.

The early days were spent with Defallah or two of his brothers, Sabbah and Eid, familiarising ourselves with the topography of the peaks and the great hidden siqs that frequently split them to such a depth and width that it is impossible to continue with a chosen route though only a short distance from a summit. On the other hand, sometimes the siqs are passable so that treks can be made through the very heart of the mountains to new panoramas in open desert beyond. Slowly we became familiar with the sandstone rocks and their peculiar architecture – as bizarre as Gaudi's cathedral. At first sight appearing loose and friable, we discovered that most were safe to use and that good climbing was possible almost everywhere.

Our main objective was always the peak of Jebel Rum, as the tourism ministry wanted us to find a route to its top. It was Jordan's most famous mountain, and thought to be its highest. Its formidable hulk rises from the desert like a huge upturned battleship embedded in the sands, over six miles long and over one wide. The plunging 500-metre sides of this behemoth have guarded its hidden summit plateau for millions of years. Only the dark chasms that split its sides seemed to offer any initial hope of access to this high 'lost world' criss-crossed by clefts and canyons between which myriad white domes of sandstone conceal a maze of small deserts offering a relatively protected ecosystem to their inhabitants. Here, long-lived junipers send their snake-like roots in a quest for moisture across the sands. Thorny shrubs cluster in shady corners. Small carpets of flowers bloom in the spring and patches of grass grow in shady recesses where hidden pools of water linger long after the winter rains. This secret world is home to the eagle and its prey, the smaller birds and desert rodents, including the ubiquitous rock hyrax. It is also home to the ibex whose sharply incised cloven-footed trail can still be found despite millennia of hunting. Despite its meagre 1,754 metres, Jebel Rum proved to be the most complex mountain any of us had been on.

Reaching its summit was a frustrating, if fascinating, experience. We had made numerous desert trips with our new friends, and been shown the various approach canyons up which they said their hunting routes went to the various mountaintops, including that of Jebel Rum. They then pointed out a huge cave, high in its east face.

'You can go there to the top,' Defallah said, adding, 'it's easy. It will only take you four hours. You won't need your ropes.'

Well, it didn't look that easy, but we were yet to learn that they had a climber's sense of humour. We decided to take one rope between the four of us, 'just in case', and were not surprised when the initial pitch turned out to be a VS crack. Then, as we climbed higher, we became lost in an immense canyon – actually the eastern end of the Great Siq, though we didn't know it at the time. Eventually, we continued up through steep, exposed and sometimes-overhanging cracks and chimneys, marvelling at the Bedouin's ability to climb alone with only a rifle for company in such wild and exposed surroundings. Plus, if they were lucky, they would be climbing back down with an ibex on their back.

We were happy to have a rope and wished we had two, which would have speeded up the climb. Eventually we climbed through a cavernous hole, initially high and wide, tapering down to body width with a thirty-metre roof – a truly unique piece of rock architecture. With time lost in route finding, the supposed four hours was well gone when we emerged on to the summit. But it wasn't the summit; we couldn't even see it. We were simply at the top of the east face, directly above our camp. We realised that, for the Bedouin, 'the top' was simply the high plateau, home to the ibex, the actual highest point not being relevant.

Behind us was what we called the East Dome. We solved up on to its top from where the true summit could be seen, but still a kilometre away. We knew we were short on time but decided to go for it, though we were soon stopped in our tracks. We discovered that the siq that we had crossed on our ascent actually cut deep into the plateau. And it was thirty-metres wide and deep with vertical walls. No chance with our single rope, but Hammad Hamdan had told us that the siq narrowed and there was a log across it that ibex used. There were even dead ibex in the bottom, below the log, he said. We did find some human footprints going to the edge, but we couldn't find the log or the narrows. In fact, we have never found either. Was it a Bedouin wind-up?

By then we knew we weren't going to get back down that day, but hurried back over the East Dome, downclimbing our ascent route. It was slow progress. An impromptu bivouac was inevitable, with no water left, no bivvy gear and no wood to be found for a fire in the long cold night. We arrived back at our camp early the following morning with throats parched, much to the amusement of the Bedouin. A bunch of them were waiting for us, Defallah and his brothers, plus Hammad and Muhammad Musa, another of the locals we had got to know well.

'Where have you been?' they asked, grinning. Round one to them! But actually, they were right; once you know the way, four hours is possible, but there are few others who would climb and descend this complex 400-metre VS without ropes.

Soon after, while out in the desert gathering firewood with our friends for a circumcision feast for Sabbah's recently born son, Defallah showed us a spectacular natural arch 300 metres above the desert, at that time unknown to all but the Bedouin. 'We thought it might be interesting,' he said, pointing upwards to it with a grin. Jebel Rum was going to have to wait. We reached it by two VS climbs up the mountain's 300-metre east face. The tourism director obviously realised its benefits, as soon after our trip our photos of it appeared in their promotional literature. However, it was the discovery of the Bedouin route to the bridge by Di and me in 1985 that led to the Burdah Rock Bridge becoming one of the local community's best assets, with increasing numbers of tourists and climbers being driven out there with Bedouin guides to look at it or to climb to the arch – only the last ten metres meriting a rope.

Returning to Sabbah's camp, people were arriving for the feast, or *mensef*. We were invited to squat on rugs by the fire alongside which three large fire-blackened kettles of tea were kept hot, with six ornate brass coffee pots nearby. As usual, Di stayed with us, being accepted as an 'honorary man'. Sabbah was master of ceremonies, roasting and grinding the beans as more guests arrived by camel or Toyota, while a constant singing could be heard from the women's tent as they prepared the *mensef*. As darkness drew in, the flickering firelight cast a glow into the black tent, illuminating the faces of the guests. Coffee and tea was served again by young boys, and then an ululating high-pitched call from the women's tent announced the meal was ready and the boys came around with jugs of water to wash everyone's right hands as six trays, each a metre wide, were carried in heaped with rice and meat, a sheep's head, jaws agape, in the centre of each, reminding me of the sheep's-head stew on the Icelandic trawlers.

Everyone gathered in groups, squatting around the trays in the low fire-light, kneading the rice and meat into balls and tossing it into their mouths. Beneath the rice, unleavened bread could be torn off to dip into the gravy. Occasionally one of our friends would flick a choice piece of meat to one of us, though sometimes, unnoticed in the dark, it would be a lump of gristle, followed by a roguish smile when it proved inedible. Eventually, having eaten our fill, we drifted away with others to where the boys were pouring jugs of soapy water on the guests' hands. When all the men had finished, the trays, still overflowing with food, were carried back to the women's tent so they too could share the feast.

More coffee and tea followed and then the young men lined up in the dark of the moonless night outside the women's tent. As they began a repetitive chant they invited Alan, Mick and me to join them in the traditional dance of the *samer*, moving repeatedly a few steps backwards and forwards, clapping to the rhythm. Initially unseen by us in the darkness of the night, two shadowy apparitions appeared shrouded in black dresses and swaying in a ghostly dance under the stars. Head and arms concealed under their black billowing clothes, the two girls gyrated forwards and backwards in unison with the line of chanting men, taunting them, but never allowing them closer than a few paces. The mesmeric dance and chant seemed endless until eventually the two black figures faded away.

The men began a different chant – a guttural grunt from the stomach as the line swayed forwards and backwards, the deep, primal sound echoing from the rock walls of the valley. The two black faceless forms materialised again under the stars, whirling and flapping ever faster as the growling chant increased in intensity, reaching a wild urgent climax only to stop suddenly and leave the night pregnant with an emotional silence as the phantom forms shrank back and vanished again. The ritualistic chants came and went through the evening and on beyond midnight so that even after we had returned to our tents the persistent rhythm of singing and clapping still dominated the valley, creating ghostly echoes in the canyons.

The feast continued next day, though we spent the morning being driven around the desert to see the starts of other Bedouin routes up Jebel Rum – and there were many, but by midday we were back at Sabbah's camp to watch the camel racing. Then more sheep were slaughtered and butchered ready for the evening's *mensef* announced again by the ululating call of the women. After dark the chanting and dancing started again, this time punctuated by gunshots, though the black billowing figures continued unperturbed. It was once again after midnight when the festivities finally stopped, leaving only the sudden silence of the night as we returned to our tents.

There was an infinity of rock to be climbed. Following our frustrated attempt on Jebel Rum's summit, we regained our honour by climbing Jebel Kharazeh, which our friends said had never been done. We couldn't resist. It was staring us in the face every morning as we emerged from our tents.

It rose almost 600 metres from the desert and we made an initial reconnaissance from the canyon to a good bivouac site over 200 metres up the face. We also made a rather alarming discovery about the safety of pegs in Rum's soft sandstone. Having used three for abseils, one fell out while being used, and another was removed by hand when we returned to do the route a couple of days later. On the actual day of our return, and for the first time since our arrival in Wadi Rum, the weather became extremely overcast. Black clouds moved in from the Gulf and we huddled in our bivouac as a cold wind swept the face – a bivouac site which two weeks later was swept by flash floods as a brief but violent storm thundered around the massif of Um Ishrin. We were told that the summit was named after a similar incident that killed twenty Bedouin in the depths of its canyons.

The following day we continued our climb up cracks and easy, yet holdless, white slabs until our chosen line vanished from view. From here on in the way was unknown, as we had been unable to see it from any viewpoint. An alarming traverse of a few feet on a shale band led to a three-metre roof crack. Then easier rock took us up a winding cleft with a few bushes: typical scorpion and snake country. Di had already narrowly missed stepping on a Palestine viper, and Mick had once put his hand in a slot only to see it evacuated by a scorpion. We trod and moved with care.

Beyond, the crack rose steeply, again giving good VS climbing for another hundred metres, an overhang above being passed by easier but unprotected wall climbing. Above the bulge new vistas appeared: a soaring 150-metre crack rose abruptly to the summit dome but appeared unwelcoming when compared with easy-angled, white whaleback slabs that swept off rightwards around a corner. We were tempted away in that direction only to be abruptly stopped 200 metres further on and just twenty metres from the top by a vertical holdless wall that proved unclimbable.

It was already past midday and we had only planned on one bivouac but the choice between descent and trying the crack line we had ignored 200 metres back down the route was obvious: we were going for the top. Still climbing in two ropes of two, and moving together sharing the same runners, we were up the crack in three pitches including a nasty bottomless VS cleft hanging out into space just a few metres from the top, which provided the crux.

Summit views, especially those from previously unclimbed peaks, are good anywhere and we lingered as long as we dare, soaking in the desert landscape and congratulating ourselves on our luck at having the once-in-a-lifetime opportunity to explore an unknown range of peaks. Time was short and we were now doubtful about getting back to our bivouac before nightfall. All our gear was there and we knew from past experience it would be no fun without bivvy gear and water – the nights are long, cold and thirsty in the desert.

Fortunately our faux pas up the whaleback slabs served us in good stead and a quick abseil down the unclimbed twenty-metre wall landed us back on their easy slopes so that we were soon well down the route. More heart-in-mouth abseils from doubtful pegs or dubious-looking sandy threads behind wind-carved fingers of rock and the occasional pitch of downclimbing landed the first of us back at the bivvy at dusk. So rapidly does the sun set, it was completely dark when the last of us descended some minutes later. Our Bedouin friends saw our torches from the valley and knew we were safe but we were told that the children cried and said we would die in the mountains and never return. The morning proved them wrong: hungry, and up at first light, we were soon down the lower abseils to be met by Defallah, eager to learn about the climb. It was an unexpected welcome, the spontaneity and warmth of which we won't forget, nor the meal awaiting us at their camp.

Days were passing. We would soon have to leave and we still hadn't found a way up Jebel Rum. When asked which of their routes went to the *actual* highest point, they directed us to Al Thalamiyyah, the 'Dark Place of the Djinn' – a massive cleft cutting deep into the east face. It seemed an unlikely starting point, being almost two kilometres from the summit, but it proved fascinating. Like the cave climb – which we later named *The Eye of Allah* – it provided continuously interesting climbing. It was also technically harder, even more complex and extremely long. It was on this climb that we found some Bedouin 'tricks of the trade', such as a pile of stones to stand on so that holds cut into the soft sandstone could be reached to pass an overhang, while another bulging wall had branches jammed into a crack to provide holds. Both were above big drops – bold places for a hunter to be soloing alone.

Here also we discovered their system of cairns: the occasional single, anomalous pebble to mark the way, a few stones indicating a turn in the route and a 'wall cairn' marking a no-go point. We found the latter when, arriving on the plateau after complex route finding, we were stopped by a barrier of bulging rock running the full width of the mountain forcing us along a narrow terrace. We could see what looked like a large cairn in the distance, but having reached it, it was in the form of a wall. Beyond, we looked down into a vertical canyon 300 metres deep on the other side of the mountain. We had lost the route, so back down we went. As a matter of interest, so many climbers have now been on the summit plateau of Jebel Rum, many of them placing new cairns then getting lost but leaving them behind, that the old system, perfect in its simplicity, is now defunct. Sad to say, but cairns are no longer a guarantee of a route, but back then we were still learning.

'Ah yes,' our friends said, 'when you reached the wall cairn, you should have gone back towards Wadi Rum. If you go again you will find the way.' Another test!

A search from the desert with binoculars revealed another terrace going left below the barrier wall. We returned, finding the key to this, only to be trapped a kilometre further on in a maze of domes between two rock crevasses. We found the way through that only by checking every part of the two siqs, finally descending in the one possible place, jumping across and climbing the opposite wall. Beyond, we circumvented two more barrier walls, finally accessing the upper hidden desert that we hurried across in anticipation of reaching the summit only to be stopped 300 metres from it by the siq we had encountered on our first attempt at climbing the mountain. We now realised it cut though the whole massif.

We had heard Bedouin tales of this chasm that bisects the mountain. While unique in itself this Great Siq also contains a number of equally impressive and unexpected features, not least of which is the 'Pit'; a huge hole in the mountain, the only exit for water in the times of flash flood being a giant natural arch through which sunlight streams in the early morning. We were well and truly stopped in our tracks, and bivouacked in an excellent cave with juniper wood for the fire, which, as Edward Abbey said in *Desert Solitaire*, 'is the sweetest fragrance on the face of the earth'. In such places, protected by the fire's glow, our ancestors have sat and talked and slept for millennia. What a magical place to spend a night.

Later, over on Jebel Um Ishrin, electrical storms played havoc with the skies, unleashing torrents of water, so that even here in our bivouac we could hear what sounded like a distant Niagara Falls. Defallah told us on our return to the valley that the roar came from floods crashing down the slabs and canyons of the route we had climbed on Kharazeh. We were lucky. On Jebel Rum, the stars shone and we revelled in the wildness of it all and wondered about the location of the log bridge that reputedly spanned the siq, giving access to the other side. When morning came we searched the domes and clefts without success, while across the Great Siq – less than half an hour away, could we but cross over – the summit smiled at us. The Bedouin footprints we had seen previously leading to the edge of the canyon were still there, and when we finally found the way to reach its other side by a different route a few days later, we found the same footprints there also. A year later, we repeated *Al Thalamiyyah*, abseiling into the Great Siq and climbing out, which is now the normal way for this route, but the Bedouin still maintain it can be crossed and no rope is needed. Those footsteps would seem to prove it. Our friends were smiling again when we returned to the valley summitless but a lot wiser that evening, having managed to connect our new climb with our earlier *Eye of Allah* climb. We were beginning to understand the mountain.

With only a few days left of our stay in Rum they finally revealed the secret of the direct way to the top via the Great Siq up a climb created by Hammad: entering the siq from the east and then climbing its south side. His father's way, which we were yet to discover, and up which Sheikh Hamdan had taken the Longstaff ladies, reaches the summit from the western end of the siq. Once deep inside the canyon, *Hammad's Route* exits by the vertical south side up some grade V (VS) rock with a dead juniper tree for aid, which had been jammed in place by Hammad. Emerging from the cathedral-like rock architecture of the siq, after some complex route finding, we then struck directly along a line of domes heading for the summit ridge. There, some mini-siqs briefly threatened our success but were bypassed by bold leaps and enjoyable detours before we finally topped out with another storm gathering and waterfalls cascading down the face of Jebel Nassrani. At only 1,754 metres it was a hard-won top. Not a difficult mountain technically, but certainly one of the most rewarding of mountain experiences for all of us. Thanks to our Bedouin friends, in reaching it we had learnt a lot about their mountain and their climbs, which are truly unique. We enjoyed the panoramic view to the full, extending as it does out to Saudi Arabia and Sinai over the seemingly endless and colourful maze of Rum's mountains, hiding remote Bedouin camps that we could now call home and offering years of mountain exploration.

Despite the storm on Nassrani, Jebel Rum stayed dry. The four of us were more than happy as we sat that final night by our bivouac fire on the summit plateau. We had found a route to the top, though certainly not one for tourists, as the tourism director had hoped. Instead he had the Burdah Rock Bridge to promote, which was more than enough to keep him happy. And we had not only discovered a wealth of climbing – the best in the Middle East, enough to keep us busy for years – but had become close friends of the Bedouin. They turned out to see us off a couple of days later and I'm not ashamed to say some tears were shed. The whole expedition had been without compare. Wadi Rum was destined to become a major attraction for rock climbers and trekkers, a World Heritage Site and a hotspot for film-makers from Hollywood.

39

EXPLORING JORDAN – PETRA'S SECRET CANYON

Once back home, I rapidly sent off numerous colour slides to the tourism ministry, with a report on Wadi Rum and its climbing and adventure tourism potential, suggesting a guidebook would be useful but would need a couple more trips to complete. We were invited back the following autumn. I embarked on a lecture tour promoting Wadi Rum, which I felt I owed to the Bedouin and the tourism ministry. Wilf Colonna, the French lad I'd met in Morocco and who was climbing with us in England at the time, came along to one and was hooked. He had previously passed through Amman airport on his way to Thailand and seen pictures of Wadi Rum and always wondered about it. He was keen to join us on our visit in the autumn, and the tourism ministry were happy to have him along.

It was a year since our first visit to Petra on our way to Wadi Rum, but our memories of it were still vivid. Emerging from the cool cavernous depths of the siq, the canyon that descends into the fabled 'rose-red city', the rock-hewn tomb of the Treasury dominates the exit. Beyond it and a second ravine, stairways worn like those of Gormenghast 'by ritual's footsteps, ankle deep in time' carve their way up to the High Place of Sacrifice. Here, 2,500 years ago, or so it is said, priests and victims raised their eyes in fervour and fear to the blazing sun and the gods. Below, the canyon widens out, passing through the heart of this once-forgotten city to an area long since devastated by earthquakes, which brought the death knell to an already dying Nabataean culture. As I write this, thirty years on from our first visit, archaeologists have been busy revealing numerous buildings including an ancient church with a mosaic floor, but back then the only sounds echoing in the ruins were those of the ravens and the Bedouin. Further on, beyond the Roman colonnades, the surrounding cliffs close again and the well-worn paths of the tourists end. The shadows of high mountains with tombs and castles on their tops draw closer and the dry bed of the wadi leaves the city, to pass through pink-flowered oleander bushes. Beyond, it finally disappears into the shadowy unseen recesses of the lower canyon.

We had looked down there one hot afternoon in late September the previous year, wondering where it went and if it could be followed. We wondered about the possibilities of ascending this 'secret canyon' into Petra. No one in Jordan could give us any information and the map obtained for us by the Ministry of Tourism from the military-controlled geographical department revealed little other than a narrow and tortuous ravine descending between steep mountain walls, eventually opening out past the Bedouin village and police post of Bir Madhkur to the inhospitable desert beyond. Here the Great Rift Valley, cleaving its way north to the Red Sea and beyond from Africa, drops down the barren, sand-duned depression of Wadi Araba through dust-hazed wastelands to the Dead Sea, then 400 metres below sea level and now down to 430 below, losing a metre a year.

A new road was being built up this valley though we were told it had not yet reached the Dead Sea, due partially to the bankruptcies of the companies involved, and partly, so our Bedouin friends in Rum told us, due to some of the Korean workers who hadn't been paid, *eating* their workmates. A highly improbable story, but told with great relish as we sat around the fire one night in a Bedouin tent.

About eighteen miles north of Bir Madhkur, a more open valley comes down out of the mountains to meet the desert road – the valley of Wadi Dana, along whose rim Lawrence had ridden his camel alone, carrying 6,000 sovereigns through waist-deep snow in the winter of 1918, and up which invading Israelis had driven their tanks almost fifty years later.

We had gazed down into this vastness of rock domes and ravines on our way along the King's Highway to Petra the previous year and remembered it along with the great canyons of Mujib and Hasa as our first views of true mountain scenery in Jordan. What better plan than to try and descend this valley into Wadi Araba, and re-ascend through the mountains to the south by Petra's 'secret canyon'. It seemed like it would offer a good adventure. Dana, which was almost abandoned at that time, is now, thirty years later, a biosphere reserve and one of Jordan's gems under the care of the RSCN (Jordan's Royal Society for the Conservation of Nature). More recently, Petra also gained in world fame having become one of the New Seven

Wonders of the World. Nowadays, National Geographic classes the trek between the two as among the world's top ten treks.

Our ministry driver, Abdul, drove Wilf, Alan, Mick, Di and me down the rough track to the village of Dana where we unloaded our equipment in what was then a mostly ruined village. The sun was already low in the west. We unloaded our sacks under the curious gaze of the very few inhabitants clustered around Dana's only street between stone-walled houses with heavy wooden doors. A tattooed, wrinkled old lady warned us about wild dogs which, she said, only last week attacked and ate someone, while someone else proffered the advice that the deep valley down which we were going was full of hyenas, scorpions and snakes. It was with some trepidation that we left the village for the steep gravel track that drops immediately over the canyon rim, leaving Abdul to go for more petrol and drive around by the Dead Sea Valley to meet us in Wadi Araba the next day. That's assuming he could find us. He wasn't used to going anywhere other than tourist sites and wasn't very happy about our plans. It wasn't just the wild animals that our urban-dwelling driver feared, it was the Bedouin themselves.

The track wound down steeply into the valley. At one point we heard the sound of rushing water in a dark, tree-concealed ravine but where the track levelled out, the wadi bed was dry. An ideal bivouac spot was found with plenty of wood for the fire, but as the first flames flickered in the fast-encroaching gloom of the setting sun, headlight beams stabbed down towards us from the canyon rim. It could be no one else but Abdul who, having gone for petrol, had overcome his fears and decided to try and drive down the canyon to meet us. Not that we wanted him, we were happier on foot.

The lights shone steeply down into the darkness, swinging crazily from side to side as he descended the rubble-strewn and deeply rutted hairpins. Little wonder that he prayed on arrival! Minutes later, after a scorpion had scuttled across the bivouac site and dogs were heard howling on the canyon rim, Abdul prayed again, and climbed on to the roof of the Land Cruiser with his mattress to sleep. I noted in my diary that none of us had ever seen so many scorpions; they were under every stone we moved trying to level a place to sleep on the wadi floor. It must be said we passed a rather restless night and it was with some relief that we watched the dawn lighting the rock walls around us to a chorus of birdsong.

We had an early start, Abdul lurching along the wadi bed while we spent most of the next two hours walking ahead of him and rebuilding the track at the many washouts. In some places the ruts were a metre deep. The washouts were so bad we began to wonder if we would get through with the car, but as we progressed down the valley we left the cliffs of the narrower upper canyon behind and the valley floor became greener and more open, with trees, bushes and tall phragmites reeds fringing the dry streambed. The scree-covered hillsides above were streaked with traces of green and red mineral deposits and mine workings could be seen with their tailing piles high above us. The oldest of these date back around 3,000 years to the Iron Age, while others were once copper mines worked by the Romans in what was effectively a penal colony. Abdul, however, was unimpressed by these historical legacies and was more concerned about negotiating another vertical metre drop into the wadi bed that had suddenly confronted us. It was obviously impossible. We scouted around up the hillside until Mick found some old tracks winding up towards a low pass to the north. Abdul reversed back and the vehicle crawled steeply up the hillside until, cresting the col, we could look down an easy path into the stony desert and Wadi Araba beyond.

An hour later we had reached the Araba road, the hills rapidly closing in behind us and concealing the entrance to Wadi Dana. Little wonder that Abdul had been concerned about finding us in this barren place. We were now below sea level and the Dead Sea was some thirty-seven miles to the north of us and another 300 metres lower still, unseen in the midday haze.

We drove south, rising all the time, until a sign pointed off left into the desert again. Somewhere up there, below the same chain of distant brown and purple mountains through which we had come in the morning, was the Bedouin village of Bir Madhkur. Tracks led us out across the dust-dry land until eventually a little fort came into view on a clifftop with a few houses clustered below. At the well, a small group of Bedouin were watering some goats as we drove up and greeted them: '*Salaam alaikum.*'

'*Wa alaikum salaam,*' came the ritual reply – 'Peace be with you too.'

And then the questions: 'What are you doing here? Where are you going?'

Once they realised our objective of walking up to Petra through the canyon, the old man of the group became almost violent. It was obvious he had no intention of us going anywhere near the place. Or had he? Was it just a ploy to get some money out of us? We decided to go up to the police post in the fort to see if we could find out what the problem was.

As always we were met politely and tea was brought while they listened to our plans, but no, we shouldn't go, they said. It was a dangerous place, we might even get shot, mistaken for Israelis as the border wasn't far away in Wadi Araba, and the Bedouin, particularly the Saidiyin of this area, were suspicious of strangers and didn't take kindly to Israelis on their lands. Finally they suggested it might be possible with a guide, and anyway without one they were sure we would never find the way.

So this was the catch we thought, it all comes down to money in the end, and who should appear at the appropriate moment than the leader of the group from the well. We had more tea and haggled awhile, going up from five dinars to ten (£20 at that time) but to no avail, and our plans of the last twelve months were rapidly sinking like the afternoon sun into oblivion. As a last resort Di produced some photos of us climbing with the Bedouin in Wadi Rum the previous year. Perhaps these helped, as the old man had seemed determined to hold out until suddenly he changed his mind. Ten dinars was not enough, he said, but we could go without him.

He escorted us down to the well, filled up our water bottles and said it would be possible to drive another six miles up into the wadi that descends from the canyon. Climbing into the vehicle alongside us he pointed us off over the rising hills and down into a distant valley with a Bedouin camp concealed in its entrance. As we descended the hillside with darkness gathering, a group of men armed with rifles came out of the tents to gather round us gesticulating and shouting loudly. Again we thought our trip was over, but the old man spoke brusquely to a couple of particularly noisy youths who moved back respectfully as he waved us on up the valley. A few years later, Mick Fowler arrived here on foot having bought our guidebook and reversed our route down the canyon from Petra. They had a similar reception to ours, meeting 'gun-toting nomads of questionable mental state,' as Mick said in his book, *On Thin Ice*.

We, on the other hand, were going the other way, up the canyon. Thankful to be moving on, and not stopping to look back, we drove on up the dry gravel bed of what was obviously a major watercourse in the winter, until the vertical sides of the wadi swallowed us up as we followed its course towards the mountains. We weren't quite sure what we had got ourselves into or just how we were going get ourselves out again, but whatever the outcome was going to be, the view ahead certainly looked impressive. As the vehicle crunched to a halt among the boulders of the wadi bed, the mountains ahead of us appeared to present a vast unbroken and impenetrable wall. On the summit of the most distant peak to the south a small white building was caught in the last light of the setting sun: the supposed tomb of Aaron, brother of Moses. Hidden beyond it was Petra, and it was on the pretext of visiting the tomb that the Swiss explorer Burckhardt, disguised as a Muslim and having spent two years in Syria, had discovered the lost city in 1812.

Assuming that our twenty-five-year-old maps were correct, the wadi we were now in was called Wadi Siyyagh, the only exit for any water passing through Petra. Close inspection of the mountain wall revealed a shadow-line across an otherwise blank area of rock, indicating the possibility of a hidden canyon. As the sun set, we gathered wood for a fire for the evening meal.

We had a good night's sleep stretched out in comfort along the sandy edge of the wadi and were woken at first light by a vast unseen army of insects humming loudly in the nearby thicket of tamarisk. As we cooked breakfast Abdul sat on top of a nearby hill looking pensively to the horizon until finally the time came to part company, leaving him to drive south then round and back along the eastern side of the mountains again to meet us.

'We'll see you in Petra,' we said optimistically.

'*Inshallah*' – 'God willing,' he replied. Abdul obviously wasn't convinced!

It was good, at last, to be off on our own, walking up the early morning canyon, hills striped with dark basalt intrusions slowly closing in around us, and then suddenly, hungrily, swallowing us into the deep recesses of a cool ravine to be greeted by that most beautiful of desert sounds: running water. Only 100 metres back down the wadi we had been in bare dust-brown hills and now, as we rounded the bend, a waterfall cascaded into a pool surrounded by a jungle of tall green phragmites. As we parted the dense undergrowth, startled birds chattered in alarm and a dark green frog plopped into the pool. Scrambling up pink granite rocks by the side of the waterfall we were astonished to find a large crab sitting on a ledge, its periscope eyes staring at us, as though it, or we, had come from another planet. Looking back out to the parched desert landscape through which we had so recently walked, this green secret paradise seemed a total anachronism. No wonder the Bedouin guarded this little Eden so jealously.

With three miles of unknown canyon still to explore we moved on with fresh enthusiasm, plunging through thickets and making enjoyable little detours across the perfect granite when boulders or cascades of water made progress up the actual canyon bed impossible. Quite soon we

36 A Rum team: Alan Baker, me, Di, Defallah and Sabbah Atieq, and Mick Shaw. Jordan, 1984.
37 The massif of Jebel Um Ishrin, and the east and south faces of Nassrani. Wadi Rum.

38 Di, Wadi Rum, 1986. **Photo**: Bernard Domenech.
39 Wilf Colonna on the first ascent of *Mad Frogs and Englishman*, east face of Jebel Rum, 1987.
40 Rowland Edwards and Brede Arkless on the first ascent of *Flight of Fancy*, east face of Jebel Rum, 1986.

41

42

43

44

45

41 Wadi Rum, seen from *Hammad's Route*, above the east face of Jebel Rum, Jordan, 1987.
42 Wadi Dana. The Dana Biosphere Reserve is Jordan's largest nature reserve.
43 Dana village, with Wadi Dana in the distance.
44 The 400-metre east walls of the two Nassrani summits.
45 'I can see you!' A blue Sinai agama lizard.

46 The magnificent Barrah Canyon conceals many quality routes. The vertical crack is the 150-metre *Merlin's Wand*, the 'super crack of Rum', first climbed by me and Wilf Colonna, Wadi Rum, 1986.

47 Mick Shaw and Alan Baker exploring the south summit of Jebel Rum, with Jebel Khazali opposite across the sands of Khor Al Ajram, Wadi Rum, 1985.

48 Approaching the summit of Jebel Rum on *Hammad's Route*, Jordan, 1992.

49 Paul Taylor and Tannith on a precarious river crossing on our Thailand trek, 1987.
50 Traditional Akha hill-tribal attire. The Akha are closely related to the Hani of Yunnan Province in China. Thailand, 1987.

51

51 Di exploring the 1,500-metre-deep 'Grand Canyon of Wadi Nakhr', one of many canyons on Jebel Shams. Oman, 1989.
52 New route in Wadi Dayqah – Wilf Colonna climbing. Oman, 1991.

53 Mick climbing in the Roman quarry of Mons Claudianus using slots chiseled in the granite. Wooden wedges
would then be inserted and soaked with water so they would expand, fracturing the granite. Egypt, 1996.
54 On Um El Amud, the 250-tonne 'Mother of Columns' in the Roman quarry of Mons Claudianus. Egypt, 1996.
55 Di in one of Shivaji's summit forts on our Western Ghats trek, India, 1990.
56 Carved out of solid rock, the Ajanta and Ellora cave temples are among the most remarkable in India and
now a World Heritage Site. Western Ghats, India, 1990.

57 Trekking near Zanskar with Mike Searle *(left)* the day before our camp was robbed and horses stolen by Bakarwal nomads. India, 1993.
58 Bihari road workers, toiling with a Dante's inferno of yellow-flamed barrels of burning tar, while continually breathing in black smoke at close to 5,000 metres. Mad! India, 1993.
59 Ben Stephenson and me crossing the Suru River, having failed to cross the glacier to Chamba. India, 1993.

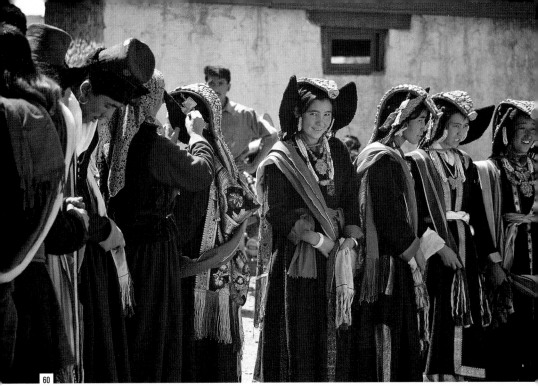

60 Festival in Ladakh. India, 1993.
61 Evening meal in a tukul with our guide. Ethiopia, 1995.
62 Shepherd boy with his fire of smouldering embers held in dried cow dung. Ras Dashan, Ethiopia, 1995.

63

64

65

63 The remote Akakus mountains in the Sahara in south-west Libya. 1997.
64 One of the numerous petroglyphs in the Libyan Sahara, many dating back
     to pre-desert times of the 'Large Wild Fauna Period' 12,000 years ago. 1997.
65 The Roman ruins of Sabratha on the Mediterranean coast. Libya, 1997.

66 The sixty-metre abseil into the Hidan Gorge, seen from a helicopter provided by Queen Noor. The abseil descends both basalt and sandstone, and the palm trees in the foreground conceal the ongoing canyon. Jordan, 1998.

67 Di on the committing sixty-metre abseil into the Hidan Gorge. Once the ropes were pulled, there was no way back. Jordan, 1998.

68 Hanna Jahshan and Di after abseiling the waterfall in the lower Mujib. Jordan, 1998.

69 Presenting Her Majesty Queeen Noor, wife of King Hussein, with our guidebook to Jordan. Our explorations would have been impossible without her assistance. Jordan, 1999. **Photo**: Palace photo.

70 The village of Wadi Rum. Mostly a cluster of Bedouin tents in 1984, but now a modern village rapidly increasing in size. Jordan, 2000.

rounded a sharp bend in the ravine where it cut south through what had, last evening, seemed to be the unbroken face of the mountain. A wide, hidden valley opened out before us twisting its way towards a 300-metre wall of steep black basalt through which it somehow vanished through a gap in the teeth.

There, in the darker recesses, the vertical sides of the canyon plunged directly into a murky pool beyond which the way on was blocked by a giant boulder wedged across the gap, its lower end leaving only a chink of light above the water. Wilfried, the French member of our team, and otherwise known affectionately as 'Le Frog', was obviously better suited than most to probe the depths of this watery barrier, so we volunteered him, grimacing as the green water rose up to his waist. He prodded cautiously at some slime-covered sticks floating seemingly innocuously in the gloom, but concealing who knows what strange creatures. Satisfied that nothing was lurking in the depths he eventually reached the boulder. Peering through the gap above the waterline he could see nothing, so with a struggle he climbed up on to its top. The way on was blocked by yet another boulder more massive than the first, completely barring any progress.

The sunlit summits of Petra smiled at us less than a mile away, while unknown to us, Abdul was going out of his way to call at every Bedouin village and police post within walking distance of Petra telling them to watch out for and not to shoot the five strangers.

We sat by the pool and deliberated, deciding to scramble up alongside the wall of black teeth until, hopefully, a way through could be found leading down to the canyon again, beyond the impasse. Sure enough, we found a way through, descending across basalt columns down into the upper ravine, to arrive at a small sunlit beach deep among the surrounding shadows. A silver ribbon of water cascaded down a granite chute over a velvet lining of moss into the beckoning pool. Sweating from our midday climb over the ridge we plunged into the refreshing water, choosing to ignore for the moment the fact that the way ahead was blocked by granite cliffs. We swam under the waterfall washing off the dust of three days in the desert and dried ourselves in the sun. By the side of the cascade a ridge of pink polished granite dropped down from the higher canyon. Without my sack, I climbed up it looking for a way through, enjoying the feel of clean rock and happy to see that once we had regained the canyon bed above a second waterfall; the way on seemed to pose no problems, at least as far as the next bend.

Now, very close to Petra, we were at last allowing ourselves a little optimism, and after a final delicate traverse above a murky pool we glimpsed some man-made walls supporting green gardens. Here, hidden from all but the most prying of eyes, in the last dogleg of the canyon was a paradise of fertility: well-tended irrigation channels, some of them dating to Nabataean times, watered terraces of fruit trees and vegetable plots hemmed in all sides by dry barren hills giving no hint of this secret place.

Passing through the oasis we disturbed a lone Bedouin working in one of the small gardens. He looked up in obvious surprise at this unexpected intrusion. As always, a ritual greeting passed before he asked where we had come from. We pointed down the canyon at which he shook his head in disbelief muttering '*Hamdulillah*' – 'Praise be to God' – as we carried on up the valley.

We rounded the final bend into the upper wadi among whose oleander bushes we had wandered and wondered twelve months ago. Looking back, the walls of the canyon had already closed in again on its secrets and we entered Petra feeling somehow different than the other tourists. Leaving the old city though the dramatic upper chasm of the siq we passed the entry kiosk with its sign: 2 dinars. At least we hadn't had to pay!

40

EXPLORING JORDAN – BEYOND PETRA

*The green slopes end suddenly and the gnome-like mountains
begin, so split and cut by millions of crevices that the whole mass is
always filled with small patches and pockets of shadow. In the heart
of these grotesque mountains is the mysterious city of Petra.*

***In the Steps of the Master**, H.V. Morton*

Di and I have been to Jordan every year since 1984, always spending time
with our Bedouin friends in Rum but increasingly exploring the rest of the
country, about which nothing was known from the point of view of climbing, trekking, canyoning and caving back in the 1980s. It was the late 1980s
when we first got the opportunity to explore further in the Sharra Mountains around Petra, though they are just an hour's drive from Rum. The area
had attracted me since I first looked down on what H.V. Morton called
'gnome-like mountains … like the devil-haunted landscapes which early
Italian painters have put behind their saints'.

Driving north from Aqaba or Rum along the edge of Jordan's high plateau,
rolling green uplands are cut here and there by stony fields in which farmers
have laboured with their horses and wooden ploughs. Sometimes there
are a few black Bedouin tents on their perimeters, the occupants eking out
a living on the seemingly barren surrounding hills. These hills plunge immediately and steeply down past a village of ancient stone-walled, flat-roofed
houses harmonising with the landscape and reminiscent of Morocco or the
Himalaya. Lower still is a petrified cloud-sea of pale rock domes. Bizarrely,
they are actually mountaintops, split by a maze of dark, mysterious canyons.
On the summit of the highest and most distant peak, a white speck brightly
reflects the morning sun; it's said to be the tomb of Aaron, brother of Moses.
Beneath it, concealed from the outside world by these 'gnome-like mountains' on to whose tops you are looking down, is the legendary city of Petra.

Beyond, in the very far distance, blue hills shimmer in the heat haze rising from the unseen desert valley of Wadi Araba deep below sea level. We always used to wonder what was down there in those unknown canyons. *Are they as inhospitable as they look? Is there any water?*

The area intrigued and tempted us as we passed by on our way to and from Wadi Rum, then in 1988, with a few days to spare, Di and I headed off in the footsteps of Burckhardt to what had been called the 'Lost City'. Though of course it wasn't lost at all, it was home to the B'dul Bedouin tribe. Having heard of temples hidden in the mountains, Burckhardt had gained entry using the excuse that he wanted to sacrifice a goat to Nebi Harun (the prophet Aaron) at his tomb on the summit of that prominent but distant peak.

His Bedouin guide took him in through the 1,000-metre-long siq, which despite some manicuring of the canyon floor by the Petra Authority is as awesome now as it must have been in Burckhardt's day; one can sense the feeling of increasing excitement and, probably, fear that he must have felt as he followed his already suspicious Bedouin guide deeper into the foreboding chasm. His emotions on seeing the immense and immaculately carved Treasury cut out of the solid rock at the exit of the siq must have been overwhelming. Beyond lay Petra itself, with its endless facades of tombs and temples.

When we arrived, only poorly defined paths wound their way up into the mountains. Little, if anything, had changed since Burckhardt's time. The local Bedouin were still very wary of strangers. Having been turned back by them on a previous attempt, we moved discreetly, concealed from prying eyes, up small valleys to the high col of Naqb ar-Rubai. The landscape opened out revealing a dramatic view to the west, over the wilderness of Wadi Araba.

The summit of Jebel Haroun was now directly above us and, to our surprise, concealed a huge underground water cistern cut out of solid rock. Above, carved steps led to the white-walled tomb. They had obviously been great chisellers, the Nabataeans.

We sat by the tomb in the late afternoon sun among a carpet of springtime flowers through which a blue lizard scuttled. The sound of a shepherd's flute drifted up from the abyss below. It was an idyllic spot and would have been a perfect place to spend the night but, respecting the summit, revered by the world's three Abrahamic religions, we moved down a short way to sleep. Hidden by cliffs and out of sight from keen Bedouin eyes, we bivouacked and watched the sun set over the distant blue mountains. I always prefer to bivvy out rather than camp as being in a tent separates you from the outside world. Perhaps more importantly in this instance we were less obvious, so less likely attract attention. Hidden in our hollow we dozed unseen under the stars, while below us in the darkened valley small fires glowed in Bedouin camps and from one of which the time-honoured ringing of the brass pestle and mortar announced to their neighbours that coffee was ready.

Five years later, in 1993, we returned to Jebel Haroun, sleeping once more near its summit, under a gnarled juniper tree. Obligingly, it sheltered us from a shower of rain that fell in the night. We rose with the dawn, keen to discover what lay beyond in those pale rock domes with their mysterious canyons that we had looked down on so often. Our 1960s map didn't give much away … no trails, no fine detail of cliff or canyon, just a thirty-year-old impression of mountains and valleys. It looked fascinating! Leaving the summit, we crossed to the head of a long valley that descends southwards for twenty-five miles to the sands of Wadi Araba. Somewhere down there was the Sabra Roman theatre on the site of the old caravanserai or southern gateway to Petra – a last staging post for travellers coming up through Rum from distant Arabia Felix (now Yemen), or through Sinai from Egypt.

Scrambling down the hillside to the green valley floor, we stumbled into a small Bedouin camp hidden beneath the cliff.

'Ahlan wa sahlan' – 'welcome to Wadi Sabra, where only Allah and the Bedouin live,' came the memorable poetic greeting from a typically small wiry figure. His temporary camp, of which he was the sole resident, was just a lean-to against the rock, with a few blankets and the inevitable blackened pans and kettle simmering in the ashes of a fire. We dined on *shraq*, wafer-thin Bedouin bread, goat cheese and sweet mint tea, and explained – as best we could – that we intended to follow Wadi Sabra, then regain the high escarpment at the old village of Tayibah through Wadi Tibn.

Our host, whose name was Awad, offered to show us a shortcut. He accompanied us down the valley to the Roman theatre, which was carved from the cliffs close to a spring, surrounded by palms, oleanders and the scattered ruins of the ancient outpost. Here, we unexpectedly left the valley floor, climbing through a maze of narrow canyons and over a concealed pass to descend to a parallel valley. Forcing his way through a small forest of oleanders in the valley bottom, Awad led us into a hidden canyon of stunning proportions: above its two-metre-wide gravel bed, water-polished cliffs rose to merge with overhanging crags, themselves rising to unseen summits. This magnificent chasm, as splendid as the Petra siq, took us for more than two miles up and out on to flower-filled meadows between the domes. The village of Tayibah with its flat-roofed houses where Awad was going was visible on the hillside above. We 'crashed out' in our sleeping bags almost where he left us; it had been a long day. It rained on us again in the night, but it didn't matter. More than pleased with our previous day's trek, we found our way back through carved passages and stairways in the tomb-filled cliffs on the eastern outskirts of Petra.

Another four years passed before we were able to return in 1997, planning to continue the journey south. We made our way down through the siq of Tibn, which was every bit as breathtaking as we had remembered. Having had a late start it was a relief to find the spring of Tibn Awad had told us about. The small tadpole-filled pool seeped out of some rocks in the midst of wild and barren mountains, offering unlimited cups of tea.

We slept by the water's edge before heading off south under clear blue skies, happy to be in unknown hills again. Having made our way up through a juniper-filled gully we emerged in a small hanging valley to find the tumbled ruins of ancient walls and dams; even here, in this hidden place, the Nabataeans had laboured at their irrigation systems. A more recently built cave dwelling in the cliffs above was evidence that Bedouin still lived here, but we met no one as we followed a faint shepherds' trail over a pass and down to an area of boulders at the far end of the next valley. Beneath, cliffs of loose red rock enclosed a narrow, tree-choked ravine.

The path, though now indistinct, continued, rising up away from the ravine, sometimes disappearing on scree slopes, but always re-appearing to tempt us on as we searched the hillside. By midday with what looked like a final steep valley and ridge to cross we lost it completely. Access to the red ravine down loose cliffs seemed most unlikely. The path had simply stopped. Perhaps Bedouin shepherds wandered the hillside, only to return to the cave dwellings or the Tibn spring at night? Our explorations in Rum had made us wary: if we continued there was no guarantee of finding water – or of getting out to the village of Rajif, our next objective the following day. *And what then?*

The sensible thing to do was to retrace our steps and go north instead, to see if we could connect the Tibn spring with the Sabra spring – another key part of the maze; it looked easy on the map as their valleys met just over a mile downstream of our last bivouac. If we could do that, we could then hopefully make a trip in from Rajif, connecting all the water sources, to finish at Petra.

Having backtracked to the Tibn valley, time was getting on. We had already been walking in temperatures in the upper thirties for most of the day, struggling up and down scree slopes and getting absolutely nowhere. Confident that Sabra couldn't be far away, we continued down the dry valley. The trickle of water from the Tibn spring, only ten minutes' walk back up the boulder-strewn wadi, had already sunk into the sand again; burnt, black volcanic cliffs surrounded us – it was a hot, dry world. We should, perhaps, have returned to the spring to fill our bottles, but we felt we couldn't afford to lose more time if we were going to make it through to Sabra that day.

Confident of our way, which looked straightforward on the map, we passed a Bedouin lad with a herd of goats, pausing only for the traditional greetings, before continuing to the confluence where the valley of Sabra entered through a deep ravine. Tired, but pleased to be making progress, we made our way up the rocky bed knowing that its spring was less than a mile and a half away; instead, we were met by the vertical cliffs of a box canyon. A trickle of water dripped from the lip to instantly lose itself in the boulders up which we had struggled.

Thirsty now, the day was drawing on as we returned a second time to the dry valley of Tibn – if there was a way through it had to be lower down, beyond the canyons through which we had just come. This was confirmed when the young Bedouin shepherd arrived and showed us a trail up a broken cliff further down the valley, its rocks polished by use. We scrambled up and around the upper edge of the box canyon. Beyond, a narrow gorge led us to the palm- and reed-fringed pools of the Sabra spring. After endless cups of tea, we finally crawled into our sleeping bags on the warm sand. High above, as the dusk light dyed the glowing cliffs blood red, a Bedouin family returned with their sheep to a small cave. From its mouth, a fire flickered into life under the stars of the darkening sky. The following day we trekked out, following Wadi Sabra for the first time to its source near the seldom-visited southern city walls of Petra. There, in the dome-shaped hills above the Petra siq, we joined the line of our previous trek to Wadi Musa.

Entering these mountains from the hilltop village of Rajif and connecting with the ancient trails coming up from Rum to Petra had to wait another year. Together with Mick Shaw, we finally had an opportunity to fill in this blank on our map. Having driven 125 miles south from the capital we started late down the stony hillside beneath the village to the rock domes, already hemmed in by two huge canyons. Though both ran in the right direction, as always, we were unsure if either could be descended. Some old men in the village had nodded reassuringly at the mention of Wadi el Bahra so we chose the one to the north. It was a good decision!

A small but distinct path led down a side valley, picking its way around boulders and through thickets of scented white broom and pink oleanders; sometimes it followed ledges in the cliffs, supported by old walls to allow the passage of loaded donkeys. It was obviously a Bedouin thoroughfare so we were hopeful of finding water. Continuing down, we entered the dry stony bed of the great ravine of Wadi el Bahra, which we followed easily west. As the confusion of bare rocky mountains slowly closed around us, the wadi was compressed into a narrow reed-filled gorge where the first signs of dampness showed through the gravel. Beyond, we reached the upper lip of a canyon from where we could see a small green oasis far below – an anachronism among the ubiquitous reds and browns of these arid mountains. The well-travelled path picked its way over a col and down past a dry waterfall. Above it, Bedouin cliff dwellings overlooked the spring of Bahra and a small olive grove painstakingly nurtured on the rocky hillside.

Despite our late departure, we still had an hour or so of daylight left, so we topped up our water supply and moved on to see if we could find the start of the way through to the Tibn spring. A promising trail led us over the shoulder of a hill to the north and down to a small dry streambed that we followed up into the hills again. Rounding a bend in the rising valley we reached the dark mouth of a narrow, forested ravine with walls of red decaying rock, and above were the screes and cliffs of high mountains. Though there was no obvious trail, the logical way on was into the ravine. It was undoubtedly the ravine Di and I had looked down into a year ago. Had we known then of the existence of the Bahra spring it would have been easy for us to continue, but nothing was lost, the key was now in the lock; hopefully, tomorrow, we would turn it.

As we brewed tea in the gathering dusk, a hawk returned to its nest in the rotting overhangs above us. Dawn, unusually, was slow to come, with dark clouds sleeping heavily on the peaks to the south, so we breakfasted in our sleeping bags before continuing to squeeze our way up the wooded gorge for a little over a mile to its abrupt end. A scramble up water-worn chimneys brought us into the boulder-choked valley above: the door was open! Jubilant, we continued north to the Tibn spring for a relaxing second breakfast as the clouds rose lazily before melting in the warm morning sun. With our water bottles topped up, we continued through the now familiar siq of Tibn and north over the gnome-like mountains to Petra. The major water sources were located and linked, and we finally felt at home in these apparently savage but no longer inhospitable peaks 'where only Allah and the Bedouin live'.

Though we didn't know it at the time, we had found trails that would soon be part of the country-length Jordan Trail.

41

EXPLORING JORDAN – MORE RUM GOINGS ON

My guide to *Treks and Climbs in the Mountains of Rum and Petra* was published in 1987 and revised editions are still in print today, though Petra is no longer included. It did what it was supposed to do: promote the area and bring climbers and trekkers to Wadi Rum for the benefit of the locals.

Its publication was not without difficulty. The tourism ministry offered to pay for it and, having received their written agreement on price, the printer that Troll worked with took the job on. When it was ready, Di and I delivered the books to Cicerone who had agreed to launch it, and faxed Nasri Atalla, the director of the Jordan tourism board, to ask for payment. He had always been very supportive, but his apologetic reply came that the accounts department were insisting the books had to be in Jordan before they could pay. Why is Jordanian bureaucracy so difficult?

After discussing the situation on the phone, pointing out that the books were next to useless in Jordan and needed to be in England where they could be sold by a publisher specialising in outdoor guides and with an international sales network, Mr Atalla suggested taking them to the Jordanian embassy in London. He would then inform the accounts office who would release payment. All we had to do was: drive to Cicerone (about 100 miles), load Troll's van up, drive to London (another 300 miles) and deliver 2,000 books to the embassy then 200 miles back home, but despite Mr Atalla's assurances to the contrary, we weren't expected. Eventually, understanding our predicament, the embassy staff agreed we could leave the books there, but the only available space was two floors up and they had no lift. Nor was any help offered, so Di and I carried 2,000 books from the van up to their storeroom.

I faxed the embassy receipt over to Jordan the next day and received a reply stating that payment would be made at the month end so we could return the books to the publisher. Which of course meant we had another 600-mile round trip to do. The month end came. 'No payment yet,' the printer said. And the same next month. It was getting embarrassing. When no money arrived after the third month I offered to pay personally, but the printer hung on.

Finally, after four months, the ministry paid up. The arrangement with them was that they would then be refunded with annual payments as the book sold, but when we returned to Jordan the following spring, Nasri Atalla said, 'Don't worry about the repayments; keep the money for the next edition'. So that's what we did. It's now in its fifth edition.

Others started to go to Rum as the first ascent names show, but strangely very few of these were British. I say 'strangely' as the climbing in Rum is very much suited to the British ethos of traditional climbing rather than bolt-protected sport climbing. Nevertheless, the majority of climbers in Rum have always been French. The increasing number of trekkers visiting Rum were also predominantly French.

The 'cream team' of the British climbing scene missed out on some superb new route opportunities. Ed Douglas said in his article 'The Changing Face of Wadi Rum', in *Climber* in 2005, 'It must be somewhat galling for Tony Howard to have pioneered so much of all that is good in Wadi Rum, and yet the place to be taken up by the French'. On our annual trips with Wilf Colonna, we were not only finding new climbs but new mountains on an almost daily basis including classic routes such as *The Beauty, Black Magic, Orange Sunshine, Purple Haze, Desert Rats, Essence of Rum, L'Apertif, The Haj* and the superb super-crack of *Merlin's Wand* in the newly discovered and magnificent Barrah Canyon. There were no other Brits there when Wilf and I climbed *Towering Inferno*, Rum's first route to touch alpine grade ED – a route that I almost wimped out on.

Di, Wilf and I had climbed its opening pitches on Jebel Rum's east face – a fun five-pitch route with a French 6b crux we called *Inferno* – and spotted thin cracks continuing up the wall. We abseiled off and left our ropes in place then Wilf and I returned the next day reclimbing it with more ropes and adding another four pitches of mixed free and aid, including a small pendulum. I led the penultimate pitch and, with only one dodgy runner in, I was wondering how to get across a seemingly blank piece of rock to a tempting crack when my foothold snapped off. Miraculously my handhold held, but unable to hang there I somehow pirouetted across the wall to security. We abseiled down from the top of the next pitch, once again leaving our ropes in place planning to jumar up the next day and complete the route.

When morning came I had a bad feeling about going back, a premonition that something would go wrong. On the other hand I knew I would be letting Wilfried down. In the end, he and Di talked me into going, though I still felt curiously uneasy. Wilf started first, jumaring a rope ahead of me. Each rope was tied into the pegs holding the bottom end of the rope above. As he clipped into the second rope I began jumaring up the first. Finally, as he reached the belay at the top of the last rope I clipped myself on to it and reached back to retrieve the previous rope before hammering the pegs out, but as I pulled myself in, they simply fell out. The surrounding sandstone had been crushed by the on–off compression of jumaring. Losing contact with the rock I dropped on to the final rope and swung down and out into space. It held, but I felt sure it wouldn't have held the two of us if the pegs had pulled while I was still jumaring. After that my worries were gone; I was no longer ill at ease. I jumared up with a huge sense of relief, then another four pitches finished the route. It was a good climb too.

By 1986, with plenty of good routes in the bag, we organised an international meet that we had suggested to the tourism ministry. There were a couple of Germans involved in the mountaineering business and the rest were all guides: Wolfgang Nairz (Austria), Alberto Re (Italy) and John Hogg (a Swiss and Canadian guide). Wilfried and Bernard Domenech, both French guides, were also there, as well as Rowland Edwards and Brede Arkless, both UK guides.

Guiding guides was a crazy but fun job. Afterwards they added a nice little new route of their own and Di and I did a new route, *April Fools*, with Wolfgang. Rowland and Brede did two first ascents, *Flight of Fancy* and *Ziggurat*, the latter moving the Rum grades up to French 7a. Rowland then returned the following year with his son Mark, adding more top-end routes including *Sandstorm*, pushing the grade up a notch to French 7a+, then *Warriors of the Wastelands*, a 450-metre corner with a French 6b crux pitch to finish, and the magnificent *Lionheart*, one of Rum's best routes, with 350 metres of French 6a and 6b climbing. Claude and Yves Remy – Swiss climbing pioneers – also turned up, climbing a new route every day.

Among the few Brits to seek out new climbs, Doug Scott added some new routes in 1987 including a couple of powerful crack lines, *Crack of Cracks* and

Guelta Grooves, and Chris Forrest and Louise Thomas found their way up *Ocean Slabs*, an aptly named 500-metre route up the swelling sea of rock opposite *Merlin's Wand*, while Alex Renshaw and Dave Green climbed their *Siege of Jericho* also in Barrah Canyon at 7a. Geoff Hornby and his friends joined the spree for a few years in the mid 1990s adding routes throughout the area, including some big slab routes on Jebel Burdah and in and around Barrah Canyon. Various friends of ours also joined the scene including my old mate John Smith who added his neat French 6b *Little Gem* in Rakabat Canyon, and Andy Perkins from Troll who powered up his French 6b layback corner, *Sheikh Yerbouti*, in Barrah Canyon.

Otherwise there have been few British first ascents other than ours, which also included two more big routes on Jebel Rum's east face. *Aquarius* was a TD+ of constant variety and interest on water-washed rock which Wilf and I gleefully raced up and down, enjoying its idiosyncrasies. The other was the delightful and now classic *The Pillar of Wisdom*, also climbed in 1986 – a bumper year – by Wilf, Di and me. The pillar, which is strikingly obvious from Rum village, rises almost directly above Lawrence's Spring. Having sussed out the approach the evening before, the climb went perfectly; one sequence of cracks leading to another, a final traverse and the finishing dome.

Rum's domes can be both bald and bold. It was Wilf's lead and he disappeared out of sight on to the crest of the pillar on what was to be the final pitch. As expected it was bulging and smooth with no protection.

'I'll place some bolts,' he said, meaning the peg-bolts that we had previously used for abseils that necessitated hand-drilling a hole and hammering an oversize angle peg in. They worked well and some are still in use after thirty years, but it would be the first time we used them on an actual climb. He put three in before the final exposed friction moves could be made to the top. Using the 'bolts' for holds it was French 6a. Clipping them for protection only, it's 6b, without them there was no protection on the whole pitch. Whether you use the bolts as holds or not, this final pitch is the crux, the pitches below never being more than French 5. Without the bolts to clip almost no one would do a route of grade 5 that finished 350 metres up with a long, totally unprotected pitch of 6b.

I have no qualms about us placing them. As with all our Rum climbs we were very much aware that as well as being flag bearers for clean climbing, we were helping to develop Rum as a climbing area for the benefit of others, not just the climbing community, but also for our Bedouin friends for whom guiding climbs and treks was increasingly providing an income. It wasn't just about making a first ascent; it was about making good routes with good clean ethics. As Dave Durkan said in *Penguins on Everest*, 'The sport of mountaineering has innate values that should be valued in their own right – understood, practiced, honoured and protected.' I hope those three bolts don't exceed those values. *The Pillar of Wisdom* has become one of the most popular climbs in Rum, but on his fiftieth birthday Albert Precht soloed *Hiker's Road*, one of his big routes on Nassrani, in the morning, abseiled down to have an unrushed lunch with us at the campsite, then soloed *The Pillar of Wisdom* in the afternoon and was back down again in the evening. You don't get cleaner than that! Good effort, Albert!

What a tragedy when, in May 2015, we read the awful news that Albert and his partner, Robert Jölli, fell to their deaths while climbing in Crete. Albert's climbs in Rum and more than 800 elsewhere are a great memorial to his climbing ethics. His arrival in the early 1990s with other Austrian climbers – most notably Wolfgang Haupolter, Sigi Brochmeyer and Josef Inhoger – pushed Rum's climbing into new terrain.

Those early years in Rum were glorious days – we were much more relaxed about our climbing. Spending time with the Bedouin was also important to us, not only as it was a valuable opportunity to learn more about their mountains, but also because they have a great sense of humour and being with them is always good for a laugh.

On one occasion Di and I were out in the desert with Eid Atieq looking for his camels. When we found them Eid said they needed water and there was a Nabataean dam nearby in one of the siqs on Burdah's east face.

'You can water the camels,' he said to me, 'and I'll light a fire and make chai.'

Having never watered camels before, it sounded interesting, so I climbed up on to the top of the dam wall to find a bucket hanging from a rope. The water was about three metres below. I threw the bucket in and hauled it out, full, then poured it down into a stone trough in the desert below. By the time I had repeated the process the camels had already drained the trough dry with a lot of slurping and sucking. This continued endlessly until Eid shouted up that the tea was ready and laughingly said the camels would be OK. I only found out later that a thirsty camel can drink thirty gallons of water in a quarter of an hour – and there were a dozen of them! Nice one, Eid!

After our first trip, the Bedouin were always one of the main reasons we returned to Rum. And during our early visits they also kept us fed as well as they were able when the tourism ministry driver failed to turn up, which was frequently. The arrangement was that the drivers would change every week, going back at the end of their stint and a new driver returning the next day at which point we would go to Aqaba to buy food and go swimming in the Red Sea. Except very few of the drivers were happy in Rum. They were used to driving tourists to Petra or Aqaba then sitting around until their guests returned in the evening, whereas we were always on the move. And they weren't used to desert driving. On one occasion when we got stuck, a young boy, barely a teenager, appeared from a nearby Bedouin camp and effortlessly drove the car out of the sand. Once, in the far south, Defallah, who was with us, told the driver, 'Now we are in Saudi Arabia'. The driver was paranoid, 'I'm not supposed to be here. It's not allowed. We will be arrested.' Quite often the driver failed to show up from Amman leaving us without food for a few days and reliant on an invite to a Bedouin camp, or eating the crusts of loaves thrown out by the desert police at the fort. For some reason their rations included loaves of bread – the only ones we ever saw in Jordan where flatbread is eaten – but they only ate the soft centres and threw out the crusts, which we ate greedily.

From the late 1990s numerous world-class climbers started coming to Rum and grades were pushed ever higher, including routes such as *La Guerre Sainte (Jihad)* at French 7a+/b, climbed in 2000 by Arnaud Petit and friends. Wilf says enthusiastically, 'The headwall remains one of the most outstanding experiences you can get on steep sandstone throughout the universe.' Two years later Kurt Albert and friends climbed *55 Steps to Hell* with pitches of French 6c to 7b. Twenty-three bolts were placed but a full rack is also needed. In 2005 the Czechs created *Rock Empire* on Jebel Rum's east face, with 300 metres of mostly French 7c+/8a connecting with *Raid mit the Camel*, ED+. Wilf commented, 'The first true Hard Extreme in Rum: Czech style means not a bolt ladder, quite committing and not always on the best rock!' In 2007 English climbers Anne and John Arran freed *Towering Inferno* with pitches of French 7a+/b (E6 6a). In 2012, *Glory* was climbed by a mixed team on Jebel Kharazeh opposite the rest house with five pitches of 8a/a+, while the hardest single pitch to date is *Wadirumela*, 8b+, by Klemen Bečan from Slovenia in 2014. Rum had come of age.

Others however have created less significant bolt-protected sport climbs sometimes alongside trad adventure routes. Ed Douglas wrote about bolts in Rum:

> It's their gradual appearance on established rock climbs and the new fashion for short sport routes that grates. One-pitch 6bs in Wadi Rum? It's like booking the Albert Hall for a pub band.

Like Ed I have to say that initially I didn't like any of the bolted routes. To me they were an intrusion and a bad example – even an eyesore, some of them turning climbing in Rum into a mere gymnastic exercise with no other skills being required, and little concern for the environment. I'm not sure if that's elitist, perverse or simply old fashioned, but I still don't like the routes that intrude into 'adventure' terrain close to trad routes. However I have to admit that in recent years sport climbs have allowed Jordanians – who are all new to climbing other than on Amman's new climbing wall – to experience climbing in Rum, usually with local Bedouin guides, so the climbs have been beneficial. Visitors from abroad are also enjoying them.

I can't say my conscience is clear either, though my own bolting in Rum has been minimal. Initially we hand-drilled our 'peg-bolt' placements for abseils only, though very occasionally we used them on climbs such as *The Pillar of Wisdom*. As I said, some are still in use. However, a few years after our first trip, at our request the tourism ministry paid for a power drill and, with Wilf in charge, we placed glue-in bolts on the most frequented descents and fitted them with abseil chains, as much to clean up the growing confusion of worn slings as to improve the safety. In doing so, we brought down a sack stuffed full of worn tapes from *Hammad's Route* on Jebel Rum. Interestingly I took some tape slings that had been sun-bleached on the mountain for a year to Troll and tested them. Instead of being over two tonnes in strength (actually rated at 22 kN), they hardly registered on the test rig as they disintegrated. Beware of old nylon abseil tapes!

There are still good new routes to be discovered. Though don't just go for the rock, have a day snorkelling or diving among the Red Sea coral reefs which are just an hour away, and spend some time with the Bedouin. If you are lucky, they may recount some of their hunting experiences in the mountains, or tell you their sometimes bizarre or bawdy stories while sitting around the fire in a *beit esh-sha'ar* with people like Sabbah Eid. He was a young boy when we first arrived, but like many others became a guide and close friend. His tent wasn't far from our camp and Di used to go out in the evening for the goats with his mother, a wonderful old lady with traditional Bedouin tattoos on her face, something that is seldom seen these days.

Sabbah is one of the Bedouin to have done a new route with visiting Europeans, famously arriving to do a new climb on notoriously difficult Nassrani, carrying his harness and a kettle with tea and sugar, but no footwear. The resultant route of 500 metres with numerous pitches of French 6a, which he climbed with bare feet, was called *Tea on the Moon*. Sabbah is always entertaining to be with. He once drove us back across the desert after a climbing trip with one wheel bigger than the others having had a puncture and borrowed a wheel off another Bedouin. On another occasion we were out in the desert with his family when the engine refused to start. The battery was flat and we were stuck in a sandy hollow between dunes with no chance of pushing it out. There was a Bedouin camp in the distance.

'I'll walk over to that camp to get a tow out,' I offered, but no.

'We'll have some tea and then I'll fix it,' he said.

An hour or so later he went down to the car, piled some stones under the rear axle then dug the sand out from under one rear wheel, put the engine in first gear and wrapped an old length of climbing rope round the wheel a few times. Together we pulled the rope, the wheel turned, the engine started and Sabbah jumped in as the car rolled forwards off the stones and off we went.

Once, driving back through the desert with him after exploring dramatic rock canyons in a remote corner of Rum, we stopped off to visit another old friend, Ham'd, a true Bedouin of the desert, his black tent concealed behind a dune far from the village. As we arrived, he rang the final melodic welcoming chimes from the big brass 'nijr' to announce that the freshly roasted coffee beans and crushed cardamom were ground and put to simmer in the coffee pot in the embers of the fire. The sun was setting behind the ragged jebels that formed a barrier of black, broken teeth to the west. Darkness crept across the red sands of the desert; it was story time. 'How's your foot?' someone asked an old man in the corner of the tent, after the formalities of coffee drinking were over.

Sabbah Eid explained: 'He was in the rocks underneath the cliffs of Draif al Muragh about three months ago when he was bitten by a snake; not the desert viper – the sand-coloured one with the horns that moves sideways – but the dark one that lives in the rocks. His wife put a tourniquet on and tried to get the poison out, but the foot swelled and he was in pain for forty days. Even now after three months he still has a limp.' This was well worth knowing; we had seen this 'rock snake' – the Palestine viper – many times in the mountains of Rum.

Another Bedouin, sipping a glass of sweet tea in the half glow of the fire, had a different story to tell. 'I saw a really strange thing the other day,' he said. 'One of those snakes was lying in the shade of a rock and I was watching it, when a big black scorpion crept up behind it.' He demonstrated with his fingers in the sand, chuckling at the memory, then stabbed the air suddenly with his curved forefinger. 'The scorpion stung the snake in the head, which then rose up quickly in the air, but the snake saw nothing and it lay down again. The scorpion then stung the snake twice more and it died, and the scorpion sucked its blood. I had never seen anything like it, and I was worried that this new creature – now half snake, half scorpion – might be really dangerous, so I killed it.' Everyone nodded their approval, but there was more to come.

'I once saw something even stranger,' another man said. 'You remember when my tent was by Jebel Khush Khashah? Well, I kept seeing the track of a big snake near our camp. I thought it would be dangerous for the children, so one day I followed the trail to its hole and dug down. It was very deep, but eventually I saw the snake and managed to pull it out with a long stick. It was very big and black, but the strangest thing was, it had eyelids and eyelashes, like one of the monsters that people say live under the ground and guard buried treasure. Because of this, I was afraid to kill it, in case it changed into something even more terrible, perhaps even a Djinn, so I sacrificed a goat and poured the blood into its hole. It came out quickly and disappeared across the desert and never came back!' Again, everyone agreed he had taken the right course of action.

There was time for one more story before the *mensef* was carried in by four boys, who struggled with the metre-wide dish of unleavened bread, heaped with mutton and crowned with the head of the unfortunate sheep, its open jaws laughing at the moon.

'I have a friend who is one of those Bedouin who can cure scorpion stings by kissing them away,' another man told the attentive audience, now into their third round of tea. 'One day his old mother-in-law came to him, saying she had sat on a scorpion which stung her. "Can you cure it for me?" she asked.

"'No problem,' my friend said. "Just show me the place." But when he saw it, he had to tell her it couldn't be done.

"'Why was that?' I asked him.

"'Because,' he replied, chuckling, "I would have had to put my nose exactly in the middle of her bottom!'"

42

EXPLORING JORDAN – BEDOUIN ROCK

It wasn't just finding new climbs that motivated us, it was discovering historical Bedouin hunting routes. Rakabat Canyon cuts though Jebel Um Ishrin all the way from Wadi Rum to the next great parallel desert valley, Wadi Um Ishrin. It is a great scramble through a spectacular mountain maze with world-class climbs in its depths. As such it has become a climbers' and trekkers' thoroughfare, but we didn't know it existed until our second visit when Defallah told us about it. He said it was a shortcut sometimes used by Bedouin to bring their goats through from the valley of Um Ishrin to Rum.

It sounded straightforward enough, so after visiting some Bedouin friends in Wadi Um Ishrin, Wilf, Mick and I decided to return through it one evening to our camp in Rum, Alan and Di opting to stay in the car and get dinner ready.

We scrambled through quite quickly, passing Bedouin ladders of stones jammed in cracks to enable goats to pass through more easily, thinking we had found the way through the maze of small canyons, only to emerge about fifteen metres up a cliff, itself above a rock plateau high above the valley of Rum. We were on a typically overhung and overhanging ledge with no way on and no way down. We had no rope and it was almost dark. Alan and Di eventually arrived on the plateau, looking for us, but there was no way we could reach them, so we had to go all the way back in the dark to Wadi Um Ishrin. Never take Bedouin routes for granted. We went back the following day with more information from Defallah and found the way from the Rum side, sneaking cunningly in across some exposed slabs fifty metres above the floor of a narrow side-canyon before zigzagging through a maze of slits to reach the main canyon.

A rumoured Bedouin way to the summit of Jebel Rum was another route that caused us difficulties. We had already found *Hammad's Route* from the east, but the way from the south proved more problematic. It was early October 1985 and we had just returned on our second visit. The summer heat had not yet relented, but having been told about another route to the summit, we were keen to discover more of this complex massif.

We were up at 5.30 a.m., but by the time we had eaten and driven down to the springs of Abu Aina at the south end of Jebel Rum, it was already seven and the sun was well up. The vultures which used to roost on the south end of the mountain were long gone – we had seen them drifting out on the thermals over Khor al Ajram towards Jebel Khazali. Looking forward to another day of exploration, we climbed enjoyably up the confines of the gully of Abu N'khala (Place of the Palms) eventually breaking out on to the south col with superb views over the desert towards Saudi Arabia.

Unfortunately, the elation didn't last long. 'It's started too well, something's sure to go wrong,' I said. The obvious way, with occasional Bedouin cairns, soon came to an abrupt halt with an inspiring view out across a siq plunging into Wadi Rumman in the west. We circled back 500 metres and continued on another cairned Bedouin way following a perfectly situated terrace below vertical pink walls and above the lip of the ravine of Abu N'khala. The black tents of our friends at their Abu Aina camp could be seen down below with the small figure of Hamda herding a flock of goats to the well.

A wide crevasse in the terrace, its depths plunging down into the canyon, caused brief entertainment in crossing it, after which we continued to reach a col, this time at the head of the Wadi Rumman siq that had stopped us earlier. The way through to the main summit two kilometres to the north now seemed open, so we moved on hoping that the mountain wouldn't have any more hidden siqs.

The next part of the route went easily enough, crossing sections of sandy ground interspersed with white whaleback ridges of sandstone. We savoured the anticipation of success while at the same time being aware that each ridge could conceal a siq. One ridge in particular seemed to lead up to the crest of the mountain and once on the line of the watershed we hoped from previous experience that we might have the most chance of meeting the line of least resistance. We followed it up. Clean white rock just a few metres wide slowly steepened towards the summit ridge, giving a hundred metres of enjoyable steep slab climbing at its top. A few metres beyond, just after we had glimpsed the summit smiling wickedly at us between some smaller domes a kilometre away to the north, the inevitable happened. A giant siq opened up at our feet: a gaping gash savaging its way westwards to form a huge ravine leading to Wadi Rumman, and cutting like a knife eastwards through the heart of the mountain to Wadi Rum. Like the Great Siq that we had found north of the summit, it completely split the mountain. We sat down in despair and named the summit we were on 'Frustration Dome'.

It was already midday and unusually hot with the temperature approaching 40 °C. We sat in the shade of an overhang, relieved to remove our sweat-soaked sacks and have a drink of our precious water. After brooding despondently over the pernicious nature of this uniquely complicated massif, we wandered off along the lip of the siq in the hope of finding a way through, but to no avail. It actually closed on the line of the watershed as we had hoped, but its south-facing wall loomed above us, featureless and unclimbable.

On the off-chance that we may be able to cross the eastern mouth of the siq above the valley of Rum, we descended our whaleback ridge, then utterly fatigued by the relentless afternoon sun, we sat in the shade again and drank lemon tea brewed on a fire. In the cool of the late afternoon we scrambled up chimneys and ridges to another new summit at the far eastern end before traversing west to the place we had been earlier, but the way on was closed so we returned for more tea, totally dehydrated. The mountain had proved again that it was not to be taken lightly. We should have remembered that for the Bedouin 'the top' simply means the vast expanse of the upper mountain where ibex can be hunted. The summit itself is of no special significance.

The isolated summit plateau, cut off from the desert by 400-metre cliffs, was however just as magical as we remembered. We bivouacked in a sandy hollow brewing cup after cup of sweet lemon tea until the water, unlike our thirst, was almost gone. Shooting stars blazed their trails beneath the wheel of the Milky Way and finally the embers of our fire dwindled in the darkness of the night. Later, the moon rose, washing out the stars with its pale radiance and once again transforming the surrounding domes into distant snowy hills.

With the new dawn, ravens and vultures rose in flocks from their unseen roosts and circled skywards over our bivouac. A downwards glance assured them that we were, at least for the moment, of no special interest as they slid through the warm morning air circling south, maybe to cruise over the silent sands of Saudi seen distantly among the peaks beyond. In recent years they have vanished completely from Rum as have the pair of rare black eagles that used to nest on the east face.

For us, with only sufficient water for a morning brew, the priority was descent. We made our way back along the twisting terraces to the ravine of Abu N'khala. Anticipating a welcome drink at the spring below the gully we made rapid progress, eager to reach the desert before the sun rose too high. Unfortunately the herd of goats from the Bedouin camp arrived at the water seconds before us, turning it into a pool of mud, so we set off on the three-kilometre walk through the red sands of Rum to our camp near the village of Bedouin tents.

It wasn't until 2002 that Gilles Rappeneau – who I had met previously in Oman – and his Bedouin friend Talal Awad found a way through by exploring south from the summit, after which Talal returned with Wilf Colonna and Patrick Gabarrou to do a south–north traverse finishing down one of our finds, the Bedouin route of *Al Thalamiyyah*. By then, finding the full traverse of the massif which involves around fifteen kilometres of rock, had become something of a holy grail, the riddle being solved by Gilles and Talal accompanied by Alban Busatta in an amazing nine and a half hours in 2005. Nine years later Wilf and Amjad Shahrour, one of Jordan's new breed of climbers from Amman, did the whole route north to south, Wilf commenting, 'It's a superb trip, one of the best mountain experiences anywhere.'

Meanwhile, back in 1985, after our failure to reach the summit of Rum from the south, we had instant success finding another Bedouin climb.

It was going to be a lazy day. We had been in Wadi Rum for a month. Wilf, Mick and I took a stroll up Wadi Shelaali, past Lawrence's Spring, to check out the first couple of rope lengths of a Bedouin hunters' route up Jebel Rum that they had mentioned to us.

We started quite late – about 8.00 a.m. in the morning – taking a bit of climbing gear almost as an afterthought, and a couple of litres of water, intending to be back around midday. We walked up the wadi and climbed to the rickety pile of stones, or 'Bedouin steps' as we called them, that we had seen earlier. They mark the start of the route beneath a most improbable wall of vertical rock festooned with typical Rum 'rock mushrooms'. Having climbed the 'steps' okay, though with some care, we scrambled up to try and discover where the route went next. Out to the left, the wall was vertical and interlaced with rounded purple overhanging slabs like bracket fungi. There, boldly but with incredible ease, went the route, winding its way effortlessly up purple grooves poised on the very edge of space, and emerging on a suspended sloping terrace with a second terrace overhanging it three metres higher. Piled on its outward-sloping floor was another delicately balanced tower of stones a metre high: just high enough to facilitate reaching over the overlap. Our curiosity aroused, we roped up and belayed Wilf while he balanced on the tottering top stone of this wobbly Bedouin construction. As he pulled over the lip of the roof at French 5 standard on to the ledges above, we marvelled at the audacity of the person who first conceived this route and climbed it to hunt ibex. Beyond, it was suddenly easy again, up another purple ramp and out on to the crest of the ridge, which is so obvious from the valley, rising at a temptingly easy angle directly towards the summit. The climbing was delightful, on the open face of the ridge, and always about grade 3 (VDiff max). We climbed fast and ropeless for 500 metres with plunging walls on either side, unable to resist the white domes of the summit plateau tempting us upwards. The route was going so well we abandoned our original plans of a simple reconnaissance and decided to go for the top.

We were in luck: everything went perfectly. In a mere two hours of solo climbing we were approaching the summit plateau, albeit with some considerable suspense as the actual top was still a kilometre away, and such is the unique complexity of the high plateau that every new dome can conceal an impassable crevasse beyond. We needn't have worried. Romping along on white whaleback ridges of sandstone we rose steadily towards the top. Just as the summit came into view, two ibex trotted across the rising domes ahead of us, to disappear over the horizon. We followed them up on to the summit ridge and continued to the top. It was only midday and four hours earlier we had been in camp.

With only a litre of water left we set off back for the valley. Having no food, spare clothing or head torches with us, we didn't fancy spending a thirsty and cold night on the mountain. The way back was via our friend Hammad's route, which Mick and I knew from the previous year. We ran down the bald white slabs from the summit with barely time for a passing glance at the plunging rift of the Great Siq that had caused us much previous frustration. Finally, we were down the ridge to the south with its curious nippled rocks, finishing with another abseil and a final scramble down the screes to the mint- and mustard-scented Lawrence's Spring with its sweet, cool water.

What an amazing day! We walked leisurely back across the desert as the shadows of Jebel Rum crept on to the sands and swifts chased flies in the tamarisk. Later, as the yellow-mushroomed walls of the great towers of Nassrani turned red in the dying sun, we sipped cardamom coffee in the cool tent of our Bedouin friends. We told them of our day and listened to their stories of this previously unknown classic Bedouin climb of *Rijm Assaf* – the 'Tower of Assaf'. Our exploration of these hunting routes continued, sometimes in the company of our Bedouin friends, mostly just following their hints and trying to discover their ways for ourselves.

Also in 1985, after a tip-off from Sheikh Kraim who had shot an ibex not far from the summit of Jebel Barrah, we climbed the vast, steepening sweep of his *Hunter's Slabs*. Later, Di and I followed Sabbah Atieq up a route on Jebel Khush Khashah from which a Bedouin woman had fallen to her death when descending with water. *Sheikh Hamdan's Route*, up which he had led 'the English ladies' to Jebel Rum's summit in 1952, proved to be delightful. From the top, we descended by his son's route, *Hammad's Route* – a magnificent mountain traverse 'of alpine proportions' and now a sought-after classic. Also from the west, we climbed *Sabbah's Route* with its exposed traverse above the void to reach the summit domes. Ten years later, in 1995, Di and I reached the top by what we called the *Thamudic Route*, perhaps the world's oldest known rock climb, still inscribed with names left by two hunters 'Kharajat, son of Sa'adan' and 'Jahfal, brother of Taym' carved in Thamudic script over 2,000 years ago.

Talking of Bedouin hunters, they have incredible eyesight and are superb shots. On an early desert trip with Defallah in response to our questioning about hunting, he produced a rifle from under his four-by-four seat. 'Watch this,' he said, and shot a swallow in full darting, swooping flight. A hurtling dot in the sky. No fun for the swallow, but unbelievable marksmanship. As was the shooting down of a centimetre-wide jammed abseil rope that two climbers had abandoned a few pitches up Jebel Rum's east face on a route of ours called *Rainbow Warrior*.

A few days later there was a cooler feeling in the air. As the gathering clouds rolled up the valley towards us, enveloping the high mountain plateau of Jebel Rum, the storm too rumbled nearer until the air seemed alive with vibrant energy. Without our realising, the echo of thunder had been replaced by the distant roar of unseen water rushing through hidden canyons high on the mountain: canyons that emerged 300 metres above us on the vertical wall of rock. Soon the heavy rain began to splash in the dry desert around us, dappling the dust of months as we looked up at the cliffs.

The water-scoured pink, lavender and purple rock of *Rainbow Warrior* became the course of a roaring river of water, bursting from a ravine high above and careering down the wall in a breathtaking crescendo of violence. All across the 5,000-metre-wide wall of the mountain, countless other waterfalls crashed from concealed canyons, some falling free for 300 metres. Suddenly, water from the largest cleft of all, the Great Siq, burst out of the centre of the face in a foaming brown flood.

Children from the tents of the Bedouin village ran through the rain towards us, and as the first waves of the torrent pushed foam and debris across the sands they danced, laughing and splashing in the rush of water. Within seconds the dry wadi became a river, the water quickly fanning out as it reached across the desert. Yet, so thirstily was it swallowed by the sand that despite the increasing torrent behind the waters spread ever-more slowly and the river, raging between boulders only a few hundred metres away, simply vanished into dampness at our feet.

Within an hour the rain had stopped. The waterfalls trickled almost instantly into oblivion and the sands sucked up the last of the flood. Blue skies appeared again. The wet, black walls of the mountain dried to purple and red in the hot sun. The damp sands of the desert turned once more to orange and yellow. Sheikh Atieq led his camel to drink at a rapidly disappearing pool near the foot of the jebel. Only those pools, the thorny bushes and tamarisk shrubs – now shiny green and dust free – and a foam-rimmed area of darker sand where the river had just been, gave any visible indication of the storm. The valley was quiet again.

Our Bedouin friends had warned us before about flash floods, but now we knew! We were forever afterwards cautious when we saw threatening clouds on the horizon, but of course desert storms are rare events and our climbing explorations continued. *Rainbow Warrior* was extended to become *Aquarius*, and further right we found *Black Magic* and the 300-metre face climb of *Captain Morgan*, after which our probings ventured out on to the mushrooming walls with the discovery of *Where Angels Fear to Tread*. We were also still looking for traditional Bedouin hunting routes; one of the last that Di and I did being *Muhammad Musa's Route* in 1992. Muhammad lived in his *beit esh-sha'ar* a bit further up the Rum valley from our camp. His sons,

Salim and Eid, used to come past every morning on their camels saying, 'If you want to ride them, they are yours,' which we did one day, though they are not the most comfortable of animals for those not used to them. We were sometimes invited to Muhammad's camp for an evening meal, after which he would play his *rababa*, a one-stringed instrument, while a young falcon perched beside him that he had captured from its nest to train before selling in Saudi Arabia. It was on one of those evenings that he told us about his hunting route behind his camp on Jebel Um Ishrin, a mountain that retained its mysteries longer than most. He was going to take us up there when we returned the following year, but in the interim he was killed in a crash on the Aqaba highway.

Behind his camp there was a granite block some twenty metres high. We did some routes there in spring 1989 and called it *Musa's Slab* in his honour. Three years later Sabbah Atieq took Di and me up what we called *Muhammad Musa's Route* on Jebel Um Ishrin. It was, as expected, long and complex. It was also the first hunting route we had actually done with some-one who knew the way. He showed us the almost indiscernible signs of where an ibex had been eating grass just the day before. Sadly he also found traces of blood in a canyon we descended later in the day where the ibex had been shot. Later, Mick and I returned to explore a variation of the route that crossed the north ridge of the mountain, eventually descending into Wadi Um Ishrin down 2,000-year-old Nabataean steps.

Defallah mentioned he had been helping an Italian archaeologist, Pro-fessor Borzatti. While looking at the maps to which he was adding Bedouin place names, he had noticed a mountain close to Saudi Arabia's border which seemed to have more contours than Jebel Rum – then said to be Jordan's highest mountain. He was right! The highest twenty-metre contour circle was at 1,820 metres, the top presumably being around 1,830 metres, so well above Jebel Rum's 1,754. Together with him and his brother, Sabbah, we went on a wonderful desert drive out beyond Rum's main massif past cliffs with Thamudic inscriptions and down through the desert canyon of Nogra before winding through some narrow and tricky sand wadis to the foot of a pyramidal peak which Defallah said was Jebel Um Adaami. Its ascent was an easy and enjoyable scramble and the summit views over Rum and Saudi were superb. It was mentioned years later in *Trek & Mountain* magazine as being number fifty-two of the world's 'Top 100 Trails'. The actual trail was a circuitous route from Wadi Rum to Petra via Jebel Um

Adaami, Burdah Rock Bridge and Rakabat Canyon.

In the summer of 1989 I arranged for three Bedouin from Rum to come over to the UK on guiding and rescue training courses. Sabbah Atieq had already been a couple of years previously, his flight paid for by the tourism ministry, to attend a course at the National Mountain Centre, Plas y Brenin. He also did some mountain rescue training at Troll and climbed with us. He was joined on his second visit by Sabbah Eid and Atieq Auda. By then our benefactor, the director at the tourism ministry, Mr Nasri Atalla, had retired. Undeterred, and with advice followed up by a phone call from a friend of ours, Sami Sabat, who had friends in high places, Di and I went to the palace and were given every possible assistance from Queen Noor who took over sponsorship of the project as she immediately understood its benefits both to Wadi Rum and to Jordan.

Atieq, who was only eighteen at the time, couldn't wait, and unexpectedly arrived three weeks early: he had never travelled before, but he changed his flight date, arrived at Heathrow, made his way to London where he found a cheap hotel, then caught a bus up to Manchester, then another to Uppermill as that was the address on Troll's business card. The first I knew about it was when the secretary at Troll said, 'There's a bus conductor on the phone, he says there's a Bedouin on his bus. Can someone come for him?'

43

TRAVELS IN THAILAND

Wilf suggested Di and I visit Thailand as he would be out there later in the year doing new routes with Bernard Domenech and another French friend we knew from Wadi Rum, 'Dolby' Monet. It sounded too good to miss.

We flew out to Bangkok in 1987 with Tannith and Di's eldest son, Paul, now both in their late teens, and stayed a few nights in a cheap 'hotel' (if you could call it that) while we visited the temples and other sites. The divisions between the bedrooms were sheets of quarter-inch ply: everything could be heard. There were two young British lads next to us, presumably students on their gap year. One evening they came in late with a couple of giggling Thai girls. The giggles became louder accompanied by the sound of creaking beds. Then the girls left.

'I wish we hadn't done that,' one lad said.

'Me too,' the other replied. 'I think we should see a doctor when we get back.'

'Serves you right for waking us up,' I said. The room went silent.

From there we caught the bus south, then a ferry to the tropical idyll of Koh Pih Pih where we stayed in a hut on the edge of a beach of squeaky silver sand fringed with coconut palms. Wilf and his friends were already enjoying themselves preparing a route on a small overhanging cliff on an adjacent island. The next day I was with them, but it wasn't my scene.

'Wilfried,' I said, 'I know climbers are supposed to be "conquistadors of the useless", but this is taking quixotism to the extreme.'

'I told you climbing new routes in Thailand would be stupid,' he said, 'especially when this is your first time here and there's so many other things to see and do.' It was OK for him; he had been to Thailand often. For me, in a country of overwhelming beauty and variety, the laborious and systematic engineering of a climb on an insignificant limestone tower capped with jungle seemed the height of futility. As Wilfried acknowledged, it was stupid for us on our first trip, he had been to Thailand five times and was ready for some rock, whereas for us, there were hopefully other adventures to be had and other sights to see, so we left them to it.

There was more coast to enjoy, and in the far north Chiang Mai beckoned with trekking opportunities among hill tribes in the infamous Golden Triangle where the Himalayan chain finally submerges itself below misty rainforest ridges, themselves descending to the rice fields, towns and dazzling golden temples.

By far the best chance of gaining access to the villages of the various hill tribes was to hire a local guide familiar with the area and the different languages of the peoples: Karen, Yeo, Meo, Akha, Lisu, Lahu and so forth. And so it was in the company of a New Zealander and a Swedish lad that we set off up a bumpy and dusty forest track with our Karen guide to the start of a trail some thirty kilometres north-west of Chiang Mai in Doi Suthep-Pui National Park.

The morning was already hot, the sun penetrating the forest cover and the sound of a nearby river immediately tempting as we wound up the path. Shai, our guide, darted ahead enthusiastically with his two rucksacks slung front and back. An early stop was more than welcome, relaxing on warm rock slabs by the top of a waterfall after plunging into its cold crashing cascade. The rest of the day took us higher into the hills through bamboo forest, past the villages of Karen, Shan and Lisu tribes to a Meo settlement on a high ridge. All these peoples and perhaps twenty other hill tribes have migrated through the Himalaya over the past two to 300 years from distant parts of Tibet and China to settle in the remote upper valleys of Burma, Laos and Thailand. Here they live by slash-and-burn agriculture, where crops include the notorious opium poppy.

Although the people are of different tribal origins and speak different languages, the villages are invariably a cluster of hardwood houses on stilts, thatched with forest leaves. The larger houses have an airy, almost open-sided communal room, through which the building is entered. Beyond that, through a low doorway, smoky shafts of sunlight reveal a central hearth in the dim inner room where the family sit and sleep in the cooler nights. Beneath the houses, black pigs, usually with a litter of young, lie panting in the dust where ducks and hens scratch a living and puppies pester the empty teats of their ribbed mothers.

We passed our first night in such a village. In the evening, the sun disappeared behind the black-forested fretwork of the hilltop skyline and the sky turned to pink and violet as inside a small group of men lying on bamboo mats gathered around the tiny yellow flame of an oil lamp. A skewer of black opium held by a gnarled, hard-laboured hand was slowly and lovingly rotated over the flame, bubbling its sickly sweet smell into the darkness. Dimly seen in the far corner, a young girl of exotic beauty gently rocked a baby in a hammock, while an older woman smoking a silver-bound, curved-stem pipe painstakingly prepared the evening meal, the smell of garlic mixing with the smoke from the melting opium. Whispered words from the men indicated the time was right to insert the skewer into the bowl of a long-stemmed pipe, and the bubbling pellet still held over the flame finally melted into smoke to be inhaled in one long deep breath in an ageless ritual of quiet contentment. The beauty of the high, hidden poppy fields and the remote unspoilt villages of seemingly peaceful people is a great contrast to the trail of greed, corruption and lingering painful death that the abuse of this same flower brings to the West.

We moved out in the early dawn, long after the villagers themselves had risen in the cricket-shrilling darkness to begin their daily routine of grinding rice and feeding the animals. By the time we set out on the narrow trail the village was quiet again, most of the people having gone before us into the forest to tend hidden crops. This second day took us even higher into the hills between giant hardwood trees and past carefully irrigated rice fields to arrive, sweating, at midday at another Karen village. In the cool shade of the thatched house we drank endless cups of locally grown tea, while the sun passed its zenith.

A rough but drivable track entered the opposite side of the settlement and here we were picked up by a truck to go further north and even higher to the Mae Taeng river area, passing the thundering Mork Fa falls, before being dropped off at a lodge where hot springs gushed steam into the thick surrounding jungle. Now in the cool of the evening, almost dark in the forest, we wound our way up a final track to a hidden village in the next valley, so hidden in fact that we lost the trail in the gathering gloom, arriving in the village after nightfall.

The New Zealander and I tried the opium pipe that night. It was one of those now-or-never things. After some discussion I had twenty-one pipefuls. It seemed a lot to me, but each pellet was only pea sized and our hosts were the undoubted experts, so in hope of pleasant opium-induced dreams I relaxed by the fire and puffed away. *After all*, I thought, *if it was good enough for Sir Richard Burton, Byron and Shelley it is good enough for me*. Later, however, I discovered that Shelley was said to have run shrieking from the room on one occasion, having hallucinated that the nipples of his wife Mary had become demonic eyes. Apparently she too had a nightmare that was the source of the plot for *Frankenstein*. I have to say I had no luck either: my hopes of sweet dreams turned into a whole night of itching. I was still awake as the sky lightened in a cool and misty dawn, but the veil of cloud clinging to the steaming jungle hollows offered no contest to the swiftly rising sun.

More jungle trails followed across ridges and rivers to the next village in a small clearing where working elephants were to take us down to the Mae Taeng river, a prospect which had seemed distastefully touristic when we arranged the trip, but which in reality was quite an eye-opener. I had envisaged a boring plod along a flat jungle path; instead we found ourselves on steep and narrow tracks, it felt a surprisingly precarious place to be, perched high on the howdah, or in Paul and Di's case, legs astride behind the ears, as the animals lurched down or across hillsides so steep I would have previously considered them impossible terrain for an elephant. On the plus side, river crossings became problem free, and the whole interlude provided an enjoyable and interesting afternoon's experience before we arrived at the next village on the edge of another swift-flowing river.

We spent a chill night on the bare boards of the house, fingers of damp mist from the nearby river spreading through the forest and dissipating slowly in the early dawn. Down at the river a couple of bamboo rafts were being constructed for the journey downstream for us and another trekking group who had also arrived in the village. All the rafts looked alarmingly flimsy affairs and we weren't too surprised to find that once we stepped on to ours it immediately sank knee deep below the surface. Even Shai seemed perturbed. Long discussions ensued until finally two more bamboo poles were lashed to the raft and a tripod of branches erected amidships to suspend our rucksacks above the water. Shai, with a disarming smile, told us to wrap our cameras up well in waterproof bags as a lot of rafts capsize or fall apart in the rapids. *That's encouraging*, we thought, but nothing ventured nothing gained. The raft builder and river guide grinned confidently at the bows as he thrust his pole against the bank, sending us gliding now only ankle deep into midstream where the current swept us away towards a bend in the river, not far behind the submerged stern of the raft of the other group.

We stood, legs apart, balancing precariously as the water swished around our legs and the larger waves slapped up against the bottoms of our sacks. Within minutes we were rounding the bend, plunging between boulders and rushing onwards past the already-capsized raft of the other group – two of whom were clutching at rocks, a third in the river – but you can't stop a raft in a rapids so on we went, all of us convinced it wouldn't be too long before we joined them, until suddenly rounding the next bend we bobbed out into quieter waters. *One down, how many to go?*

On the smoother stretches of the river it was a pleasure to look around as the river licked our legs and the miles rippled by. Jungle-covered hillsides tangled in creepers formed an apparently impenetrable green wall on either side from which monkeys called. The deeper we went into the forest, the more we wondered how we would get out if the flimsy craft we were stood on fell apart. Passing other rafts smashed to pieces on the numerous midstream rocks did little to increase our confidence.

The worst rapid came after about two hours. Just as we thought we were getting good at the game, we swept around a bend to be greeted by the roaring of more white water. The raft careered down a narrow chute between huge rounded boulders, the bows plunging deep below a series of waves that swept across the raft in swift succession so that we found ourselves waist deep on a wildly lurching platform. The river surged around us as we struggled to balance the raft, at one moment tipped on edge almost to the point of capsizing, then rolling just as swiftly to the opposite side as we counterbalanced chest deep in the water. To our great surprise we made it through, and the rapids that followed were never quite as bad. With some relief we arrived at a village downriver.

Lunch as always went down well – the food in Thailand is a daily delight – before we walked up a pleasant forest trail to our last village, an Akha settlement. Its inhabitants were one of the most colourful groups we saw on our trek, the dress of the women resplendent with embroidery and appliqué, and studded with polished metal and beads. I wondered if they had donned their traditional dress especially for us – the tourists – and hoped our visit was less intrusive and more financially beneficial than most of the intrusive touristic visits to Bedouin camps in Rum. They were in fact very friendly, and their village was in a small clearing high on a ridge overlooking the surrounding forest, which formed a perfect setting for the end of our trip.

As the darkness crept up from below to join a lavender evening sky, we walked down to meet our truck for the long and dusty drive back to Chiang Mai. Only four days in a forest, but a wealth of good memories. Dare I say it: it beat hanging around on a limestone cliff.

44

OMAN ODYSSEY – A SURPRISE CHRISTMAS

I had been researching Oman and was given the address of Alec McDonald who, I was told, was a climber with a top job, employed by Sultan Qaboos. I got in touch, and before long Di and I were on our way out to be hosted by Alec.

Oman's infamous deserts, once inaccessible mountain strongholds and piratical coastline have always intrigued yet been unattainable for the vast majority of travellers. It wasn't until after our arrival there that the doors creaked marginally and tantalisingly open to allow tourists in on two-week visas. Oman is a magnificent and varied country and two weeks is hardly time to scratch the surface. It had fascinated me for years, partly due to Wilfred Thesiger's incredible journeys with the Bedouin in the late 1940s through the wild, unknown, unmapped and forbidden Empty Quarter: the Rub' al Khali, the world's largest sand sea.

These journeys were made 'when the interior of Oman had remained one of the least known of the inhabited places of the East, even less well-known than Tibet', and all described in his book *Arabian Sands*, an inspiration for anyone interested in the tribulations and total commitment of self-sufficient travel in one of the world's most inhospitable places. Like Knud Rasmussen in the Canadian Arctic, Thesiger and his indigenous companions were in inhospitable terrain, reliant on no one, with no outside contact and consequently with no chance of help should it be needed. As Thesiger rightly said, a few years later the desert could be flown over and driven across in vehicles, making a journey such as his – on foot with camels – superfluous.

His feats in some respects make a mockery of today's desert and polar adventurers repeating historical journeys with their modern equipment, clothing, maps and Google Earth, GPS navigation, permanent contact with the outside world and backup teams ready for rescues. A lot of people today climb, run or even carry bizarre and cumbersome objects of furniture up mountains purely as 'a challenge for charity'. Others pay tens of thousands to go up Everest (I won't say climb). There's nothing wrong with raising money for good causes, but it seems people are forgetting that mountains are places of inspiration and beauty, and to climb them for pleasure in good or wild weather, summer or winter, for no other reason than that they are there is sufficient in itself. I was simply intrigued by the unknown. I had heard rumours of trekking and climbing to be had in the barren mountains that fringe Oman's deserts. The final reason for my growing obsession with the place was that there was almost no tourism. We would have it virtually to ourselves. Permits to enter were unobtainable for individuals unless you happened to work there, or had an approved 'sponsor'.

Europeans were not, however, unknown to the Omanis, as the country had over 6,000 expatriates – mostly British – resident in the modern suburbs of Muscat or out in the oilfields, though the days when Thesiger slipped surreptitiously through on the other side of the mountains risking his life as an infidel were not long gone. His Bedouin friends, Bin Ghabaisha and Bin Kabina, still lived in a desert village to the south. In 1970, Sultan Qaboos had assumed power from his ageing father who had ruled with little deviation from the customs and lifestyle of the last thousand years or more, but was to spend the rest of his life in exile in London. His son was then only thirty; he had been educated in India then England where he graduated at Sandhurst. As soon as he took over, he flew to Muscat where he reversed his father's restrictions, surrounded himself with advisors (mostly British) and started to modernise the country.

With increasing oil wealth in the 1970s, Oman moved irrevocably, for better or worse, into the twentieth century and became an exemplary Arab nation rather than a collection of feuding tribes, making Sultan Qaboos one of the most benevolent, well-loved and respected Arab leaders. A pro-gramme of modernisation commenced: towns and cities were built with schools, universities and hospitals. Roads and tracks were carved out of solid rock to the smallest and remotest villages hitherto inaccessible except on foot or by camel. Their creation left ugly scars across the mountain land-scapes but turned journeys of days into those of hours. An eyesore to us when we arrived, but the villagers weren't complaining.

We were there to explore the mountains. Alec had not only arranged our

'No Objection Certificates' but he also arranged our accommodation and, being one of the very few climbers resident in Oman, he pointed us in the right directions, while his friend Gilles Rappeneau, another climber and director of a French oil company, provided us with the absolutely essential four-wheel-drive transport.

Together, Alec and Gilles introduced us to the dubious pleasures of Omani limestone on the 100-metre-high roadside cliff of Wadi Adai. The crag is just outside the capital and is rather akin to the slabs and buttresses of the Avon Gorge, having nothing of the remote mountain atmosphere one normally associates with Arabian climbs. The rock was dark, disappointingly flaky and suspect, totally unlike the creamy coloured and beautifully rough rasping limestone of Morocco's Taghia canyons, or Iran's towering cliffs near Kermanshah. It was nevertheless climbable. We were assured that the higher mountains were likely to hold greater promise and Di and I left the next day in our Land Cruiser for the massif of the Eastern Hajar, east of Muscat.

We took the only road south over the mountains then east across the gravel plains, on past the northern fringes of the great Wahiba Sands whose dunes rise to 100 metres, and into the ancient port of Sur – one of the last places in Arabia that the traditional shipbuilding crafts are still used to build, without plans or templates, the beautiful wooden 'booms' and 'shuais' that are still used along this coast by traders and fishermen.

From Sur we backtracked, turning north and leaving the modern highway in the evening to drive across the stony plains towards the distant blue mountains of Bani Jabir. As the hills and darkness closed around us, we bivouacked by an acacia tree that cast a pale shadow beneath the bright crescent moon and the million stars of the silent Arabian night.

In the morning, we continued over a high pass and down to the village and oasis of Wadi Bani Khalid. Like all such oases in these austere bare-boned mountains, it nestled like a rare emerald in the dark deep cleft ahead of us, all the more luscious for its isolation in these apparently arid peaks. We walked through the terraced gardens which were shaded by date palms and fed by cold, crystal-clear, fish-filled waters from a 'falaj' – a centuries-old irrigation channel, one of over 4,000 in Oman which, like the *qanats* in Iran, run underground for long distances beneath the otherwise dry wadis bringing water for crop irrigation, drinking and even for fish – a rare harvest in the desert.

Higher up the valley, another oasis could be seen and we drove on up the worsening track, glad to reach a point beyond which we could only go on foot. We had hoped to find a canyon with good climbable rock. Instead we were greeted by cliffs of a now all-too-familiar doubtful nature, but concealed below their water-worn bases were deep pools of ice-blue water where laughing children swam, enjoying to the full this most rare of Arabian delights. Further on, we climbed up to a small cave entrance in the side of the canyon but without a torch were unable to investigate. A young boy told us that 'there is a room inside big enough to hold five 747s'. I treated this with great suspicion, so it was with considerable surprise that on our return to Muscat Alec told me that, although that wasn't the cave we had found, there was indeed a cave in that area of that size called Majlis al Jinn, 'The meeting place of the Djinns'. It had been explored by an American, Don Robinson, five years earlier in 1983. Many years later, in 2014, its 300-metre-high and totally overhanging walls were climbed in thirteen pitches and graded French 8b+ by Stefan Glowacz and Chris Sharma who spent two weeks creating a route up and out of what is currently the world's fourth-largest cave chamber. It is now also a hotspot for BASE jumpers.

Caving, however, was not our *raison d'être* and as the upper reaches of the canyon, though inspiring in themselves and giving an enjoyable trek, contained no potential for climbing, we descended to the car and wound our cautious way back over the steep rubble-strewn pass to the main track and the highway. Further north again, as suggested by Alec, we cut back once more on to desert tracks and spent our second night beneath the stars. Baked potatoes in the embers of the fire had never tasted better.

In the cool of dawn with the crisp light of early morning outlining row upon row of blue shadowed jagged hills ahead, we crossed another thirty miles of gravel plain to reach our next hidden oasis at Sumayyah where a sweep of smooth slabs showed promise of good climbing but ended nowhere among the shattered rocks of the surrounding peaks. We drove on down the wadi – in places an active river – which we crossed and recrossed axle deep, removing the dust of the previous days, and finally entering the mouth of Wadi Dayqah.

This tremendous gash cleaves through the heart of the Eastern Hajar. In its upper reaches its perennial river cascades through deep pools between sensually smooth boulders. The cliffs on either side are 100 metres high or more, but unattractive to the climber. For the walker, however, the journey through the nine-mile canyon is superb, following an ancient caravan route to the sea and the port of Quriyat through the only break in these otherwise impassable mountains. Descending the upper canyon we found a rope in place which, not too long ago, was used to haul goods up the massive boulders to allow the unencumbered camels to slowly make their way round a devious and awkward bypass on the opposite bank.

Climbing down the rope we continued down the ravine towards its eastern exit, sometimes following the riverbed, sometimes on the waterworn slabs of its right bank, polished to a height of five metres or more by flash floods that have more than once swept away the unsuspecting traveller. Reaching the last bend, a series of savage and almost inaccessible cliffs rise 1,200 metres from the north bank in a maze of clefts and towers to a final dramatic headwall. Simply to reconnoitre such a climb would be an undertaking in itself and with no obvious attractive line we left it untouched. To contemplate the savagery was sufficient and the journey through the canyon had been memorable enough, with a refreshing swim in a deep pool to end the day. We returned to Muscat the following afternoon feeling that we were beginning to know the mountains.

We were now ready for a foray into the Jebel Akhdar massif west of Muscat in the company of Alec and Gilles. Our particular objective was the remote peak of Jebel Misht, rising to 2,090 metres and crouching sphinx-like, facing south-west into the desert where Thesiger's 'landscape of black rocks and yellow sand sloped down to the Empty Quarter … [and] stretched away unbroken for 1,500 miles to the orchards round Damascus and the red cliffs of Rum'.

For the climber, the attraction of Jebel Misht is the 7,000-metre-wide wall of its south and south-east faces, rising for much of its length to over 1,000 metres and composed of Omani exotic limestone, which we hoped would be better than the other rocks we had seen or climbed on in the past few days. Our trip was to be a simple reconnaissance to see if any unclimbed lines were feasible, as the wall already had three routes. Two were climbed by English geologist Mike Searle and friends, one of which is a short 200-metre route to the little west summit, the other climbs the full height of the south face up a natural line. The third route on the wall is on the superb dominating 'nose' where the line of the cliff changes, curving back from south to south-east. Though now free, its first ascent with mixed aid and free climbing took Raymond Renaud and two other Chamonix guides three days, the lucky trio being whisked off the summit by the sultan's helicopter for a feast at the palace.

We arrived late in the afternoon, but still had time to inspect the wall before sunset. Inspired, Alec and I left early the following morning to toil up two hours of scree, reaching the foot of the wall as the sun swept down its eastern flank to greet us. Our new climb was excellent. A ramp led out from a high tongue of scree to a platform 500 metres up the wall. A good place to begin, already high on the cliff with bands of what looked like bad rock on the lower section already well below us. Clean, enjoyable slabs of prickly rock swept up for three rope lengths to a prominent crack line. Two superb pitches of English 5a and 5b brought us out close to the end of the steeper section. They suited me fine, though they were hard enough to get a good sweat going in temperatures of around 25 °C in the shade and over forty in the sun. Above, after a pitch sneaking out deviously around a roof, the angle eased and with it our apprehension: the top was in sight and we emerged on the crest just after midday.

The descent of the rubble-strewn, easy-angled slabs of the northern side was a bit of a nightmare with no respite from the sun and seemingly eternal cautious stepping from rock to rock. We envied the French and their helicopter trip, whereas for us, the sight of Di and the Land Cruiser parked in the shade of a large tree taunted us for two and a half hours until we finally arrived, dusty and thirsty. On our arrival the local sheikh of the Bani Rawwal invited us into the cool spaciousness of his house in the nearby village for coffee and fruit.

After Alec left, Di and I walked through the remote villages and dramatic canyons on the south side of nearby Jebel Akhdar. The canyon of Al Hijri seemed particularly spectacular with smooth black walls rising tier upon tier for 600 metres. The ancient *falaj* taking water from its upper reaches led into the ruins of a once beautiful traditional village, bombed into ruins twenty years ago by the British air force supporting the old sultan in a feud with his rebellious imam.

Christmas Eve was celebrated in a cafe in Nizwa's souk, and we rose early next morning to make a new climb on the Nizwa Towers, a small but attractively jagged group of rocks. Our 200-metre route in the pleasant shade of the west face finished with an amazing little pinnacle of rock as bristly as a hedgehog's back. Di, who really enjoys topping out, took the lead and perched herself on its perfect – if sharp – summit: a present for Christmas Day. The town of Nizwa surrounded by date palms was spread out beneath us, while to the south, the 560-mile road to Salalah pointed like an arrow into the heat haze where the desert merged in a shimmering glare with the sky.

The descent was quick and easy and the drive back to Muscat on the excellent road enabled us to spend an hour in the sea.

On our third week we drove or trekked through the valleys and canyons that abound on both sides of Jebel Akhdar and culminate in Oman's highest peak, Jebel Shams, at 3,009 metres. It is unfortunately crowned with a radar dome that robs it of any mystique, but just below on its southern slopes we found the 1,000-metre abyss of Saydran Canyon. Walking along its lip, we spotted two Egyptian vultures, their backs to us, perched on a prow overlooking its depths, like Tennyson's eagle, which 'clasps the crag with crooked hands / Close to the sun in lonely lands'.

Further on, in the uppermost recesses of the cliffs, we met a troglodytic Bedouin family, babies crawling contentedly at the cave mouth on the edge of a 1,000-metre drop. It seemed a total anachronism in modern Oman that people should cling so resolutely to the old life, while just above them the incongruous radar dome ballooned like a monstrous green carbuncle. With typical Arabian benevolence they asked us to share coffee and dates with them in the morning. The entrance to the cave was along a narrow ledge some fifty metres below the lip of the canyon, while beneath it the cliffs swept abruptly down like those of the Grand Canyon to the narrow silver ribbon of the wadi bed. It was a magical place with their adjacent, small terraced garden built on the lip of a giant overhang with a stupendous view down the full length of the canyon: perhaps they weren't so crazy after all.

Later, on the other side of the mountain, in valleys guarded by massive and ancient castles, we inspected its eastern bastions. A savage arena of cliffs tumbled chaotically for 1,200 metres to the remote village of Madruj, awe-inspiring and climbable but loose on their lower walls – up which I did a quick pitch, tossing holds off as I went, and who knows what problems lay ahead on the summit towers. Further east, but still on Jebel Akhdar, 'the Green Mountain', we wandered among the neatly terraced villages of Ghubrah and Wadi Bani Kharus and found some delightful little routes in the canyon mouth of Wadi Bani Awf. Beneath the cliff a whip-like snake, the well-named wadi racer, languished in a small pool – a remnant of the last rains but now more fish than water – choosing passing mouthfuls with casual indifference to their frenzy.

Our last few days were spent near the sea and revealed a new world. To the west we drove for eighteen miles along the beach of the Batinah coast watching fishermen bring in catches of sardines which were spread out to dry on the sand, acre upon endless acre of flapping silver gasping and dying in the heat. The men fished from simple traditional 'shashas', palm-frond boats through which the sea runs at will, or huge dugout 'houris', canoes from India's Malabar coast.

East of Muscat, we climbed in Wadi Mayh, finding time to add a route of our own inevitably named *The Scorpion*, with its last pitch 'sting in the tail'. The rock wasn't the best in the world and both our previous belays had been dodgy, so I was relieved when I pulled over what turned out to be the crux moves of the final overhang on to the safety of the top. Afterwards, down at the canyon's seaward exit, a lone fisherman crouched in the surf where it took only a matter of moments to hand cast a net and immediately bring in twenty or more kilos of startled fish. Even more stunning, an osprey flew overhead smashing into the waves and reascending, a struggling fish in its talons, to be leisurely eaten on a nearby pole before casually repeating the process. Kingfishers and waders of various shapes and sizes were everywhere, and herons darted, strutted or stalked the shoreline as a memorable sunset filled sea and sky with blazing orange, concluding a journey of far more variety than the burnt black hills had first implied.

Before leaving, Alec introduced us to a contact at the department of tourism who was interested in developing their adventure tourism, which was virtually non-existent. Luckily I had recently dreamed up the wheeze of n.o.m.a.d.s: New Opportunities for Mountaineering, Adventure and Desert Sports, a ploy to enable Di and me to become adventure-travel consultants, not only for Jordan's Ministry of Tourism, but also to get us to other mountains and wild places. It wasn't that we wanted a new job – we were still more than happy at Troll – it was simply a ruse to be able to get permits and perhaps sponsors to reach otherwise remote and restricted places. In return, we would advise on environmentally aware adventure-tourism potential, while ensuring that the local communities would be the key beneficiaries of any resultant adventure tourism – as had happened in Romsdal and Jordan. Our future travels would then be ensured of a more philanthropic aspect. As our website says, we could 'help to open these areas to climbing, trekking and adventure tourism in a way that will minimise change to the environment and maximise any potential benefits to the lifestyle of the indigenous peoples. This is a delicate path to tread but one which we care deeply about, and which offers an opportunity for us to give something back in return for a lifetime of climbing and travel.'

Our first opportunity to make use of this came in Oman. We presented our n.o.m.a.d.s. portfolio with information on our magazine articles, guidebooks and activities in the UK, Norway, North Africa and Jordan, and some photos of us with Queen Noor. Seemingly impressed, they said that was exactly what they were planning and invited us to return, which we did with an international team. As well as the two of us, Paul Seddon from Troll came along to do some cave exploration with his friend Dave Brook, one of Britain's top cavers with some major discoveries to his name. Wilf and Bernard came from France; and Mario Verin, a climber and photographer friend from Italy, together with his girlfriend Verena from Switzerland. We were also joined for some of the time by Mike Searle, a professor of earth sciences at the University of Oxford, focused on the geology of the UAE/Oman ophiolite as well as the Himalaya, Karakoram, Tibet and South East Asia. We were all given a house in Medina near Muscat and three Toyota Land Cruisers plus all expenses, and left to get on with it. Happy days!

45

OMAN ODYSSEY – MUSANDAM TO DHOFAR

We spent three months in Oman in the winter of 1990 as guests of the department of tourism carrying out a 'Survey into the potential of the mountains and deserts for adventure tourism'. We explored 'grand canyons' tumbling from Arabia's highest summits, sometimes forested with ancient junipers, into jewel-like green oases in their deepest fastnesses; we found other mountains less harsh, where ancient villages and forts perch above cascading terraces of pink and white fruit blossom sheltering gardens of vegetables; we travelled through the lunar dunes of Wahiba which roll end-lessly into the blue Arabian Sea, driving for half a day along empty beaches where sand, sea and sky unite in primeval harmony.

We plunged through caves and canyon rivers, abseiling through icy water-falls and swimming in subterranean lakes of gargantuan proportions with the cavern roof squashing our noses close to the water, and winds howling like djinns through narrow passages. We refreshed our memories of the 1,000-metre cliffs of Jebel Misht brooding over the oasis of Al Ain and glowing angrily red as the sun set in the desert. Further north in Musandam, home of the Shihuh people in their lonely mountain eeries, there was a dead leopard strung from a tree. In the south, there were great flocks of flamingoes and the bizarre plants and trees of Dhofar, land of frankincense, inhabited by the desert and mountain Bedouin with their warm and friendly welcome, as well as the Jebali with their warlike reputation; the mind reels with contrasting images. Never again would we think of Oman as just another desert country.

Everywhere apart from a few small military zones was open, and for accommodation out of the cities, as one of our Omani friends told us, 'All of Oman is a hotel!' Only Musandam, which is separated from the rest of Oman by a strip of the United Arab Emirates, posed entry problems that may have been insuperable for most visitors at that time, but we had permits for what proved to be a dramatic fjord-riven, rock-bound isthmus, thrusting into the Strait of Hormuz. We drove the length of the peninsula through narrow canyons and along airy mountain ridges with glimpses of wild Shihuh villages, their stone 'winter houses' perched on distant ramparts in rocky, arid terrain. A shepherd had killed the dead leopard we saw hanging from a tree, its mate had since been heard howling in the mountains. They were two of only a handful of Arabian leopards left in Musandam; sadly now only their ghosts haunt these mountains.

Back in the Muscat area, we travelled around the massifs of Jebel Akhdar and the Eastern Hajar, passing through ancient castelled market towns bustling with all the activity of rural Arabia. We were actually on our way with Paul and Dave to explore a cave we had been told about. Our hosts from the tourism department accompanied us there to show us the location, and we simply slept out in the desert, which they were very concerned about as we were their guests, but finally convinced we were happy, they left us to enjoy the stars. We woke early the next day and were just about to cook breakfast when we heard the noise of an approaching vehicle and their Land Cruiser appeared over the dune. They opened the back and brought out silver tureens of food, a veritable five-star breakfast. Paul was massively impressed. From then on my absences from Troll were christened Howard's Softie Tours.

Breakfast eaten, we entered the cave, crawling along the entry passage on hands and knees before descending into a larger chamber with small stalagtites but no long ongoing passages despite our searches. We were just about finished when Paul said he could hear a drumming sound. Dave reckoned it could be rain, though there had been no sign of it when we went in. We decided to exit quickly, shocked to find a trickle of water in the previously bone-dry entrance passage. When we emerged from the cave mouth, the reason was obvious: it had been raining so heavily there and in the distant mountains that the wadi, which was only just below the entrance, had flooded. The desert beyond the wadi, over which we had driven the previous afternoon, was now a lake extending to the far mountains. Having walked in to test the depth we realised it was too deep to drive through, but our dilemma was soon solved when another Toyota arrived, its driver offering to show us the way round.

Flash floods are notorious in Oman. Mike Searle, who had spent considerable time in the country, mentioned that he had once been bowled over in a Land Rover while crossing a wadi. Although he knew it had rained high in the Akhdar mountains there was no sign of water where he was driving, but just a few metres further on, as he was bumping across the stones of the wadi bed, a flood surged around a bend and rolled his vehicle.

Mike joined us on our Wahiba Desert trip, like us, happy to be back in Bedouin country and driving across its vast and seemingly endless dunes. Sheikh Said bin Jabber bin Hilays was our host: a tall and elegantly charismatic Bedu moving with ease and certainty between the two worlds of the ancient desert ways and modern Oman. The Royal Geographical Society's Wahiba Sands Project, headed by Nigel Winser, had finished its work there just a year previously and Sheikh Said remembered with a happy smile a camel journey with his friend 'Naigi'. We spent a day in his camp, making a journey with camels and finding, as Nigel had indicated in *The Sea of Sands and Mists*, that the Omani Bedouin camel-riding style, perched behind the hump, is not the most comfortable in the world unless you were 'born in the saddle'. The rather more luxurious sheepskin-lined saddle atop the hump – as used by the Jordanian Bedouin – is certainly more forgiving to uninitiates!

Driving south-east through the dunes from the camp of Sheikh Said, the next day was unforgettable, an unearthly landscape unrolling before us. On reaching the distant coast, we passed by an isolated family of Bedouin eking out a living in this wilderness of sea and sand. Where they got their drinking water from, or feed for their goats, I've no idea. Continuing along the deserted coast we passed tracks of foxes and turtles and saw whales and dolphins out at sea. We camped for the night on a beach surrounded by dunes and awoke to a blood-red sun rising from the Arabian Sea.

Had we had time, this coastal four-wheel-drive journey could have been continued through a land of infinite variety virtually the whole of the way to Dhofar in the south. Instead, still with much to do, we took the shortcut out across the southern end of Wahiba to the desert highway and on past the fringe of Thesiger's Empty Quarter to Oman's southern region where, to our surprise, cattle vied with camels for grazing. There, the unexpected and bizarre landscape squashed between the desert and the hostile mountains and canyons varies between that of the Scottish Highlands and the Derbyshire Dales. The plants and wildlife are no less varied on this south-eastern strip of Oman and Arabia which is uniquely caressed by the mists and rains of autumn's monsoons, locally known as the *khareef*. Reaching Salalah, the only town of note on the south coast, I looked around for somewhere to get some torn clothing mended. Finally I found a small Indian shop with someone busy sewing inside and the name of the business over the door: 'Sewerage'. Beyond, the beaches of Dhofar were superb and were then untouched by development, while not far inland, huge caves and giant sinkholes tempted the explorer. Above them, the massive escarpment of Jebel Samhan snaked eastwards like the Great Wall of China, forming a barrier between the harsh interior and the coastal plains, tempting the trekker to follow it for days into a little-known wilderness.

Despite warnings from an ex-SAS guy who was in the area's capital Salalah – keeping an eye on things after frequent Yemeni cross-border skirmishes had stirred up tribal unrest – we fancied a trek through nearby Wadi Darbat.

'I wouldn't go if I were you,' he had said. 'There are Jebali guerrillas up there so it's a bit dodgy.'

But uniquely for Oman it was also said to be green, with lakes and forests; Wilfred Thesiger had been there, and leopards and hyenas were reputed to live there. There were even rumours of limestone cliffs with climbing potential. It sounded far too good and mysterious to miss, so I was keen and Di, who equally enjoys a challenge, was happy to give it a go. So, we left Paul and Dave to go on their cave exploration down the gaping Tawi Atair sinkhole on Jebel Samhan and set off to chance our luck, plunging down from the hills into the forests at the head of the valley, hoping to follow it to the lakes and the sea.

It was difficult going through tangled, thorny trees, but occasional paths led us on. Where the trail climbed steep rocks, claw scratches were evident and some of the bigger tree trunks had deeply incised claw marks made by leopards marking their territory – Darbat and nearby Jebel Samhan are their last retreats. Then we began to pass by overhangs with man-made shelters beneath them; some were well-built stone structures, others just makeshift 'benders' of saplings. Perhaps they were shepherds' bivouacs, or were we in Jebali country? It was all getting very interesting!

We walked on, emerging above a cliff like that in Malham Cove, spanning the valley and blocking forward progress. Forced on to the steep hillside, we lowered ourselves from branch to branch through dense thorn scrub to reach the lower valley that was filled with large boulders, forcing us to jump along them for a considerable distance during which I severely twisted my ankle, making it painful to walk. There was no easy way back now, but having left the boulders we were in a greener, more pleasant world and began to feel more at ease as the coast wasn't too far away. Ahead were the reed-fringed pools where Thesiger had camped 'under great fig-trees'. 'There were mallard and pintail and widgeon and coots' he wrote in his epic *Arabian Sands*, adding, 'that night Musallim shot a striped hyena'. We walked on in eager anticipation. Overhanging cliffs along the valley sides still concealed shelters, but we had seen no one all day; the threat of Jebali guerrillas seemed unfounded until a ringlet-haired character emerged silently from the trees alongside us, AK47 in hand, cartridge bandoliers across his chest.

We've really done it this time, I thought, while simultaneously saying, '*Salaam alaikum*,' with what I hoped was a welcoming smile. I presumed he would understand Arabic although the Jebalis have their own language, but there wasn't much else I could do and 'Peace be unto you' seemed a good start. The next move would indeed be up to him and was totally unexpected.

In immaculate English he replied, 'Do you want a photo?' Well, I did, but what with balancing on one leg due to my bad ankle, and the surprise at meeting this politely spoken 'terrorist', the photo was totally out of focus.

Six hundred miles back north in the Akhdar massif we explored the 5,000-metre-long cave of Hoti which Andy Dunsire, a British expat living in Oman, had told us about. There was a lake inside its lower entrance with blind fish that had been named *Garra dunsirei* after him, following his discovery of them in 1980. Although the lake could be reached directly from the outside by descending a boulder-filled passage, it was fed by a stream which started in a pothole 5,000 metres back up the mountain. The stream entered the lake through a short flooded passage. It would be the biggest cave trip that Di and I had ever done, but we were definitely up for it, even with the sump exit. Then Dave – who was our expert in all things subterranean – said he wasn't sure about the weather and wasn't a good swimmer. He would wait on the lake side of the sump to check us out. I wondered if he was sacrificing his chance to go through the cave in case there was a flash flood and we needed rescuing. Paul however was still up for it, as were Wilf and Di, which left me with my sprained ankle. But how could I miss it? We abseiled in and Paul scampered off down the passage as happy as Tolkien's Gollum.

Di and Wilf were close behind and I hopped along as best I could, calling out a plaintive 'Wait for me!' as they disappeared into the darkness.

We scurried along the 5,000 metres of passages, descending subterranean waterfalls and swimming the lakes, wondering all the time if the weather had broken. If so, we would be trapped in rising floodwater in the cave's last reaches where sticks and grass hung from cracks in its roof. Then, during a long swim with the roof getting increasingly lower until our heads were scraping against it, we heard an unexpected noise. My first thought was rushing water and flooding, but it was the sound of rushing air. Ahead we saw a pinpoint of light through a small hole just above where the roof finally dropped below the surface. Peeping through, head half in the water, it was just possible to see the lake. All we had to do now was dive the sump and we were out, hopefully with Dave at the ready to pull us though if necessary. Which, to my relief, he did. A small rise in the water level would have flooded the cave for 100 metres or more; not a place for the faint of heart. The accessible part of the cave around the lake is now called Al Hoota and is a show cave billed as 'one of the largest cave systems in the world'. I hope our report helped.

Still in a watery mood, we explored the north side of the mountain, descending the great canyons of Bani Awf, which once again involved abseiling down waterfalls and swimming through cold, dark pools – a total anachronism in this hot, dry land. This time however, the trip was less claustrophobic as we could glimpse blue sky between high cliffs. Mario's girlfriend Verena couldn't swim, so she put a large inflated ball in her sack to keep her afloat. It worked when we tried it in Alec's pool, but it wasn't a good plan!

The river emerged from the canyon through an unexpected twisting cave, its dark interior concealing a logjam. Wilf went first with a rope, then Verena next, tied on to his rope with me swimming close behind carrying the spare rope. Verena had real problems in the logs. Her 'float' had forced her face down in the water (why hadn't we thought of that?) and she was drowning. She grabbed me but I was already finding it difficult enough swimming with one hand, carrying a heavy waterlogged rope and trying to push logs out of the way with the other. I went down with Verena clinging on top of me, but fought my way back up shouting at Wilf to pull on Verena's rope. The more we got into the logjam the harder it became and I went down again, this time for longer. Then an arm grabbed me and pulled me up; it was Di. At this point, the logs moved and Verena shot though the water pulled by Wilf. Panic over!

Afterwards, we climbed in the canyons of both the Eastern and Western Hajar where we found some excellent cliffs with one- and two-pitch routes on perfect Omani limestone, which are now popular. We also trekked over trails of ancient rock-hewn 'Persian Steps', sleeping rough at night or camping, or accepting the hospitality of the mountain people, staying in the 'majlis', the communal meeting rooms of the villages. Food was given freely and indeed a journey can stagnate if one accepts every offer of fruit and coffee. Trekking on Jebel Shams, we experienced one of the not infrequent winter storms, which persisted through the second and third days of our journey. Our Bedu companion who was soaked to the skin and shivered through the night by a small fire beneath an overhang was happy. '*Hamdulillah*' – 'Praise be to God,' he said, as the water dripped from his clothes and lightning flickered in the darkness across the unseen cloud-covered desert. His donkey was happy too, its nose in a bag of dates that it ate while cleverly spitting out the stones, followed in the morning by dried fish for breakfast. They also remained happy throughout that day, perhaps because they were heading for home, guiding us miraculously through thick mist in a wet and featureless limestone landscape to his village.

Unbelievably, our time was up. I prepared a 200-page report, sections of it and hundreds of photos and transparencies being contributed by the team. Our route descriptions became part of Alec's guide *Rock Climbing in Oman* and the caving information was used in the *Introduction to the Caves of Oman*. Not long after, Jerry Hadwin made use of our trekking explorations in his book *Adventure Trekking in Oman*. About ten years later I was back out in Oman and pleased to see that our photos were still being used by the Department of Tourism.

Oman is an adventure – don't miss it!

46

EXPLORING EGYPT –
SINAI AND THE RED SEA MOUNTAINS

Dedicated to George William Murray 1885–1966

> He spent forty-five years in the Desert Survey, one of a group of
> dedicated men who spent their best years exploring and mapping
> the Egyptian Deserts … when news of his return to Sinai spread
> from tent to tent, old friends mounted and rode, often several days
> journey to greet him. A tired camel's grumbling protest would
> announce the arrival of a visitor and all were made welcome.
> ***Dare Me to the Desert***, G.W. Murray

In 1987 Di found a book in a second-hand bookshop called *Dare Me to the Desert* by G.W. Murray. We were always poking around in the dusty corners of their travel shelves in the hope of finding ideas for future mountain trips. 'You might like this,' she said when she got home. Its title sounded mildly promising. On opening it the frontispiece had a photo of 'The author at work', though all he was doing was standing with a couple of Bedouin. It was a black and white photo from the 1930s. He looked rather cherubic in a neat short-sleeved shirt and baggy shorts with a Boy Scout-type hat above a chubby face, and his ankle socks were pulled up high and neatly on what looked like legs untouched by the sun. He didn't look at all inspirational.

Nevertheless, flicking through the photos there were numerous tantalising mountain scenes with captions like 'Giant granite pinnacles on Shayib', 'Grim pinnacles that guard the flank of Umm Shomar', and 'The Qattar Range'. The more I read, the more I was fascinated by his mentions of mountains, 'the topmost pinnacle, 5,230 feet high, stands … like a King at chess between two Bishops', or, 'the 2,000 foot cliff stood behind us like a wall', and, 'the bald red summit had been planed smooth as ice … we were ob-liged to venture in bare feet … the top of Chephren's pyramid, still enclosed in its original casing, had not seemed to me so alarming or exposed'. Or mys-terious Elba, the only part of Egypt touched by the monsoon and often cloud covered. It consequently has over 300 species of plants rarely found elsewhere in Egypt and almost never in Europe. To quote Murray, Elba is 'wooded to its summit with dragon's blood trees, acacias and weird euphor-bias, carpeted underfoot with magic plants which heal sword-cuts and harbour the souls of the departed'. And out in the desert is 'the great granite bell of Gebel Sila'i, "Baldpate", a thousand feet high and as sheer and smooth and unclimbable as the Hill of Glass', plus, above the coast, 'the Berenice Bodkin, sharper and more vertical than the Aiguille du Géant', which Murray 'left alone in its austerity'. And if I may mention one more of many in this intriguing book, 'the serrated ridge of Shayib, eight miles long, towered 5,000 feet above us', its highest top 'a monstrous webbed hand of seven smooth fingers, themselves unclimbable'.

There are few words quite as magical as 'unclimbable', but I wondered if he really was a climber until I read his mention of the Aiguille du Géant and other Alpine mountains. I checked with Margaret Ecclestone, the Alpine Club's very helpful librarian who was by now familiar with my unusual requests, and discovered he had not only been an Alpine Club member, but also the director of Egypt's Desert Survey in the 1920s and 1930s. During World War One, 'Joe' as Murray was known, served in the sappers in the Palestine campaign, and won the Military Cross. He was also awarded the Founder's Medal of the Royal Geographical Society (RGS) in 1936 for his Egyptian explorations and, two years later, elected a member of the Institut d'Egypte, of which he was a vice president from 1945–1947. He was elected to the Alpine Club in 1925 on an alpine qualification supported by Tom Longstaff noting that he 'opened in 1923 in the Valais with a number of stan-dard routes on the bigger peaks, as also in 1924. In 1925 he paid a visit to the Dolomites before going to the Valais again (Saas, Zermatt and Arolla) and in later years, in the intervals between climbing seasons in Egypt and Sinai, he returned regularly to his old alpine haunts; in 1928 he and his wife, Edith [née Cairney] were busy in the Mont Blanc range and in the Oberland, where they made the first complete ascent by the south ridge of the Lauter-brunnen Breithorn.' Additionally Edith was 'a noted member of the Ladies' Alpine Club' with many years of Alpine climbing including an ascent of the

Matterhorn on her honeymoon with Murray. She was awarded Life Fellowship of the RGS. He was known to the Bedouin as 'The father of the Ababda', a tribe in southern Egypt, and to quote from the *Alpine Journal* in memoriam files, he and Edith 'were travellers in the Egyptian deserts of almost legendary fame'.

Murray knew his stuff, but more importantly for us it seemed no one had followed in his footsteps in Egypt's Red Sea Mountains or in Sinai, leaving us with a wealth of projects. Where Rum had provided us with around 600 square kilometres of unexplored desert mountains, the Red Sea Mountains that extend for 600 kilometres offered at least ten times that. We were hooked. Di's discovery of that book led to four trips to Egypt and concluded with us in a military jail! We managed to make our first exploratory trip in spring 1988. After a stay with our Bedouin friends in Rum, we set out alone to Sinai. It was something of a pilgrimage, partly out of biblical curiosity, but also a quest for a holy grail of unclimbed rock and mountains.

From Rum not far to the west across the waters of the Red Sea, the mountains of Sinai rose against the same night sky, though looking less hospitable, even less beautiful to our eyes. Even so, they were peaks which had inspired not only Murray, but were also inextricably linked with Old Testament deeds, despite there being no pharaonic records or scientific evidence to support the story of the Exodus. A web search reveals that, though not accepted by Christian and Jewish literalists, 'mainstream history and archaeology now consider the Exodus never to have happened, and the story to be an entirely fictional narrative put together between the 8th and 5th centuries BCE'. As the late Uri Avnery, of Gush Shalom, an Israeli peace activism group, said, 'In spite of all the frantic efforts of a hundred years, no archaeological evidence has been found that there ever was an exodus from Egypt, a conquest of Canaan by the Children of Israel or a kingdom of David and Solomon'. Nevertheless, according to the Old Testament, it was on the summit of a mountain in the heart of Sinai, now named Jebel Musa, that Moses reputedly received the Ten Commandments from God, laying the foundations of Judaism which, followed by Christianity then Islam, altered the course of history forever, inspiring a third of the world's population. This has given impetus to and excuses for many of the world's wars and hatreds both great and small. Similarly, the reputed subsequent sighting by Moses of the 'Promised Land', which is a central tenet of Zionism, has excused Israel's occupation of Palestine.

So it was that, having taken the ferry to Sinai, and reached the top of this 'Mountain of Moses' in the heart of the peninsula, I sat and pondered history and wondered if John Lennon's simple message, 'All you need is love' wasn't a better credo. Moses on the other hand supposedly had no doubts why he was there: we are told he had been called there by God to receive the Ten Commandments. Unlike our visit he had no distractions: there was no small temple on the summit, no church or mosque; no heaps of litter or smell of human defecation in the hot midday sun; no graffiti; no well-worn trail or 'Steps of Repentance' from St Catherine's Monastery below; no monastery either for that matter, just a wild, windswept mountain in the wilderness to whose summit he is said to have climbed alone.

Sadly the peak is now lacking in spiritual grandeur and the way from the monastery is a wide, well-worn scar on the landscape but, hidden on the other side of the mountain to the west is a quieter, less obvious path. From the village of St Catherine's we had noticed a wadi going south into the hills and we walked up on the evening of our arrival to check it out, only to be stopped by a guard from an Egyptian military base at its entrance. We asked for permission to go up the valley, but to no avail – it was forbidden. We had the impression that everything in sight was also forbidden. Indeed we felt sure the guard didn't really know what his job entailed but if he refused access to everywhere he would surely not be failing in his duty. This meant the great 500-metre cliffs of Jebel Raba immediately above our camp were obviously out of bounds, which was a pity as we had hoped to climb there. However, it did seem that we might be able to enter the valley by discreetly approaching up its opposite shoulder and if that worked we could also get some climbing in on the cliffs of Jebel Fara beyond.

As a consequence we set off early next morning and sneaked into the valley, finding a path between crumbling granite boulders, their surface like those in Sudan, shattered by the extremes of desert temperatures. Ahead, a well-tended oasis nestled between the rocks, emerald green and smelling of herbs. Ancient cypress trees, date palms, nut, olive and fig trees cast their shade over the neat, irrigated garden: a jewel in the bare harshness of our surroundings.

Further up the valley we passed the seemingly abandoned Convent of the Forty Martyrs and beyond, the busy farmyard sounds of a Bedouin village coming to life in the morning sun. We continued up the path that rose above it, not wishing to confront its occupants in this apparently forbidden place.

At this point the path split, the lower one winding off up a narrowing rubble-strewn canyon to the west, to the highest summit of Sinai, that of Mount Catherine at 2,642 metres. To this place, so legend goes, the body of St Catherine was 'transported by angels' from Alexandria where she had been tortured on a spiked wheel and then beheaded for her belief in Christianity. *Here we go again*, I thought, continuing my mountaintop meditations on religious idolatry. Our chosen path however led pleasantly and gently up and across the western slopes of Jebel Musa with ever-increasing vistas of the wild surroundings. Curving round the shoulder and over the col to the south, we joined the 'tourist track' below the summit walls. Just beyond this point we met the final rock-hewn 3,000 'Steps of Repentance'. The cutting and laying of these steps which lead almost directly from the monastery to the summit was a self-inflicted task carried out by one of the monks of St Catherine's as a penance, though reaching the top was for us, as I have said, a singularly disenchanting moment and we quickly moved away to more remote rocks where there were fewer disgusting signs and aromas of human presence.

Descending the hill on its more usual side, we passed the small hollow where it is said 'the seventy elders of Israel stood' waiting for Moses to descend from the mountain, and where Elijah hid from the wrath of Jezebel and was fed by the ravens. Down below, now shimmering in the midday heat, the ravens of today flew above the wall of the monastery itself. Built 1,600 years ago, this magnificent fortified hermitage with its medieval walls and streets conceals a macabre ossuary of monks' bones carefully preserved over the centuries and, deep in the gloom, an ancient church. Incense fumes fill the darkness through which an icon of Moses is dimly seen on the far wall, the 'burning bush' flaming behind him against a golden sky, for it was here that the famous apparition supposedly occurred. The monks seemed to have absorbed much of the mystery and serenity of their chosen mountain retreat, smiling with beatific contentment and, hopefully, transcending and coping with the ever-increasing numbers of pilgrims and tourists arriving at their door. We ourselves carried on down the valley after only a brief stay, feeling ourselves intruders in this ancient sanctuary.

Murray's Red Sea Mountains in Egypt's eastern desert were waiting and time was short, so we moved on. Local buses rattled us up to Suez, narrowly avoiding a desert storm and washed-out roads, and on down to mainland Egypt's Red Sea coast. There, we were greeted by three days of stinging sandstorms that eventually obliterated the road and all else from view.

To the west, the cliffs of Jebel Galala were rumoured to hold potential for the climber, the only way in being by tracks leading to yet more monasteries, those of St Paul and St Anthony. Sixteen centuries ago, the 'Desert Fathers' had independently retreated into the desert to a life of ascetic solitude in the caves and canyons of these mountains, in so doing founding the world's oldest Christian monasteries, pre-dating even St Catherine's. The *Vitae Patrum* – a Latin collection of their lives and sayings written in the fourth century now translated in Helen Waddell's book, *The Desert Fathers* – reminds us that, 'inhumanity towards one's self had often its counterpart in an almost divine humanity towards one's neighbour'. My initial interest had been the cliffs, but having read the book I was, more than ever, intrigued. We hitched in for eight miles up a sand-covered desert track to the remote monastery of St Paul during a break in the sandstorm, being given a lift by a Coptic monk driving a battered pickup. We felt the inner glow of contentment in the aura of the monk as we travelled through the barren landscape. The same smile radiated from the face of the monk we met sitting in happy solitude in the shadow of the monastery wall. Their search it seemed was over, while ours continued, as having found no climbable rock in the vicinity, we hitched another lift back down to the coastal road later in the day.

The now increasingly fierce winds quickly turned the sky ochre with sand from the deserts of the Nile and perhaps even further beyond, from the mountains of Tibesti, and, who knows, from the Hoggar and the Atlas Mountains, as the Sahara is the world's biggest desert extending virtually from the Red Sea to the Atlantic, spreading its sandy fingers into every nook and cranny. It's also the world's biggest source of wind-blown sand, and that day we were surrounded by it. Hidden in the whirling dust were some of Egypt's highest peaks – Gharib, Qattar and Shayib, all said by Murray to be of good red granite, and further south the 'aggressive needles of El Farayid', with a huge rock bridge that he said, 'seemed to sway and throb in the wind', and the needle of the Berenice Bodkin, known to the Bedouin as 'El Meibar', a vantage point from the vicinity of which you can't be seen in times of war or danger. Beyond that the fabled cloud-capped and forested Elba Mountains stood guard on the Sudanese border, but unless the sandstorm abated we were going nowhere. We could see nothing, not even the road – even breathing was difficult. The chance of a lift seemed zero. We weren't even sure we could survive long out there but then a car appeared out of the murk less than two metres away from us, crawling along the sand-covered road, its wipers struggling hopelessly to clear the whirling sand from its wind-screen. It stopped! We needed no request to jump in, slamming the doors quickly behind us. 'I take you to Ras Ghareb,' the driver said. It was the first town down the road and suited us fine.

It was a run-down place with a squalid-looking 'hotel'. With no choice, we booked in then dashed out to get some food in a small cafe. When we got back there was a magazine under our door – not a tourist brochure but a porn mag. Was the receptionist or the person in the next room having fanta-sies about Di, I wondered? In the evening someone knocked on the door and invited us for tea in his room – well, nothing ventured nothing gained. Travel is about meeting people, so we accepted his offer. He seemed pleas-ant enough and, chatting away in good English, having noticed I was rub-bing my back he said he had been a physio in London.

'Do you have a problem?' he asked.

'Yes,' I said, 'just an old injury but it's okay.'

'I can fix it for you,' he said.

I very much doubted it, but the Canadian truck driver who had invited me into a vibrating bed with him had turned out to be a genuine guy, so, curious about the unfolding events, I said 'Okay,' stripped to the waist as requested and lay on his bed.

After a few minutes of his physio massage, which was useless, he announced, 'All done, now I massage your wife.'

'No need,' I said, 'my wife has a good back. She's fine.'

'Massage good for lady anyway,' he said, but finally convinced Di wouldn't be taking her blouse off he said he had to go, and showed us the door. So we never got our cup of tea.

Next day with the sandstorm easing we caught a bus down the coast road to Hurghada hoping to get our first look at one of 'Murray's mountains', Jebel Gharib. Its 'beautiful red granite' had not only been climbed by Murray in 1937 but also, so my enquiries had revealed, by a character called James Burton who had gone to Egypt 'as an excuse for not returning home to fulfil his father's wish that he "find himself some gainful employment"' – something I could empathise with. Today's Bedouin doubt that the summit has been climbed by either.

Having found a decent hotel in Hurghada, which was then just a fishing village rather than the tourist resort it is today, and with clearing skies, we tried to contact the Bedouin living near Jebel Shayib, as it wasn't far to the west, but no luck; we found people who could help, but were told we needed permits from the army and they could only be got – if at all – in Cairo. This was particularly frustrating as that meant we were unable even to approach the mountains to see Murray's 'serrated ridge of Shayib'.

Having then failed to get past checkpoints to the south, it wasn't until 1996 that we got permission to return. And I used to think desert climbing wouldn't involve as much bureaucracy and paperwork as Himalayan expeditions …

47

EXPLORING EGYPT – SOME YOU WIN, AND SOME YOU LOSE

By 1996, eight years had passed since our frustrated first visit to Egypt's Red Sea Mountains, but they hadn't been forgotten. Spasmodic correspondence outlining the benefits of adventure tourism to various people using our n.o.m.a.d.s. ID eventually culminated in an offer from the Egyptian Tourism Authority to arrange the necessary permits, but we were still faced with six more months of letter writing, phone calls and visits to their London office before we finally had a firm promise not only of permits but also of sponsorship for a five-week exploratory visit.

We flew out to Cairo with Mick Shaw in keen anticipation of climbing in new mountains. It was a fiasco! It started impressively enough as guests at the Nile Hilton, but the next day we were told that our trip had been cut to six days. How do you explore 370 miles of mountains in six days? Determined to make the best of it we headed south immediately with our off-road vehicle and driver and the necessary permits. Though about 500 miles from Cairo, Murray's 'unclimbable "glass-dome"' and Egypt's 'most aggressive mountains', the Farayids, were our first targets, in particular Murray's rock bridge and another unclimbed top, 'the threatening tip of Berenice Bodkin'.

Beyond Hurghada, checkpoints became increasingly difficult to pass. A day and a half from Cairo, we reached Berenice: our peaks were just beyond in the Nubian Desert, but the officer at the checkpoint was adamant.

'Your permits are no good,' he said.

'Why?' I asked. 'We have military and tourism permits from the tourism authority,' adding, in the forlorn hope of sympathy, 'and we have just driven 500 miles from Cairo.' He wasn't interested. Only after considerable pleading did he relent a little and allow us to drive another twenty-five miles to take a photo of the impressive but still distant needle of the Berenice Bodkin, Murray's 'Aiguille du Géant, rising on the Tropic of Cancer'. Having been instructed that we mustn't even step off the road, and with only four and a half days of our ridiculously short six days left, we then headed immediately back north 190 miles to Hurghada.

Next day, frantic driving through stony deserts left us only sufficient time to photograph Shayib's northern peaks and climb briefly on Qattar's impressive 1,000-metre cliffs of remarkably good rock. It was while there that we made the satisfying discovery that some of Comici's 'missing climbs' were in fact on this mountain and not somewhere in Sinai as had previously been thought.

Using Murray's book, we next visited Roman quarries at Mons Claudianus where the immense and complete but badly cracked 250-tonne 'Mother of Columns' lay in the sand. Had it not cracked, it was to be manhandled sixty miles across the desert to the Nile for shipment to Rome. But at least the quarries gave us some good bouldering in a unique location, using slots that had been cut into the granite for wooden wedges which, had the job been completed, would then have been soaked in water to make them expand and split the stone. As some boulders had been left unsplit, the holes made perfect finger slots.

On our last day, we drove along the foot of Jebel Gharib, but with no time to look around we failed to identify a route to its top, which wasn't surprising as both Murray and Comici had taken two visits to find the way. As we had to be in Cairo that night, that was the end of our explorations. We were a little bit wiser, but had now made two almost abortive trips and hardly touched rock. Now with time to spare, we went climbing in the Sinai mountains around St Catherine's where the exfoliating granite reminded us of Jebel Kassala in Sudan. We had a fun week there, one day taking advantage of some bolted routes close to the monastery, although we felt that bolting single-pitch climbs in these wild hills and in the close proximity of one of Christendom's most ancient and holy places was even more sacrilegious than usual.

Back home, we didn't forget Murray's mountains, and the Berenice Bodkin and the remote Elba Mountains continued to tantalise us. I was determined to return.

48

INCREDIBLE INDIA – THE WESTERN GHATS AND BEYOND

In the winter of 1990 to 1991, Di and I finally succumbed to the lure of India. Our logical destination should have been the Himalaya, but we both fancied seeing India itself. I asked Doug Scott if he knew anything about the Western Ghats, and he put me in touch with Harish Kapadia who sent me some info. The Ghats is a range of hills stretching almost the whole length of the west coast of India. Very few people go there other than to visit the few sites such as the splendid 1,500-year-old rock-carved temples of Ellora and Ajanta north of Pune. We were keen to explore.

We flew to Mumbai, and were greeted by streets of poverty and squalor where the homeless struggled to survive with dignity and cleanliness, on the edge of gutters running with filth. Next day we left by train from the grandiose mock-Gothic splendour of Victoria Station (now the Chhatrapati Shivaji Terminus), to Pune high in the Western Ghats ninety miles to the east. A notice on the window of our ticket kiosk read, 'Freedom fighters and Foreigners' – we were in the right queue!

Pune was a breath of fresh air after Mumbai. Once a hill-station where the British colonials took refuge from the coastal summer heat, it was a typically Indian, chaotically busy market town with a statue of Mahatma Gandhi striding purposefully out above the streets. Below him, vendors, beggars and holy men with tridents, painted faces and dreadlocks, bustled or shuffled around among the barbers, dentists and ear-cleaners plying their trades on the pavement. Pune was then the site of the late Bhagwan Shree Rajneesh's ashram, peopled by hundreds of Westerners seeking spiritual enlightenment through free love and liberation from materialism. The fact that the great guru had previously had a fleet of ninety-three Rolls-Royce cars seemed not to matter. He had also started a commune in Oregon that had collapsed in 1985 after criminal acts including a poison attack on the citizens of Dallas, after which he was arrested and deported. After twenty-one countries denied him entry, he eventually returned to Pune, where he died a couple of years prior to our arrival.

We were trying to catch a bus south to the villages in the distant hills, but failed to get started. Burdened by rucksacks, how do you compete with fifty or more people all trying to jump on to a bus? Especially one that is going past without stopping because it is already so full that people are hanging out of the door? We eventually gave it up as a lost cause and haggled with the driver of an auto-rickshaw to take us on the next leg of our journey. The rickshaw driver probably enjoyed the journey as much as we did, escaping from the bedlam of Pune out into the quiet green of the countryside, past ox carts, well-kept fields, small villages and forested foothills. High above, the fortified summit of Sinhagad, 1,317 metres, the site of the 'Lion Fort', could just be seen and the ascent kept its promise of a hot afternoon trek until we rose above the treeline to enjoy the breezes coming in from the Arabian Sea to the west.

The uphill trail was both well constructed and well worn, zigzagging through woodland and past a small hamlet to the gates of the ancient fort, with a pastoral scene spreading below us reminiscent of the Lake District. From the summit, surrounded by ancient castle walls, more fortified peaks were visible in the blue distance of late afternoon; a wild landscape of hills, lakes and forests, from where the great Marathi leader, Shivaji, had harried both the Moghuls and the British Raj 300 years ago, a master guerrilla fighter in his perfect mountain stronghold.

Within the fortifications, almost on the summit, a natural spring of cold clear water fed a deep pool making the ten kilos of water we had diligently carried up with us superfluous. We bivouacked on the far western battlements, high on a clifftop up which Shivaji's warriors are reputed to have climbed in the night, storming the fort and capturing it from another Marathi chieftain. Legend has it he used lizards to climb the cliffs, dragging ropes behind them. It was a mystical place to spend the night, the sun setting beyond lakes shining amber and red in the black-forested valleys of evening. The panorama was unimpeded by other hills when viewed from this perfect vantage point, the last high summit on this rim of India's Deccan plateau.

We were up with the dawn and refilled our water bottles. Having found the only exit south through the double-walled fortifications, we set off down into the distant valley where an early morning cloud of aromatic wood smoke hung suspended over a patchwork of fields and a small village. Our initial objective was the ridge of hills on the far side of the valley. Without maps we had two choices – a direct line down to the village and up the other side, or contour around the head of the valley along connecting ridges. With the prospect of a brew of chai and some food in the village set against the possibility of having to find a way between cliffs hidden by minor summits on the latter route, we chose the former.

It was an enjoyable descent by small trails winding down to wooded pastures up to which shepherds and cowherds were bringing their animals in the cool of the morning. They greeted us with welcoming smiles, yet looks of puzzlement as it became increasingly obvious that few, if any, Westerners passed this way. Once into the cobbled village streets winding between thatched crofts, we struggled with sign language to locate the local shop or cafe without success, as there wasn't one. The village was virtually self-sufficient, the few extraneous needs being purchased in a larger village far down the valley. This was to pose a real problem since we had planned on buying provisions as we went along and had virtually no food with us.

As the day was growing hotter we carried on up into the next hills hoping to reach the summit ridge by midday, but without a map the simplest of journeys can become quite infuriating. The path was obvious, or so it seemed, but following it led us out across the hillside into steeply sloping hayfields. We staggered up their edges, following the rapidly disappearing track until it stopped at a thorn hedge. Being well committed by this time and feeling complete fools under the puzzled gaze of half a dozen women working in the fields below us, we struggled carefully over the hedge and sweated up the ever-steepening hillside, thistles and burrs clinging to our clothes and tearing at our fingers as we toiled.

As we could see only a few feet ahead through the tall tangled grass we were increasingly concerned about snakes and leopards, which we had been told inhabited the hills, but once out on the shoulder above we found the correct path, wide and obvious. Happy again, we followed it, the panorama now opening out behind us, with last night's fortified summit guarding the horizon to the north. Ahead, the shoulder narrowed and steepened to a ridge at which point the path split: a narrow poorly used one went on upwards winding between small outcrops of rock, while a well-trodden track contoured to the south-west and appeared to be heading towards the col that was our next objective. Why go up and down when you can go across? We took the low road and once again were to regret it.

In the cool dark shadows of the western slope, the path disappeared into dense, shrubby jungle dripping with dew, and eventually vanished completely; it was obviously a cattle track, vanishing to grazing areas on the grasses and leaves of the steeply sloping forest. There was no way on, but it was also too late for us to go back, so we crashed on upwards through the tangle of the jungle, hopefully making so much noise in the process that any self-respecting dangerous wildlife would keep well away. In fact, it wasn't easy to climb through tangled bushes with a rucksack, especially at midday with the Indian sun at its zenith, but it was well worth it to top out on the narrow ridge carpeted with the dry golden grass of autumn.

In the far distance was our next objective – the magnificent mountaintop citadel of Rajgad, its black ramparts already visible. This time we were lucky in our choice of descent: a narrow trail, at first almost inconspicuous, picked its way down between densely wooded bluffs and out on to a long, gently sloping hillside. Cattle grazed in clearings between eucalyptus trees, small children giving us curious looks as we passed by until we eventually reached a village hidden in the trees.

Faces peered from small stone terraced cottages on either side of the single narrow cobbled street.

'Chai?' we asked hopefully.

'No chai,' came the smiling, head-shaking reply. Seemingly nothing was available in this hillside village either, but as we were about to shoulder our sacks and move on we were beckoned into one of the dark houses and given tea and nuts, enjoying the spontaneous smiles of welcome and curiosity that typify village people in remote places the world over.

Refreshed, we thanked them and moved on down the valley, following a maze of interconnecting paths criss-crossing the rice fields. These would, we hoped, take us to the next village partially concealed by more trees on the lower slopes of Rajgad. Crossing a river by stepping stones, we disturbed an old lady searching for edible frogs among the rushes and a young boy poised, thigh deep in the river, spear in hand, waiting patiently for passing fish.

Once at the village we were able to buy a few samosas, the main ingredient of which was chilli, and more chai but nothing else. Beyond, the trail began to rise, still winding between fields, crossing another river then up steep jungle-covered slopes. Passing through small settlements of thatched houses where cattle shared the split-level accommodation, we asked repeatedly for water and were eventually given a cupful from one of the large stone jars stored in recesses. Above the last and highest settlement we managed to locate the well some ten minutes from the village and filled up our almost empty bottles. Water, it seemed, was a precious commodity, the streams all being some distance from the hillside villages, hence everyone's understandable reluctance to give away what they themselves had had to carry from the wells.

We camped in the woods above, small boys from the village making signs indicating that there were dangerous animals, but we had an undisturbed night and left before sunrise for the high peak of Rajgad. A good trail took us up through the trees to greet the dawn on a narrow shoulder high above the valley. The black walls of the fortress loomed above us and monkeys prowled the hillsides and battlements, grimacing and gesticulating as we appeared at the entrance to *their* castle.

Once through the first archway in the outer wall, we scrambled up to the second fortress where a hole in the wall just one metre square, forced a rather ignominious entry on hands and knees – easy prey to any guardian of the gate. Inside, stone steps led up between the battlements to an open area with a huge pool of spring water. Here we met a group of four Indians trekking the fortified ridge of Rajgad: they had spent the night up there knowing, unlike us, of the existence of water which we had once again carried with us.

We carried on towards the main summit still high above at 1,376 metres, reaching it through yet another gateway guarded by a carving of Hanuman, the monkey god, and followed by stone steps cut into the cliff face. On the top itself were more pools cut into the rocks of the summit, and the ruins of ancient buildings looked out in all directions, the battlemented ridges falling away impregnably into the jungle covered hills. While we were descending from the summit fortress, a snake – it looked like a viper – seemed to fall on to the path, rolling sideways with increasing speed towards Di until both she and the snake tumbled, fortunately in opposite directions, off the path and down the hillside. No harm was done, but my laughter wasn't appreciated!

We spent the following hour searching the battlements of the east ridge for an exit to the next valley but without success, the only small gateway in the wall led immediately to a drop over a cliff, the reason for which we learned later in the day. Baffled, we retraced our steps, meeting the Indian trekkers. They too didn't know the way down to Lake Bhatghar but had just met someone who lived in the area and who had come up here to collect flowers and plants for herbal medicines. They introduced us to him, speaking in Marathi, the local dialect. He was a wild-looking character carrying a large bundle of herbs, and he offered to take us to his house where we could spend the night as his guests, after which a friend of his would take us on down to the village by the lake the next morning. Since both men were going in that direction anyway, his fee was only ten rupees. This was not only ridiculously cheap but also solved both the problem of how to get to the lake and what we would eat that night.

The journey started well, following 'Herby' – we never discovered his real name – along a fascinating path contouring below the summit fort, and out on to a narrow multi-battlemented ridge thrusting westwards above the forested hills like the bows of a battleship. Descending through one of the walls a dark spiral staircase ahead exited over a cliff, like the one we had seen earlier: it was a trap for invading forces who, rushing down the steps, would be forced on by those behind to fall over the abyss beyond.

The correct exit lay less obviously on the opposite side down narrow walled passages and through numerous stone arches on to the open hillside beyond. Now in the late afternoon, we carried on down, losing height easily on the ridge, the jungle-covered slopes below separating us from the twisting ribbon of the lake.

We reached our guide's thatched hut on the last knoll of the ridge at dusk and started putting up the tent. At this point, the inevitable problems commenced. With much waving of arms, we got the picture: a rather sly-looking character sitting in the darkness of the hut would take us on down to the lake tonight and Herby wanted his ten rupees now. That, of course, had a number of implications, not least of which being that we obviously wouldn't be eating that night; secondly, that the journey would cost more than the agreed ten rupees since the arrangement made with the help of the Indians was five rupees at the house and five more at the lake. While this was a trivial matter, it also meant we would be descending through the jungle in the dark which didn't sound like fun, especially after what had already been an unexpectedly long day.

Having not eaten anything substantial since dawn we would have preferred to camp and move on in the morning, but our protestations proved to no avail so we paid up and agreed another ten rupees for Mr Sly to show us the way down through the now black jungle. *What's 25p between friends,* we thought. However, no sooner had we descended by an unseen track into the trees and become uncertain of our whereabouts in the darkness than he demanded we pay him his money immediately. He had us over a barrel and knew it, so we paid up knowing it was a bad move.

We stumbled on through the trees marvelling at the night-eyes of our guide as we tripped over roots and boulders or walked into overhanging branches until we eventually reached a drivable dirt track. We felt sure that if we followed it downhill we would reach the lake but Mr Sly wanted another ten rupees for getting us to this point. Feeling there was still a chance of finding a village and perhaps some food before midnight, we decided to be generous and paid him his extra ten baksheesh and fell into his trap.

No sooner had we paid and made moves to set off on our own down the track when more arm waving signified the lake wasn't down the road at all but simply across it and down through the forest. It didn't feel right, but in the middle of the night surrounded by jungle our choices were once again minimal. Feeling sure we were about to be conned yet again, we followed our decidedly cunning companion down into the trees. Some fifteen minutes later we emerged into a muddy clearing by some thatched huts: no lakeside village tonight. We pitched our tent while curious faces peered from smoke-filled doorways in the darkness. No hillside hospitality here: a bowl of warm milk was offered at a highly unrealistic price which we refused on principle, sliding into the luxury of our sleeping bags and tucking into our remaining biscuits and water after a fifteen-hour day.

I told Di to get some sleep while I stayed awake for a while since people were obviously prowling around, but Di told me in the morning I fell asleep immediately. While we were repacking next day, someone ran off with a cup and a major row ensued before it was recovered. Mr Sly then emerged and after insisting on yet another ten rupees took us back up the hill to the track we had been on the night before. The way on was of course down the road.

He stayed with us all the way along the track, through the village – no shops for breakfast – and down to the lake where a small group was gathering on the hillside, waiting for the morning boat. Another ten rupees was demanded; this was getting ridiculous – the sum involved was irrelevant but the principle was important – we argued, a crowd gathered and we partially succumbed to the pressure paying a begrudged five rupees to a disgruntled

Mr Sly. Feeling well and truly conned but having completed a memorable trek through a fascinating and seldom-visited part of India, it was with a mixture of relief and sadness that we saw the small ferry appear in the misty distance of early morning.

Returning to Mumbai six weeks later having circumnavigated India via Goa, Hampi, Kerala, Varanasi, Khajuraho, the Taj Mahal, Rajasthan, Pushkar and several other now overdeveloped tourist ticks, we got chatting to an Indian guy at a bus stop. He asked in perfect English with a distinct Lancashire accent, 'Are you from England?'

'Yes,' I said, pre-empting his likely next question by adding, 'not far from Manchester.'

'Me too,' he said. 'I live in Oldham but I'm visiting my family here. How do you like India?'

'We love it,' we said. 'It's a fascinating country. We've been here for two months. It's so varied, there are so many different cultures and the people have been so nice.'

'I can't stand it,' he said. 'I've been here two weeks, and I can't wait to get back to Oldham.'

49

INCREDIBLE INDIA – LADAKH AND BEYOND

In 1993, Mike Searle mentioned he was off to the Himalaya again. He's always off to the Himalaya! Twenty years later, his book *Colliding Continents* was published. It's a masterful blend of geology and adventure during a lifetime of exploration on the roof of the world. He asked if we would like to join him, Ben Stephenson – a PhD student of his, and some other Oxford University geologists on a trip to Ladakh and the mountains around Zanskar.

We left in August heading out in a hired bus from Delhi to Manali in the Kulu Valley, 'the Valley of the Gods'.

The journey over the Himalaya from the Kulu Valley to Ladakh isn't your average bus journey. The rough and winding road crosses numerous 5,000-metre passes and reaches an altitude of 5,317 metres at the Taglang La with its sun-bleached, wind-shredded prayer flags. Just a few days prior to that, we had been in Delhi, which isn't too far above sea level. When the bus finally wheezed over the top of the pass, the engine had been struggling for most of the last three days, coughing out unburnt diesel fumes through numerous holes in the floor. Everyone had headaches. Most of us were sick. Even so, we didn't envy a gang of Bihari road workers, toiling with a Dante's inferno of yellow-flamed barrels of burning tar while continually breathing in black smoke. The air was black. Their clothes and nearby camp were black. It was a vision of hell, but as we passed, white-toothed cheery smiles lit their tar-smeared faces.

The scenery was magnificent. We had left the forested gorge of Kulu behind to rise up past herds of bleating sheep and goats, and vehicles trapped in mud slides, finally reaching the wide-open spaces of the Himalayan plateau. Dwarfed by vast distances and high mountains, scattered yak herders and the occasional nomadic tent were visible on the horizon. By the roadside, other rosy-cheeked Tibetans supplemented their income by offering food and accommodation in their well-kept parachute tents.

Going down the other side, the bus – and we – breathed more easily. The air was clean and fresh. We passed by flower-dotted green meadows on the banks of foaming rivers. Buddhist monasteries rose from rocky hills beneath a backdrop of snow-capped summits. Above the narrow cobbled streets of Ladakh's old capital, Leh, welcoming strings of prayer flags flew from the stone turrets of Sankar Gompa, sending out their benevolent message, 'May all beings have happiness and the causes of happiness. May they all be free from suffering and the causes of suffering.' We were in one of the last refuges of Tibetan Buddhism.

Well acclimatised by our journey to the thin air of Leh at 3,500 metres, it nevertheless took a day to clear our lungs of diesel fumes while appreciating the simple joys of taking it easy, eating well and walking in the nearby hills to Leh Palace and Soma Gompa. Mani walls with their delicately carved ancient Buddhist prayers lined the paths, protecting the walker and the villages from evil spirits. Prayer wheels, turned by sparkling streams, spun eternal prayers for the benefit of all sentient beings into the skies: 'Om mane padme hum.'

The next day was a festival. The town was vibrant with sound and colour. Old men from the mountains, sporting jaunty hats above richly tanned faces like gnarled oak, greeted us with warm smiles. Wrinkled old women and pretty, fresh-faced young girls came in from the villages and mountain pastures wearing thick sheepskins and traditional dress including increasingly rare hats and necklaces full of turquoise stones. Youths in their finery were laughing together, ready for the dances. Monks in their plum-coloured robes chatted together. Drumming and the sound of temple horns echoed their shrill or sometimes reverberating sepulchral notes around the valley as the dancers ebbed and flowed, entertaining the watching crowds. There were few outside visitors; flights were not easy to get and the 250-mile road up from Kashmir was little used by tourists due to its ongoing border and independence struggles. Alternatively, the high road from Kulu, as we had discovered, has its own idiosyncrasies.

In the evening, we walked up to nearby Sankar Gompa with its image of Avalokiteśvara, the personification of compassion, a bodhisattva dedicated to helping all sentient beings to be free of suffering with a thousand helping hands of compassion coupled with the eyes of wisdom in each palm. We sat on the wooden balcony while stars came out over Leh, and watched the sunset glow on the snowy 6,121-metre peak of Stok Kangri as shadows slid rapidly up its lower slopes.

We took the local bus up the valley to the point where a rough track sneaked into the mountains, leading to the hidden and ancient monastery of Hemis Gompa. It was a pleasant walk, ideal for testing legs and lungs in the high, clear mountain air. Eventually, the track narrowed to a stony trail between mani walls as we entered the village of Hemis above which the gompa merged with the cliffs. Inside it was dark; incense drifted through the rooms and corridors; monks chanted sonorously and repetitively in front of ancient thangkas and mandalas, or sat in quiet contemplation.

Back outside, the path led us up into a ravine where hermitages perched among the cliffs. Higher still, from the rocky ridge crowning the main gompa the mountains of Tibet were visible across the valley.

We spent the night in Hemis village, enjoying happy hospitality in a small but immaculately clean house where copper pans gleamed with pride on the kitchen wall. In the cool of the mountain-shadowed dawn we left the monks to their incantations and walked back down to the road where we waited among green fields for the bus. When it finally arrived, it wasn't too much of a surprise to see that it was full, but it stopped and Di squeezed in leaving me to leap on to the back where a few young lads were hanging on and enjoying the bumpy ride.

Halfway down the valley the classic hilltop monastery of Thikse proved irresistible. We jumped off and wandered up the many steps to experience once more the now-familiar quiet peace of these time-worn holy places. Within the gloom, a magnificent gold-leaf covered statue, once again depicting Avalokiteśvara, smiled serenely down. On the steps outside, some young monks chatted idly; beneath, in the green irrigated valley, farm workers were returning home. It was time for us to continue our walk down the valley and back to Leh.

In the morning, feeling fit and relaxed, we walked up to Leh Palace, home of the ancient kings of Ladakh, passing giant mani walls. Then it was time to go. Mike and Ben were heading down to Kargil en route to the Suru Valley in Zanskar as Mike had a project over there. We left the remote valley of Ladakh reluctantly. Its tranquillity seemed too precious to lose and was emphasised when, having crossed the barren Fatu La and Namika La passes, both around 4,000 metres, we descended to Kargil with its rain, mud, litter and ceaseless heavy trucks pumping out diesel fumes into the thin air. It was also a time of festivities, though a startling contrast to Leh. Mike had been there previously during the festival of Ashura when Shia Muslims whip themselves with spiked chains until their backs are red with blood to commemorate the martyrdom of the grandson of the prophet Muhammad at the Battle of Karbala in AD 680. It was a polluted and noisy town and it was good to leave the next day in jeeps, and to head back up into the mountains past the snow-capped peak of Nun, the highest peak in the Zanskar massif at 7,135 metres.

We left the jeeps to cross the fast-flowing Suru River by a cable. Having heaped all the sacks by the riverside I asked Mike what the plan was. 'Well, you're the expert,' he said, 'you work at Troll.' How that made me an expert in Himalayan river crossings I'm not sure. Once across we camped a short way upstream to wait for two more friends of Mike who were coming up the valley with horses to join us. I knew Micky Fox as he worked for Black Diamond so we had met at trade shows. Cathy Speakman had come out with him as she was on her way to Nepal to visit the place where her boyfriend, Mark Miller, had been killed in a plane crash on the approach to Kathmandu the previous year.

Sitting round the campfire as dinner was being made in the evening, a bunch of Bakarwal nomad shepherds turned up, a couple of them stopping to squat by the fire and enjoy some chai and chapatis with us. I have to say they were dodgy-looking characters, big men with beards, hennaed hair and shifty eyes glancing around our tents and their contents. We obviously had considerably more material possessions than they did, and already knew that a couple of trekkers had been stoned to death in their tent before being robbed not far from here the previous year. Rightly or wrongly the Bakarwal had been blamed so, perhaps unfairly, we were wary of them. Eventually they moved on, out of sight, presumably on their annual migration between the high mountains and the Kashmir Valley. They were nowhere to be seen the next day when we stashed our gear on the horses and trekked alongside the river and across the fast side rivers as we headed further into the mountains to within view of the hilltop Rangdum Gompa across the Suru Valley.

That night, Di and I camped with the porters as they were good to be with and the fire was nearby. The others camped some distance away by a lake, being disturbed before dawn by hands reaching into their tents stealing any loose items. As they shouted, they heard the sound of horses heading off down the valley. Not only had they lost some of their gear, but some of the horses had been stolen. It was the first time Mike had been robbed in twenty-eight years of Himalayan exploration. We gave the horsemen a note for the police and they set off back down the valley with the remaining animals. Mike's plans were then thwarted by the weather. He had hoped to traverse to the south side of the Himalaya as part of Ben's project, and in so doing also see if there was a way through to the Ravi River, but next day it was raining and the cloud was down. We made a brief attempt at exploring the glacier, but it was almost zero visibility, and as it was unmapped it was not only dangerous but pointless carrying on as Mike and Ben were unable to do any work. Disappointed, we packed our bags and with no improvement the next day made our way back to the river. Though it was still in spate we had no option but to cross it hand in hand, before making our way up to the Zanskar road and hitching back down to the first village. There, we checked in with the police who said they had caught the thieves but retrieved nothing. We were ushered into an almost windowless and consequently dark room where a cluster of identically bearded henna-haired men were stood. 'Are these the men who robbed you?' we were asked.

Well, how could we say? We didn't even want to say. If we accused any, it would have to be all, and how could we know if they were the men? They would undoubtedly have been jailed for who knows how long, causing untold difficulties for their wives and children. So we said we didn't know. The police weren't happy, but if the accused men actually were the robbers I hope they appreciated what we did for them.

Next day we made our way back down to Kargil then on to Kashmir and Srinagar where Mike knew the owner of the Rolex houseboat on Lake Dal. And what a luxurious place that was to spend a few days, even if we could hear machine gun fire in the night, presumably from the ongoing separatist insurrection.

Moving on entailed catching a bus and they were being targeted by 'terrorists' who had stopped some and shot the passengers. Not a nice thought, but needs must. Di and I had planned to do a trek through the seldom-frequented Chenab River valley on our way to Dharamsala, home to Tibetan Buddhist refugees and the Dalai Lama. Having reached Srinagar earlier than expected the others decided to join us, though Ben would have to leave after a few days. The two-day bus journey was, I'm happy to say, problem free, though on the second day as we drove on an increasingly narrow road sliced into the vertical cliffs of a deep gorge with the river far below, it was scary to see the outside rear wheel regularly leave the road and hang suspended over the drop as we went round tight bends. Best not to look!

Arriving in Atholi, starting point for the trek to Cerro Kishtwar, we were surrounded by young lads wanting jobs as porters, which suited us fine as we were able to leave immediately for the village of Shol.

Having spent most of the previous day geologising with Mike, Ben set off back the next morning leaving us to walk in incessant rain to Darwas where we were given a grubby room for the night, piled high with lumpy sacks and plastic bottles on which we tried to sleep. Luckily, by morning the weather had cleared and the trail continued along a spectacular narrow ledge halfway up a cliff to reach a nice camping spot down by the river. The next day was the crux of the trek: a nine-hour day up over the snow-covered Sach Pass at 4,420 metres, beyond which a lonely Tibetan camp served very welcome chapatis, dhal and chai. We camped close by, and having eaten well again, continued next day down a long and beautiful forested valley to a rest house where a double bed collapsed beneath four of us in the night.

A short walk and a bus ride then took us down to Chamba where we found a small hotel. When Di pulled the bedcover back, hundreds of fleas were revealed, jumping up in the air. I shouted down to the receptionist who came up, brushed his hand across the bedsheet a few times saying, 'All gone now sir, no problem'. We slept in our sleeping bags worrying that the fleas might join us as permanent travelling companions. The others left the next day; their time was up, but we still had plans. Two days later we were in Dharamsala where we spent most of the morning eating 'Lonely Planet' food: eggs on toast, banana pancakes, apple pies and German cakes, washed down with lemon tea and milky coffee. We stayed around town for a few days soaking in the Tibetan culture and hiding from violent and impressive thunderstorms before returning to the Kulu Valley for a final trek over the mountains to see the Manikaran Spires.

The start was a real uphill slog, climbing steeply and ceaselessly for six hours to a high ridge which not only had superb sunset views over the Himalaya, but also a small spring which solved the water situation.

Two Norwegian lads arrived just as it was getting dark.

'Can we pitch our tent here?' one of them asked, taking his sack off.

Why do people do that? They had the *whole* mountain to go at but they pitched up just a few feet from us. They talked loudly and endlessly in Norwegian into the night until I shouted in Norwegian, '*HOLD KJEFT!*' – 'SHUT UP!' It seemed to do the trick.

We woke to find thick frost on the tent, making for an early but chilly start the next day up to and over the 3,600-metre Chanderkhani Pass, beautifully located with a great view of the Manikaran Spires, before descending to the village of Malana, its location said to have been chosen by the Hindu god Shiva as a secluded place, full of nature's bounty.

It's an ancient and idyllic village with richly decorated wooden houses and a large Shiva temple, but visitors are considered untouchable and have to use specific paths without touching any of the walls, houses, plants or people otherwise there is a penalty requiring payment for the sacrificial slaughter of a lamb to purify the object touched. Being a Shiva village, our approach path went through fields of head-high marijuana, bunches of which were hanging to dry from all the balconies of the houses, where children sat outside rubbing and rolling the leaves and flower heads into a paste for hashish. It's consequently a hippy Mecca and the special guest-houses set aside for visitors were full of stoned-out oddballs incapable of speech, sitting or lying in a haze of hash smoke. Luckily we found an empty room to sleep in before moving on down to Jari and up to Manikaran for a night then back down to the Kulu Valley. At breakfast we asked for fried eggs only to be told after half an hour they had no fried eggs but could make boiled eggs. There's nowhere quite like India!

50

EXPLORING ETHIOPIA – THE ROOF OF AFRICA

Most of the Europeans who were lucky enough to return from
Ethiopia wrote wondrous accounts of the mountain empire, and
gradually the name of Ethiopia or Abyssinia became synonymous
with beauty, danger, solitude and mystery. Often the lure of such
places operates subconsciously. Then one fine morning the traveller
wakes and surprises himself by saying – 'I'm going to Ethiopia'.

In Ethiopia with a Mule, **Dervla Murphy**

We had first enquired about visiting Ethiopia in the late 1970s but Meng-istu's Marxist government had been in power since 1974 having ousted Emperor Haile Selassie, reputed descendent of King Solomon. It wasn't a good time to go. Wilfred Thesiger had written to me saying, 'The country is dominated by bloodstained thugs'. I also had a letter from Duncan Forbes, author of *The Heart of Ethiopia* confirming my suspicions that, 'there is certainly a lot of rock-climbing potential, much of it never approached', but going on to say 'the country is not only under communist control, but virtually at war', and 'Sudanese Muslims are knocking Christians about in the south'. He finished by saying, 'You will have a hard time getting permits … and even if you do you could be in danger of being mistaken for a Cuban by the Eritrean Liberation Front'. He was right: getting permission was fraught with bureaucratic obstacles, and our continuing quest for information revealed that people were living in fear of murder, torture and rape.

In 1987 Thesiger published his autobiography, *The Life of My Choice*, which revealed a different picture of the country. Anyone reading the enthralling tales of his early days in ancient Ethiopia (then called Abyssinia and incorporating Eritrea) and the pageantry of Haile Selassie's coronation will be aware of a rich country of great ethnic, cultural and geographical diversity. Known as the 'Roof of Africa', the land sweeps up from the Great Rift Valley to culminate on the windswept 4,550-metre summit of Ras Dashen; enough to tempt any lover of wild and mysterious mountain places. But the Marxist regime remained in power until the end of 1991, when the northern province of Eritrea separated and became independent. Our plans to visit Ethiopia remained dormant.

Then, in October 1995, the year we sold Troll, and with another proposed climbing trip to Egypt's forbidden Red Sea Mountains having yet again fallen through, I pulled our big *Times World Atlas* down off the shelf. Ethiopia and Eritrea were the only two countries we hadn't been to in North Africa. Eritrea was still a dodgy area, so, like Dervla Murphy, we surprised ourselves by saying 'We're going to Ethiopia'. It seemed to be just our scene: a vast and varied land with its myriad tribal peoples, its ancient cultures, big mountains and hopefully a chance of finding unclimbed rock. Ras Dashen was then given as 4,620 metres, though it has since been relegated to 4,550 metres –the tenth-highest mountain in Africa.

We flew out to Addis Ababa and a few days later, after an inexpensive flight in a small eighteen-seater plane doing in a few hours what would have taken days on dirt roads in a rattling bus, we were wandering through wooded hills to the fabled Blue Nile Falls. Just eighteen miles from the source of the river at Lake Tana, the 400-metre-wide smoothly flowing river abruptly plunges forty-five metres into a narrow transverse ravine. Down at the foot of the falls, the air was filled with the roar of water, a fine refreshing spray covering us and creating rainbows against the blue sky. We revelled in the exuberant excess of elemental colour, light and sound, and felt at last we had arrived in Ethiopia. From Lake Tana we travelled north by bus, with all the usual hassles that entails, to Gondar, over 2,000 metres up in the mountains and once the castellated home of the ancient kings of Abyssinia, which, in another atrocity of war, was bombed by the British in November 1941 as it was the last hideaway of Mussolini's Italians in East Africa. Fortunately the ancient walls withstood the attack. Standing on the turrets looking northwards towards the high Simiens was a magic moment.

From there we once again submitted ourselves to the early morning ritual of 'the battle of the bus', travelling north again across rolling country to Debark in the foothills of the mountains. Here we made arrangements for the compulsory guide, gun-toting guard and mule-man, the minimum permitted entourage for travel in the Simiens, along with a pack pony and a riding mule. Our guide provided his own horse, and the whole deal, food included, worked out at less than £10 per day each for two of us.

Our team were an amiable lot: Muhammad – 'The guide with the wrinkled leg', as the Simien mountain park officer described him rather cruelly – despite his slight limp caused by a childhood hospital accident was as nimble of foot as he was of mind, always thinking ahead and going out of his way to ensure our journey was not only successful but enjoyable. Naga the mule-man was young and quietly efficient, and Brahanu the armed guard – who was the eldest of the three but with a tireless, easy gait ending each day as fresh as he started – was constantly solicitous of Di's wellbeing; a true gentleman.

We loaded up the following morning eager to be walking into high mountains and a new adventure. The temperature was pleasant with the cool breeze of early morning carrying birdsong and the earthy, spicy smells of an African hill market town. Ahead a few heavy clouds clung somewhat ominously to the distant tops, though not enough to darken the day or our high spirits as we walked briskly across the rolling hills carpeted in purple thyme. Small settlements of thatched tukuls and plantations of quick-growing eucalyptus dotted the hillsides. The eucalyptus had been imported from Australia in a last-ditch effort to stop total deforestation of indigenous trees for firewood.

We rose easily up into the hills on tracks well used by the highland people going to market with their livestock and crops from the high 'ambas'. These vast stepped plateaux are typical of the region, Ras Dashen and its environs being the result of a huge basaltic lava upthrust on the western edge of the Great Rift Valley some forty million years ago.

Having reached a small village six miles from Debark and about 300 metres higher, we stopped at a tukul where freshly roasted green beans and coffee were prepared for us on the fire. The smoke-blackened thatch and rafters were hung with gourds and simple wooden tools worn to a rich shiny amber by hard-working hands. The communal bed was a simple straw-covered platform suspended over the warmth of the stable at the side of the entrance. Our hostess, squatting by the fire with a child slung contentedly on her back in a homespun cotton shawl, was friendly and welcoming; it was great to be back home among mountain people.

We recommenced our journey rising ever higher until we crested a top, abruptly and unexpectedly reaching the edge of the great north-facing escarpment. This extends almost thirty miles and plunges over a thousand metres to the so-called 'lowlands', which are themselves more than 2,000 metres above sea level. The panorama was magnificent, the partially forested cliffs plunging down to the rolling foothills, a patchwork of crops and thatched villages extending to the far horizon with the blue-hazed towering remnants of volcanic cores standing sentinel over the landscape.

We camped a little further on at Sankaber on a high ridge sheltered by six-metre-high heather trees trailing long grey-green moss beards in the breeze. Shafts of cloud highlighted by the setting sun radiated out across the upturned dome of the sky from horizon to horizon in a bizarre atmospheric effect. Soon after the tents were up, Muhammad had the chai ready, rapidly followed by 'doro-wat', a spicy chicken stew. With eighteen miles behind us we slept well despite the sudden onslaught of heavy rain in the early hours of the morning.

We continued our journey riding the spare mule occasionally and eating freshly picked peas, beans and wheat handed to us by people working in the fields despite their poverty and our refusals. The crops extended as far as the eye could see, almost to an altitude of 4,000 metres, and often on land so steep it is difficult for the ploughman and ox to stand. Sadly, this, coupled with population growth, is inevitably leading to considerable erosion problems causing land loss and the need to plough ever higher and steeper ground; a tragic vicious circle that the Simien park officials are trying to combat by teaching the art and necessity of terracing.

With such perennial toil where every plant is hand nurtured and vital, and where the people, otherwise, have so little, one wonders at the generosity of giving handfuls of fresh grain or armfuls of bean shoots to passing strangers who obviously have so much more in the material world. In our own society where we place such great emphasis on eliminating toil and maximising profit, the farmer with his mechanised lifestyle and multi-acres of flat arable land would perhaps be less eager to give armfuls of his crop away to passing strangers.

Up in the high Simiens, the overwhelming polite, friendly hospitality seems, as yet, untainted either by the sometimes degenerate side effects of relief aid, or by tourism and its inevitable commercial overtones. The urban children's mantras of 'Mr, money', or 'Mr, pen', or the incessant chanting of 'You, you, you, you … ' are rarely heard in the mountain villages. The latter refrain allegedly originated with Cuban soldiers billeted in various parts of Ethiopia during Mengistu days. Their frequent commands of 'You! Come here', 'You! Do this', had left its legacy, but up in the mountains the traditions of hospitality were still strong. We walked on our way munching happily on peas and beans.

The track descended to a river that could be seen plunging over the abyss a little further down the valley then a steep climb followed to the higher village of Geech where we camped in the late afternoon. Muhammad worked miracles with the evening meal and the locals again treated us to the coffee ceremony and some home-brewed 'tella' – wheat beer as thick as mushroom soup and still fermenting, but cold, bitter and refreshing.

The following day was what Muhammad called 'a day of rest' which actually entailed an easy five-hour stroll among yet more unique and spectacular scenery. We wandered up a gradually rising slope of moorland which, were it not for the giant lobelia, would have passed at a glance for the moors of our home in the Peak District. Here again we emerged on the edge of the high amba, this time at the famous Geech Abyss on the rim of an amphitheatre of cliffs plunging over a thousand metres down to the gentler farmland. We were lucky to see two families of the rare Walia ibex on the cliffs – endemic to the area, less than 200 remain.

Birdlife was abundant. Vultures, buzzards, kites, eagles and lammergeiers nested on the cliffs and cruised the thermals. Takazze sunbirds fed on the flowering giant lobelia and red-hot poker plants and a myriad of smaller, frequently colourful birds darted among the rocks and grasses.

We lunched on the crest of the abyss, on the summit of Imet Gogo at 3,926 metres before strolling further along the edge of the escarpment to find ourselves among a troop of hundreds of gelada baboons. Busily tearing up grass roots and chattering away among themselves, they were, for the most part, unconcerned by our presence, except perhaps for the watchful large lion-like males protecting their harems. Occasional squabbles would burst into frenzied chases and fights with fierce grimaces and fang displays, but all subsided equally quickly as dominance was re-established.

This was a great day out and more village hospitality was followed by an early night, which was just as well as more heavy rain came just after sunset. To our amazement our old tent survived yet again and we awoke to blue skies, a thick covering of ice on the flysheet and a heavy frost on the ground. At this altitude wood is a precious commodity and the few glowing embers of the fire on which our coffee was prepared did little to warm the ragged half-naked occupants of the tukul, making us uncomfortably aware of the harshness of the environment and the poverty of the people among whom we sat, embarrassed by the luxury of our fleece jackets.

Another 'easy' day took us over rolling hills to the campsite at Chenek, perched on the very edge of the abyss. Like Sankaber this had been an official park campsite with stone buildings for visitors. Unfortunately their use by freedom fighters had led to bombing and strafing by Soviet MiGs and all are now destroyed. The few standing walls did however provide shelter from the icy wind that swept up the narrowing valley. Otherwise, the night was undisturbed and within half an hour of sunrise we were off on a crucial day, the crossing of Buahit, a 4,430-metre summit barring the way to Ras Dashen.

The climb up was pleasant and surprisingly easy. We arrived at a little saddle just under the top and Muhammad surprised us with potatoes and eggs gleaned from one of the villages the previous day and cooked while we were sleeping. The summit of Ras Dashen – which we hoped to reach the next day – still looked a disturbingly long way away in the heat haze, and we were not too keen on the prospect of having to descend 1,500 metres down a steep and rocky hillside to get to the foot of the objective.

I had already been very impressed by the footwork of our equine companions on difficult terrain but had generally opted out from riding except, as I said to Di, 'for the hell of it'. Di, on the other hand, was very much into it and thought nothing of traversing on a horse along a line of footholds across a crag for which I couldn't justify using the term 'ledge', or of ascending and descending small cliffs on horseback. I chose to scramble down, and as we descended the temperature rose and the vegetation became more tropical, until we were walking down pathways hedged with giant flowering cacti, lavender, aloe and other exotic flowering plants.

Having crossed the river in the valley bottom in mid-afternoon, we climbed up another 500 metres following a side valley to the small settlement of Amiko on the slopes of Ras Dashen. In a large tukul almost hidden by trees, the chanting and drumming of an ancient Ethiopian church ritual reminded us of Buddhist ceremonies in the high Himalaya.

We left at dawn, disturbing an African wildcat on the prowl. As we climbed up the frosted path to the head of the valley, blue smoke was rising through the thatched roofs to the highest settlements as the highland farmers warmed themselves by the embers of their fires, wrapped in their woven cotton 'shammas', drinking chai and eating heavy hunks of unleavened 'dabo' bread before starting the day's work. We met the sun just before we crested the first shoulder, enjoying its welcome warmth as we contoured ridge after ridge to scramble up to the final plateau at 4,400 metres. Even up here a few small shepherd boys dressed in sheepskin rags and thick woollen hats were looking after their livestock, calling and singing to each other across the vast sky-filled emptiness of this final high amba.

Summits are always magical places to linger on. We relished Ras Dashen to the full and stayed as long as Muhammad would allow before starting our journey back down to the campsite. Two more long days followed, back over Buahit and down to Debark the short way, breaking the journey in villages, one of which had a huge, almost palatial, tukul fifteen metres in diameter and with ancient carved wooden furniture around the fire; it was an inspiring place to spend our last night.

For the next few weeks we travelled by local transport around the rest of the highlands. The first bus we took was stuffed with guns beneath the seats. On another we crossed a high pass; winding slowly up the hairpins we crawled past another bus, its back half hanging precariously, balanced over the drop like the closing scene in *The Italian Job*. We visited the twelfth-century churches of Lalibela, the remote centre of Ethiopian Christianity, which are concealed below ground, hidden from prying eyes, and carved out of solid rock like the temples of Ellora in India's Western Ghats. They are decorated with murals, many ancient and blackened by incense, including a depiction of St George slaying the dragon. On holy days, incense and the chanting of priests permeates the air.

Moving on, we wandered through Axum, once capital of the ancient Axumite Empire – legendary land of the Queen of Sheba. There, the church of St Mary of Zion is home, so it is claimed, to the Ark of the Covenant. Only the guardian of the ark is allowed to see it and no one has ever been permitted to check its authenticity. This legendary, many say mythical, artefact was reputedly made about 3,000 years ago by the Israelites to house the stone tablets on which the Ten Commandments were written. Biblical accounts describe it as made of gold-plated wood, crowned with two large, golden angels, but between 597 and 586 BC, when the Babylonian Empire conquered the Israelites, the ark vanished from history.

We were always hunting for climbable rock on our trips, though we had no gear with us as we had decided before starting to concentrate on enjoying the country while making it a climbing recce. We had learnt years ago that it's difficult to travel and trek with sacks loaded with climbing gear, especially when it might not be needed. So far, we hadn't seen any cliffs worth climbing in the region of Ras Dashen other than the small summit cliff, which we enjoyed. There was plenty of rock, but it was overgrown and home to gelada baboons.

With rock in mind, we also trekked out for a closer look at some impressive basalt domes and towers that seemed to offer opportunities for climbing near the 2,700-year-old ruins of Yeha, and further east in Tigray, where we spotted sandstone towers west of the Mekele road. Not long after our trip, and using our information, Andre Hedger climbed in these areas and reported good routes, followed later by Pat Littlejohn and Steve Sustad who climbed on the 'Arizona style' sandstone towers of Tigray twenty-five miles north-west of Mekele. They climbed three towers over eight days in traditional 'adventure' style, up to E5 6a.

Having at least found rock, if not touched it, we continued through the villages and towns of Tigray along the eastern fringe of the highlands where Afar nomads come with their camels carrying salt from the sun-scorched salt lakes of the Danakil Desert, one of the lowest and hottest places on earth. Thesiger had been one of the first Europeans to explore the area, despite the Afar having a reputation for castrating intruders.

From there we journeyed out by train on the 600-mile single-track railway to the holy Muslim city of Harar close to the Djibouti border on the northern edge of the Ogaden in Somalia. Hyenas yelped and howled beneath our window at night having been welcomed into the walled city and fed as part of an ancient custom. On our return we had a bizarre journey with trouser smugglers (!) being chased wildly up and down the carriages by the police. We couldn't help but wonder: *how much profit is there in smuggled trousers?*

Finally we went south past the rolling Bale Mountains following the Great Rift Valley with its forests, savannahs, lakes, amazing birdlife and myriad tribal peoples. Having been told there were crocodiles in one river we went along for a look, walking through deep grass along the edge of a high riverbank, but we saw nothing. Then, alarmingly, and just as I was in the midst of suggesting we turn back, a three-metre croc lunged from the grass just in front of me, almost knocking me into the river with its tail as it plunged down into the water. We went back, keeping further from the edge while being serenaded by unseen grunting hippos in the reeds. Finally, having reached a remote village not far from the Omo River, it was time to head for home.

51
A LIBYAN INVITATION

At the 1996 World Travel Market (WTM) in London, armed with our n.o.m.a.d.s. business cards, we called in to the Libyan stand to check out the possibility of going to the Akakus Mountains, 600 miles south of Tripoli. Although the Akakus aren't far from Algeria's Tassili n'Ajjer sandstone towers, they are considerably bigger, the massif extending for 125 miles, its summits rising about 500 metres above the desert. The area is also rich in rock art, some dating back 12,000 years to pre-Sahara times, and depicting animals of the African savannah. We knew of no one who had been there.

Wings Travel who were based in Tripoli were keen to develop their adventure-tourism side and the director, Hakim, was interested in our proposal, saying he would get in touch to arrange an exploratory trip. He and his partners, Isam and Alaa, were nice guys, so we were cautiously optimistic.

Libya, for the British at least, doesn't spring readily to mind as a travel and tourism destination (either then or now). In fact, relations between Libya and the UK were considerably strained since the shooting of WPC Fletcher outside the Libyan People's Bureau in 1984. The Lockerbie disaster in 1988 had exacerbated matters further and since then there had been a UN embargo on flights to Libya, placing it with Iraq as one of only two countries in the world it was impossible to fly to. The country was controlled by Colonel Gaddafi who was a supporter of revolutionary movements across the world, not conducive to attracting visitors.

The situation was not quite so politically tense with other European countries. A few Germans, Italians and French – the latter always ardent lovers of the desert – visited Libya each year. Travel however was difficult. The flight embargo meant that most people flew to Tunisia before continuing to Libya by road. The air embargo also meant that air travel within Libya was almost non-existent as their air industry was suffering from increasing maintenance problems. For us however it couldn't have been better, as Libya was not only devoid of mass tourism, but its mountains were virtually unknown – not just the remote Akakus, but also Jebel Akhdar, the 'Green Mountains', along the north-east coast. Chad's Tibesti massif where Doug Scott had been in 1965 even had a finger of mountains protruding north into Libya called Jebel Nuqay that, like the Akakus, was reputed to have magnificent desert scenery cut by ravines and with bizarre rock formations as well as fine examples of prehistoric rock art. Unfortunately Jebel Nuqay was well off Wings' itinerary, but having a Libyan travel company to arrange our visas and provide transport and accommodation elsewhere around the country made it irresistible. Isam and Alaa met us at the Tunisian border, helping us to change money on the black market, which was ten times greater than the official rate.

Chatting with our hosts over dinner in the hotel in Tripoli, I noticed one of the ubiquitous photos of Colonel Gaddafi on the wall. Like all North African and Middle Eastern countries, having a framed photo of the country's leader was de rigueur whether you liked him or not. Naively, I asked what it was like having Gaddafi as leader, but all I got in reply was a hushed, 'Ask me later when we are in the desert'. Walls obviously had ears. Tripoli, then with a population of one million, perhaps a fifth of Libya's total, was a typically North African city, a blend of ancient and modern: finely minareted mosques, the souk with its arched alleys and passages, and the massive-walled Red Castle mingled with remnants of Italian colonial architecture and modern tower blocks. Inside the medina, the souk sold the usual eclectic mix of goods, but little or nothing specifically for tourists – a refreshing experience. However, there was a craft area where copper and brass were beaten into decorated trays and pans, and where rugs and silk dresses were woven. The jewellery shops mostly exhibited the fine goldwork beloved of modern North Africa and Arabia. The traditional heavy silver bangles, bracelets and necklaces worn by the Berber and Tuareg people were less in demand.

Before leaving the coast, we visited the real jewels in Tripoli's historical crown: Sabratha and Leptis Magna, each an hour's drive away. Both these wonderfully preserved Greco-Roman cities fan out extensively from their once-perfect harbours. To the west, Sabratha was founded by the Phoenicians and passed through the hands of various peoples, finally falling into disuse when the Arabs moved the centre of trade to Tripoli. There are numerous temples and some fine, but unprotected mosaics which would be unlikely to survive the trampling armies of future tourists should the country ever be safe to visit again. The second-century Roman theatre dominated the site, at that time splendidly restored, the magnificent colonnaded three-tier backdrop with its marble reliefs and statues only partially concealing the nearby blue waters of the Mediterranean. Tempted by the sea sparkling in the sun we walked down for a closer look, finding some small sea cliffs, not worth roping up for but giving me some fun soloing on good sea-salt etched limestone.

Heading east, Leptis Magna also had its origins in Phoenician times, before flourishing under the Greeks and Romans with its Hadrianic Baths, colonnaded street and huge marble-floored Severan Forum. Its harbour had silted up long ago, but the circus and amphitheatre, which were once on its shore, are massive, well preserved and magnificent – it wasn't difficult to imagine the roar of the crowds at the chariot races and gladiatorial combats.

Almost 600 miles east again, beyond the bay of Sirte – Colonel Gaddafi's hometown, where he gave notoriously interminable speeches – is the extensive hump of coastal hills called Jebel Akhdar. It was one of our objectives and Isam was keen to go despite it being in Cyrenaica, a rebellious province even then. So much so in fact that beyond Benghazi all the road signs had been removed, making it difficult to find anything as we had no road maps. Additionally, it was raining. In fact, rain is common there from October through till March and the area provides much of Libya's fruit and wheat, having once been part of 'the bread basket of Rome'. We were not too surprised therefore when we eventually arrived at the town of Al Bayda high on the centre of the Akhdar plateau in a torrential downpour with a thunderstorm lighting the sky.

Al Bayda, in common with most Libyan towns, had little of architectural merit, being mostly utilitarian concrete blocks with, here and there, remnants of the Italian occupation exhibiting the occasional artistic flourish. Bizarrely, in the countryside it seemed usual to use the ornate Italian buildings as cowsheds while the people lived alongside in modern concrete homes. We checked into the grandly named Qasr Al Bayda (Bayda Castle) Hotel – an imposing if singularly unimaginative Italian construction of the 1930s, built on a massive scale but more akin to a military barracks than a hotel or indeed a castle. Draughts from air conditioners blew through faded dusty curtains and wafted along the cavernous lower floor. Wide, empty corridors echoed as we made our way to our rooms. The fixtures and fittings, it seemed, were original, and consequently getting a little worse for wear: sprung steel beds struggled against time and gravity not to become hammocks, the bath and toilet were stained with the drips of unattended plumbing. The carpets had long since given up hope.

As always in Libya, the main evening meal was substantial if equally predictable: Libyan soup, Libyan salad, meat (beef or chicken) with rice or chips, sometimes strangely preceded by spaghetti bolognese, and usually concluded with fresh fruit. Breakfast, as always, was considerably more frugal, being bread and jam with coffee or tea. The Qasr Al Bayda was the least pleasant and welcoming of all the places we stayed in during our three-week trip. It was the exception that proved the rule: even if sometimes a little frayed around the edges, hotels were otherwise always clean and adequately maintained, and the staff friendly. It's a pity that it was the only accommodation on Jebel Akhdar, since North Africa's fabled Greek city of Cyrene was just over the hill, with its nearby beautifully located harbour town of Apollonia, a historical gem by the rocky and totally tourist-free shores of the Mediterranean.

Cyrene is the most remote of the Libyan cities of the Greek and Roman period. It was idyllic, almost forgotten by the outside world and seldom visited by tourists. We saw no one during the day we spent there, or at Apollonia and lesser sites along the surf-washed coast with its deserted coves and beaches. What a tourist idyll they could be. After our almost day-long drive in the rain, it was a real delight to wake to blue skies and wander among the 2,500-year-old relics of Cyrene, picking our way between marble columns, tumbled statues and carpets of flowers. The massive Doric columns of the Forum of Proculus dominated the hillside, and the nearby Acropolis was unexcavated, hiding who knows *what* treasures.

Dr Fadel Ali Mohamed, the resident curator, told us with a smile, 'We find new things every day'. In his inner sanctum there were magnificent milk-white, silky-smooth marble statues of Aphrodites, Hercules, Hermes, the three muses and many others. All had been resurrected from their sandy graves and were still uncatalogued, as were the marble heads that peered from the drawers of dusty filing cabinets waiting to be united with their bodies in this archaeological treasure trove.

Beyond the Acropolis and the colonnaded area of Cyrene's Agora, or square, with its surrounding streets and mosaics, we reached the edge of the plateau and appreciated for the first time the true beauty of the setting. Below us was a narrow wadi and spring, its ever-running water rising from a cave sanctuary to feed cleverly designed pools and saunas before the valley opened out into the Sanctuary of Apollo with its temples, statues and magnificently located theatre. Further down the hill with its necropolis of 3,000 graves, the coastal plain extended to the shining blue sea and the concealed port of Apollonia.

The hills of Jebel Akhdar concealed deep wadis from which springtime breezes carried the perfumes of flowers. Clifftop walks took us among crags of limestone, their rounded tops grey and sharp edged, plunging into the red-rocked and overhanging depths of cave-filled gorges. There looked to be some possibilities for climbing, but we had bigger mountains in mind. The Bedouin however had made use of them, making their homes there over the centuries in the many large caverns despite their seeming inaccessibility.

All along the 190-mile coast of Jebel Akhdar and Cyrenaica, the sea crashes or whispers on rocks and beaches, empty except near the few small towns and villages, waiting for tourism that has never had the opportunity to develop. West of Apollonia, the tranquil ruins of Tolmeitha cover an immense Greek water storage cistern hidden below its forum where water piped from the jebel twelve miles away collects in a man-made chamber of maybe 15,000 cubic metres. Beautifully detailed mosaics and statues were lovingly shown to us by their curator, who sadly bemoaned the fact that the site, which covers a vast area, had hardly been touched by archaeologists. Indeed, there had been no excavations there since 1964.

Cyrenaica was a beautiful if very neglected area. We felt some good treks could have been made there above and along its empty forested coast. There were also many opportunities for caving and possibly climbing. In fact, the region was ripe for both cultural and adventure-tourism development, though twenty years on it's impossible. Following the killing of Gaddafi in 2011 it is now a self-proclaimed autonomous region trying to throw off 2,000 years of colonisation having been first a Greek then a Roman province, then more recently under Italian rule, then British military administration and finally as a province ruled from Tripoli which reaped its resources and left it impoverished. With the bitter, armed struggle ongoing, who knows when the region will open up.

Heading back west from Benghazi, the coast, no longer supported by the thrusting backdrop of hills, slips south to the bay of Sirte where Gadaffi was killed, then a quiet place, and a modern coastal city with the vast Sahara to the south reaching all the way to Niger, Chad and Sudan. Having left Jebel Akhdar far behind, we sped south on a modern road following the old trade and slave route – an elongated snake of a road striking into the very heart of the desert. Mirages incessantly retreated ahead of us in evaporating pools of light as we rose and fell across the barren undulating land, carrying our apparently unchanging sphere of horizon with us beneath its dome of blue.

After one and a half days we passed a couple of soldiers in a sand-blasted sentry box in the middle of nowhere, after which we finally reached the ancient desert town of Ghat, beyond which and ever deeper into the desert were the Akakus Mountains in Libya's furthest south-west corner: a seeming nuclear devastation of rock, contorted towers and impressive arches standing in petrified silence in the vast emptiness. Siren rocks with twisted faces and bodies cracked and wrinkled like elephant hide beckoned us to seek their hidden charms and repulsed us with exfoliating flakes of rotten rock.

The highest towers seemed to offer what we were looking for: compact rock cleaned by the desert winds with attractive ridges and walls offering hopes of worthwhile climbs to their summits, but access from the west up big screes beneath the doubtful-looking lower walls was far from attractive. The best approach to the enticing upper towers seemed to be from the east and we asked Isam if it would be possible to circumnavigate the massif to verify this possible illusion, but in the limited time available there was no possibility.

Around the foot of the towers, whirling dervish dunes swirled their skirts in the dancing breezes. They swept up to smoking crests graceful enough to enhance any alpine summit. All around, hidden in caves and recesses, ancient figures inscribed in stone or painted in fading ochre told stories of a better land: long-horned cattle, mighty charging elephants, giraffes, ostriches, rhinos, hunting dogs and human figures delicately depicted with the tools of their trade – bow, arrow and a kind of bolas or 'trapping stone'. Flint arrowheads still lay in the dust of the desert, eagerly gleaned by the very few Tuareg that live in this savagely beautiful but dying land. For a few coins we bought a small collection that had last been used some 5,000 to 10,000 years ago and later in the day we camped with a Tuareg family who, despite their poverty and our objections, killed a goat for us as custom dictated.

Since the ancient Garamantian people and their ancestors walked this land of savannahs and green canyons, leaving only their art and their tombs before vanishing as the Greeks and Romans settled in the north some 2,500 years ago, the whole area has succumbed to desertification. Nowadays, it almost never rains, though fossil water still appears here and there as small lakes concealed in a wilderness of dunes. Such are the lakes of Gaberoun, Mavo and Mandara, hidden among the endless dunes of the great Ubari Sand Sea in an area known as the Ramlat Dawada – the 'Sands of the Worm Eaters'. We reached them after travelling north for a day from the Akakus; the latter half of the journey was over a giant switchback of massive dunes. We camped high on a dune above the lake of Gaberoun from which the people in this lonely oasis had harvested shrimps as a mainstay of their diet, becoming known as 'the worm eaters'. Now most have moved away and the sands were increasingly encroaching on the disappearing gardens of this small oasis.

As the sun set, the long hungry shadow of the dunes swallowed the lake and its surrounding palms, their crests still glowing red in the evening light. Out of the gloom, a cheery voice rose in the gathering night. It was a young Nigerian from the small camp by the lake. He joined us by our fire and we asked what he was doing at Gaberoun in the middle of nowhere: his father was an ambassador, he said, so he had easily obtained visas for Europe. Travelling up from Mali to Tamanrasset in the Algerian Sahara, he and his companions had been robbed 'by those Bouzou boys'. Whoever they were, they had taken everything – money, passports, the lot. He travelled on eastwards across the Sahara and somehow managed to get into Libya avoiding the numerous checkpoints (and the lone soldiers in their hut) before hearing about the Gaberoun oasis. Here, lost among the dunes far from any roads, he had found his sanctuary, never returning to the outside world. He had been here for eight months and managed to save a little money towards his hoped-for journey back home, his hopes of reaching Europe abandoned.

'Sometimes,' he said, 'I think that God sent me here to this strange faraway place so that when I am old I can tell my grandchildren about how it was when I was a boy living in the desert with the worm eaters. Why else would he send me all these problems? I can also tell them about you, the English people who gave me soup with no food in it,' he added with a grin as he sipped a cup of instant soup we were having for a quick warm drink in the rapidly cooling night.

Next day we returned north over Jebel Nafusa, the scenic mountain stronghold of Libya's Berbers who were to play an important role in the fall of Tripoli in 2011. Their traditional villages perched on the edge of a long escarpment high above the plains were the location of the magnificent twelfth-century multistorey granary of Qasr al-Haj. At the time of our visit, its ancient grain silos – some dating back to Roman times – were still in use, and springs rose from caverns, some many miles long, as in Jebel Akhdar. Both these limestone areas have much to offer the speleologist, with vast cave entrances and sinkholes beckoning the adventurous.

Our journey almost over, we arrived back in Tripoli. A shopkeeper shouted to me as I was leaving his shop.

'Are you a politician?' he asked.

'No, why?' I replied.

'Then why does it say "Think Green for the Future" on the back of your T-shirt? You should think anything but green – even red might be better than green!'

Then I realised what he meant. Behind him on the wall of his store below the green Libyan flag, with his cheerful smile, fist raised in a 'power to the people' salute, was the inevitable picture of Colonel Gaddafi, author of *The Green Book*: the thoughts of the leader, the 'Third Universal Theory', neither communism nor capitalism, but a third way. It wasn't popular!

That brief exchange seemed to epitomise the feelings of the Libyan people towards the self-styled 'leader of the revolution' and his policies. Though we had mostly avoided the issue of politics with our hosts, the few conversations we had with them and others all pointed to discontent with the regime. At the time they seemed to us to be a naturally relaxed and stoic people with a great *joie de vivre*, able to carry on smiling despite what was generally felt to be unnecessary adversity. Returning home via Djerba in Tunisia, we happened to meet, quite by chance, a friend of ours at the airport. He ran a Tunisian tour company and the conversation inevitably turned to Libya.

'You know,' he said, 'last year I took my first group to Libya. I was very afraid as everyone thinks they are bad people. So I was very happy to find it's not true – they are very nice, maybe even nicer than us!'

As usual with n.o.m.a.d.s., we prepared a report on adventure-tourism potential for Wings Travel together with a set of colour slides for their use. We were also invited to work on their stand at the WTM in London for the next couple of years, where we successfully introduced them to some British tour operators. It had been a worthwhile project for all concerned.

No one expected Gaddafi to be killed and the country to be trashed by civil war. Since 2005, the use of seismic hammers to send shock waves through the rock to locate oil deposits has placed the precious Akakus rock art in danger. Also deliberate vandalism has destroyed many sites. Libya's cultural heritage in the UNESCO World Heritage Sites of Sabratha, Leptis Magna, Cyrene, and Ghadames is under threat, and 8,000 gold, silver and bronze coins dating back to Alexander the Great have been stolen from Benghazi. In Tripoli, precious ceramic tiles have been removed from the iconic Karamanli Mosque and a depiction of a nude woman with a gazelle destroyed. What a sad world we live in.

Libya was and hopefully still is an amazingly varied country steeped in history and rich in culture. There is potential for trekking and caving in Cyrenaica and around Jebel Nafusa. We were told there is also amazing diving on submerged Roman ruins in the Mediterranean. Jebel Nuqay in the deep south and jebels Arkno and Uweinat far away in the remote south-east near Sudan and Egypt are all intriguing mountain destinations with ancient rock art. There may or may not be climbing there, but simply getting to them would be a great trip. As with the Akakus where we had hoped to climb, we had them all on our list for a return trip, but we never got back. Right now it's all impossible, Libya has been torn apart by war and the UN Security Council reported early in 2016 that ISIS is attracting outsiders to fight in the failed state. It's a tragedy; Libya's people were truly hospitable. They deserve a better future.

52

MIDDLE EASTERN MEANDERINGS

The year 1998 started badly. Bill Tweedale, my long-time Rimmon friend and companion on the Troll Wall and numerous other escapades, died in February. He had been working abroad and I hadn't seen him for over a year, the last time being when another of the Rimmon and Romsdal lads, Wayne Gartside, died. Bill had said at his funeral, 'We must get out climbing together again'. I agreed, but we never did. Sad times. Grasp the moment.

I was invited on a trip organised by the British Department of Trade and Industry to assist the development of British tourism in Yemen, Oman and the United Arab Emirates for both our and their benefit. Arriving first in Oman, it was good to see the tourism department promoting some of the sites in Oman that had been part of our project eight years previously. I was also pleased to see that photos from our exploratory visit were still being used in their presentation.

Travelling around Yemen was especially interesting. What a fascinating country it is, with its ancient high-rise buildings, frankincense trees, wild mountain scenery, and equally wild-looking dagger-carrying men, the traditional curved 'janbiya' being de rigueur and often accompanied by a rifle slung over the shoulder.

Yemen was different. Even our meeting with the tourism minister was wacky – it seemed that chewing qat, an illegal drug in many countries, was essential in any meetings, indeed it was part of everyday life taking up much of the afternoon for the vast majority of Yemeni men. Even the British ambassador had permission to chew qat as it's the only way to do business, but it did nothing for me, sitting there with ridiculously bulging cheeks, chewing endlessly on a great bunch of bitter leaves. I was told that, sadly, growing qat had become more important than growing food. The beautifully terraced hillsides that traditionally grew food for the villages had been taken over for the lucrative cash crop of qat, making food ever-more expensive and less available.

The following year I had a similar trip, this time to Lebanon courtesy of Middle Eastern Airways and RIDA International Travel. That too was an interesting trip, but with insufficient time to do justice to Lebanon's numerous remarkable sites: the coast and the buzzing metropolis of Beirut, the 'Paris of the East'; the magnificent Roman temple of Baalbek; the Bekaa valley where Lebanese wine is made (and Red Lebanese hashish), as well as being home to Hezbollah who announce their presence with their yellow flags. Further east, the country-length Lebanon Mountains form a barrier, snow capped in winter when there is skiing above the famed 'Cedars of God', which we visited. There are very few cedar trees there now, just the protected last remnants of a once-extensive forest that provided resin for Egyptian mummification and timber for Phoenician, Assyrian, Babylonian, Persian and Roman ships. In 1876 the remnants of the grove were surrounded by a protective stone wall courtesy of Queen Victoria, but in World War One British troops used the timber to build railroads. Nearby, I was pleased to call in at the village of Bsharri, once home to Kahlil Gibran, a Maronite Christian, poet and author of numerous books including the mystical prose-poetry of *The Prophet*, which became a worldwide bestseller.

There was lots of scope for adventure tourism. There is now a popular 292-mile Lebanese mountain trail, and the Middle East's highest summit, Qurnat as Sawda' (3,088 metres), offers both winter skiing and autumn trekking. Below its western slopes, the impressive limestone Qadisha Gorge is being explored by climbers, and the whole area is riddled with excellent caves.

53

EXPLORING JORDAN –
THE LOWEST ADVENTURES ON EARTH

The view which the Modjeb presents is very striking … when
viewed from above, the valley looks like a deep chasm formed
by some tremendous convulsion of the earth, into which
there seems no possibility of descending to the bottom.

Travels in Syria and the Holy Land, **Johann Ludwig Burckhardt**

Returning to the 1990s, Jordan still had numerous challenges waiting for us. I couldn't wait to try to descend the great chasm of the Mujib Gorge, Jordan's answer to the Grand Canyon. What had really grabbed my attention in 1984, apart from the immensity of it when you first arrive on its upper rim, was the river in its depths and its mysterious disappearance into distant mountains. Now Di and I were back, once again heading south along the ancient King's Highway, a route which reputedly dates back 3,000 years to the kingdoms of Ammon, Moab and Edom.

As the road abruptly reached the upper edge of the gorge, we looked down into the abyss where the sunlit river snaked between tumbled boulders. To the east we could see the forked tongues of its tributaries descending from the high desert plateau. The far southern rim, three miles opposite us across the gorge, was equally bare and rocky. Even so, the river, 600 metres below, had mustered its waters from unseen springs and was making its way to the Dead Sea concealed beneath blue mountains and a heavy heat haze about eighteen miles to the west and 400 metres below sea level – the lowest point on earth.

We didn't know if it would actually be possible to follow the river, and as there was – as far as we were aware – no other way out, it seemed that failure to make our way to the Dead Sea and up the coast would mean totally retracing our steps – a rather grim prospect. And our road map, which was all we had, showed no road along the Jordanian side of the Dead Sea. All we knew was that a road was being built, but not how far it reached, so we had to plan for a possible additional twenty-five-mile walk all the way out north to the Jordan Valley, making about fifty miles in total. We took four days' food and hoped for the best.

Having arranged a lift down to the point where the King's Highway crosses the river (now a reservoir), we threw our sacks on our backs with a determined flourish and waved a positive and cheery goodbye to our bemused driver. It was already close to midday and hot, but this was not an occasion for seeking the shade; the unknown twisting canyon disappearing between hazy blue mountains beckoned irresistibly.

Initially, shepherds' paths wound around fields scattered with poppies and beneath riverside cliffs of white limestone. The barren hillsides rose ever higher above us, inhospitable and forcing the eye back to the sparkling waters of the river that cascaded between boulders and banks of pink-flowering oleanders with the delightfully refreshing sound that running water always has in otherwise parched lands. Occasionally the cliffs closed in, forcing boulder hopping. Once or twice we passed Bedouin shepherds or farm boys at water pumps, their rusting irrigation pipes snaking crazily up to small thirsty fields hidden by the folds of the gorge. They looked at us quizzically:

'*Salaam alaikum*?' – 'Where you go?'

'*Wa alaikum salaam, al-Bahr al-Mayyit.*' – 'The Dead Sea.'

'*Inshallah!*' – 'Not possible!'

… was the usual reply, or 'Big problem, many snake, maybe hyena, not good to sleep,' was a more optimistic response. Always we were welcomed to drink 'shai' (tea), as is the Bedouin custom, while we wondered what lay ahead. We moved on as quickly as politeness and tradition would permit, pointing at the lowering sun and making our excuses.

We found a perfect campsite some distance above the river behind a huge boulder, yet still in the upper driftwood zone. The weather was settled so hopefully no flash floods to sweep us away in the night. Relaxed and glad to be in unknown country we ate well as the stars of the desert night appeared, far above the black, gaping jaws of the gorge into which we had been swallowed.

We slept late in the shadow of the boulder, but were soon off, walking

71 The Andringitra National Park, the big walls of Tsaranoro in the background. Madagascar, 1999.
72 Sailing with fishermen in their outrigger pirogues. Madagascar, 1999.
73 The remote and untouched south-west coast of Madagascar, 1999.

74 Climbing at Tsaranoro, with Twid Turner just visible behind on his new route, *Always the Sun*. Madagascar, 1999.
75 Me with Mark Khano looking over the Monastery of Mar Saba, Palestine, 2000.
76 Olive picking in Palestine is sometimes a dangerous business! 2000.
77 Our first view of the rock bridge of El Farayid. Egypt, 2001.

78 Mark Carr and me on the first ascent of a route to the summit of the Farayid rock bridge. Egypt, 2001.
79 Exploratory trekking in the Dzüku Valley, 'the best trekking in the area'. Nagaland, 2002.
80 One of Meghalaya's amazing 'living bridges'. Made from the living roots and creepers of banyan trees (*Ficus elastica*), they are the only structures that survive the monsoon rivers. Some are two tiers. India, 2002.
81 A surprise meeting with demon dancers in Arunachal Pradesh, eastern Himalaya. India, 2002.
82 Tawang Monastery – India's oldest Tibetan Buddhist monastery, in Arunachal Pradesh. India, 2002.
83 Konyak tribesmen at the Hornbill Festival, in Kohima, Nagaland. India, 2002.

84 Malian transport. The Hand of Fatima mountains in the background have good climbing. Mali, 2005.
85 Trekking through the Dogon mountain villages. Mali, 2005.

86 Tuareg at the Festival in the Desert on the silver sands of Essakane beyond Timbuktu. Mali, 2005.
87 The world-famous mud mosque at Djenné, now a World Heritage Site. Mali, 2005.
88 Our guide Abdina. The monkey skulls are believed to protect the inhabitants from wild animals. Mali, 2005.

89 Mark Khano and me on a first exploratory visit to the surprisingly green Wadi Sirin, North Jordan, 2010.
90 Al Ayoun, with Mark, Julie and Gabriel Khano in Wadi Zubia. North Jordan, 2009.
91 Exploring the Bedouin way into Wadi Khorma, south of Petra, with Tarek Abul Hawa, Jordan, 2005.
92 The spectacular rock arch above Wadi Khorma, south of Petra. Jordan, 2007.

93 Me exploring Zubia Cave, then pristine but much of it now damaged by tourism. North Jordan, 2007.
94 Di and me making the second ascent of our route *The Haj* in the far south of Rum, as part of the BBC climbing series *The Face*, filmed by Triple Echo. Jordan, 1992. **Photo:** *Triple Echo*.
95 Di doesn't get the first drink at the end of filming our climb *The Haj*. Jordan, 1992. **Photo:** *Triple Echo*.
96 Mark Khano and our first view of the Red Sea from the Aqaba mountains while exploring a route for the Jordan Trail, 2014.
97 It was a joy to discover the beautiful hills of Al Ayoun in North Jordan in the spring. North Jordan, 2009.

96

97

98 Sunset from our camp above Wadi Feid on the Jordan Trail.
99 Di and Mark Khano exploring the route for the Jordan Trail, here in the Jordan Valley almost 300 kilometres from the sea, but still 100 metres below sea level. Jordan Trail, 2013.
100 A friendly welcome in a village on the Brahmaputra River. India, 2013.
101 The fearless Di. Exploratory trekking in the Bodoland National Park. India, 2013.
102 Osama Cori and friends high above the Mujib Gorge. Jordan, 2014.

103 Di sitting on the steps leading to Petra's High Place, with the Garden Tomb in the background, Jordan Trail exploration, 2014.
104 Petroglyphs in the Wadi Rum with Osama Cori and Amjad Shahrour, 2014.

105 The ancient village of Ma'tan, high above the canyons of Wadi Labun and Buseira. Jordan, 2015.
106 Di and me exploring the Jordan Trail, 2015.
107 The end of the trail. L–R: Mark Khano, me, Di, Amjad Sharour and Osama Cori finally reach the Red Sea, 2014.

108 Bedouin guide Mahmoud Bdoul from Petra leads the way through the amazing Aheimir Canyon on the way from Petra to Rum. Jordan Trail, 2016.

109 Entering Petra with 'extreme adventurers' Sean Conway *(left)* and Leon McCarron *(right)* on the Jordan Trail, 2016.

110 Di with Sabbah Eid, one of Wadi Rum's Zalabieh tribe and one of our closest friends. Jordan, 2016.
111 Her Excellency Lina Annab, Minister of Tourism and Antiquities, and trekker, with Di and me. Jordan Trail, 2016.
112 On a two-day trek through Wadi Hasa, one of Jordan's superb canyons. Jordan, 2016.
113 On the inaugural through-trek of the Jordan Trail. Standing in the centre, Queen Rania; Bashir Daoud, CEO of the Jordan Trail Association on her left; on her right, same row, Muna Haddad, then the president. 2016. **Photo:** Palace photo.

briskly in the precious cool of the morning. As the hills drew closer, so the cliffs grew steeper, plunging directly into the river and forcing us finally to walk in the water. Hot springs cascaded in from hidden side valleys. Bright green frogs and large freshwater crabs jumped and scurried from under our feet. A mongoose dashed for cover into the reeds at the water's edge. A porcupine rattled through the scrub on the shore. Eagles flew overhead.

A tent-sized beach under the cliffs offered a home for the night; driftwood was piled five metres above us by the floodwaters, but the weather was still settled so we slept well.

Half an hour's walk downstream next morning brought us out of the 'narrows' into more open terrain, though still with no sign of the Dead Sea. Just beyond, another river entered from the north, a waterfall spouting from the mouth of an extremely narrow canyon. We consulted our woefully inadequate map: it was the Hidan Gorge and it looked every bit as long and impressive as the Mujib – something for the future we thought, but it was going to need a rope to escape from the canyon without being swept over the waterfall.

Walking on downstream, we saw the combined waters of the two rivers disappearing into another narrow and ominous-looking canyon. I took my sack off and waded in, only to find that it was immediately necessary to swim. The fast-flowing water swept round a bend into the unseen chasm beyond: there would be no way back. It would, anyway, be impossible with our sacks. I came back thinking dejectedly that we weren't going to make it, and unless we could find a way out to the Dead Sea we had a two-day walk to do to retrace our steps.

Di, however, didn't live on a hill farm without knowing donkey poo when she saw it. She had commented on it once or twice on the way downstream and there was more, with accompanying human footprints, on the beach.

'Bedouin come down here for water,' she said. 'Maybe there's a way out up that ravine.'

Climbing up through foliage above the beach, she shouted down excitedly. Sure enough, there was an old trail. It eventually widened to a long-disused and washed-out four-wheel-drive track which we followed up over a bizarre moonscape of dried mud hills, topping out to a view of the Dead Sea immediately below us and less than a mile away. We were out!

We picked our way down to the salt-crusted coast then along its edge to the downstream end of the canyon. Just to the north, a road construction camp could be seen, but, reluctant to leave the mountains, we camped hidden inside the mouth of the gorge.

Next morning, we knocked on the workmen's cabin door, which opened to reveal the surprised faces of its occupants. 'Where you come from?' We explained to a gathering of bemused faces over a very welcome breakfast. Then we had to hang around as they were still blasting a way through, before we got a lift out to a military checkpoint. Again, more questioning: where were we from, what were we doing and, of course, why? At first they suspected we were Israelis and had somehow crossed the Dead Sea, saying, 'It's impossible to get here from the King's Highway'. Then we showed them a letter from the director of tourism and they made some phone calls. Finally we got our passports back after everyone had inspected them. Accepting that we were just 'crazy English' and not spies, we were given a lift out to the first village.

Five years were to pass before we were able to revisit the Mujib in 1998. By then, it had become the heart of the newly created Mujib Nature Reserve run by Jordan's Royal Society for the Conservation of Nature (the RSCN). They told us that people had been through the final canyon of the Mujib Siq and that ropes were required: it sounded good.

We thought we would approach it through the Hidan Gorge, that other provocatively tempting canyon we had seen all those years ago with its waterfall exit into the Mujib. We were joined by Mick Shaw and Hanna Jahshan, a friend from Amman. Hanna was into horse riding in a big way but enjoyed the outdoors and had already once got himself into difficulties trying to descend the Hidan. His tale of a 'huge waterfall' sounded most intriguing.

With permission from the RSCN to enter the reserve, we arrived in the upper Hidan Gorge late one morning. It was very impressive, the river winding through high cliffs of basalt columns. We had ropes with us and were confident that two or three days at the most would see us through. We were nevertheless surprised to be already wading chest deep in water between such spectacular cliffs so far upstream: a different proposition altogether to the neighbouring Mujib.

It was mid-afternoon when we reached Hanna's 'huge waterfall'. We heard it long before we reached it, the telltale roar of the water increasing as we approached the edge of the concealed abyss. What greeted us as we peered over was totally unexpected: a vertical drop of what looked like more than fifty metres led the eye down organ pipes of black basalt, sliced off beneath us by an overhang of unknown proportions. Beneath that was a sandstone cauldron streaked lime green and bright orange and festooned with hanging palms and foliage. In the depths was an obviously deep, dark green pool into which the white curtain of the waterfall cascaded. *What to do?* Not only had Hanna never abseiled before, but we only had ropes for a fifty-metre abseil and having thrown the ends down they didn't reach the pool. *And what was beyond?* The river disappeared into a narrow and dark chasm that wound out of sight into barren hills – its confluence with the Mujib was still over seven miles away. The decision made itself: we backtracked upstream to spend the night on the beach.

The only disturbance – apart from an incessant cacophony of frogs – was caused by me waking up to feel a soft, snake-like body sliding down my stomach. I grabbed it and threw it out of my sleeping bag into the dark, waking everyone up in the process. We searched around with our torches, finding an unbelievable number of extremely large and colourful oleander hawkmoth caterpillars rampaging among us. Let me assure you, waking up with what feels like a snake heading for your groin is no joke!

We trekked back out of the gorge the next day and had a chat with our friends at the RSCN – the final canyon of the Mujib Siq was, they said, impassable at the moment due to considerable spring rains. By the time we could attempt it a few weeks later, Mick had returned home (well, some of us have to work … !). Hanna, however, was still keen and had now done a couple of short abseils with us in Rum, so the three of us took the shortcut in along the newly constructed Dead Sea Highway and over the 'mud hills' that had provided the escape for Di and me five years earlier. They are, apparently, the alluvial remains of the old riverbed left high and dry when the Rift Valley – of which the Jordan Valley forms the northern end – had one of its spasms in prehistoric times, cracking its sides and forming the chasm or siq through which the Mujib now runs.

The water level was a metre lower than it had been last time Di and I were there, and we had no heavy sacks – just the abseil gear and cameras and our secret weapon – buoyancy jackets. Wading and swimming and leaping into pools from boulders we made our way into the darkening chasm, the walls echoing with the increasing noise of the river as we approached a waterfall. There, huge boulders split the river into falls both over and between the rocks. An old sling under the surface of the water tempted us to abseil into a 'cave' under the largest block, disappearing through the inner waterfall as we did so, which was a novel experience. Emerging from it, the roaring outer waterfall then blocked the view downstream. We made a second abseil behind it, swimming out through a narrow passage of foam-flecked waves between it and the cliff. I was first down, finding it difficult to swim while dragging the ropes that the falls seemed determined not to relinquish. Having pulled the ropes, we swam on down the chasm: no way back now, but as it turned out, nothing to stop us either, though the cliffs closed in shutting out the light as we roped down another small fall, then slid down water-worn chicanes in the boulders, finally swimming out through a long flooded passage to reach the sunlight on the shore of the Dead Sea.

All we had to do now was fill in the gap from the Hidan's 'huge waterfall' where we had turned back on our previous visit to its junction with the Mujib. But almost six months elapsed before we were able to return in October, hoping to complete our explorations. Logistically, we needed some transport for this and other planned trips, but we failed to raise any support or even interest from the tourism ministry for our ongoing activities, as the director, Nasri Atalla, who had supported us almost unquestioningly since 1984, had retired. From then until very recently it seemed the ministry were only interested in cruise ships, Petra and five-star hotel tourism. Undeterred, as we were now exploring the whole of Jordan – not an easy task without a vehicle – Di and I went to the palace.

Having been welcomed by Queen Noor, we explained that we were gathering information for a guidebook to Jordan's treks, climbs, caves and canyons, in the hope that – like our Rum guide – it would bring visitors to lesser-known and comparatively poor parts of the country, enabling villagers to become guides and tourist drivers and perhaps to open homestays. As she already headed the Noor Al Hussein Foundation founded four years previously to 'facilitate lasting change in underprivileged communities by creating economic opportunities and sustainable community development', she understood exactly the potential benefits of our activities.

The support that she gave us with her letter of introduction and the continuous help of her secretary, Dana Toukan, were indispensable. As were the palace car and driver that she put at our service. At first the driver couldn't understand that we wanted to walk to our final destination each day, saying why walk, when he could drive us there, but he soon realised what it was all about and it worked perfectly. Occasionally he would even appear earlier than expected, struggling up the rocky wadis in a four-wheel drive. With the queen's permission he soon stopped wearing his military uniform on his daily trips with us and he took particular pleasure in racing through police speed traps, knowing the palace insignia on the car gave him impunity. Additionally, our friend Sami Sabat who was going abroad, gave us the keys to his house outside Amman, so we now had a base.

Supported by Queen Noor, new doors were opened. Having explained that we were finding it impossible to get maps, we asked if she could get us a set covering the length of the country. A few days later she had them. 'I see what you mean,' she said, 'even I found it difficult!' So we finally had maps, even though they were from the 1960s and 1970s which meant many of the villages on the maps were now towns, and some of the paths were roads, but they did the job, and still do.

'The map office said you have to return them when you've finished with them,' she said, but we are still using them. We also pushed our luck and asked if there was any chance of a helicopter to have a look at the Dead Sea canyons. A couple of days later we were in the air, doors open, flying along the length of the Hidan Gorge and over the ominous black cleft of the final Mujib Siq through which the merged Mujib and Hidan rivers passed unseen in the cavernous depths to enter the Dead Sea. The upper Hidan also proved too narrow and dark to see into, retaining its mysteries. The only way to discover what problems it entailed was to do it. The pilot also obligingly gave us a quick flight along the other Dead Sea canyons before returning to the airport.

Returning to the Hidan with Hanna and Mick, we now had sufficient rope with us. We had also heard a rumour that someone had been down, which seemed to be confirmed when we found a new bolt at the top of the falls. We threw our extra-long rope down to see the end splash satisfyingly, but disturbingly far below, in the pool. Mick volunteered to go last, to ensure that Hanna was OK, leaving me to go first on the single ten-millimetre rope, knotted to a five-millimetre retrieval cord. It was a big and committing abseil, down the basalt columns then suddenly into space over the edge of a sharply defined and huge roof. Spiralling on down, the ropes hung below, eventually touching dripping rock, wet from the waterfall and the hot springs emerging from the surrounding cliffs. On down the lower wall, gloved hands heating up, to a splashdown in the pool, my sack pulling me under as I struggled to unclip.

Once off the ropes, I swam for the beach at the far side of the cauldron, pulling them with me so we could haul them down afterwards. The thin red retrieval line tangled round my feet, which still couldn't touch the bottom; my sack was soaking water up too, which didn't help. Nor did the dark object bobbing in the water, looking disturbingly like a cobra's head – at the RSCN they had said 'Watch out for Egyptian cobras!' I was beginning to think this wasn't my day, but then I managed to untangle the ropes and swim on cautiously, one eye on the 'cobra', which I eventually realised was the tip of a sunken palm branch.

We slid the rest of the sacks down on the ten-milimetre rope, which made life easier for the others, then Di came down, then Hanna with commendable nonchalance considering his minimal abseil experience, and finally Mick. The abseil rope was retrieved with ease by pulling the five-milimetre cord and we were in. What lay beyond was anyone's guess.

The next 1,000 metres of the canyon was through a narrow siq: wall-to-wall water and lots of fun in spectacular surroundings with hot and cold showers cascading in on us from both sides. We emerged into a jungle of phragmites reeds through which the river, still trapped between cliffs, flowed for another 2,000 metres. Visibility ahead was sometimes zero as we forced our way through the tall matted reeds, thinking all the time about cobras. Then, tiring of the jungle warfare, we tried a detour over a fallen palm below the cliffs. Being in front at the time, I came close to standing on a viper; had it not raised its head I wouldn't have seen it. I stopped and we stared each other in the eye. Neither moved. I went into slow reverse. The snake remained poised and motionless. With relief, we half submerged ourselves again in the warm reed-filled river, to re-emerge at an area of hot springs just before dark.

We were up with the dawn, back in the river and having fun until we were swallowed once more into the jaws of a siq. The walls closed in claustrophobically, but we passed a small waterfall with ease. Then the whole river rushed down a metre-wide chute into a pool, above which a rusty bolt seemed to indicate someone had been down – or at least tried. We clipped in and this time Mick went first. With no option but to cross through the fall near its end, he moved into the full force of the chute, which instantly picked him up and slammed him against the opposite wall. Winded and unable to breath, he hunched up in pain under the cliff, hanging on the ropes and still half submerged. We looked on aghast: this was no place for an accident. I followed him down, managing with the benefit of Mick's experience to cross safely, but he was still in pain: we wondered if he had broken some ribs. Signalling to Di and Hanna to wait, we swam on cautiously down the dark, cavernous siq, but another small fall lay ahead, then more pools, then a bend. If we pulled the ropes we would be stuck.

With Mick in a bad way, we binned it and decided to try to find a way round, then, if possible, to check the canyon from below. My memory of a big waterfall spouting out from between vertical cliffs when Di and I had looked up from the confluence with the Mujib didn't help. *Better safe than stuck in here*, we thought; we could always come back next spring. We climbed back up the ropes, a struggle for Mick, the pain becoming worse as the day wore on and the adrenaline wore off. Back out of the siq, we found a side gully that led us up into the barren hills to the old riverbed. This too had been left high and dry 200 metres above the siq, on the ancient depositional shore terraces of Lake Lisan that, between 70,000 and 12,000 BC extended 125 miles up the Jordan Rift Valley to Lake Tiberius.

Following its edge we found our way with surprising ease to the canyon exit known as Malagi, 'the Confluence', where the Hidan meets the Mujib. It was almost concealed by huge boulders and strangely the waterfall that Di and I had first seen from the Mujib had gone. Presumably a boulder dam had been swept out of the canyon in a flash flood during the intervening years? We dumped our sacks and swam up into the chasm through pool after pool of warm green water between twisting overhanging walls striated with the bright stains of minerals. A water snake plopped into a pool as we swam by, struggling to swallow a loudly complaining frog.

It was a magical cavernous place, and a joy to swim in without sacks. 'As warm as a womb,' as Mick said, with surprising prenatal recall. It was therefore with disappointment that having climbed two falls we failed to get up the third one, deep in the heart of the canyon. Just beyond it, a bend was visible – it looked identical to the one that Mick and I had looked down on. We could have gone through after all, but we were alive and well – apart from Mick's ribs, which were in a bad way. We trekked out downstream and over the hills to the Dead Sea feeling reasonably content.

In 1998, we finished our guidebook – *Jordan: Walks, Treks, Caves, Climbs and Canyons*. Other than my two guides to Wadi Rum it was the first book to cover these activities throughout Jordan. These books have been credited with kick-starting Jordan's adventure tourism. Amazingly, we have now had over thirty glorious years of exploration, the last few in the company of Jordan's increasingly active young people. How lucky we were to be in there first.

54

MADAGASCAR – MYSTICAL MOUNTAINS

In 1998 I received an unexpected letter from François Lenfant who we had last climbed with in Wadi Rum twelve years previously. Since then, he had been wandering the planet sending us an occasional letter before finally settling in Madagascar. He wondered if we would like to spend some time with him checking itineraries for an adventure-travel company he was starting with his Malagasy girlfriend.

I had first realised the potential for trekking and climbing in Madagascar back in 1981 when I saw a photo of the Andringitra mountains in the Reader's Digest *Book of Natural Wonders*. The picture, depicting blue-grey mountains 'scoured by torrential rains … deeply channelled with crevices and ravines', captured my imagination. The article alongside described 'giant isolated domes that stand 500 metres high … a series of massive, dramatically eroded mountains, including Imarivolanitra (formerly Pic Boby) – at 2,658 metres, the highest of the massif'.

Six weeks later we were in François' Renault army truck and on our way. The road south-west from Antananarivo – the capital, known to everyone as Tana was one of the few 'good' roads in Madagascar, winding ever higher past interesting-looking crags and rocky peaks. Their Malagasy names are inspirational: the 'Hand of God', the 'Door to the South' and many others were all unclimbed, and maybe still are. Their bare sweeps of rock rise into wind- and rain-sculpted *cunettes* – deep fluted grooves more typical of limestone, but also found on Brazilian granite. As we drove beneath them, rows of workers bent, stoop-backed in the reflected blue of the sky, toiling in the patchwork of water-filled rice fields.

On our second night we arrived in the foothills of the Andringitra mountains. After seventeen years I got my first view of the peaks I had originally seen in that photo. The night was spent with a friend of François', in his two-storey thatched house, home-made of local red clay bricks in the classic style of the Betsileo tribe. Smiling faces made us welcome, the air smelt of wood smoke – it was great to be among hill people again.

Next day we drove slowly up the deeply rutted zebu (humpbacked cattle) track and through rivers, rising ever higher into the hills where great domes of rock thrust out their obvious challenges. It was strange to think they had only been discovered by climbers a mere four years ago. Almost above the village, a prominent dome had been climbed for the first time only the previous week by an American team. As we rounded a bend in the valley the incredible walls of Karambony and Tsaranoro came suddenly into view – magnificent towers of granite.

During the early years of exploration this had been a true wilderness area, the only people in the valley being the local farmers. Since then, Gilles Gautier, one of the pioneers, had built Camp Catta among beautiful boulders an hour's scramble below the cliffs and close to a 'sacred forest' where colonies of ring-tailed 'catta' lemurs live. The name is also a pun on 'quatre', or 'four', and in some respects it has the ambience of the famous Camp 4 in Yosemite, if a little more upmarket. It's an idyllic place. Arriving there after the difficulties of travel was luxury: solar-heated showers, rustic bungalows, idyllic camping, excellent food and, of course, beer, wine and Malagasy rum and impromptu musical entertainment in the evening by the staff. At the camp were Americans, French, Spanish and other nationalities all intent on new route adventures on the big walls. The Brits were there too – Twid and Louise Turner, Grant Farquhar and Steve Mayers. We met them as they were coming down from a new route they were working on. It was a good excuse for us all to sample some of Madagascar's ubiquitous Three Horses Beer – good value at 40p a large bottle. The rum and local talent show came later!

Next day, despite my headache from the journey (or was it the rum?), we sampled the granite, picking the line of *Alien* put up by Michel Piola. As expected, bolts were the order of the day. This made for a pleasantly relaxing climb – there's nothing like bombproof gear beneath your feet and more not far above your head to tempt you upwards.

The initial pitches were slabs – holdless and no line except that created by Piola. I was hoping for more interesting rock above and feeling rather puny beneath the magnificent seamless 400-metre wall that the 'Turner Team' were engaged on a hundred metres away. Destined to be called *Always the Sun*, it looked superb. Fortunately, as we climbed higher, the rock steepened and we had a nice pitch with some French 5+ and 6a climbing to look forward to, though it turned out to be an easy touch at HVS. Regardless of the grade, the rock was a joy to climb; too good to be true in fact, and François pointed out other excellent-looking climbs to look forward to. Right now, however, we had projects of our own: Alun Davies, the editor of *Adventure Travel*, had commissioned a trekking story so we were going to Pic Boby, after which François had to go to the west coast on what sounded like a good exploratory trip. We expected to return afterwards, but the unpredictability of travel in Madagascar was to dictate otherwise.

The following day, as planned, we set off to Boby, the focal point of the Andringitra National Park. It's also Madagascar's second highest summit, the highest being Maromokotro, 2,876 metres, way up north in the Tsaratanana Reserve. From Camp Catta, Boby should have been visible to the south, but since our arrival heavy clouds had concealed it, so we weren't too optimistic. The situation was unchanged when we arrived at the hamlet of Morarano further up the valley, where a WWF sign marked the park's northern limit. There, we hired the necessary guide, setting off for the col south of the aiguilles of Pic Dondy. Piola had been on this top too, by the 1,600-metre alpine west ridge. Apparently the rock was covered in 'weird plants and hairy lichen' giving rise to unpleasant climbing. No doubt this will put other climbers off, which is perhaps as well, given the comments on conservation we were to hear later from the park manager.

Though a bit of a sweat in the heat of the morning, the walk up the hillside trail was surprisingly enjoyable. It was great to be walking in beautiful and bizarre mountain scenery with lemurs calling from small areas of nearby forest, and palms, cacti and other strange plants adorning the hillside. It was also good to meet local people coming down the rocky track: women carrying babies, and tough, wiry men with axes and spears. They passed us by with a friendly '*Salama*', waving as they moved on down the path, to the disappointment of their dogs that glowered at us suspiciously.

Beyond the col, the trail turned south, up the broad valley of the Zomandao River, towards its headwaters in the distant foothills of Pic Boby. We passed through an area of lush forest before entering the village of Mahasoa with its dancing, laughing children chanting what had become a familiar mantra '*Bonjour vazaha*' – 'Hello foreigner'. The next stop was

Antanifotsy where we arrived in the late afternoon, expecting to get permits to enter the park. We also believed we could buy food there, and stay the night – but we were misinformed.

Bakole, François' Malagasy girlfriend, was able to talk to the locals who told us that we needed to go to Ambalamandry for permits. This was not good news, since it was five miles away in the wrong direction and it was already dusk. We decided to ignore the bureaucracy and instead to head for the hills – the park entrance was, we were told, just a few miles up the track. Maybe someone up there could resolve our permit problem? Well, it was worth a try. Or at least we thought so until we met someone in a suit coming down the track on a motorbike.

'Where are you going?' he enquired.

'To the park,' we told him, adding, 'can we get our permits there?' We should have known better: never trust men in suits – especially in the mountains! He was both officious and uncaring.

'Permits must be purchased in Ambalamandry,' he said, confirming our fears. Then, seemingly oblivious to the gathering darkness, he warned us that, 'You can't get any yet as the park isn't officially open. You must come back in two weeks, after the ceremony.' With that, he kicked his bike into gear and drove off into the gloom.

This left us with a dilemma: should we respect official procedures, or do we continue and hope to meet someone less zealous? We decided to continue, then, as luck would have it, a pickup came down the hill and stopped. The driver, a happy, welcoming man of the sort we had come to expect in Madagascar, listened to our story.

'Jump on and I'll take you up to the park camp. The WWF man is up there – he'll be able to help.'

It was well after dark when we arrived at the park. Scott, the WWF advisor, confirmed that it wasn't open for a couple of weeks but, having read the request from Alun Davies for a story on trekking in Madagascar, he said, 'No problem, you can use the unfinished campsite and ask someone to go down for the permits tomorrow'. Happy again, we finished off most of the food we had with us and called it a day.

As we had only one tent with us, Di and I offered to sleep in the open air as we often did, but this time enjoying the constellations of the southern sky. François' tent had recently been burnt along with his climbing gear in one of the thousands of fires that blaze annually in Madagascar. *Tavy*, or 'slash and burn', is still a common practice used by Malagasy farmers, converting forests to farmland which becomes unusable within about twenty years, not realising that they are slowly destroying ever more of the land on which they depend. Eighty per cent of Madagascar's jungle has now been lost to *tavy*, putting the long-term survival of its unique, endemic species at risk of survival, though efforts are now being made to restore some of the lost forest. If you're camping wild, it's worth remembering to pitch your tent where it can be seen, though in some parts of Madagascar, bandits and zebu rustlers are said to be more of a threat than the fires.

Next morning our guide collected our permits. He was back by midday with more food, the compulsory official park guide, a porter and an extra trainee guide to add to our rapidly growing little expedition. As he didn't seem any worse for his twelve-mile round trip, we were soon on our way, winding steeply up through thick forest to the high plateau of Andohariana. From it, two waterfalls plunged into deep, clear pools in the forested river gorge in which we had spent a lazy morning.

The plateau is rather like a dry version of Rannoch Moor in Scotland. It's a magical place, wild and breezy with granite crags rising up on the horizon. Our bivouac was by a cold, clear stream in a hollow beneath the southern cliffs of Boby. Lying in our sleeping bags and sheltered by three-metre-high 'heather' we realised that the clouds that had been sitting on Boby ever since our arrival at Tsaranoro had gone. Overhead, a dome of stars never seen in the northern hemisphere rose from the black chalice of surrounding cliffs. Beside us, in the pre-moon darkness, our guides huddled for warmth in their blankets by the still-glowing fire. As the full moon rose, we sunk deeper into our sleeping bags and slept contentedly.

We awoke to see the cliffs above us lit with the warm glow of the unseen rising sun while the bright lantern of the full moon still hung over the distant hills. Our guides were already up, squatting round their fire from which a ribbon of smoke uncoiled. We joined them for coffee and breakfast and by the time we left, the sun was up and the sky was blue.

Scrambling up the hillside and across blue-grey slabs fringed with bizarre plants, we reached the foot of tempting granite cliffs mottled orange, gold and white with lichen. Beneath us, to the east, was a sea of clouds, while to the north, the rocky summit of Boby rose up in contorted flutings into a clear blue sky. The rock was wonderful. The sweeping *cunettes* of this artistically draped curtain of granite offered innumerable lines begging to be climbed – some even looked possible without bolts. This was all very frustrating as Scott had explicitly asked us to stick to the trail and not to climb. 'The park is still not fully surveyed,' he explained. 'It's possible that unknown species of flora and fauna could be discovered and it would be a tragedy to trample them, unknowingly, underfoot.'

Who could argue with that? It was a justified request that could well become a regulation. As such, it may contradict our assumed rights to 'the freedom of the hills', but perhaps rules are necessary if we are to conserve what few wild places are left on our small planet. Happy to comply, we contented ourselves with a delightful scramble to the summit, enjoying the superb rock friction and magnificent location. A final series of curvaceous grooves brought us quickly to the top. Intrigued by this rare human intrusion, a falcon swooped down to join us as we looked out across its craggy domain. Then it was time to head off again, back down the rough rock of the summit dome, over a gently rising col on carpets of flowering moss and down to our bivouac. From there, we headed off northwards across the plateau. Already grey fingers of cloud were groping at the cliffs around us. Halfway across the plateau, we walked through an area of burnt-out, dead vegetation; nothing was growing. Our guides said lightning had caused the fire. Hopefully they were right, but it seemed to us that even here, within the limits of the park, this was possibly more evidence of slash and burn.

By mid-afternoon, we were approaching the bizarre crab-shaped summit of Anakandriam-Itoboroke, with its great overhanging rock claws clutching the sky. As we scrambled up to cross a col to its south, squalls of rain started to gust across the cliffs, but our guides knew their mountains – within an hour we were over the top and sheltering under a huge overhang. Nearby, ring-tailed lemurs leapt across the wet crags with a speed and agility that would be the envy of any climber. *Why do we bother?*

By the time we had cooked our evening meal, the rain had stopped. The clouds were sinking back into the dark valleys into which night had already arrived, leaving the sun to set the sky on fire over the towers of Tsaranoro. Dawn was equally magnificent, the big cliffs thrusting forcefully upwards above the sea of clouds.

The clouds rose again as the day warmed and we descended through clusters of wild palms and thickets of flowering shrubs to reach the valley and its remote hamlets. By midday we were back at Morarano. Camp Catta and its tempting towers were going to have to wait, but we had saved a day to try to finish a half-completed route on a dome named the Bishop's Hat, with the proportions of Ayer's Rock, down near the Tana-Tulear highway. Gilles Gautier had been up the lower pitches of a 300-metre line, climbing with natural protection, which must be unique in Madagascar, so we were optimistic that it might be our style. Unfortunately Gilles hadn't mentioned a hanging garden of trees in the unclimbed upper section. Maybe the climbing would be okay, but after the beautiful, clean and open rock we had become familiar with, it somehow didn't seem too tempting. The rest of the thousand-metre face was, as we had come to expect in Madagascar, very impressive, but impossible without bolts. Remembering our chat with the WWF advisor, we thought it was best left undisturbed.

A few days later we reached the sea: a beautiful tropical dream into which we plunged uncontrollably. We camped on the beach and sailed in a pirogue with local fishermen out across the lagoon towards the white surf of the reef, to snorkel among the coral. Continuing south along the coast we spent another night in the forest camped near a flooded cave in which blind fish swam lazily, seeming uncertain what to do or even which way was up; not even knowing, as François said, that they were supposed to be fish! Moving on, we camped again by the sea, unable to resist more time sailing in pirogues and snorkelling in the transparent sunlit water. We dined on lobsters and tropical fish speared by our French friends and local fishermen, and slept to the sound of the surf on the reef.

The giant bulbous baobabs, one of the strange denizens of these unique forests, provided unexpected 'bouldering' opportunities, using holds cut in the silver bark by honey hunters and fruit gatherers. The boulders alongside the beautiful beaches of the Laka peninsula near Fort Dauphin also provided fun in an idyllic location. As always, we climbed chalk free, leaving the rocks unblemished for others to enjoy in their natural state. Overlooking them, a beautiful 200-metre granite cliff with sweeping slabs leading to twisting towers demanded closer inspection. Unsurprised by the lack of cracks, we forced our way up the side of the cliff through thick, matted jungle. Having tied a bunch of palms together on a ledge fifty metres up, we were then able to have fun crimping, frictioning and tiptoeing up the immaculate rock on our top rope. Finally, it was time to leave Tana for home. As we drew out of the bus station, the driver turned his tape deck on. Being familiar with the battered speakers and raucous music usually found on this type of transport we were surprised to hear good quality sound and the vibrant voice of Bob Marley urging us on.

We pulled out on to the street, narrowly missing a hat seller with a tottering tower of trilbies on his head. The driver was unconcerned – he too was into Mr Marley! 'Move it!' Bob sang, and the driver obeyed, heading up out of the busy streets and on to the open road.

'Move it!' he exhorted us again as we swerved to pass a convoy of zebu-carts heading down to market.

'Move it!' Marley demanded once more, as some laughing children shouted '*Au revoir*' up to our strange white faces.

55

WELCOME TO PALESTINE

*Wandering around our America has changed me more than I thought.
I am not me anymore. At least, I'm not the same me I was.*
***The Motorcycle Diaries**, Ernesto 'Che' Guevara*

After our Libyan trip, Di and I had been invited to help on the Libyan stand at the WTM in London. The Palestinian stand was directly opposite. Two things caught our attention: a help-yourself bowl of pistachio nuts, and some leaflets promoting the Nativity Trail, which we had never heard of. We had always been interested in Palestine but resisted the temptation to visit the West Bank despite its proximity to Jordan due to the Israeli occupation which we had no wish to condone by our presence. Intrigued, we went across to the stand and were greeted by a guy called Mark Khano.

He told us that he and a few others had created the route with a friend of his, Marwan Tarazi. When we gave him our n.o.m.a.d.s. card he realised who we were and told us he had our Jordan guidebooks.

'Could you come out and write a story about the trail?' he asked.

Having explained our concerns about visiting Israel, which you have to do to enter the occupied West Bank, Mark said, 'Come and see the situation for yourselves, then you will come closer to understanding what is really happening'.

The following spring we took the bus over from Amman. The Israelis don't make life easy at the border checkpoint. At the Jordanian side you can be stamped out on a piece of paper which you keep in your passport. The theory is the Israelis will then stamp you in on the paper and back out when you leave so you don't get an Israeli stamp in your passport, or even a Jordanian stamp at the Israeli border, either of which prevents travel to places like Syria and Libya. In fact it shouldn't even be an Israeli border, it should be Palestinian, but that's how it is. The West Bank is surrounded.

Despite our reservations we were determined to keep an open mind, but got an idea of life for ordinary Palestinians after we got out of the bus outside the old Damascus Gate of Jerusalem's walled city. We were an hour early for our meeting at Mark's office just up the road so couldn't resist walking into the old city, but we had only just gone through the ancient gate on to the street of El Wad when the black-booted foot of a young Israeli soldier appeared suddenly from behind us. With one well-aimed kick he sent an elderly Palestinian lady's basket of almonds spinning down the cobbles. He also shattered our last hopes of visiting Israel with open minds. Di stopped to help her gather up the basket of nuts while I remonstrated with the soldier who simply shrugged his shoulders and walked off. The lady, neatly dressed in her embroidered Palestinian dress, was old enough to be his mother. She gave Di a smile of gratitude mingled with a look of resignation.

Having met Mark he drove us to his house and gave us the key. 'My wife's away right now,' he said, 'but make yourself at home. There's plenty of food, and I'll be back later.' We had barely met him at the travel show and now he had given us the freedom of his house – the kind of Middle Eastern hospitality we were more familiar with.

Before walking the Nativity Trail we returned to Jerusalem or Al-Quds as it is known in the Arab world. It is steeped in politics and religion and sacred to the three monotheistic faiths of the children of Abraham: Jews, Christians and Muslims. We walked the Via Dolorosa where Christians sang hymns at the Stations of the Cross. We followed a pilgrim as he walked this 'Street of Sorrows', hunched beneath his cross, to the Church of the Holy Sepulchre on the hill of Golgotha, the site of the crucifixion. We visited the Western or 'Wailing' Wall where Jews of all sects come to pray, including the distinctive black-clothed Hasidic Jews with their unshorn ringlets. Above the Western Wall stood Al-Aqsa mosque, dominated as all else in the Old City by the golden Dome of the Rock. Shining in the sun, it forms a sanctuary over the exposed rock at the summit of Mount Moriah on which it is believed that Abraham prepared to sacrifice his son, Isaac. Here also was the reputed site of Solomon's and, later, Herod's temples. It is also to here that the prophet Muhammad is said to have made his night journey from Mecca on his winged horse Buraq, ascending from there to heaven to meet Abraham, Moses and Jesus.

Beyond, outside the Eastern Wall, rises the Mount of Olives down which we walked early one morning. We escaped briefly from the multitudes into the quiet gardens of the Church of Mary Magdalene with its beautiful Russian Orthodox 'onion domes', before rejoining them in the Garden of Gethsemane, marking the site where Jesus was arrested.

Already immersed in the history and religion of this ancient land, we were soon to learn yet again that its turbulent story is still unfolding. Travelling with Mark, our car was stopped on the perimeter of Jerusalem at one of the numerous Israeli checkpoints.

'Your ID and your driving licence,' the soldier demanded.

'You are not a policeman. You have no authority to see my licence,' Mark replied, while showing his ID.

'I can see anything I want,' was the arrogant reply. 'I can search your car, inspect your engine, anything. Show me your licence.'

'It's not your job, you are a soldier,' Mark persisted, pushing his luck I thought, though he was determined to establish at least this minimum right.

'I can get a policeman. There is one here.'

'I would prefer it.' Mark had made his point. The policeman checked his licence and waved us on.

We were experiencing daily life for Palestinians trying to retain a degree of dignity amidst constant humiliation. Some – those living outside Jerusalem and the West Bank – need permits to enter. It is one of many daily frustrations. On our way to Bethlehem one day, Di and I were crossing a checkpoint on its outskirts when Israeli soldiers stopped us.

'What nationality are you? What are you doing here?' one said in a strong American accent.

'We are English and we are on holiday in Palestine,' Di replied, disillusioned with the Israeli occupation and its everyday hassles.

'There is no Palestine,' he said, but waived us on with his gun ignoring my retort:

'There is and always will be.'

Later, we continued through the Shepherds' Field, to the Church of the Nativity built over the cave where it is said that Jesus was born. Continuing south, we went on to Hebron – a place that often makes headline news. In the heart of this city where over 120,000 Palestinians live, about 400 fanatical Jews had occupied and fortified what were previously Palestinian homes but were now guarded by around 1,500 Israeli soldiers. The reason for this seeming insanity is that Hebron is regarded as the burial place of Abraham, Isaac and Jacob and is consequently holy to Jews, Christians and Muslims. Ahead of us, two young Jewish boys strolled deliberately slowly up the centre of the road. As passing Palestinian cars crawled cautiously past them, they spat at the drivers through the windows which were open due to the heat of the day. They did the same to a passing Palestinian woman. No one resisted or spoke. It was a street of quiet persecution and fear.

We didn't just walk the Nativity Trail once. Having completed it in spring we were asked if we could write a guidebook.

'I wish you had asked us before,' I said. 'I don't have any of the necessary notes for a book!'

'That's okay, you can come again in the autumn,' Mark said. 'Maybe you can also find a publisher?'

We jumped at the chance, and Cicerone Press, to their credit, took the project on and received a firm order from Palestine's Bethlehem 2000 millennium project. We consequently did the Nativity Trail twice in 2000. What follows is a story of the events that occurred along the way on our autumn visit.

Our timing was bad: the Camp David Summit in America had collapsed in July 2000, failing after years of frustrated effort to deliver a Palestinian state. Two months later, the Second Intifada, also known as the Al-Aqsa Intifada, began exactly at the time of our arrival, caused by a deliberately calculated provocation by Ariel Sharon. Knowing the predictable result of his actions, he entered the Haram al-Sharif, the third holiest site in Islam, site of the Dome of the Rock and the Al Aqsa mosque just as the faithful were coming out of prayers. He claimed he was asserting the right of all Israelis to visit what they call the Temple Mount. What made that even worse was that he had been found to bear personal responsibility for the massacres of Palestinians in the refugee camps of Sabra and Shatila in Lebanon, the memorial anniversary of which had just passed. The inevitable Palestinian demonstrators threw stones at the Israeli bodyguards before being dispersed by the Israeli army using tear gas and rubber bullets with a resultant high number of casualties. The intifada rapidly spread, the final death toll, including both military and civilian, is estimated to be about 3,000 Palestinians and 1,000 Israelis as well as sixty-four foreigners.

It wasn't the best time to be in the West Bank but at least we were better able to appreciate the life of the Palestinian people as we walked the 160-kilometre trail through its hills and villages. We had been invited to walk it for the millennium, 2,000 years after the birth of Christ, 'to encourage tourists and pilgrims … and to enhance the economic development of Palestine as a crucial part of building peace.' As Mark had said, 'It's more than just a trek, it is a pilgrimage for social justice,' which was something we came to appreciate as the journey unfolded.

The trail starts in Nazareth at the Basilica of the Annunciation where the story of Christ began. From there we drove out to the foot of nearby Mount Tabor, a strategic location that shows signs of use by man dating from 80,000 BC. Rising to 588 metres above the fertile plains of Jezreel, it overlooks the hills of north Jordan that we were so familiar with. It was strange to be on the other side of the Jordan River after all these years.

We walked up through pine trees to its summit where the Church of the Transfiguration stands on the site where some of the disciples reputedly saw Jesus talking to the Old Testament prophets Elijah and Moses. Beneath lay the pathless agricultural plain, so we, like the creators of this new trail, contented ourselves by descending on foot from the summit and continuing by car to the small West Bank village of Faqqua in the biblical hills of Gilboa.

Having overnighted in the Faqqua village council rooms, our breakfast arrived at 5 a.m.: locally produced hummus, lebaneh (thick, strained yoghurt) and tomatoes with freshly baked unleavened bread served on communal trays with mint tea. We set off in the cool of the dawn, passing Palestinians waiting to be taken to work, ironically on land that was once theirs but was now occupied by Israel. Continuing down the grassy lane we passed through orchards and olive groves. Cactus and wild flowers grew in abundance. We walked on through limestone dales where a shepherd with his herd of sheep offered us tea. Overhead, buzzards searched for height to continue their migration.

We arrived in the village of Zababdeh, having completed twenty kilometres. We were on the old Roman road from Nazareth to Jerusalem in one of the villages of Samaria with numerous archaeological remains of biblical origin. Our accommodation was a building dedicated to Naim Khader, a martyr of the Palestinian struggle. In the village, Father Louis Hazboun, a contagiously enthusiastic man, showed us around his multifaith, mixed-sex school of which he was rightfully proud. He escorted us through the village where the smiling inhabitants rushed to greet him. We were welcomed into a traditional stone house, where a brass coffee pot simmered on the charcoal fire, and we chatted about life in the village, sipping at the black coffee. In the evening, gunshots echoing across the darkened hills from a nearby Israeli military camp reminded everyone that this is an occupied land.

On our third day, we walked up into the rolling hills again through olive groves, meadows of flowers and pinewoods. An eagle, resting on the lazy morning breeze, drifted by as we stopped for an early lunch on a hilltop. Descending again, we passed by a farmhouse whose owner invited us for a drink before we continued along a lane smelling of sweet lemon blossom and juniper. Ahead lay the spring of al-Far'a in the biblical land of Tirzah, the first capital of the Northern Kingdom in the time of David.

Next day, faced immediately with the ascent of Jebel Saalim, which rose to over 700 metres behind the house, we breakfasted at 5 a.m. before starting on our climb. Among the hillside flowers, delicately veined Nazareth irises nestled in a north-facing hollow. Above, Bedouin were camping with their sheep as they do each spring when the grazing is good.

Avoiding the summit, we followed a track over a pass. Below was the village of Beit Dajan through which we were inevitably unable to pass without accepting another invitation for tea. Refreshed, we continued over a low hill, then sweated up to a summit where we were greeted by the barbed wire fence of yet another new Israeli settlement spreading its scar across what had until only recently been a wild mountaintop.

'This is what the delays in fulfilling the Oslo Accords are all about,' our friends told us. 'They are building on all the commanding summits, ringing our villages, separating one from the other. Every settlement and 'bypass road' has a cleared zone on either side. If you happen to live in those areas you are evicted from your home which is destroyed with no compensation.'

We picked up the trail again on the other side of the hill along a path carpeted with blue mountain lilies. Beneath was the village of Ein Yanun with its permanent spring which, we were told, is now sometimes disrupted by the settlers. Further down the valley we ended our fourth day, a little tired and a lot wiser at the hamlet of Yanun. There, we spent the night in an old compound among Ottoman ruins, enjoying the hospitality of Abu Yassin and his family. As we relaxed in the warmth of late afternoon we were entertained by some birds on a nearby dead tree: on its broken top, a peregrine was tearing at its prey, feeding its newly fledged young. Below it, a Syrian woodpecker tapped busily at the trunk. Lower down still, a goldfinch hid in the shade while on another branch a crow struggled to crack an almond held in its beak.

After the previous day's hard, hot trek over the hills, it was then an easy stroll to the village of Duma, and our next overnight stop at the schoolhouse. We took a trip into nearby Nablus, a town in full Palestinian control. Above was Mount Gerizim with its modern Samaritan buildings built with money from the Vatican in gratitude for the drink of water given by the 'Good Samaritan' to a man who had been beaten and left by the roadside, ignored by others. As George Rishmawi, one of our Palestinian friends, said, 'You put a glass of water in the bank and 2,000 years later you get a city – not a bad investment!'

First impressions of Nablus were comparable to images of Northern Ireland, with resistance posters and graffiti everywhere: slogans supported the Popular Democratic Front for the Liberation of Palestine and posters recalled the martyrs of the intifada. The object of our excursion however, was the Turkish bath built in 1480. In the baths, we sweated on the hot stone floor heated by underground fires. This was interspersed by dips in hot and cold water, then a steam bath. A cold shower followed, then back to the hot room for a final soap down and shower and out, tingling fresh and ready for the next half of the walk.

Back in Duma, Mark, Di and I walked down to the village shop, partly for a drink, partly to meet the locals.

'You may be the first woman to enter this shop,' Di was told, much to our surprise.

We were asked back to someone's house and while we had tea, coffee and almonds we chatted about life in the village.

'It used to be very good here,' the man said. 'The land is rich, and we had enough water. Now the population has grown but the Israelis have sunk artesian wells, taking water for their settlers, so it is not so easy.'

On the fifth day, Habib, a local who was following in his family tradition of gathering honey and birds' eggs from the surrounding cliffs, accompanied us, setting a brisk pace down into Wadi Rashshash – the Valley of the Gushing Spring. It was a great day out, in gorges rimmed with ragged cliffs and riddled with caves.

A fast-flowing stream appeared abruptly from beneath a rock. We plunged our hot feet into its refreshing coolness. There's nothing quite so magical as water in the desert – for we were now entering the desert on the western fringe of the Jordan Rift Valley, about 300 metres below sea level. We spent the night in a Bedouin camp. As the sun sank behind the hills, the smell of a barbecue drifted through the tent, followed by the sweet smelling *nargile* and its accompanying sound of bubbling water, which is, perhaps, one of the reasons for its popularity in desert countries. Drinking repeated cups of sweet mint tea we listened to more tales of woe: the Bedouin, it seems, live under a constant threat of eviction. As traditionally nomadic people they have no documents of title to the land and are therefore considered as having no rights.

Next day was the second of our 'easy days'. Walking south across the stony desert we reached another Bedouin camp with a temporary school. The teacher, discovering that we were English, said while offering us tea, 'You gave our homeland to the Israelis, but you are welcome.'

Above us was the Mount and Monastery of Temptation up to which an incongruous cable car rose. We took the hard way (which was not so hard), entering the monastery in the early morning. It is built around the caves where it is believed that Jesus fasted in the wilderness. As we entered 'the cave of Jesus', the Greek Orthodox priest dismissed a Muslim family that was also present. 'You do not know much about these things, I will talk to the others.' It was uncalled for religious bigotry – a missed opportunity to share his beliefs. Disappointed, we wandered on through the monastery and up the path that winds its way to the summit of the mountain.

Returning to our Bedouin camp for a second night, we were detained in the darkness by Israeli soldiers while a military exercise passed by. Then, back at the tent we were woken in the night as a pole crashed down in a sudden gust of wind, covering all of us in the heavy goat hair tent fabric. 'Don't move, continue to sleep,' commanded George, one of the Palestinians, having miraculously sprung erect from his sleeping bag to form a human tent pole. A rather pointless bit of advice as it was almost impossible to move anyway.

The sun rose over the hills of Jordan and our eighth day began. We picked up the trail walking out of Jericho past Herod's winter palace and following the line of his aqueduct. As we followed the path up between the cliffs, rock hyrax scurried ahead, disappearing into the many caves used in the Byzantine period by Christian hermits. Further up the cliff-bound wadi we glimpsed the walls of the fifth-century Monastery of St George linked with Elijah and St Joachim. Among the icons and relics are the bones of monks martyred by the Persians. As we left the monastery, the silence of the hills was disturbed, as had often happened during our trek, by the noise of low-flying pilotless surveillance drones. We were being watched.

Our ninth day of walking was planned to take us up to the monastery of Mar Saba in the Kidron Valley, but fate had other plans. After walking for five kilometres along a deserted road we were stopped by an Israeli military vehicle.

'The area is closed for exercises,' we were told.

'But we have just walked over 100 kilometres all the way from Nazareth,' we said, hoping to appeal to the soldier's better nature, but failing. 'Could you drive us through, it won't take you ten minutes?' we pleaded, but he wouldn't. So we missed our walk up from the fringes of the Dead Sea into the mountains and resorted to our mobile phone to ask George, who was our liaison man on the trek, if he could meet us with the vehicle and take us round by road.

Sadly, this meant that we missed ten kilometres of the trail, arriving directly at the magnificently located monastery of Mar Saba built into the cliffs halfway between Jerusalem and the Dead Sea. The surrounding lime-stone hills were wild and wind-worn with panoramic views across the Dead Sea to Jordan in the east and to the hilltop fringes of Bethlehem and Jerusa-lem to the west. It was a joy to spend the afternoon on the breezy tops and in the quiet valleys with only kestrels and buzzards and the occasional flute-playing shepherd for company.

We arrived in Bethlehem with mixed feelings – the walk had not only been varied and interesting, sometimes challenging and always enjoyable, but most importantly, those of us from outside Palestine had become aware of the struggles of the Palestinians to live in peace and dignity. It had been a life-changing experience. Our guidebook *Walks in Palestine and The Nativity Trail* was published soon after, and the trail, or sections of it, is still regularly walked in guided treks by the ever-resilient Palestinians.

I can only conclude this chapter by extending Mark's invitation to 'Come and see for yourselves'. You won't regret it.

56

EXPLORING EGYPT –
IF AT FIRST YOU DON'T SUCCEED ...

Our first two failed attempts at climbing in Egypt's forbidden Red Sea Mountains were followed by five more years of persistent emails, phone calls and visits to the Egyptian Tourism Authority in London. Then, in January 2001, Di and I met Tamer, the young owner of Egypt's Nomad Adventure Tours, at the Adventure Travel Show in London. He was instantly enthusiastic.

'Yes,' he said, 'I can get you the permits. I would love to join you for some exploration.' Two months later we were on our way, this time with old friends of ours, Mark Carr and his partner Christine Evans.

Tamer emailed to say he could get permits for three weeks so we could head straight off to the desert as soon as we arrived, but Egypt being Egypt, it didn't work out like that. On our arrival he said there had been problems, it would take another five days, but he had made some alternative arrangements. Hany Amr who had a company called Desert Adventures, would take us on a trip to Egypt's Western Desert while he stayed in Cairo in case there were any further problems. *Here we go again*, I thought, but with no choice we went on what turned out to be a fun trip with Hany.

Having driven west along the coast to the battle site of El Alamein, we headed south into the desert to the remote Siwa oasis, which had been on my list of places to visit for a long time, but all I could think about was our climbing objectives, which were slipping yet again. Siwa is an interesting and ancient place and had been visited by Alexander the Great to seek knowledge from its oracle. It's way out in the Western Desert, which is so vast it encompasses most of Libya and Egypt. Remarkably it had been explored in the 1930s using Model T Fords by Ralph Bagnold. He formed the British Army's Long Range Desert Group during World War Two, though they were called the SAS in a British disinformation campaign to deceive the Axis into thinking there was a paratrooper regiment with numerous units operating in the desert instead of a small commando force behind enemy lines.

As is illustrated by a map in his fascinating book, *Libyan Sands*, the desert is comparable in size with India. Simply crossing a small corner of it from Siwa was impressive, winding our way through to Wadi Al-Hitan with its fossilised whale skeletons before heading for the Nile. Had we not had other plans it would have been tempting to continue south across the dunes of the Great Sand Sea and along the infamous Darb el Arbain – the forty-day road – used by the old slave trade route. And what an awful journey that must have been, leaving the Sudan with up to 80,000 slaves only a quarter of which would survive the journey. Following it would have taken us past the great escarpment of the Gilf Kebir to the lonely mountain of Jebel Uweinat, both of which have always intrigued me but, as I said, we had other plans, so we returned anxiously to Cairo wondering if Tamer had finally got our permits.

He had! 'I have all the permits,' he said, 'the military intelligence, the coastguard intelligence, the tourism authority and state security. I also have permits for the drivers, and permits for both compulsory vehicles.' And then came the bad news: our three weeks had now been reduced to ten days.

We started early the following morning with two vehicles driven by Hany and Tamer who had brought his Canadian girlfriend Nancy along. Almost to our surprise, the permits worked. We left the coast road 430 miles south of Cairo soon after Marsa Alam. The soldier at the checkpoint removed any remaining doubts. 'You can enter the desert from here but you will need a military escort with you for security.' So we had to have an escort, but we were in! He arrived a couple of hours later and was quiet and friendly, quickly removing any concerns we had about having someone from the army with us. We camped in the desert, Di and I sleeping out under the stars.

Using Murray's 1935 1:100,000 maps provided by the RGS and still, as far as we could discover, the best maps of the area, we continued into the emptiness of the desert. Mark, jokingly known as our 'navigation officer' as he had a GPS, was almost immediately redundant: cresting a rise, the huge domed inselberg of Jebel Sila'i dominated the otherwise flat surroundings.

As Murray had said, it initially looked seamless: 'a thousand feet high and as sheer and smooth and unclimbable as the Hill of Glass.' He thought some summit stones may have been a cairn, but having walked around the mountain and briefly explored the upper slabs from a high col, he and his companion Ali 'slapped hands on its smooth sides and left the mystery unsolved'. Viewing its atrociously exfoliating faces, huge scabs of rock ready to fall at a touch, we felt he may be right about it being unclimbable. Nevertheless we were here to climb it and were already inspired by the remote location of our camp under its south face. It was an idyllic spot made all the more remarkable by the presence of three deep pools of water hidden in the slabs above us.

We were up before dawn, armed to the teeth with climbing gear and loaded down with water. It had taken fourteen years to get here and we weren't going to be turned back easily. The best approach was obvious, up a boulder slope to the east col, thereby neatly bypassing the apparently impregnable lower tiers of this three-tiered dome. The final tier overhung the second for most of its length but looked accessible from the col, though Murray had tried that way without success. Remarkably he had missed the solution to the puzzle. Concealed beyond the col and lower down on its opposite side, a ramp curved through the flaking rock of the 300-metre north-east face. We scrambled into it with ease. Unable to believe that climbing gear wouldn't be needed, we roped up and padded skywards on large creaking crisps of granite, imagining inadvertently 'surfing' down on one for 200 metres to the desert. Murray could have climbed it with ease. By eight in the morning, we were on the summit. The view was awesome though marred by desert dust blowing up from the south, concealing the even more remote Elba Mountains on the Sudan Border. Otherwise, the void stretched out towards the Red Sea and the Nile, black dykes of basalt leading the eye out to other distant desert mountains.

The cairn was unmistakable, but was it the one Murray thought he had seen? Or was it more recent? Had the military been there, perhaps by helicopter? It didn't matter – it was a wonderful top. In the heart of the desert, between Aswan and the Red Sea and just north of Sudan, we had finally climbed G.W. Murray's Hill of Glass. After a fourteen-year quest we were at last standing on the first of our summits in what we now called 'Egypt's Forbidden Mountains'.

Despite its simplicity we were more than happy with our ascent and our minds were already moving on. With an unexpected half day to spare, we grabbed the opportunity and headed south-east through the desert into a blank area of Murray's map marked 'Unsurveyed', and there're not many of those around these days. His neat writing indicated that it was 'Rocky terrain with small hills' but interestingly there was a 'Remarkable pinnacle' on the far side. It would have been a bonus just to locate it, but with limited time and after losing ourselves in complex canyons, home to herds of gazelles and flocks of sand grouse, we abandoned our search. If nothing else it was good to know the desert was still alive and it would be a good area to come back to another time. We then headed south for another thirty miles to look for the Farayid Mountains, 'the most aggressive in Egypt', their sharp spires being known to the Romans as Mons Pentadactylus, the Five Finger Mountain. The following morning we looked for the Bedouin well of Bir Girid. It was marked on Murray's map but we couldn't find it, so Di and I went to search about a hundred metres away in some bushes which seemed to us to be the obvious place until Mark shouted, 'It's here, right on Murray's coordinates'. It was covered by branches, which were covered in sand. We would have missed it were it not for Mark's GPS, which proved not only that a GPS was useful, but also the impressive accuracy of Murray's 1930s survey.

Further on we met a small group of Ababda Bedouin eking a living from charcoal making and raising camels. They were fuzzy-haired characters, one of whom unsheathed his sword and performed a welcoming sword-dance. They told us about their life, making charcoal to sell at Bir Shalatein, a four-day camel journey away; or travelling all day for water and spending the last six months trying to dig a new well but without success. 'Would you like to stay and help?' they asked. It would have been an interesting experience but time wasn't on our side. We declined, but filled their goatskin to the brim with precious water, and gave them some oranges; the smiles on their faces were sufficient reward.

Their women, they said, were camped further down the valley and we stopped as we reached a few 'benders' of palm matting spread over gnarled branches, and called out a greeting. Di and Christine walked over for a chat with the black-clothed women who were adorned with rings, decorative headpieces, bracelets and earrings of silver. Mark and I were tempted to join them but it wouldn't have been etiquette so, having exchanged greetings, we drove on leaving them to the quiet solitude of their traditional desert life.

We were happy to have met them, but hoped that the inevitable encroachment of modernity and the possible advent of desert tourism would bring genuine benefits rather than cultural disaster.

Reaching the frontier town of Bir Shalatein, with its problems of gun-running and drugs due to the proximity of the Sudan border, we were allowed through the checkpoint for a couple of hours for fuel, water and provisions. It's predominantly a shanty town, bustling with Sudanese selling camels and goats and eager to boost their income by selling their swords or knives, though few other than Egyptians reach this remote and distinctly wacky place. We then turned north to find the Farayids which rise spectacularly from the coastal desert across which the turquoise sea offers a tempting alternative. Resisting its seductions, we drove west into the mouth of a tree-lined wadi encircled by high-pinnacled summits, blue-grey in the afternoon light. Murray's description of the location of a dramatic rock arch was vague but, since Bedouin – or mountain people anywhere – know everything worth knowing about their local hills, we were pleased to see a couple sitting in the shade of an acacia.

After the usual greetings, we asked about the bridge. 'Come with me,' the elder one said, obviously happy that he could help, dashing off immediately – a broken sandal flapping madly as he strode across the sands. Sure enough, within 200 metres a shaft of sunlight speared one of the summits to reveal an amazing and unique piece of rock architecture. From an elephant's head of rock just under the summit, a long slender trunk arched down the seaward face with a bulbous 'wart' growing up from its dangerously narrow centre. Murray's 'preposterous flying buttress that seemed to sway and throb in the wind' was undoubtedly the weirdest rock feature we had ever seen.

We slept surrounded by a ragged array of granite peaks. Rising in the pre-dawn, we were already making our way up a gully filled with house-sized polished boulders when the sun turned the Red Sea into shimmering beaten gold. It was going to be hot! We continued, urged upwards by glimpses of the bizarre rock bridge, but reaching its foot, it became obvious that its ascent was out of the question – we opted instead to climb the cliff beneath it then pass beneath its slender arch to reach its top.

It was nice to be climbing, the dubious rock added to the interest. Murray had photographed it from the side, so it was a real delight to be the first to climb beneath the ludicrous trunk, reaching its summit at midday.

To the south, the last of our three objectives could be seen – the aiguille of the Bodkin. Eastwards, the sea now shone silver. The surrounding peaks were burning in the sun. Rock hyrax, perching in an acacia in the gully beneath us, dashed for the safety of the cliffs as a sharp-eyed eagle attacked. It was hot and getting hotter. We descended through a high valley of polished rocks and white sand, sun blasted, burning like a solar oven at 40 °C. Logs jammed high in its mouth told of flash floods roaring through these barren hills, which also explained the giant boulders jammed in the gully below. Its descent was as arduous as the ascent, but as we relaxed around the fire later that evening, the rock bridge smiled at us from the darkening peaks.

Next day, using Murray's book and maps, we managed to locate the approach to the Bodkin up a hidden wadi concealed by a sand dune, and identify a possible route to its narrow top, but with our permit about to expire, like Murray we 'left it alone in its austerity'. We did however note with interest what I called some 'little big walls' further up the desert valley. Their summits were marked on Murray's map, one of which was named Purdy Peak after US Colonel Purdy who had done a recce along the coast for a railway in 1870. I hope Murray would have been as pleased as we were with our achievements, following in his footsteps. I also remembered the advice of Don Whillans, 'Always leave something to come back to'.

57

EXPLORING EGYPT – NUBIAN NEMESIS

It takes a lot of optimism, after all, to be a traveler.
The New York Times, Paul Theroux

We returned to Egypt later in 2001. The world was still in turmoil following 9/11. Almost 3,000 people were killed, resulting in President George Bush's 'war on terror' after which the Middle East has never been the same.

It wasn't the best time to be in an Islamic country, but apart from problems with bureaucracy all our previous experiences in the Middle East had been faultless. You couldn't wish to meet more friendly and hospitable people. It was to be our second trip to 'Egypt's Forbidden Mountains' after fourteen years of both natural and man-made obstacles in the form of sandstorms, military checkpoints and bureaucracy. It was also our fourth attempt to visit the Bodkin and the little-known Elba Mountains in Egypt's Nubian Desert near the Sudan border. We were keen to return and explore further, and I had spent eight months since our last visit asking Tamer and anyone else including the Egyptian Tourism Authority and Hany to obtain permits for December for all the Red Sea Mountains.

Having had no response from the ETA and a very apologetic one from Hany saying permits were impossible to get, I finally had an email off Tamer to say he could get them, so we booked our tickets and a week before we were due to fly, Tamer emailed to say 'I have the permits in my hands'. *Could it really be true?*

When we arrived in Cairo we met Hany, who was worried about Tamer's permits. So much so that he said he wouldn't be joining us.

'Have a good trip, but be careful,' he said.

Tamer however was confident, and the next day we were headed south loaded with food and equipment for three weeks in the desert. This time he was accompanied by his new young Spanish girlfriend, Kristina, who was wearing a crop top exposing her bare stomach and navel ring. Hardly appropriate for an Islamic country, but it wasn't our place to tell her.

We travelled speedily south for 400 miles to Quseir, mysteriously avoiding the Hurghada checkpoint.

Next day an early start brought us to the Marsa Alam checkpoint, now about 500 miles from Cairo, which we neatly bypassed when the world was sleeping late, as it does during Ramadan. Unperturbed, Tamer suggested we continue. We began to wonder if there was more to these early starts than simple enthusiasm to get to the mountains, but arriving at the next checkpoint, there was a soldier there. It didn't worry Tamer. A donation of Ramadan sweets seemed to work miracles and we drove on with only one more checkpoint to pass at Berenice before entering the desert above which a half moon hung in a pale blue-rinse dawn sky. To our surprise, this final hurdle was neatly bypassed, making a huge detour through stony wadis. 'It's Ramadan,' Tamer said. 'No need to disturb them.'

As we approached the village of Sheikh Shadhili the first scattered Ababda camp came into view and we detoured west again through the desert. It all seemed very odd, but we made it to the foot of Jebel Sila'i – our first objective – exactly at nightfall. We wondered why we didn't need a military escort with us from Marsa Alam, as had been necessary in the spring, but Tamer seemed unconcerned. He had the permits so we thought no more of it, at least, not until having climbed to the summit with him the next day. We looked down and saw an army vehicle at our camp. The elation of topping out on this remote mountain was replaced by anxiety about this unexpected visit. We returned down the plunging slabs of the south-east face to see what fortune had in store. 'Don't worry,' Tamer said, 'there's no problem.'

Back at camp we were asked for our passports and permits. A four-hour radio call to military HQ ensued. Permits were read repeatedly. Passports were checked. Something, we felt sure, was wrong. A soldier was detailed to accompany us, and I overheard the officer telling Tamer to be in Bir Shalatein – the last village down the coast – in a couple of days. This was odd as we had much to do before reaching Shalatein, but questions got us nowhere.

Determined to make the best of it we set off with our military escort for our next objective on Murray's map, the well of Bir Abraq, where we found inscriptions of cattle, hyenas and a pharaonic boat of the style seen in Egyptian tombs – strange to see so far out in the desert though the well is strategically located on a shortcut between the Nile and the Red Sea, so perhaps goods once travelled this way. We however were looking for rock and the map showed a winding twelve-mile canyon called Wadi Dib that looked as though it might offer climbing potential. It was a great desert drive, twisting through the mountains, but the rock was completely shattered.

Emerging from the desert at Shalatein, our passports were collected again and we were asked to stay in the vehicles until the officer arrived. It was hot, far too hot to be in the car, but the delay dragged on for over seven hungry and thirsty hours and despite repeated requests we weren't allowed out. When the officer finally arrived, more calls to Cairo HQ ensued. By midnight, we had the verdict.

'You must go to Cairo for new permits,' he said apologetically. 'You will get them in one hour, then you can return and I look forward to joining you for the rest of your trip. The Elba Mountains are beautiful and the Bedouin will welcome you. I know them well. Don't worry,' he said sympathetically, 'you can be back in two or three days.'

By now none of us were really convinced but we tried to remain optimistic. Driving there and back – 1,250 miles in two days didn't seem like fun, but if that's what we had to do, we weren't giving up on eight months of planning just for two days of inconvenience.

We crashed out wondering what tomorrow would bring and if we really would reach our long-planned destination on our return. Unknown summits beckoned, 'mountains with granite cliffs surrounded by forests so dense that loaded camels couldn't pass between them. Where Bisharin Bedouin lived a life of plenty with unlimited water.' *Could it be true?*

By six, we were on the road. Fifteen hours later, we were negotiating the polluted, congested streets of Cairo to arrive at 10 p.m. at the high-walled guarded gates of the military security; it was obviously a prison. We were escorted through the darkness into a large, dingy office. A soldier was asleep on a table. The others seemed to be transfixed by Kristina's bare stomach and navel ring. About 3 a.m., we were escorted to see 'the General'.

'You know why you are here?' he asked ominously, with a sneaky glance at Kristina.

'Yes,' we replied, 'to get a new permit,' trying to be optimistic in the hope that we could still rescue the situation and be on our way back 'within an hour' as promised, but no such luck.

'No,' he said. 'You have been travelling in a forbidden area on false permits.'

Well, this was news to us. His next question was even more confusing.

'Do you know anyone called Nancy?'

'No,' I started to say, then remembering that Tamer's previous girlfriend was called Nancy, I started to add, 'oh, sorry, yes', but was cut short by Tamer:

'No, not her, there must be another Nancy.' It was all getting rather strange. We had been up twenty-two hours and were ready for bed.

'Is there anywhere we can sleep?' I asked. Having been offered 'some nice accommodation', we were then driven across town, arriving at another high wall with huge steel doors. It opened to reveal armed soldiers with fixed bayonets. A dimly lit corridor giving access to prison cells lay ominously ahead.

'Women first,' the jailer said. It was all getting rather out of hand.

'No,' I said firmly. 'Either we all stay together or we phone the British embassy now.'

The officer changed tack. 'No problem, we have just the place.'

We were lead down a narrow prison corridor, half expecting to be pushed into individual cells, but emerging in a courtyard, we were shown a separate block – still with a barred door and windows, but with showers and toilets. The door was locked behind us and we were in bed within minutes, waking four hours later when swords of sunlight divided by the bars at the window pierced our room reminding us – if it was necessary – of our current location locked in a military jail in Cairo. I walked over to the door. Through its bars a massive, padlocked bolt was visible. Beyond, a sleepy-eyed armed guard shook his head and grinned when I asked to be let out into the yard. There were obviously going to be no more new mountains to explore on this trip.

Later, we were allowed into the high-walled compound where, to our surprise, we were given a good breakfast. It was quite pleasant really, in the centre of Cairo but quiet, with a few trees casting shade under which we sat and read. Di and Kristina did their washing, hanging their 'smalls' on the trees to the bemusement of the guards. Each of us was individually interrogated during the day, and we finally discovered what the problem was: we had been travelling on last spring's permits. Tamer had altered the dates and added new areas without telling us. Kristina was – unknown to her – travelling on Nancy's permit.

Meanwhile, Tamer had 'disappeared'. We never saw him again. The few bags that we had left in the vehicle had been searched and an unused film destroyed. Luckily, Di, quick-thinking as ever, had suggested keeping our used film with us. When I asked why they had ruined an unused film the officer replied, 'I didn't know it was unused'.

I should have taken all our bags with us into the cell as Di had also suggested with her usual common sense. Then they asked for our other films and cameras but we refused.

'Not until we have spoken to the embassy,' I said. Once again they backed off.

Then Di had another good suggestion, 'We can show them some photos'. Among them were not just pictures of us with our families and with Bedouin that we used for conversation when invited to stay with strangers, but pictures of Di and me with Queen Noor. The guard obviously thought he recognised her.

'Who is that?' he asked, bemused.

'It's Queen Noor,' Di replied. 'She's a friend of ours.'

They seemed impressed. We were taken back to the 'General's' office 'to attend court'. There, after more laborious questioning, all of which was painstakingly translated into Arabic and written down by a soldier, we eventually arrived at the 'summing up'.

'It is obvious that you did not know the permits were false,' the judge said. 'You will be released and your travel agent's company has been told to arrange a free hotel for you.'

'But what about the new permits your officer in Bir Shalatein promised us?' I asked, with pretend naivety, guessing what the answer would be.

'First you must find a reliable agent, then you will need to wait three weeks,' he said. 'Will you be coming back to Egypt?'

'After all this mess, I'm not sure,' I said.

The 'General' seemed quite upset. 'You have been travelling illegally in a forbidden area. You could have got lost or had an accident. We are very concerned for your safety.'

So that was the end of our trip. Hany commiserated with us and said, 'I told you there was something wrong, but maybe we can try again sometime. I would be very happy to go with you.'

Tamer lost his tourist licence and spent three months 'inside' with his unfortunate drivers. But I have to say he meant well and we wouldn't have achieved what we did in the spring without him. He now has a hotel in the Western Sahara and I wish him well. I have made enquiries about Murray's mountains every year since, but I'm told that travel in the southern Red Sea Mountains is still impossible.

58

INCREDIBLE INDIA – THE NORTH-EAST FRONTIER

'If you can keep your head when all about you / Are losing theirs … ' is one of Kipling's better-known lines. It also used to be a matter of genuine concern rather than metaphorical for any strangers entering Nagaland in north-east India. A few tribal elders still recall their warrior days. Indeed, rumours persist that heads sometimes still go.

Di had her hip operated on in summer 2001. A month after the operation she was able to walk a few miles. In two months she was beginning to climb again and walking up to ten miles in the hills without problem, so we were keen to get a trip organised for the winter.

At the WTM in November we found someone from Assam who was interested in the possibility of developing trekking tours with his company, Ashoka Holidays, to Nagaland and other parts of India's previously closed north-east states. He said, 'You will find some wonderful places on your trip to this almost virgin land which remains under-explored. Experienced hands like yours can do a lot of good for this region, which nature has richly bestowed with great variety.'

Nowadays, though permits are still required for some parts of North-East India, which includes the eight states of: Assam, Arunachal Pradesh, Nagaland, Manipur, Mizoram, Tripura, Meghalaya and Sikkim, the region is open. The indigenous peoples are developing village lodges, arranging treks and rafting trips, and assisting caving, trekking and climbing expeditions. There are also excellent and little-visited national parks and colourful festivals in an area rich in wildlife and tribal culture.

Nagaland itself sits high on India's north-east border – another example of a tribal group being split in half in the British colonial era when their land was divided between India and Burma (now Myanmar). Its dense jungles, deep ravines, high mountains and previously inhospitable and feared Naga headhunters meant that much of it remained 'unadministered territory' until India's independence in 1948. Border incursions from China in 1962 and tribal skirmishes including interstate and cross-border raids, as well as movements for a free and united Nagaland, kept the Indian army busy and the north-east predominantly closed to the outside world until the end of the twentieth century.

With only twenty days allowed to experience the diverse culture and wildlife and any opportunities for adventure, we were stuck for choice. Fortunately our hosts, Ashoka Holidays, solved our dilemma. Nagaland would be just one of the places on our list.

In late November, we left Guwahati, the 'Gateway to the North East', with Dave Cummins, a photographer friend of ours, and Ashoka's manager, Partha Pratim Das, a young lad, enthusiastic to learn more about adventure and ecotourism. We headed off up the tortuous road, dodging slow-moving trucks on our way to Meghalaya and Cherrapunji, high up in beautiful jungle mountains and with a surprising panoramic view over the watery plains of Bangladesh, a country we had never expected to see. Cherrapunji is also 'the wettest place in the world'. Not an obvious attraction for anyone coming from the English Pennines, but when we were there it never rained, whereas in the monsoon it can drop over four and a half metres of rain a month on to your tin roof – not a nice thought! The rain has also carved out the limestone to form most of India's and South Asia's longest caves.

The great thing about caving is, it's always good to re-emerge again, to newly appreciate the beauty of the blue sky and mountains and realise how lucky you are not to be a caver! But the seven-kilometre-long Krem Mawmluh is one of the more amenable ones. It was easy going, with a nice river passage, although the roof was unusually decorated with shredded poly bags swept in from a nearby cement factory. We emerged into vertical jungle, escaping to eat lunch above Nohkalikai Waterfall which the locals told us is the world's fourth highest. When I checked later, it wasn't even on the world's 'highest waterfalls' list, though I was pleased to discover that three of them are in Romsdal.

We then heard tales of some possibly unique 'living bridges' – eco-friendly constructions built by the Khasi and Jaintia hill people by training the living roots and creepers of banyan trees (*Ficus elastica*) across the rivers, initially through hollowed-out areca nut tree trunks. They date back perhaps 200 years but undergo continuous maintenance as new shoots are woven into the old. One of the bridges is two-tiered. They are truly spectacular and the only bridges to survive the annual monsoon floods, well worth the steep descent on jungle trails. We were told – probably wrongly – that we were the first outsiders to see them.

We also found a daily archery competition in Shillong, where a dozen or so archers from the Khasi and Jaintia hill people, who are Mongolian in origin, fire off as many arrows as possible in a limited time. Bets are placed on the number of arrows that will hit the target – which is a lot! The people have obviously not forgotten their hunting and fighting skills. We lost our few rupees but, like the locals, fully enjoyed the experience before heading down to Assam's famous Kaziranga reserve. There, we rode elephants through the tall grasses as the sun crept over the hills, banishing the morning mist. We came within a few metres of India's rare one-horned rhinos. Otters played in nearby pools over which kingfishers darted. Wild elephants trumpeted a greeting to the dawn. Deer and wild boar barked and grunted.

Next day found us winding up into the jungle-covered hills of Nagaland to Tuophema village, its entrance protected by huge and ancient stone mono-liths and its houses displaying the skulls of mithun (large humpbacked mountain cattle, 'the pride of the north-east') commemorating 'Feasts of Merit' given by the owner where once human skulls had pride of place. The disparate Naga tribes who previously raided each other to add to their head collections had since formed the Naga Nation, proud of their heritage. Their capital, Kohima, was hosting the Hornbill Festival, ritual dances being performed by tribes such as Konyak, Rengma, Chang, Ao and Angami, each in their own style and brightly coloured traditional dress.

Food, as always in the north-east, was excellent and spicy, though perhaps more meat oriented than elsewhere in India. Cafe menus included pork fat curry, venison, wildfowl and the curious 'tadpole delicacy'. Needless to say we didn't see much wildlife in Nagaland. Sadly, even the hornbill, the tail feathers of which adorn the Naga headress, is only found in one protected area. Despite missionaries' efforts to declare Nagaland a 'dry' state, the local rice beer and ubiquitous Kingfisher were easy to buy, but the presence of Christianity is seen in many villages which are sometimes dwarfed by the often huge churches largely paid for by tithes from the Nagas who, though apparently willing, could scarcely afford it. We were also told that the young were losing the strong traditional respect for their ancestors who, not being Christian, wouldn't be able to go to heaven. How sad is that?

Following the festival we had intended to climb the highest nearby peak, 3,084-metre Mount Japfu, home of the world's tallest rhododendron at twenty metres, but its summit remained obstinately cloud capped. Instead, we opted for the Dzüku Valley, 'the best trekking in the area'. Its approach involved a four-hour sweat up vertical jungle. The three young Nagas, Avile and the two porters who led the way, were, as hill people always are, supremely fit. Climbing effortlessly they set their pace by calling the traditional Naga war cry to each other: '*He-haa*' … '*Ho-haa*'. It echoed eerily from the jungle ahead as the omnipresent gloom deepened with the rapidly setting sun. Little wonder that the chant terrified the intended victims of Naga raiding parties.

We emerged from the jungle at over 2,700 metres, just as the sun sank across the valley, to be welcomed by a sign nailed to a tree: 'Come to me, all you who are weary and burdened, and I will give you rest. Matthew 11.28.' Well, maybe he would, but it was more than rest we needed, it was liquid refreshment and a pan full of the always-excellent Indian food. Jubilant to be up, we contoured the precipitous hillside through waist-deep dwarf bamboo.

A bird with a high-pitched squeaky call like an old door hinge seemed to be following me through the bushes. When we stopped to look for it, the shrill whistle stopped. When we started again, it began again. After a few repeats of this we suddenly realised what it was. It wasn't a bird, it was Di's hip: every time she moved, it squeaked, which worried us at the time. It was too remote an area to have a serious hip problem, but there was no pain and no problem the next day or the rest of the trip. When we eventually got back home we mentioned it to the surgeon who said she had probably been dehydrated and the joint lacked lubrication.

We reached the hut well after dark. Despite their cumbersome loads, the Naga boys were there first, dinner was being prepared and hot drinks were soon ready. Next morning, veils of mist parted beneath our sun-warmed eyrie to reveal a thick carpet of frost in the Dzüku Valley, its dwarf bamboo turned white by the cold. As we walked down into it, the clouds lifted, revealing a bizarre landscape of eroded mountains heaving into the distance. It would have been good to trek on for a few days, but having other things on our agenda, we returned along a narrow hillside trail before descending into the jungle again and down to Kigwema with its terraces of rice and maize and fat black pigs in bamboo styes.

Next day we visited the hilltop fortified village of Khonoma where the British fought and won a battle against the Nagas in 1879 as evidenced by memorials to the dead of both sides. A stone archway guarded the village entrance, carved symbols on its doors recording 'deeds of merit'. Despite our ancestral conflicts, we were, as usual, treated to home-brewed rice beer while we chatted with the locals in the village square. Women and children were washing at the spring. Two boys were splitting bamboo and weaving baskets. Down in the fields, a few people were working. A pig lay idly sunning itself in someone's garden. Wild flowers grew from the walls. We had another rice beer before leaving to pay our respects at the World War Two cemetery above Kohima where I remembered my Uncle Roy, 'missing in action, believed dead', in the jungles of nearby Burma, while only a teenager.

From there, our route took us through Assam, over the Brahmaputra River and up towards the Himalayan mountains of Arunachal Pradesh where we were delayed briefly by soldiers demanding to requisition our vehicle. Fortunately they changed their minds following discussions with Partha and the fortuitous arrival of another car behind us. In the morning we visited Rabgelling Gompa. As in the rest of western Arunachal Pradesh, the people are Tibetan Buddhist and we were treated to the traditional welcome of yak-butter tea. Once more on the move we wound up the ceaselessly twisting road to the Sela Pass where prayer flags streamed in the icy wind at 4,170 metres. We spent a long cold night there in a Buddhist shrine with headaches due to the fast rise in altitude of about 4,000 metres in one day from the Brahmaputra.

In the morning, the sunlit snow-capped 6,488-metre pyramid of Gori Chen glinted on the horizon. Bill Tilman had attempted it in 1939 but the expedition had succumbed to malaria. It was finally climbed 'illegally' by Dutchman Ronald Naar in 1993 who had been unable to get permits, but our destination was India's oldest Tibetan Buddhist monastery at Tawang, 'Chosen by Horse'. The founding lama had travelled over the Himalaya from distant Lhasa to start a new monastic retreat. While meditating in a cave, his horse disappeared. He found it pawing the ground, indicating the spot on which to build the biggest Buddhist monastery outside of Lhasa. Tawang is now home to 700 monks and steeped in the serenity of centuries of prayer. The huge Buddha that dominates the prayer hall was brought in pieces on yaks from Tibet.

We spent a couple of days there, walking trails between villages and gompas, one of which stands on the birthplace of the sixth Dalai Lama. We also visited the Tawang war memorial, built after the Chinese incursion of 1962. Then we were back on the road again, by now used to its twists and turns, precipitous drops and regular warning signs: 'Drinking whisky, driving risky', 'Be gentle on my curves', 'Don't read this sign, keep your eyes on the road', and, most bizarrely, 'In 2005 an MIG 37 will land here'. Was that written by a mad road builder or a prophetic Himalayan mystic emerging from years of meditation? Either way, it didn't happen!

Descending towards Assam, we entered a valley in search of some black-necked cranes – an endangered species – that we were told were overwintering there. We found them stepping daintily through a paddy field but were distracted by the sound of chanting to the rhythm of a Tibetan drum and the tortured notes of a trumpet. Overlooked by the balconies of stone and timber frame houses, a cluster of Monpa villagers were watching some wildly gyrating, strangely masked demon-dancers. Their origins date back to a time when, troubled by demons, the people went to an ancient lama who, after much contemplation, conjured up five celestial beings to wander the earth, ritually dancing demons away wherever they find them. The drumming and dancing was incessant. Chang beer was flowing freely. There wasn't a tourist in sight – we had been in north-east India for almost three weeks and hadn't met a single one.

Next day, we rafted downriver into the jungle of the Nameri reserve in which elephants could be seen and heard, crashing through dense vegetation, and disturbing the monkeys. A sambar deer leapt into the undergrowth ahead of us and deeply incised tiger tracks told of a recent buffalo kill, but the tigers themselves remained frustratingly elusive.

Then we were back in Guwahati, in our hotel on the banks of the Brahmaputra, but our time with the Nagas and other hill tribes, and the sights seen in the north-east states had been ample to justify a positive report for Ashoka.

59

INCREDIBLE INDIA – SARAMATI SURPRISE

Next year we were in Nagaland again with Ashoka Holidays. Our objective was Saramati, which although only 3,837 metres high, is the highest mountain in Nagaland, situated precisely on the Myanmar border. Not a major summit in the general scheme of things, especially being within view of the Himalaya, but an obvious potential attraction for trekkers being in such a remote, wild and culturally interesting area, three days' drive from the capital, then a trek through the jungle with its otherwise inaccessible Naga villages.

We were told no outsiders had ever been. We met our porters in Salomi and loaded up to trek to Thanamir, a delightful Yimchunger Naga village on Saramati's lower jungle-covered slopes, where we stayed in a village house. Living with the locals is always a pleasure, and we were able to explain the benefits of trekking and ecotourism.

Having had eight porters to get six of us to Thanamir, we were surprised to find about twenty-five villagers would be accompanying four of us as 'guides and porters' the next day. There were also six armed village guards 'for our protection'. It was only later that the reason for this army of people became apparent.

My map, copied from one in the British Library, indicated a good ridge heading for the summit, but we unexpectedly plunged off it, repeatedly descending and ascending steep slippery ground in the gloom of the jungle, climbing up and down tree roots and creepers, the Nagas cutting a trail ahead of us with their *dao* swords. We had been told there was a trail. If there was we certainly weren't on it, but despite the difficulty we were moving surprisingly fast. The Nagas were, as Doug Scott said of the Nyishi jungle tribesmen of nearby Arunachal Pradesh,

… totally adapted to living on steep mountainsides covered in dense jungle, [they] displayed all the attributes and energy of real mountaineers … moving over the most precarious terrain with grace and an economy of effort … through the tangle of root and mud, creeper and thorn bush … by slippery logs or slimy boulders … they were also warm and spontaneous, producing laughter and amusement at every opportunity.

We were therefore surprised when after six hours it seemed we had only covered about three miles. We stopped at nightfall to clear a small area for our camp having only twice glimpsed views beyond our immediate vicinity. It seemed to us that we were well off route. But, it was a good and totally different experience to be away in this remote jungle with the Nagas.

Next day we woke before dawn as we heard distant gunshots and chanting deeper in the jungle. The fire was rekindled in the darkness; something was happening. We soon discovered the reason for the excitement. They had known that a female bear was in the area with twin cubs. Some of our Nagas had gone in the night and managed to kill one of the cubs. So that's what it was all about! And that's why the Naga jungles are so quiet. Anything that moves gets eaten. And one of the purposes of our trip was to encourage them to develop ecotourism.

We were told it would now take two days, not one, to reach the summit, so we had a problem as permit regulations were strict with potential fines. Abandoning our Saramati plan wasn't just a matter of conforming with the permit, I was also really annoyed about the bear killing after our eco talk the other day. Disappointed, we decided to return to Thanamir and do a village-to-village trek on the slopes of Saramati to experience the life of the Yimchunger Naga. Hopefully it would get us back to Kohima on schedule. Partha agreed, saying, 'Trekking isn't just about "getting there", it's about enjoying the journey'. It turned out to be an excellent decision.

We set off back, leaving the locals to cook and eat the bear cub. Summiting Saramati had been the major objective of our trip so it was a big personal disappointment. The forest itself is magnificent prime monsoon jungle with giant hardwoods festooned in moss, ferns and other plants. We are still of the opinion that Saramati could be a big attraction for trekkers if the correct trail is followed, though we were later informed that it's best climbed in November and April. It's a pity we weren't told this before going in October on the monsoon roads which were knee deep in mud, and it's a great shame our Naga companions had taken no heed of our earlier chat about the wild-life aspects of ecotourism. Throughout Nagaland we had been shocked at the absence of wildlife. Though sound doesn't travel far in dense jungle, the forests were devoid of sound except for the crickets. Of the very few birds we saw, two were dead: one was in a Naga hunter's bag, the other was spread on a branch to dry the meat.

Our inter-village trek was good. The first day had its ups and downs and a couple of entertaining footbridges made from logs jammed over the side-rivers – not to mention a few leeches. We arrived early in Fakim, which is perched nicely high above the river at an altitude of 1,888 metres. Somehow they knew we were coming and to our surprise we were greeted outside the village by the elders and escorted to our accommodation in the headman's house where we were welcomed. The walls were decorated with mithun skulls, as well as spears, farming tools, a handmade gun, *daos* and other tools of daily life. As we arrived, a group of chanting villagers came down the hill pulling a reluctant mithun with a cane rope through its nose – apparently they had bought it in a Burmese Naga village and brought it twenty-five miles over the hills that day. They weren't supposed to cross the border that had divided their nation but they did it all the time. It made me wonder about coming back on another trip and trekking down off the summit of Saramati into Burmese Nagaland.

As usual, the village was full of pigs, hens, dogs, puppies and kittens, all of which Di was upset to find are part of the Naga diet. Strips of pork were hung to smoke above the fire, though the pigs also perform another valuable service: cleaning up all village waste – including human waste – which means you have to be very quick going to the toilet in the jungle or the pigs get there before you've finished. This happened to Partha who had to beat one off with a stick. Seeing a chicken being killed for our dinner with an accurately aimed catapult using handmade pellets of hardened clay while it was contentedly clucking around the kitchen floor was another unusual experience. Life as we know it is generally too far removed from the reality of life and death.

We were told we were the first foreign visitors to come to their village. I wasn't sure if it was true, but following dances by the women in their trad-itional dress, I was asked to join hands in a celebratory dance round the fire with the men who were wearing hats decorated with bear fur and claws, boar tusks and hornbill feathers. Some had tiger-tooth necklaces. All had traditional dress and most carried *daos* or spears. I'm not usually into these things, though dancing the *samer* with our Bedouin friends was a great experience and this also seemed special. Afterwards, our guide Stefan translated the song for us:

> Thank you for coming to our village. Your visit has brought us good fortune. We have nothing but you are welcome to our hospitality. The visitor is dancing with the Nagas. He is the first to learn our dance. Welcome again to our village.

For Di and me this evening was a highlight of the trek and we hoped that others would follow in our footsteps. It seemed the village headman was a forward-thinking person who had already allocated a considerable area of jungle as a sanctuary, through which he said there was a way to the top of Saramati.

Next day we set off on the short trek to Penkim where we once again had time to enjoy the village, visiting the morung – a type of community hall – and seeing for the first time one of Nagaland's giant log drums. From there a short walk took us to the car. Just after driving through a checkpoint, a small group of armed Nagas emerged from the jungle and stopped us.

'How many soldiers were at the checkpoint?' they asked.

A tricky question! 'We aren't sure,' I said. 'Some of them were inside.' It wasn't helpful, but they seemed satisfied and we drove on wondering who they were and what they were doing.

Flying out from Guwahati a few days later when our permits had expired, the distant Himalaya were shrouded in cloud. To the east, the jungle mountains inhabited by some of the most welcoming, colourful and interesting of India's tribal people rapidly disappeared into the distance.

60

PALESTINE – IS THERE ANYBODY OUT THERE?

It's a dangerous business, Frodo, going out your door.
The Lord of the Rings, J.R.R. Tolkien

On both occasions that we walked the Nativity Trail in 2000, Di and I had been shocked by the rapidly expanding Israeli settlements and the daily difficulties experienced by Palestinian families living under occupation. We were impressed by their stoicism, resolution, welcoming smiles and hospitality. Though things were bad, there was a feeling that they would improve in the new millennium. After all, the Berlin Wall had come down and anything seemed possible. We returned four years later in 2004, this time with Mick Shaw – not to trek but to find out what had happened to the trail and the hopes of the Palestinians.

Things had changed. The Israeli wall was going up, and though it brought the Palestinian qualities of resilience and fortitude to the fore, there was a feeling of despondency. Since the unleashing of President Bush's war on terror, the occupation had become increasingly inhuman and oppressive. Travelling anywhere in the West Bank had become difficult, and only Israelis and tourists on Israeli Holy Land tours escaped the numerous dehumanising checkpoints.

Bethlehem's Church of the Nativity at the end of the Nativity Trail had been bustling with pilgrims in spring 2000 but was empty on our arrival four years later. The nearby souvenir shops were closed. Across the town square a cafe owner invited us in for hummus and falafel, thanking us for our visit and wondering when life would improve again. Checkpoints were everywhere; crossing them can be interminable. We, not being Palestinians, could possibly have avoided them, but we chose to queue with them in solidarity. Arriving at the infamous Kalandia checkpoint outside Ramallah, Di was stopped by a young, armed, female Israeli soldier.

'Woman,' she said, 'over there,' pointing to a queue of Palestinian ladies.

Di was indignant. 'No,' she said. 'I'm staying here. Would you be separated from your husband?' Though we weren't married at the time.

The girl pointed again. 'Over there,' she repeated, 'with the other women.'

'I'm not going,' Di replied. And quite right too. Behind us we could see the supportive Palestinians enjoying Di's resistance. The queue was stopped but they didn't care. They were used to it. It was stalemate. A male soldier came over and asked what the problem was then waived us through. Impossible for Palestinians who suffer similar inexcusable hassle on a daily basis, even being randomly turned back while trying to get to a hospital or visit sick friends in a once neighbouring village, or to go to university near Ramallah. Women have even miscarried at checkpoints due to being refused passage through. For some the checkpoints are simply insuperable. Many people are captive in their own towns and villages, cut off from relatives, schools, hospitals, work and their land by the encroaching wall, while tourists in Israeli tour buses bypass them completely on 'Israeli only' roads with little or no awareness that they exist.

In the outskirts of Bethlehem in the Shepherds' Field we stopped at another cafe in a Bedouin tent where we had eaten a celebratory meal on the last day of the Nativity Trail. This time we listened to tales of settlers shooting and killing someone near the cafe. Next day we reached Hebron with its settler-occupied buildings in the town centre, with their 'protective' Israeli soldiers holding the town and its people hostage. We walked through the old market, which had been alive with the calls of stall owners selling souvenirs, cloth, fruit and vegetables on our previous visit. The smells of colourful spice stalls and sizzling falafels had filled the air. This time, only the falafel maker remained, so we bought some while he pointed out the wire netting that had been fitted above the narrow alleys to prevent settlers throwing rocks and worse on the people below. Conversely, the settlers have welded the front doors of Palestinian shops and homes so their occupants have to use ladders and rooftops to access the souk, while being refused access to their own front street where settlers regularly attack Palestinian children under the watchful and unresponding gaze of soldiers.

Even in 2000, Hebron had been a grim place where we had seen settlers' children spitting on elderly Palestinian ladies walking in the street. Four years on, an Israeli military rooftop outpost still dominated the market, its machine guns ominously threatening innocent civilians. Across the way, the ancient mosque on the reputed site of Abraham's tomb had been partially occupied and all access controlled by the army. We walked past accompanied by a couple of people from the Christian Peacemaker Teams. Also with us was a Palestinian lady who guided us through the town, to the annoyance of the soldiers.

'Why do you make these problems for us?' they said to her. 'All we want is peace.'

'Yes,' she said, gesturing at the settlements, 'a piece of this and a piece of that.'

Just up the street, we visited a Palestinian family whose house was close to buildings that had been occupied by settlers. Their olive trees and garden had already been destroyed. Their neighbour's pre-teen son had recently been shot by settlers – as evidenced by the bullet hole in the window and the scar on his leg. Tea had just been served when we saw a detachment of soldiers approaching the house. Two of them took up defensive positions at the gate while the others rushed the door. There was no polite knock before they entered the house and our room in full battle dress, guns ready, saying, 'No one is allowed to leave'.

Continuing upstairs, they took up positions on the top floor, leaving our hostess to comfort her frightened children. Anxious and red-eyed but defiant, she phoned her husband who soon arrived at the gate but was not allowed in until, an hour later, the soldiers left.

'It happens all the time,' she said. 'If it isn't our house, it's our neighbours'. What have we done to deserve this?'

We found a similar tale of woe on the outskirts of town where we visited a farmer and his family. They too now had settlers nearby.

'They confiscated my family's mountain,' the old man said. 'The settlement is built on it. My great grandfather's house was there and last night they bulldozed my son's home and cut down my vine trees.'

He showed us the vineyard where trees with springtime buds had been sawn through. The once-neat rows of irrigation pipes had been torn up and burnt. 'How am I going to support my family?' he asked.

His son stood by a pile of rubble. 'This house was my dream,' he said, gesturing sadly at the ruins.

Heading north we negotiated more checkpoints in the hope of reaching Nablus and the villages at the start of the Nativity Trail. On the way we visited the hamlet of Yanun where we had stayed on our fourth night of the walk. There were just a few houses in an idyllic location surrounded by orchards and olive groves: the epitome of traditional Palestine. Or at least it used to be. Now, the military antennae and red roofs of a settlement peer down from the hill above the village. Dead animals have been thrown down their well. Armed gangs of settlers attacked the village so often its occupants eventually fled, only daring to return with the support of Rabbis for Human Rights and volunteers from the World Council of Churches, four of whom from Scandinavia were living in the village as a visible deterrent to the settlers. While we were there half a dozen Israeli teenagers strolled past armed with Uzi sub-machine guns. They walked down towards the olive groves, the trees now deep in tangled grass and no longer cared for as they had been four years ago. A villager explained: 'We are afraid to go in now. The settlers shoot at us but if we don't look after the land for a year the Israelis will take it from us. What can we do, the olive trees are our life?'

Moving on, we were eventually stopped at the outskirts of Nablus. While on the Nativity Trail, we had bathed here in the beautiful Turkish bath, but reports had come through that they and much of ancient Nablus had been destroyed. We never found out: the road into town and to the north was closed 'for security reasons'. This was nonsense: the soldiers knew – as did the Palestinians – that the checkpoint was there just to make life even more difficult for anyone needing to travel. To circumvent it, the Palestinians had carved out a rough track of unavoidably treacherous steepness over the mountains. To drive over the pass was not only dangerous but took around three hours just to return to the road a few miles beyond the checkpoint, still in view. Security indeed!

Having crossed the pass we arrived at the bottom of the mountain dusty and thirsty, but Palestinian hospitality came to the rescue as a tractor came past. 'Welcome to my house for tea,' the farmer said, seemingly unperturbed by the insanity inflicted upon life in his village. This was the third place we had slept in when on the trail, though what had been the ascent of a quiet, flower-filled hillside on the fourth day was now destroyed by Palestinian trucks churning up or skidding down their enforced bypass road.

With no time to visit the villages further north – even if they were accessible – we drove south down the Palestinian side of the Jordan Valley. Always part of the West Bank, it was soon to be cut off from the rest of Palestine by 'the wall' and checkpoints, leaving Jericho isolated in a ring of Israeli trenches and fences with only one exit and entrance. Elsewhere the wall was still being built and now extends for over 700 kilometres, believed to cost around $2 million per kilometre, paid for by the USA. On the outskirts of Jerusalem we watched as old ladies squeezed through a remaining gap to visit friends and family, or to shop – perhaps for the last time. Uncaring soldiers turned back any men, while young Israeli volunteers of the Checkpoint Watch organisation monitored the human rights abuses but to no avail.

The nightmare of the wall twists and turns like a tortured snake around Jerusalem and the western edge of the West Bank, looping round settlements and cutting off Palestinian villages. In the Biddu area alone, 50,000 people and ten villages had already been enclosed and cut off from the West Bank. The village of Fukin just inside Palestine had previously had reasonable relationships with the Israelis over the 1967 border, but now they were threatened by a new settlement to their east. We arrived there one morning to be welcomed by the head of the village with a tale of woe.

'When I went up into our olive groves this morning,' he said, 'there was a notice on every terrace. It read: "We are expanding the settlement. Remove these trees or we will remove them and send you the bill." What can we do? They are our only income. Without them we have nothing.'

Everywhere, the wall had left a trail of destruction – all on Palestinian land – as thousands of olive trees have been uprooted and houses destroyed. Israel served eviction orders on the village in September 2014. It was happening before our eyes almost everywhere we went and we in the West – 'the civilised world' as Mr Bush was so fond of saying – are allowing it to happen. It's a prison wall. Three million Palestinians are trapped within it, two thirds of them without work. Much of the best of the West Bank is lost to the wall and only twelve per cent of original Palestine now remains to the Palestinians. Even this is being bisected into 'Bantustans' by sub-walls and the Israeli bypass roads which connect the settlements to each other and Israel proper, forming an impassable cobweb which Palestinians are neither allowed to travel along or cross, making a viable two-state solution impossible. Jerusalem itself is now all but surrounded by settlements.

As for the Nativity Trail, which we all had high hopes for in 2000, we walked some of it that is still being walked in 2018. We also had a great day in Wadi Qelt, 'the valley of the shadow of death', despite being looked at suspiciously by a family of Israelis, their ringlet-haired men carrying their Uzis while they picnicked by the river.

61

EXPLORING JORDAN – THE KNIFE CANYON

In the spring of 2004, Di and I were guests of Jordan Beauty Tours who were based in Wadi Musa, the gateway to Petra. The owner, Yousef Hasanat, had asked us to join him on an exploratory trek up Wadi Sakakin – the 'Knife Canyon'. Named for the numerous Neolithic sharpened stone tools found near its entrance, it forms the shortest link between Feynan and Petra.

We had realised on completion of our Jordan guidebook in 1999 that it should be possible to link some of our treks to create a country-length trail – a Jordan Trail – and thought this trek might be a useful addition. However, after the death of King Hussein, also in 1999, Queen Noor was no longer in a position to help and the tourism ministry wasn't interested so we had been exploring unsupported which wasn't easy.

Just before we arrived in Jordan, Yousef injured his knee, so he arranged for a local Bedouin guide, Ibrahim, to go with us. We left the idyllic eyrie of Dana village mid-morning to trek again down the Dana valley – Jordan's first nature reserve. Ibrahim pointed out a chameleon tottering with a drunken sailor's gait across the track, ungainly off the thin branches on which it normally tightrope-walked with a slow purposeful elegance. Above us was its objective: an acacia, off which the pendant-frilled red blossoms of the parasitic *Ziziphus spina-christi* (by some traditions, the plant from which Jesus's 'crown of thorns' was made) dangled in profusion, attracting numerous insects.

'You know,' Ibrahim said, noticing our interest, 'often I guide groups who never see anything. They walk at full speed, with heads down, poles in each hand clack-clacking, and all talking at the same time, yakkety-yak, yakkety-yak. At the end of the trek they will say, "We walked 150 kilometres in a week", but they saw nothing.'

Walking alongside the dry riverbed, we passed scattered oak and juniper trees before reaching a spring and an Ammarin Bedouin camp. An elderly lady and four children, friends of Ibrahim, called us in. To pass by would have been unthinkable so we stopped for sweet mint tea and a chat, the wild-haired children looking on quietly while half a dozen kid goats snoozed in the shade of the tent, waiting for their mothers who were out grazing in the hills. One snored like an old wooden door creaking in the wind; the others coughed in that peculiarly human way that goats do.

We stayed the night in the award-winning new eco-lodge among the Roman copper mines of Feynan then, on the second day, it all started to go wrong. Next morning, we left an hour later than planned, then Yousef's driver who had joined us at the lodge had problems finding a way through the rocky wilderness of Wadi Araba, losing us another hour. It also left us with an unexpected hour's walk in the oven of Jordan's Rift Valley just to reach the start of the Sakakin canyon. It was now eleven o'clock; we were three hours late and already well into our water supply.

Then, to make matters worse, our Bedouin guide got lost, something we have never known before or since. Having toiled for half an hour up steep scree to avoid what he had assumed was an impassable section of the wadi, he decided we had taken the wrong way, so we returned hot and frustrated to the canyon bed. By now it was midday and we had hardly started the trek which Yousef thought would take nine hours.

Sitting in the shade of some oleanders we asked Ibrahim what the problem was and discovered he hadn't been in this part of the canyon before. Almost no one had, he said. Bedouin shepherds used the lower canyon where we were and where a trickle of water and surrounding greenery provided sustenance for their flocks, while hunters from Petra, including Ibrahim, had entered the upper canyon from above. In between, where cliffs blocked the canyon, was no man's land. We had to find the connection. If we had known all this before, we would have been prepared for the unexpected. Instead, we debated the logic of continuing.

'I don't want to walk for three hours in the dark,' I said. 'We need to take photos, and anyway I want to enjoy it.'

Ibrahim was adamant we could do it in six hours. 'I walked with you yesterday,' he said. 'It won't take you nine hours.'

'OK,' Di said undaunted. 'You're a Bedouin so we trust you.'

I wasn't so sure. We knew the Bedouin well, and young Bedouin hunters are fast, very fast, and as agile as their prey, the ibex. They often had difficulty comprehending the relative slowness of visiting trekkers and climbers. But Di was up for anything – she hadn't won her school's victor ludorum for nothing – so off we went.

The next section of the canyon was excellent, following that miracle of nature, a rippling stream. It stopped all too soon at another waterfall cascading into a shaded pool, but was bypassed by a short climb before continuing through increasingly tangled undergrowth. Ibraham had disappeared leaving only the occasional footprint in the wet sand to show the route. Then he reappeared.

'We go too far,' he said. 'The wadi is blocked. We have to climb out above the waterfall.'

'This is getting silly,' I said, finally losing faith.

'Don't worry,' Ibrahim replied. 'Once we are up I will know the way. I have been up there hunting.'

I wasn't convinced. 'Are you sure there's water ahead?' I asked. We had started with only a litre each as Ibrahim had told us that there was a spring high in the valley. I didn't want to spend a long night in the mountains without water. It wasn't a survival problem, but we knew from experience that being without isn't much fun after a long hot day, nor for that matter is being without sleeping bags in early spring – even in Jordan.

'Don't worry,' Ibrahim said again. 'There is water, and anyway, I'm sure we'll reach camp before dark.'

So we retraced our steps through the tangled bushes back to the waterfall before climbing steeply up more scree and small cliffs to a col from where we could finally see the next stretch of the canyon.

'Now we go back down the other side,' Ibrahim said. It was steep and loose but led us directly into the canyon above the impassable section. The scenery was spectacular, the canyon cutting a deep, savage cleft between 300-metre columnar basalt cliffs on our left, and ragged towers and screes to our right. Ahead, the wadi led us on through more oleanders, but the way was blocked again almost immediately by more cliffs. 'We have to climb again,' said Ibrahim, making this the third unexpected ascent of rock and scree in little more than two hours. At the next col we once more descended into the canyon where a roughly built screen of stones and branches concealed a cave. Ibrahim was finally happy.

'I know this place,' he said with a grin. 'This is where we hide when we are hunting.'

Having been on the go for five hours we finally stopped in the shade of the cliff to grab a quick bite of bread and cheese. The wadi was now dry but, reassured that there was a spring ahead, we finished the last of our water. Twice more the canyon was blocked by cliffs, but finally we reached a pool, cold and clear where a trickle appeared from the rocks. We refilled one bottle, but there was no time to stop as the shadows were lengthening.

As we rose up towards the headwaters of the canyon and the hills in which Petra had been concealed for almost 2,000 years, the scenery changed. The canyon and its savage cliffs vanished to be replaced by pastel-hued sandstone domes with junipers clinging tenaciously to their dry slopes. In the fast-fading light, Ibrahim pointed out a pass on the darkening horizon. 'From there we will see the camp.' We finished the last of the water before scrambling up to the col to see the distant glow of Yousef's fire.

A convenient ledge of purple sandstone took us around the hillside as the sun sank into the clouds and the distant Wadi Araba disappeared into darkness far below. By the time we reached the campsite and accepted the first, very welcome, cup of tea, it was pitch black and the stars were out. We drank endlessly, but despite our best efforts we couldn't finish off the huge bowl of stew that had been simmering on the fire. Tired and satiated, we collapsed into our tent – we had done a nine-hour trek in six hours, having already walked for two hours to find the start. The next day, we were sure, would be easier.

We made a lazy start, first being driven a few miles up a new road through the scenically beautiful Wadi um el Elda (the Valley of Oaks), to reach 'Little Petra' with its canyon, carvings and nearby remains of a 9,000-year-old Neolithic village – one of the places where men first turned from being hunter-gatherers to pastoralists. From now on we knew the way, so we continued alone towards the domed cliffs concealing Petra, that most magical of ancient cities from where first the Nabataeans, then the Romans, ruled the caravan routes of western Arabia.

Even before reaching the ancient city, telltale signs of man's presence two millennia ago were evident in paths and steps carved into the colourful mountains past ruined dams that once fed fountains and gardens. Finally, we reached the monastery, one of Petra's finest monuments, before descending the impressive rock-hewn stairway to the temple of Qasr el-Bint and the cafes run by the local Bedouin community. The tea stop was de rigueur and provided an opportunity to chat with old friends before continuing up the paved Roman road past the Roman theatre and the magnificent treasury into the chasm of the siq, the thousand-metre-long, narrow canyon which is surely the most naturally awesome of all city entrances.

By mid-afternoon we were relaxing with Yousef at a cafe in Wadi Musa outside the Petra gates. Tourists came and went in a steady stream, few knowing that beyond the polished paths of the old city, the surrounding mountains conceal some of Jordan's best adventures.

Our plan for a Jordan Trail running the full length of the country was taking shape bit by bit, though this direct route through Sakakin was soon to be replaced by a more scenically varied but longer two-day route leaving the wadi just beyond its entrance, then winding up through the spectacular Wadi Feid to reach the Petra mountains via a spectacular and scenic mountain ridge.

62

MALI – MOUNTAINS, MAGIC AND MUSIC

I heard about Timbuktu's Festival in the Desert when it first started back in 2001, and in 2005 Di and I decided it was now or never – before the festival became too popular and lost its roots. Having searched around for contacts, I put my n.o.m.a.d.s. hat on and emailed Thangi Mannen at West Africa Tours in Mali's capital, Bamako. As luck would have it, she was the cousin of Manny Ansar, the Tuareg who had founded the festival and who continued to organise it. Between them they provided accommodation for Mick, Di and me above their Bamako office and festival tickets including transport out across the desert to the festival from and back to Timbuktu, as well as our return flight to Bamako.

They would also have arranged for transport all the way out from Bamako, but we had other plans. Having wandered round the town's market, shocked by its fetish stalls selling monkey hands and skulls, pots of lion fat and the skins of various wild cats and other increasingly rare animals, we squeezed on to a battered bus to head east along the dust-dry hot plain of the Niger River into which fishermen cast their nets and where women in colourful dresses worked the land. We were accompanied by the mesmeric drumming and singing of Malian music. The scenery slid by easily: sandstone cliffs, scrubland, cattle and goats, mud-walled villages, and markets – jostling, colourful crowds selling drinks, fruit, cakes and skewers of meat each time we stopped.

We travelled in supposedly half-day journeys that inevitably extended to full days. Arriving in Ségou we stayed the night in a delightful hotel with a palm-fringed swimming pool. The next stop was Djenné, one of the 'must sees' of Mali, being the location of the world's largest mud-brick mosque, the original of which dates from the thirteenth century. Now a World

Heritage Site, the current mosque's dried-mud 'banco' surface is a masterpiece and has a unique aesthetic beauty due to its gentle, flowing contours but, because of the material, it has to be repaired annually following the summer rains. From there we continued to Mopti, a colourful town from where riverboats go downstream to Timbuktu, but we still had our other objectives.

Arriving in Douentza, a dusty staging post on Mali's only road from Kayes in the west to Gao in the east, we stepped with care over a condom in a smelly open sewer seeping out of a hole in the nearby mud-brick wall. The path continued between piles of rubbish and tattered sun-bleached polythene bags. Ahead, a blue metal door hung open disconsolately at the entrance to a hotel. 'I think this place is going to be a dump,' said Mick, but to our surprise he was wrong. Opening the door, we entered a courtyard fringed with plants. Beyond were small but adequate rooms, and in the corner of the yard a toilet and 'bucket shower'. Luxury!

From Douentza the 125-mile desert track to Timbuktu headed north beneath the first of the impressive Hombori towers. Hundreds of cattle with their Fulani herdsmen had just passed by on their annual migration north to the great Inner Niger Delta, the waters of which were once again crossable, being well into the dry season. Outside the campsite, half a cow was being cooked on two sheets of corrugated iron over the red embers of a log fire. Similar barbecues were taking place at other truck stops along the dusk-dark street.

We were continuing east the next day to see more of the Hombori mountains, which meant we had to be up at four for the only bus. It was pitch black both off and on the bus, but we were pushed onboard only to discover it was full – I mean African-full. The corridor was a mass of unseen luggage and sleeping bodies, most of whom we trampled on before we too could squash ourselves and our sacks into previously non-existent spaces while the bus rumbled into the night once more accompanied by the rolling rhythms of the ubiquitous Malian music.

Black precipitous mountains emerged from the pink predawn sky, before a blood-red sun rose to greet us from behind the pinnacles and towers of Hombori. The village was just beyond, where we found pleasant traditional accommodation in round mud-brick houses with conical straw roofs and a very welcome breakfast of doughnuts, jam and coffee on the flat roof of the main building. As elsewhere in Mali the local Songhai people who had dominated the western Sahel in the fifteenth and sixteenth centuries were friendly and welcoming despite living a hard life. For the girls the first duty of the day was to haul water from the well to fill goatskins. They then had to be carried considerable distances to their homes. Then there's the wood to fetch and the washing and cooking and all the other chores of rural life in Africa. And the days were hot. We wondered about the climbing in Hombori; it looked good and we knew there were maybe a hundred routes of between 100 and 500 metres, mostly in the upper grades, but what it would be like on the hot rock in mid-afternoon was anyone's guess.

We hadn't brought any climbing equipment – we knew from our own experiences in the Sudan and elsewhere that travel and climbing don't mix easily. There's just too much gear to hump about and keep an eye on. Better to travel light and see the country, then come back later if the climbing looks good. It doesn't stop you getting into the hills, and we had a great couple of days wandering the mountains, playing on boulders and walking out to some huge orange dunes to watch the sun set behind the spectacular pinnacles of the Hand of Fatima.

Back in the village, market day was a sight to see: the Tuareg had arrived with their camels and swords, and the Songhai with surprisingly well-fed donkeys loaded with sacks of millet and charcoal. Hundreds of longhorn cattle – and I mean *longhorn* – were also raising the dust as they arrived on their annual migration up from Niger with their nomadic Fulani herdsmen. There was no doubt it would be charcoal-grilled steak for dinner that night. Then it was back on the bus to Sévaré where we arranged our Dogon trek with a young likeable lad called Abdina who had a broad welcoming grin and a wacky Dogon hat. In a land where many places are sacred, a guide is essential to avoid breaking any taboos.

We spent Christmas Day in nearby Mopti, enjoying the hustle and bustle of the port. Among other goods, slabs of salt that had been carried for twenty days by camel from the salt mines of Taoudenni to Timbuktu and then shipped upriver for three days, were being unloaded. Next day we drove out with Abdina to Bandiagara and on along the unmade road to Djiguibombo where we started our trek. I say trek, but when people talk about a Dogon trek, they usually lift their arms and waggle their fingers about to mean 'trek' in inverted commas. It's not that it's impossible to walk in the midday heat, it's just that the villages aren't far apart and it's very pleasant walking for a couple of hours in the early morning then having lunch before exploring an ancient cliff village and meeting the locals, then moving on for another hour or so in the evening to the next village. Dogon trekking is very enjoyable and easy-peasy!

Arriving on the top of the Bandiagara escarpment was when the magic of Mali really hit us, as we first looked out from above the cliffs into Dogon country. Not that we hadn't already seen some fascinating sights, but here, on the clifftop, we were finally setting off on our own two feet to spend eight days in dramatic scenery, among people with their own unique culture. Far beneath us the tree-dotted orange sands of the Sahel extended south to the heat-hazed border of Burkina Faso. Almost concealed high up in the vertical cliffs, ancient Tellem houses, their clay walls blending into the sandstone rocks, perched precariously on overhanging ledges. Below them the Dogon cliff dwellings of flat-roofed houses and curious conical thatched granaries hid in the shadows at the base of the escarpment, or spread out among the baobabs on to the plains beyond.

The Tellem people, who were hunter-gatherers and who the Dogon believe could fly to their seemingly inaccessible homes, had disappeared without trace about four centuries ago with the arrival of the Dogon who, not being able to fly, built their larger villages in the lower cliffs as a refuge from the raids of slave traders. Since then, the unique and colourful Dogon culture had flourished and is still very much a part of daily life. The trek along the Dogon escarpment and the festival were the prime reasons for our visit. The first time I had seen the cliffs was in a film that showed a young Catherine Destivelle soloing lithely up the escarpment in 1987 to the sound of a Malian band in one of the villages. I had asked about climbing there but was told the cliffs were sacred and housed a burial place, which reminded me that Catherine had climbed past caves containing skeletal remains.

By now we had already been in Mali for a couple of weeks, slowly making our way east from Bamako along the line of the Niger River. We were not in a hurry – it doesn't work in Africa. And it was *hot*! Even in mid-December, in the cool season, the temperature can reach 30 °C by midday and stay there until late afternoon. Furthermore, travel is rarely straightforward or comfortable; some of the buses are not too bad, though they are frequently overcrowded, but the battered Peugeot 'bush-taxis' into which a dozen people and luggage are packed look like they've been rescued from a scrapyard after the crusher has started work. Even so, it had been a joy to meet and travel with the local people who seemed blissfully unaware of any hardship and were always on the verge of laughter with welcoming smiles.

Descending the escarpment from the clifftop was a pleasure, winding down a worn rocky trail between canyon walls to reach the village of Kani Kombole. As the sun dropped and shadows lengthened, we explored the old cliff village and shaman's house before visiting Abdina's parents and family in their cosy farm where hens clucked busily in the yard, scattering as cattle and goats were brought in for the night.

We slept on the roof of the village guesthouse beneath the black star-filled night sky across which shooting stars burnt themselves out in arcs of light. As the stars faded in the dawn we breakfasted on hot, fresh doughnuts before setting out to Dogo Le, concealed in the cliffs an easy three hours away across a small rocky saddle. Here again we were able to explore the old cliff village before lunching where an old man was nimbly and meticulously sewing goatskin bags for sale in the market. We returned to Kani Kombole by oxcart, which was not without its moments as not only did it have a tendency to capsize, but the cow pulling the cart had diarrhoea which it continually showered around with its tail. Unfortunately I was sitting at the front; it wasn't the first time in my life that I'd been shat on!

Next morning, a short walk took us to the cliff village of Téli, then on to Endé. Here too was a magnificent cliff village beneath a huge overhang. Down below, the locals were warming up for a festival to celebrate the opening of a hospital. As musket shots echoed round the cliff we wondered if the vast overhang would collapse to join other obvious rockfalls. Drumming had started. Bizarrely masked figures, some on stilts, danced and gyrated, while another more ferociously masked figure chased the children away as they were too young to see the performance. The festival continued throughout the day, punctuated by the musket shots of local hunters whose ancient guns almost exploded with each shot.

That night, a sandstorm made sleeping on the roof rather less of a pleasure than it should have been, but at dawn the village was alive with drumming again. By the time we arrived the drummers had gathered around a group of girls pounding millet in hollowed-out logs. Despite the speed of the beat urging them on, three girls not only managed to work in one mortar, following each other with perfect timing, but they also managed to throw their log-sized pestles into the air and clap hands between each thump of the millet. It was a virtuoso performance that turned a daily chore into a dance. The drumming and masked dancing continued through the morning and could still be heard in the distance when we finally left for the walk to Yabatalou.

Next morning's walk was different, rising up through almost tropical jungle into a canyon with beautifully kept gardens beyond which the village of Benje Matou perched on the clifftop. After the usual large lunch there was ample time to wander along the cliff and appreciate the superb panorama before setting off past more canyons and concealed gardens for the idyllic village of Konsogou with its ancient burial cave hidden below the clifftop. It was here we spent New Year's Eve, sleeping out beneath the stars before another enjoyable walk along the escarpment to Dourou. After lunch we continued along the edge of the high plateau with its magnificent views, finally plunging down through a narrow cavernous canyon to emerge in the oasis of Nombori cliff village.

Next was the Festival in the Desert, a celebration of Tuareg culture far out in the desert dunes beyond one of the world's most famously remote towns, Timbuktu, the reputation of which originated in 1324 when Mali's emperor Mansa Musa commenced his pilgrimage from there. He crossed the Sahara to the Red Sea and Mecca, carrying with him in his camel train thousands of gold bars, giving so many away that, in so doing, he depressed the value of gold in Cairo's bazaar. His altruism also created Timbuktu's reputation as a faraway place of legendary wealth.

We had intended to get there by riverboat from Mopti, but the water level of the Niger was already too low. The last boat had gone two weeks earlier. Instead we hired a Land Rover taxi and headed off on a 250-mile drive to Timbuktu, the last half across the desert. This meant we fully appreciated the remoteness of our destination, arriving in the evening and crossing the Niger by ferry together with Tuaregs in their robes and turbans as the sun set, turning the river red. Timbuktu was a laid-back place in which to spend a few days – apart from the festival and the end of the Tuareg rebellion, nothing much had happened there since the sixteenth century when it was a centre of Islamic learning and Saharan trade.

A couple of days later Manny Ansar organised a car to get us across the sands to the festival where goatskin benders concealed among the dunes with food tents not far away maintained the Tuareg ambience. If ever a festival was 'far out', this was it, both musically and geographically. It started with a revival of the traditional gathering or *takoubelt* of nomadic Tuareg families who, after the end of the Tuareg rebellion in 1996, were able to meet annually at the oasis of Essakane, thirty-five miles out in the desert from

Timbuktu – itself 125 miles from the nearest road. It was soon to become 'the Woodstock of the Sahara' thanks to the efforts of one Tuareg – our host, the cousin of the lady who organised our tickets – of whom Habib Koité, one of Mali's leading musicians, said, 'I was thrilled that it was my friend Manny Ansar who had the power and the vision to make this happen.'

Who could have imagined it would be possible to create an international festival in such a remote place, difficult to reach, yet exquisitely beautiful, almost lunar, with its surreal snow-white dunes rolling wave on wave out of the endless tree-studded Sahel? Most of the 1,500 visitors were Tuareg, many coming in from the desert with their camels, families, tents and benders, creating a truly ethnic ambience. We saw them arriving in their indigo or otherwise colourful flowing robes, swords slung over their shoulders, sitting high on their decorated camels.

Living in a bender was great, the food was plentiful with good breakfasts and main meals. There were even toilet cubicles and showers (though water ran out in the showers after the first day, but what do you expect over thirty miles beyond one of the Sahara's remotest towns?). Strangely some Belgians expected more – they left mid-festival complaining that their bender had no door, the food and the toilets weren't up to standard, and the showers didn't work.

Mornings – as at all festivals – were lazy, music playing in the distance, Tuareg assembling for camel races and demonstrations of riding prowess and swordsmanship. By mid-afternoon, dancers, singers and musicians including Tuareg groups such as Tiris and Tartit who have appeared internationally, were coming together in tents and at the small Dune Stage. The women performing the *tinde* dancing and drumming were in their finery, their hands hennaed and silver jewellery braided into their hair. The men, flamboyant in their coloured robes, assembled in a circle for the strange 'love dance' of *takamba*, meaning 'give me your hand', in which seated dancers make slow, sensuous t'ai chi-like movements of the arms and hands.

As the dune shadows lengthened and the full moon rose, the main stage came into use, a hidden generator soundlessly powering amps and lights for the night-time gigs which continued into the early hours. There was even a beer tent! How wacky can life be, crashed out opposite the stage on a silver dune one night and up close with Tuaregs on camels on other nights for the full-on audio-visual experience of colourful and renowned Malian and African bands.

The festival continued for three days of camel races, great music and culture with bands from across West Africa. A South American dance group gave a remarkable performance of Native American and African music and a couple of Irish bands with bodhrán and didgeridoo brought a change of sound that fitted the atmosphere perfectly.

We left early the morning after the festival; getting back across the desert to Timbuktu proved tricky. The beat-up car that we were in collapsed when it hit a bump. The rear spring connection had broken, but the driver wasn't worried. Having chopped a small tree down, he cut it into two short pieces and hammered them into the joint, forcing it open and lifting the body of the car marginally off the wheel. He then tied the wood in place with a piece of rope and we limped into town.

We hadn't climbed in the Hombori mountains, but the Dogon trek was unique, as was the festival, altogether an unforgettable celebration of Mali's varied and vibrant sub-Saharan culture. What a tragedy that in 2012 the region around Timbuktu became a battleground for al-Qaeda and other terrorist groups. Music and TV were banned, icons destroyed, and people forced to wear conservative dress instead of the often-colourful African clothes on pains of being publicly punished with amputation, whipping or stoning. Additionally, they not only destroyed some of the world's oldest Islamic manuscripts, others having been hidden, but threatened to cut off the fingers of musicians and the tongues of singers. In a country where music and musicians were everywhere, the ban was calamitous. It's a bad, sad world we live in.

63

EXPLORING JORDAN – NEW DISCOVERIES

It's best to know what you are looking for before you look for it.
Winnie-the-Pooh, **A.A. Milne**

We were out in Jordan in spring 2006. Mick was with us, hanging out with our Bedouin friends, enjoying the occasional climb and unexpectedly picking off a nice new two-pitch crack line from inside the jaws of a popular trekking canyon. As sunset beckoned, the red rock deepened in colour in late afternoon. The approach up a big orange dune that slowly avalanched at every step felt harder than the actual climb!

After Mick returned home, Di and I went a short way north to the little-known mountains and canyons of Jebel Mas'uda between Rum and Petra. Together with our friend Mark Khano we set off early one morning to try to find an impressive rock bridge we had seen when trekking through Mas'uda's Khorma canyon the previous year. Luckily we knew the way in as few would find it by chance – a series of Bedouin bridges constructed of juniper branches lead us down towards the canyon bottom. Then came an unexpected find: halfway down and easily missed, hidden behind a buttress of rock, we found another bridge of branches traversing away from the main descent into a side canyon. Soon after, we located a massive pile of rocks forming steps leading directly to the rock bridge on the main canyon lip, but who had built them and why? All around were shards of pottery, some decorated; we showed a piece to an archaeologist who thought they were Edomite, making them around 3,000 years old, but whatever their age, why were they there? This was no place to live; was it a military lookout post, concealed below the bridge from where there are superb views?

Later that day we continued down more Bedouin bridges and ladders to the canyon floor, wondering at the climbing potential of the surrounding walls before enjoying a delightful bivouac in the comfort of the sands.

Next day we trekked back out and climbed back to our starting point, spotting ancient terraces spread out below us on barren slopes. The area, it seemed, had previously been kinder in its climate, supporting hard-working people on its hillsides. Today the only remaining greenery is near the few springs that succour well-watered orchards higher on the hills.

But water is no problem above the Dead Sea, where huge canyons tempted us back to enjoy the experience of a day abseiling and walking through the hot-spring rivers that gush down the cliffs to end in a salty death 400 metres below sea level. It was a nice surprise when, over the next few years, we discovered numerous crags further north. Never more than thirty metres in height, they are mostly overhanging walls of pocketed limestone totally devoid of cracks – there is little protection without bolts. We top-roped a few routes and young climbers from Amman soon developed the cliffs as excellent sport-climbing venues. We also found a few trad lines on immaculate rock that suited us perfectly, linking both climbing and trekking exploration.

Traditional tourism numbers were down due to the deteriorating situation in the Middle East following the Iraq war and the endless problems caused by the Israeli occupation of Palestine. As someone said, Jordan was 'stuck between Iraq and a hard place'.

In 2009 we were invited by USAID (United States Agency for International Development) to hold a seminar in Amman to explain and promote the advantages of adventure tourism. It was well attended but only a few paid little more than lip service to it. Those that did were either Bedouin companies from Wadi Musa and Rum that already understood its grassroots benefits, or the new breed of entrepreneurs and outdoor enthusiasts from Amman who have since become leaders in their field.

Others in Jordan remained mostly unconvinced, believing adventure tourism contributed little to the economy and represented the downside of tourism, being more about risk than reward. We told them that it leads where others follow as happened when the Victorians began climbing in the European Alps and the early explorers opened up the Himalaya. I had also made this point in my proposal to the tourism ministry in 1984 prior to our first exploratory visit to Rum and had been happy to see the World Bank's acknowledgement of this, which noted that it was only following the arrival of climbers in Wadi Rum that the real tourism influx began.

It was also at this time that we met Brian Hodgkinson again. Fifty years earlier Brian had been one of my regular climbing friends and we had done a lot of new routes together in our home hills in the Peak District. It was consequently great to meet up with him, and he joined us on some of our new treks in the north of Jordan and climbing in Wadi Rum.

USAID partially sponsored our northern explorations, providing a driver and car as well as the luxury of a temporary base at Amman's Marriot Hotel. We spotted a possible trek that would later become the basis of the first day of the Jordan Trail project, heading down from the high hills of Greco-Roman Um Qais up near the Syrian border and on to Pella. This meant it linked into a two-day walk we had done previously between Ajloun Castle and Pella, camping in the hills and walking through forests, meadows and olive groves – a total contrast to the desert mountains of the south.

Soon after, we were invited by Ramez Habash, who was also working with USAID, to join a project developing adventure tourism based in the villages of the Al Ayoun community just north of Ajloun. Daniel Adamson of the Abraham Path Initiative became involved in order to link trails in Jordan to those in the West Bank. His idea was that if we could find more treks and climbs in the area, people might be tempted to stay there longer thereby benefiting the local community. An offer of three weeks of exploration in a part of Jordan we knew would be at its best in the spring sounded perfect, and all in a good cause: exactly what we liked doing.

Since then, we have returned every spring at the personal invitation of the mayor, Abu Ibrahim, and villagers Mahmoud Hawawreh and Eisa Dweikat, whom we have got to know well. We were given a house for the project, superbly located on the end of a ridge overlooking the Jordan Valley. Our new Al Ayoun friends helped us settle into the house and provided a sack of logs for the welcome fire as it was still cool, but we had our plans: having remembered the view into a thickly forested valley below Zubia Cave, which we had explored earlier, trekking through it was our first objective.

There were no paths on our map, but the seemingly unique opportunity of exploring a forest in Jordan seemed too good to miss. Eisa and Mahmoud came with us the next day, driving us up over cliff-rimmed hills, to descend into the upper reaches of the valley, parking among extensive Roman ruins. Nearby, a deep, tennis-court-sized Roman cistern was carved into the limestone to act as a reservoir, while the remains of buildings had to be clambered over as we headed out towards the start of the wadi which was concealed below in the tangled trees.

We thought we were going alone, but they insisted on joining us. So on we plunged through the bushes, and soon we found a small but well-trodden path heading down the valley at the side of the dry streambed, hemmed in and overhung by the forest – it looked good and like nothing else we had seen in Jordan where we were more used to open hills, big cliffs or awesome canyons.

The path unexpectedly wound all the way down the valley, frequently in thick forest, but often emerging into flower-filled glades, sometimes descending past limestone chutes and basins in the dry riverbed or past long-abandoned, overgrown terraces and once passing an intriguing cave entrance with a spring flowing out of it.

Continuing our journey, the path helpfully forked after about six miles, allowing us to climb up gently past cliffs and out of the narrowing valley to reach pine-clad hilltops. Beyond, we descended to a village on the lip of the Jordan Valley where Eisa and Mahmoud replenished our long-since-finished food and water supplies before phoning back to their village for a car. Sitting by the fire that night, with maps spread across the floor, we retraced our journey; the valley had been a great discovery and it very soon became a valuable contribution to the Al Ayoun community, walkers from Amman trekking through it regularly guided by one of our friends and enjoying a home-cooked meal of locally grown food in one of the villages, sometimes staying the night in a homestay.

Surprised with our discovery, our attention was quickly drawn to other possible trails, soon finding a choice of nice treks through more forested valleys, and over rolling hills, sometimes passing ancient olive groves with gnarled trunks five metres in girth; could they *really* be of Roman origin as the locals believe?

Among our last Al Ayoun area discoveries was a long and tempting valley we had found further north called Wadi Sirin. We were joined by Mark, his wife Julie and young son Gabriel, not yet eight but as fit and fast as a puppy off its leash. Mahmoud dropped us off at the head of the valley where a path wound between scattered trees and anemone-filled fields, but it soon ended abruptly, leaving us to plunge immediately into forest, the only tracks being those of wild boar rooting in the undergrowth. The dry streambed closely overhung by tangled trees was frequently the only way on, though occa-sional small paths used by shepherds or woodcutters provided easier going, mysteriously appearing and disappearing in the shadows of the forest.

Just before midday we unexpectedly crossed a small lane, presumably linking villages in the hills above, but the forest beyond was undisturbed. From then on, the going became tougher: paths were few and far between and only Gabriel was small enough to run nimbly beneath the hanging interwoven branches. Walking down the stony wadi bed was often the only way on, but we had a cunning plan: some big oxbow bends were shown on our old map; maybe we could eliminate them by taking a direct line, cutting across the necks of the bends and at the same time get a view of the valley.

Finding a little path out was a real stroke of luck: some cliffs ahead seemed to indicate the first oxbow bend and there, just where we stood, we found a small path heading up into the trees. We took it and within a hundred metres were on a limestone pavement level with the clifftops. It obligingly took us out on to a beautifully located peninsula in the heart of the first oxbow with a magnificent panoramic view across the second one, which swept round a huge cirque to our left. It was good to be above the trees for the first time that day.

A scramble down cliffs took us back into the valley and dense forest, and with the day passing we began to wonder if it would be possible to continue – the valley was becoming a gorge and there was every chance that the dry streambed plunged over cliffs. As always we had a short rope with us, *but would it be enough*? Our worries were unfounded; there were indeed numerous small falls, but all easily negotiable and in fine, cliff-rimmed surroundings.

We had now descended so low that we were dropping beneath the treeline and our valley soon began to open out, harbouring the occasional olive grove – a sure sign we were nearing its end. Mahmoud arrived shortly after and whisked us back to Al Ayoun. It had been another good day, not an easy one, to be sure, but a great little adventure.

More recently we have also discovered some underground houses reputedly dating back 3,000 years and which are possibly unique in the Middle East. They are as yet unsurveyed but will undoubtedly be another attraction along with Al Ayoun's nearby dolmens.

Based on the treks we developed over this period, our guidebook *Walks, Treks, Climbs & Caves in Al Ayoun Jordan* was published by Vertebrate in 2011, the costs being met by Fadi Ghandour, a Jordanian businessman and philanthropist, in recognition of which we donated our royalties to the Al Ayoun community who, not long ago like most other Jordanians, couldn't understand why anyone would want to walk from one village to another when they could go in a car. But the treks in this area are unique in Jordan. In springtime they are more reminiscent of the south of France than most people's expectation of the Middle East. It is a botanist's and ornithologist's delight, flowers and birds are everywhere, including birds migrating up the Jordan Rift Valley from Africa. Since our guidebook, the whole area has become very popular with trekkers from abroad as well as Jordan, and the local villagers are reaping benefits from guiding, providing transport and opening their houses as homestays.

64

EXPLORING JORDAN – THE JORDAN TRAIL

*I knew, deep and safe, beyond mere intellect, that there is nothing
like a wilderness journey for rekindling the fires of life.*
River: One Man's Journey Down the Colorado, Source to Sea,
Colin Fletcher

My *Troll Wall* book and our Al Ayoun guide were published by Vertebrate in
2011. Back from Jordan we visited our friends Mark Carr and Christine
Evans in their Shetland west coast croft. They surprised us by getting married. There were no guests and the four of us had a really nice day. Next year
Di and I also got married in Shetland and the following day went new routing on a sea cliff we had found. Later in the year we went trekking with them
near Everest having previously done the Annapurna Trail together.

We were then domiciled over the winter months, partly as Di had to have
two cataract operations: the same problem as me, the optician said, 'Too
much desert sun', but also because my right arm was giving me increasing
problems in both the elbow and shoulder. A bicep tendon had partially torn,
but not to worry, Di's eyes were fixed and having a bad arm didn't stop me
walking, which was just as well as we had an invite from Mark Khano to go
out early to Jordan and into some new territory as there was some exploration to be done up north for the Jordan Trail. It was just what we needed.

Mark, Di and I went up to Um Qais, high on the shoulder of the plunging
Yarmuk Gorge that separates Syria, with all its war-torn troubles, from peaceful Jordan. The Golan Heights, captured from Syria by Israel, was opposite,
directly across the gorge, with the Sea of Galilee below.

Immediately behind us were black basalt columns and a Roman theatre,
remnants of what was originally one of the ancient cities of the Greek
Decapolis dating from around the first century BC. It was the first of
March. The sun was shining, a few puffball clouds drifted slowly eastwards

carried on a faint breeze. The smell of warm herbs rose up to meet us from Jordan's Rift Valley 550 metres below us and 200 metres below sea level.

Just ahead of us an attractive-looking limestone valley with pines on its upper slopes sheltering red anemones, purple geraniums, pink flax, the delicate white star of Bethlehem and a myriad of other flowers and herbs lead the eye down into Wadi Arab. Beyond that, the distant Jordan River formed Jordan's border with Israel and Palestine. We were setting out on our first day along our proposed Jordan Trail which, if all went to plan, would one day wind for over 370 miles down the length of the country all the way to Aqaba. In addition to routing it through the best of Jordan's wild places and varied scenery, we planned to include the numerous antiquity sites such as Um Qais, Pella, the Islamic Ajloun Castle, the crusader castle of Kerak and of course Petra as well as Jordan's unique nature reserves in the Dead Sea canyons, the Dana Biosphere Reserve, and Wadi Rum, to end with a swim in the warm waters of Aqaba's coral-fringed Red Sea.

Our first objective was to complete the northern section from Um Qais to the Dead Sea, a walking distance of around 125 miles. Di and I had tried to initiate the project in the late 1990s, to link up some of our earlier trekking discoveries, but no one was interested. Now, however, with increasing numbers of young Jordanians discovering their unique outdoors and climbing, canyoning and trekking, they soon realised the possibility of a country-length trail and began exploring possible routes. Some had already been found by Hakim Tamimi and Murad Arslan, two of Jordan's leading outdoor activists.

Once out of the pines, we scrambled down a hillside through scrub and herbs. Overhead, cranes and raptors were a familiar springtime sight, taking advantage of the thermals on their annual spring migration up the Jordan Valley. Smaller indigenous birds were busy in the trees and, as always, lizards scuttled to the safety of their familiar havens at our approach, as did a Palestine viper that had been warming itself in the morning sun.

Once down the hillside we reached the lip of the ravine through which the Wadi al Arab still flowed after last winter's unusually heavy rain and snow. The resultant flash floods had scoured the riversides clean down to slate-blue bedrock on which limestone boulders rested, but crossing it was easy. We were already 100 metres below sea level. It was consequently hot, but just as we were wondering if there was an alternative to walking the steep road, a car stopped and offered us a lift. I've always been pragmatic about these things; there was nothing to be gained by slogging up a road for another three miles. The driver dropped us at the main highway where, as luck would have it, a battered old taxi rattled to a shaky halt 100 metres down the road and took us to the recently opened Sharhabil Bin Hassneh EcoPark where we were camping.

Next day, an early start found us back near yesterday's finishing point, in the village of Zabda. Hakim had already found a way from there to the ecopark that he said was good and passed a ruined monastery, but Yehya, our ecopark driver, and once a Bedouin shepherd from this area, suggested trying Wadi Quseiba as an alternative.

'It's very nice,' he said, 'and finishes close to the ecopark.' So why not? You never know until you go.

The day began down a steep ravine descending directly from the road, cutting its way through bands of limestone to a junction with another deep valley. We lunched in the early afternoon, sitting among wild rocket and mustard plants on both of which we grazed greedily while eating our bread and cheese: a beggar's banquet. As we set off, a tortoise crossed the path ahead of us, one of many we were to see along the trail.

By now the once-high hills on either side were shrinking away into the sub-sea-level Jordan Valley, but a good track took us south past palms over three low and easy passes and down to the ecopark below the Ziglab dam. The unexpected greenery and birdlife felt more akin to the tropics and was far from the usual image of Jordan.

Next day we continued south, reversing a trek of ours through the foot-hills with its views to the hills of Palestine that we had pioneered the pre-vious year. Leaving vineyards, orchards and the heat of the valley behind, we crossed a small stream where gasping tadpoles were struggling to grasp their last opportunity to metamorphose into frogs before the long, hot, rain-less summer dried the pools. Ahead were more hills up which we climbed steadily to meet a welcome breeze rippling fields of wheat peppered with red, blue and purple anemones. A cluster of Bedouin tents decorated the hillside as they have done for millennia. Far below were the Pella hot springs, but we bypassed them over a natural arch spanning the wadi then up over the next hill to Pella, which has been inhabited for the past 6,000 years including Neolithic, Bronze Age, Greek and Roman periods.

Next day we once again reversed one of our treks going from the columns of the Greek antiquity site up the steep-sided valley of Wadi Jirm.

Continuing up the valley we entered the pretty Wadi Sir leading to the mosaic-floored ruins of a Byzantine church and, just beyond, the 'Jesus Cave' which, though unproven, is – according to local legend – where Jesus stayed before his baptism. A little further on, the village of Beit Idis perches on its hilltop. A homestay had been opened there but we were met by our friends from Al Ayoun and whisked away by car for a 'homecoming' feast and a night with them.

We returned to Beit Idis the next day to walk up our beautiful Zubia Forest Trail, the first trek we had discovered in the area, following a dry stream-bed up the wooded dale through clearings carpeted in flowers. Higher up the valley, where the trees thicken, the ruins of Roman Qabla with its huge water storage cisterns proved elusive, though when walking down the valley in the opposite direction, Qabla is the easily located starting point.

Next day we enjoyed a path through woods of oak, pistachio and sensually smooth, red-barked strawberry trees to the hilltop ruins of Mar Elias at 900 metres. A superb viewpoint, the mosaic-floored ruins of one of the world's oldest Byzantine churches were only discovered in the mid 1990s. Continuing south, we plunged down into the next forested valley where wild boar had been rooting among the many fallen acorns. Then up the long hillside ahead to reach the archetypal hilltop castle of Ajloun standing strategically aloof at an altitude of 1,000 metres.

Our seven days were up, but looking south, more forested hills rose tier upon tier into the blue distance where Hakim and other Jordan Trail enthusiasts were continuing to enjoy their 'Arab spring'. They were heading literally hotfoot for the Dead Sea, to complete the northern section of what would soon be the country-length trail. However, what we thought would be the difficult bit still lay ahead.

65

INCREDIBLE INDIA – A WALK ON THE WILD SIDE

We were still in touch with Partha, with whom we had been twice to north-east India, so we were very pleased to get an invite to check out the adventure tourism potential in Manas National Park in Bodoland.

Manas is home to the Bodo people and has formed part of their ancestral land for over 2,000 years, since they migrated there from eastern Tibet. Following the annexation of Assam into India by the British in 1838–1839, the Nagas, Bodos and numerous other tribal peoples of the region, as elsewhere in the world, had been marginalised by the British colonialists– 'alienated in their own land'. The jungles of Manas became the last refuge of the Bodos. This situation continued under Indian rule, so that Manas inevitably suffered as a result of deforestation for agriculture and poaching of wildlife.

Bodo freedom fighters, known as the Bodo Liberation Tigers, lived in the jungle, using its resources in their struggle for independence from, or autonomy within, India. Then, in 2003, Bodoland was recognised as a 'state within a state' with its own autonomous territorial council. One of their prime objectives was to save Manas from further depredation and return it to its original nature in a project aptly named 'Back to the future'. As a result, it is now an acclaimed World Heritage Site and Partha hoped that adventure tourism would provide some of the necessary funding. For this reason we had been invited to join a group of Bodo forest rangers (all ex-poachers) to survey and write about trekking, elephant safari and rafting in Manas.

We flew out in November of 2013, arriving at Manas Jungle Camp on the eastern edge of the 'core area' where we were introduced to our team of rangers, one of whom had lost an arm in a tussle with a boar. Armed with kukris and old rifles, they turned out be a great bunch of guys, happy and fearless in the jungle, as well as being knowledgeable and good company.

That evening we went for a walk with them only to be met by a dozen Asian elephants foraging among the tall trees alongside the track. It's one thing to look for tigers, rhino and bison from the safety of a vehicle. Quite another to be aware of wildlife being all around and possibly close when on foot. It was reassuring to see just how alert the rangers were, seeing buffalo or bison staring aggressively from between tall grasses close to the path while we were blissfully unaware of their presence, or spotting birds and monkeys in the treetops that we otherwise wouldn't have seen.

The next day we had an easy downhill walk from the Bhutan border, followed on the third day by a trek through the 'buffer zone' of the park, past numerous small villages. We had lunch with a Bodo family, quenching our thirst with rice beer. Then on through tea plantations worked by the descendants of tribal people from Orissa, brought there by the British when the Bodos refused to accept the poor working conditions. We walked up a deepening river valley to camp by the riverside. A slender sickle moon rose into the night sky, seemingly chased in its trajectory by the diamond-bright pinpoint of Venus.

We followed the river up the next day hoping to find a trail to a Bhutanese village in the encroaching foothills, but if a path existed it had been washed out, and anyway, we had no permits. Something for the future, perhaps? Instead we bathed in the river with fish nibbling at our skin before being driven back to Manas Jungle Camp. No need to wonder what was on the menu: rice and dhal is the staple diet, with veg curry, or meat or locally caught fish if it's available. Not being unduly hungry, we turned down an offer of fried silk worm caterpillars.

The next two days were typical of Manas, starting just after sunrise and, unlike Nagaland, accompanied by a dawn chorus of jungle birds, soon spotting elephants and buffalo along the way as well as rare golden and capped langurs. On our sixth day we reached Daimari Forest Camp, not far from a place where the river had eroded the hillside to expose rock salts that were visited frequently by elephants. Having pitched our tents, Di and I walked up the almost-dry river valley in the evening, almost bumping into a couple of bison, but no elephants to be seen.

Later, after our evening meal, I wandered off alone into the jungle. Out of curiosity, I turned my headlamp off, listening intently, senses alert. Utter blackness! Any moonlight was blocked by the treetop canopy from which leaves as large and crisp as popadums drifted down noisily to cover the ground, rustling at the slightest movement. *Is something out there? A cobra maybe? Or a tiger?* I remembered a nightmare I had in my teens: I was killed and eaten by tiger. It was awful, but what was even worse, having woken and discovered much to my relief that I was still alive, I finally managed to get back to sleep only to find the tiger waiting for me. It ate me again! Standing there in the jungle it all came vividly back. Had it been a dreadful premonition? I turned my headlamp back on and returned to the welcoming fire.

'Wake up, wake up, it's a brand new day-ay-ay.' It was Partha's alarm jingle in the next tent – 4.45 a.m., time to get up. We were getting used to these semi-alpine starts. It was simply a matter of making the best of the day before the temperature became too hot. Emerging from our tents into the cold early morning, we pulled on our fleeces knowing that by the time we had eaten and were ready to start our day's trek we would be packing them away again.

Through the blackness of the jungle night the pink eastern sky hinted at the rapidly approaching dawn as I walked down to the stream, a last remnant of the monsoon rains splashing over water-polished stones. The mud by the water's edge was deeply incised by the tracks not only of a tiger – so there had been one snooping around – but of buffalo, gaur (Indian bison) and the dinnerplate-sized footprints of elephants whose cairns of cannonball-sized poo marked their route up the valley. I could hear them a thousand metres upstream, where the jungle-covered hills of Bhutan finally cascaded into India. Their roaring and trumpeting filled the valley as they scraped the exposed rock salts away with their tusks.

By now, we had been trekking through the park for six days. Its core zone covers an area of around 500 square kilometres and is part of an almost 3,000-square-kilometre tiger reserve along the southern border of Bhutan. Based on forest reserves and wildlife sanctuaries created in the early 1900s, it is part of a planned 'tiger corridor' extending along the whole of the Himalayan foothills. As well as tigers, Manas is also home to elephant, rhino, buffalo, gaur, sambar and hog deer, boar, porcupine, cobras, pythons, lizards, capped and golden langur monkeys, and numerous other creatures. Twenty-two species are 'endangered' and twenty-seven 'vulnerable' – by far the greatest number of any protected area in the country. There are also over 400 species of birds including peacocks and the equally impressive great Indian hornbill.

We set off downstream. Overhead, a flock of parrots flew by noisily as we lunched in the shade of the forest. Later, out among the elephant grass in a hollow almost hidden by tall rushes, we passed by the half-eaten remains of a boar before reaching the next forest ranger post. From there we continued on elephants over a river and through the tall grass as far as the next watch-tower. Along the way I lost my hat, knocked off by a low branch. No need to worry though, the elephant behind casually picked it up and passed it to me!

In the evening we went out again on elephant safari, surprising a wild herd almost hidden in the five-metre-high grass. The matriarch charged at us thinking a calf was in danger, but our *mahout* was unperturbed, encouraging our elephant on with his two-pronged steel *ankush* so that the wild herd backed off and disappeared into the long grass, trumpeting their alarm call.

Next day we once again split the journey, on foot in the morning and riding elephants in the afternoon to arrive at the next watchtower.

'It's too dangerous to camp,' we were told. 'The animals come in at night.'

And they did. We slept on the roof, waking to find ourselves surrounded by elephants. Then the buffalo came, then the bison. In the morning some of the trees were smashed or stripped of bark up to a height of ten metres. The rangers were worried about their domestic elephants but they had moved off and returned unscathed at sunrise.

A day later we reached Mathanguri Forest Bungalow on the edge of the Manas River which we crossed the following day by local riverboat, to explore the jungle opposite. Once again tiger prints were everywhere. Next day we drove up a few miles into Bhutan's adjacent Royal Manas National Park where their rangers were disappointed that they had been given no credit for telling a BBC film crew where the tigers were, the pro-gramme having given the impression that no one knew about them. We returned downriver with a Bhutanese rafting company. No big rapids but some tricky navigating between huge trees that had been swept downstream in the monsoon. Rounding a blind bend in the river, overhanging branches swept most of one team out of their raft, but no harm done – more of a laugh than a problem. Just as the sun was setting, we beached close to our final destination at the luxurious Musa Jungle Retreat.

Woken the next day by peacocks, we went by jeep safari out into the grasslands, seeing boar, sambar and hog deer before visiting an elephant training camp, a fascinating place. Like breaking in a wild horse, taming a wild elephant isn't an easy task and takes days of alternate harsh treatment and kindness, but the end result is that a ranger's elephant has a good life, cared for and ridden by a *mahout* who will be its constant companion. The two may spend their lives together forming an inseparable partnership. In the evening, we joined in the fun as the elephants were washed and scrubbed in the river.

Afterwards, as I was standing on the riverbank, someone shouted, 'Look out, rhino!' and sure enough the first rhino of the trip had just lumbered past behind me.

66

EXPLORING JORDAN – BACK ON THE TRAIL

Dream the impossible – and go out and make it happen.
I walked on the moon. What can't you do?
The Last Man on the Moon, Eugene Cernan

By 2014 about fifteen years had passed since we first had the idea of a Jordan Trail. We had continued to add to it whenever opportunities arose during our annual springtime visits, and the previous spring Mark, Di and I as well as Hakim's team had explored the north of the country.

I should point out here that trail making in Jordan isn't easy. Maps are extremely difficult to get. We only got ours, which were from aerial surveys in the 1960s and 1970s, with help from Queen Noor. The terrain hasn't changed much since then, but often what looked like wild country on the map is now dissected by roads with villages, olive groves and farmland covering the hills. More recently our friend Mark managed to get some modern maps. These, of course, showed most of present-day Jordan's continuously creeping urban sprawl, but strangely rarely showed any paths, whereas the old maps had a few paths on them, which sometimes proved essential in finding the best route, especially when checked against Google Earth. Equally strangely, although our old maps had a grid that remarkably correlated with GPS and Google Earth (though the map could be a couple of hundred metres out), the new maps had a seemingly indecipherable grid system. Even so, despite all the technology or lack of it, what often proved most useful was local knowledge from Bedouin shepherds. Unknown to all but them, a filigree of time-worn trails that speak silently of biannual migrations or daily travail traverse the hills and valleys of Jordan, and it was these that were to form the basis of the trail.

Our plan in 2014 was to try to find a good route to and across the formidable Dead Sea canyons, which are between 600 and 1,000 metres deep.

To our surprise, by the time we returned home after six weeks, we had not only reached and crossed the canyons, but where necessary using Mark's four-wheel drive and accompanied on various occasions by Mark and Amjad Shahrour, we had located what turned out to be the full 400 miles of the trail, identified the route and, wherever time and opportunity permitted, walked sections of it. I was particularly pleased when my suggestion for an off-road route from Wadi Rum to the Red Sea worked out well.

From the mountains of Rum we passed through the intricate maze of domes in the orange desert to its south to reach the remote Bedouin village of Titin. Beyond, the inhospitable-looking granite and basalt Aqaba mountains barred our way to the Red Sea and the end of the trail, but after two days of searching we found a high pass approached by a delightful hidden valley. Finally we saw the Red Sea. The descent down scree soon reached a long sandy wadi and before long we were on the beach. Meanwhile, Hakim, Murad and others were pushing the trail south, also crossing some of the Dead Sea canyons. The trail was suddenly gathering momentum and coming close to being a reality.

A while after this trip, an email from Mark asked: 'Would you like to come out in the autumn and finish the trail?' Who could resist?! We were back in early October, ready for six more weeks of exploration with Mark, Amjad and Osama Cori of Explore Jordan. The way south as far as the Dead Sea canyons was already established, but some of the trail across the canyons followed tortuous roads. In search of better alternatives, and with advice and help from Bedouins of the local Bani Hamida tribe, in particular Abu Saif, we started again by an almost forgotten Roman road, part of which we had already found on the Dead Sea plateau. Its continuation took us down to the basalt columned gorge of Wadi Zarqa Ma'in. We then followed a pleasant mountain ridge reminiscent of the Lakeland fells up to the south rim of the gorge with the remains of the Roman road visibly snaking along beneath us.

From there, still following Abu Saif's advice, we trekked down a limestone ravine unexpectedly discovering dolmens – probably from the early Neolithic period – on the lower slopes, before reaching a natural swimming pool in the verdant depths of the Hidan Gorge. At this point, I have to admit to cheating. We didn't go up the south side of the canyon as we should have done, we went down it, but with good reasons: it's always easier to find paths when looking from above, and Abu Saif was going to show us the start of the descent.

We were joined by more friends for the next three days of exploration. Up on the south rim of the Hidan, Abu Saif showed us the start of a path used by Bedouin shepherds. It looked unlikely but what a joy it was. The trail twisted through the summit cliff and followed a ridge down, passing what seemed to be the remains of an ancient stone circle before descending exactly to 'our' pool. Looking back up, the way was invisible. Two canyons done already, and three to go!

We returned to the top by car and slept on the roof of a watchtower perched on the apex of the west-facing rim of the high plateau dividing the Hidan and Mujib gorges which converged far below. As we arrived, the sun was sinking behind blue-shadowed hills, lighting the Dead Sea 1,200 metres below our eyrie with a golden glow.

Stirred by a cold morning breeze we were soon up and on the way. We picked up the trail from yesterday's descent into the Hidan Gorge and walked south along the plateau rim as Hakim's team had suggested, except that, armed with Abu Saif's knowledge, we soon arrived at a descent into the Mujib Gorge, which was even more unlikely than his shepherds' path to the Hidan. Bedouin used it, but would it be a way we could safely take the trail? Unsure, we started steeply down through the cliffs, finding an incredible route into the canyon.

Reaching a remote Bedouin camp we were greeted by snarling dogs, one with a collar ringed with protruding nails and its ears half cut off, both done to protect it against wolves or hyenas. Not that there were many about, but Osama had pointed out some jackal tracks and, later in the day, hyena droppings, white from eating bones and left on a thorny bush as a territorial marker. Apparently the Jordanian striped hyena is a scavenger rather than a predator, but the Bedouin don't think so. With the dogs getting too close for comfort, an equally wild-looking tangle-haired Bedouin also appeared, calling them off while laughing at our wariness. He assured us that the path continued down into the final ravine, which was still far below.

Despite his advice, we briefly lost the trail on easier ground before a profusion of small paths converged at what proved to be the only possible way down a cliff which extended along the canyon as far as we could see, seemingly blocking access to the river. Huge mounds of rocks had been heaped up against the cliff from the hillside below to support a man-made path that had been worn and polished by the passing of shepherds and their flocks for millennia. It was the key to the canyon. Once down, the river enticed us with its rare sound of running water. We waded through, knee deep, with fish swimming between our legs, finding our way through head-high phragmites reeds to a good campsite and another deep pool. Now all we needed was Abu Saif to find his way down a maze of four-wheel drive trails on the south side with our food and camping gear. As night approached we began to wonder if he would find us. We should have known better. He arrived, smiling as always, just after the sun set, the welcome lights of the car swinging erratically as he wound slowly down into the darkening wilds of Jordan's 'Grand Canyon'. With Abu Saif cooking a Bedouin favourite of *galaya* – tomatoes, onions, garlic and chilli, eaten with wraps of flatbread, we didn't go hungry.

The following day we cheated again: having learnt the trick of walking down what would become the ascents of the south sides of the canyons, Abu Saif's offer of driving us up to the south top to show us the next Bedouin trail was too good to refuse. The road zigzagged up steeply and seemingly forever. We were glad it wasn't the way we would be walking out. Even more so when Abu Saif showed us the start of a path down yet another wonderfully located ridge descending towards the depths of the canyon. At its end, a track contoured the hillside before winding down to our camp where we washed off the dust of the day in our new pool. As in the Hidan, looking back up the hillside we would never have found the trail from below.

Early next morning, we drove up to the rim of the southern plateau again in the four-wheel drive to reach the start of the previous day's walk. We just had time to check out Hakim and Murad's route along the plateau, some of it once again on a Roman road. It avoided the fourth canyon, Ibn Hammad, by traversing its rim until within view of the imposing walls of the crusader castle of Kerak. This left one big canyon to cross, Wadi Hasa, but it was time to head for Wadi Rum to see our Bedouin friends.

And we had a job to do down there: when we had been previously been exploring the Aqaba mountains above the Red Sea we had spotted what looked like a lower pass through to the coast. It needed checking. Unfortunately, having found a delightful campsite at the start of the last day in a secluded valley used only by Bedouin, the descent from the new pass proved to be dangerously loose, but such is life. With the Red Sea in sight, we scrambled up to regain our original route then once again down the scree and sandy wadi all the way to the beach and the warm, turquoise, tempting, Red Sea.

All of which didn't leave much of the trail to explore as the eleven days from the historic village of Ma'tan north of the RSCN reserve of Dana and on to Petra and Rum had been walked or driven by us in the 1980s and 1990s. Variations of it were now done regularly by different Jordanian trekking companies and the Dana to Petra section had been given the accolade of 'one of the world's top treks' by *National Geographic*, and 'one of the ten best hikes from the Middle East to South East Asia' in *Adventure Travel*. I'm not sure that treks can be compared, but it is good, passing as it does through wild country and a variety of ecosystems from mountains to canyons and deserts and ending in Petra. I'm happy it's part of the Jordan Trail.

With all that part of the trail checked, there were now only about five more days to explore from just north of Kerak Castle to Ma'tan to complete the missing link. After returning from Aqaba we were on our way again, walking happily south on Hakim's route to Kerak and being offered tea by a Syrian shepherd who had escaped the ongoing destruction of his country for the peace of the Jordanian hills. Further on we entered a narrow valley following a path down to its polished limestone bed then, unexpectedly, up to steps leading through the old castle wall beneath the Christian Tower. The next day we made our usual early start, heading south through an unusually striated limestone valley to the little-known ancient village of Ainun perched above an oxbow bend. Only one family remained, sadly but proudly showing us around the derelict homes and offering their own house as a homestay for walkers. Thirty years ago the village of Dana was similarly abandoned when we first trekked past it, yet it's now well and truly on the tourist agenda. Maybe the Jordan Trail could do the same for Ainun?

Beyond, we passed more ruined villages, now forlorn piles of rubble with no hope of restoration, on our way to the edge of the plateau overlooking the southern end of the Dead Sea, now 1,600 metres below. A few late-rising clouds were drifting gently up, lifted by the heat from Jordan's Rift Valley. Enjoying the morning breeze and the superb panorama, we walked south along the rim, crossing a side valley where more shepherds offered us tea, bread and olives, before we finally reached the yawning gash of the last Dead Sea canyon: the thousand-metre-deep Hasa Gorge – a seemingly awesome obstacle to progress.

A nice-looking ridge tempted us down past some unusual cave houses beyond which we discovered the superb cliff of Tor Taboun: over a kilometre of untouched limestone with huge boulders at its foot all waiting to be climbed, but it would have to wait; we had little time left to complete the trail. With rain threatening, we phoned Abu Samer, a friend of Osama's at Ma'tan village, our proposed destination two days' walk to the south, and accepted his offer of a night's stay.

Ma'tan was an abandoned clifftop village with awesome views down a maze of sandstone cliffs, whittled and worn into cracks and domes by aeons of wind and water. Some of its old stone houses have since been converted to chalets. Like Dana, it should be a great place to stay the night and watch the orange dawn light creeping down the cliffs. We, however, had no time to linger. We still had two days of exploration ahead of us including crossing Hasa Gorge. Heading north, a path alongside an irrigation channel full of running water led us from the village and up through orchards towards gently rolling hills along which we headed north to the small town of Ais. There we had a memorable cafe lunch of hummus, ful medames (fava beans), falafel, olives and perfect taboon bread – round and thin, soft yet sometimes crisp, served hot and fresh from the oven.

Little-used lanes then took us north again on to a high, wild ridge with dramatic views over the Hasa Gorge into which a track continued, passing an encampment of Jahalin Bedouin. The tribe had been evicted from Israel where they had come under increasing pressure from the Israeli forces to leave their ancestral lands. The demolition and burning of homes on the pretext that they had no papers of ownership and the fatal shootings of at least five of the tribe eventually drove them out. The Zionist movement claimed that they were merely nomads who had no permanent connection or private ownership of the land that they had lived on and cultivated for centuries, although in fact, land was traditionally passed down from one generation to the next and had been previously recognised and honoured by the successive governments that ruled Palestine until the end of the British Mandate.

Arriving at Burbeita hot springs in the depths of Hasa, we camped surrounded by greenery on the edge of the river, enjoying its hot-spring pool. From it a track crossed the shallow river to orchards on the north side. *Could this be the final key linking the north and south sections of the trail?* It wasn't on our our maps, which was no surprise. Leaving early we went 'just for a look' up the track beyond the orchards, reaching a wadi where we found a spring and pool. Having scrambled down into the stream and up the other side we discovered a washed-out track. There was no going back now, so in penance for walking down all the canyon sides that we should have walked up, we walked up this one, which we should have walked down! It was a long climb out, but the long-abandoned track emerged exactly where we had hoped at the cliffs of Tor Taboun. Job done. While there were still some loose ends to check out, the route of the trail had been identified and we still had time to do a new climb, the first on the crag, a French 5a which we called *Bonus Track*.

67

MEMORY LANE

Don't stop doing things because you are growing old,
because you will only grow old if you stop doing things.
Advice from Di's mum, 'Granny Barlow', then aged ninety

Though we had now checked out the whole Jordan Trail, there were still a few sections that we felt could be improved or needed revisiting. One of them was the walk to Dana, as we hadn't done it since the 1990s. Apparently there was a shorter route. Another part that concerned me was the last day of the trail over the Red Sea Mountains that descended loose screes above a narrow cliff-walled ravine. Some said it was okay, but Di and I thought descending steep scree above a cavernous drop might not be everyone's favourite day out.

These were our initial objectives in spring 2015 when Amjad, Osama, Di and I were joined by my old mate Alan Baker for a couple of weeks. We went to check the route from Ma'tan to Dana first and were joined by Abu Samer who was keen to show us around his ongoing renovations of the village. He said he knew a good route down into the canyon 500 metres below, passing cave dwellings that had been used prior to the village being built. It wasn't what we had planned to do but it sounded interesting. Unfortunately it was also dodgy, initially following narrow and loose paths between cliffs – one slip and you were over the edge. It also entered the canyon in its upper reaches, which was fun and impressive as these places are, but took too much time. There was no chance of reaching Dana in the day.

Later, with new advice from Abu Samer, we left Ma'tan by an almost-lost path, zigzagging down through abandoned hillside terraces before meeting up with one of our 1990s treks that crossed the canyon directly. Some perfectly placed hilltop lanes then brought us out on top of the cliffs that guard the upper approaches to Dana village. A zigzag path then took us easily down past a spring and through orchards to its centre.

That just left time to check out an alternative to the last day of the trail that I had found on Google Earth. I had chatted to our Bedouin friends in Rum about it. They said, 'There could be smugglers down there close to the border with Saudi Arabia, but you should be OK'. It looked like a good route, so after a few days in Rum we drove round with Alan, Amjad and Osama to the start of the walk. A sneaky little ravine barely a metre wide soon opened out into a sandy wadi that rose gently and very pleasantly up between the mountains. We had hardly gained any height before we reached the pass and a view of the Red Sea. Ahead a wadi edged by granite boulders wound gently down towards the coast. We couldn't believe our luck!

Reasonably sure we could follow it down, Amjad set off back, running down the way we had come to get the four-wheel drive and drive around the mountains to meet us. Less than a minute later, gunshots rang out close to where he had just disappeared. Then nothing, just silence.

'It must be a Bedouin hunting,' I said hopefully, remembering the warning of our friends in Rum. Then more gunshots echoed round the hills as Amjad reappeared running madly towards us and looking horrified.

'There's a madman back there!' he said. 'He says he'll shoot us if we don't go back!'

We couldn't see anyone and wondered briefly if we could dodge into the boulders and make our getaway, but then there were more shots which made our minds up, and we set off back along the wadi.

'This could be an interesting day,' I said, trying to be cheerful.

Rounding a corner, he was just ahead of us, standing on a rock, his feet level with our heads, a military rifle held loosely in front of him. And he was wearing a black kaffiyeh. No one wears black kaffiyehs in Jordan, their head-scarves are either red and white dog-tooth check or, Palestinian style, black and white. Totally black looked ominous to me. Definitely redolent of ISIS. Amjad and Osama were quickly engaged in conversation with him, trying to explain what we were doing, which was difficult as walking for pleasure was still unheard of down there. I couldn't follow the detail although it seemed to be going okay, but just in case, I eased forward a couple of steps. If it became necessary I reckoned I could grab his feet and have him off his rocky perch before he could aim his rifle.

It was very much an extreme last resort, but Di had also been thinking, and being infinitely more sensible than me, suddenly butted into the conversation, saying, 'Aren't you going to make tea for us? Bedouin always make tea when we meet.' He obviously didn't have a kettle, but he understood and smiled, everyone relaxed and soon after he waved us on. Amjad reassured us that he was happy to go back alone for the car and we continued down the valley. The man walked down with Amjad and surprisingly gave him his phone number in case we ever came back and needed a guide.

When we mentioned our experience later to our Bedouin friends back in Rum, they laughed and said he must have been a smuggler thinking we were the Mukhabarat – the secret police. We had gone too close to the Saudi border, which is notorious for smuggling. Once he was satisfied that we were simply strangers walking to the Red Sea he was happy. Nothing to worry about, they said, though I'm not sure it's an experience I could recommend. It seemed the last day would still involve the dodgy scree descent, though while looking on Google Earth I had seen another possible route.

The Jordan Trail was complete. But I still wanted to improve the last day …

68

THE END OF THE TRAIL

> To truly find what is worth seeking we must travel to the lesser-
> known spots, taking on the challenges that confront us to get there.
> ***The Road Headed West***, Leon McCarron

In 2016, given the uncertain Middle East circumstances due to the Syrian tragedy and the natural wariness of potential visitors to Jordan, tourism had collapsed, but we returned to Jordan in spring as usual, partly to hang out with Bedouin friends in Rum. Most of them were now back shepherding and living the traditional life in the desert. It was great to spend time together in the *beit esh-sha'ar* without our friends being busy guiding groups. 'The old life is much better,' Sabbah Eid said. 'Now I have time to spend with you and my family.'

A week or so later we returned to our Jordan Trail project, meeting up with two remarkable trekkers, Leon McCarron and Sean Conway. Leon had not only walked the notorious Empty Quarter crossed by Wilfred Thesiger, but cycled across America and walked though the Gobi Desert, plus other impressive projects. When we met up with him in Petra he was walking his way round an amalgam of trails around the Dead Sea. He was starting and finishing at Jerusalem, and completing a total distance of around 1,000 miles.

Sean is an 'extreme endurance adventurer'. In 2011, he was, in his words, 'miserable and depressed with the life I had built for myself, so I decided to sell my photography business for £1 and vowed from that day on to fill my days with experiences rather than things'. He then sailed, ran and biked the length of Britain, setting the record for the fastest sail at just under eighty-four hours. In 2012 he attempted to break the world record for cycling around the world and it seemed as though he would achieve it, but he said, 'My dreams were shattered in America when a driver ran me over doing fifty miles per hour. I suffered severe whiplash, concussion, torn ligaments and a compression fracture to my spine. This ruined my dream of the world record but I still wanted to continue in order to follow my dream and raise money for a charity called Solar Aid. My average speed dropped down to 140 miles per day and it became a race to get back to London in time for the Olympics. I arrived there with a week to spare having covered 16,000 miles, 12,000 of them with a fractured spine.' Incredibly, the following year Sean also swam the length of Britain, Land's End to John o'Groats, including Ireland, in four and a half months, growing his famous beard along the way to protect him from jellyfish. Beat that if you can! He was awarded the 'Adventurer of the Year' in 2014 by the Scottish Adventure Awards and when we met he had just joined Leon on the Jordan Trail from Petra to Rum.

We shared some days with them enjoying the wonderful wild mountain scenery between Petra and Roman Humeima, which was first settled in the Neolithic period about 6500 BC. It's a great five-day trek with its multicoloured sandstone, numerous canyons, the occasional huge dune and some rugged mountain vistas revealing further possibilities for exploration in this little-known part of Jordan. It was a happy trek through a spectacular ever-changing landscape, some of which we had previously missed, and made even more pleasurable by the rest of the team including Mahmoud Bdoul, our Bedouin guide, our old friend Mark and his friend Nasser Tabaa, a keen trekker and mountain biker, plus our back-up man, Suleiman the driver, who managed to access our pre-arranged campsites from the road in Wadi Araba.

Leon and Sean were good company, happy to swap yarns along the way, Leon enjoying his peanut butter or instant noodles when we stopped for a break and Sean sharing his whisky in camp at night on Di's birthday – an event to which I have to sadly admit I contributed nothing, though Suleiman had collected two used bullet cartridges and a long bent rusty nail along the way and made an amulet for her. Mahmoud too put me to shame by giving Di a nice brass 'Salaam Alaikum' – 'Peace be with you' – amulet.

At the end of the trek Di and I went north to spend time with Eisa in Al Ayoun, to trek more of the Jordan Trail among the springtime flowers, such a contrast to the desert mountains of the south, and to do a spot of climbing on the immaculate limestone crags. While there, I remembered some German and Jordanian archaeologists had discovered an amazing Roman aqueduct. It was tunnelled through the rock around 2,000 years ago to bring water 105 miles from Syria to Um Qais. Its incline never exceeds one degree and it is reputedly the longest man-made water tunnel ever. A remarkable piece of surveying and engineering technology for the time, connected where necessary by aqueducts crossing deep valleys. The discovery of the Um Qais tunnel had only recently become common knowledge, but none of Jordan's increasingly active adventure community seemed to have checked it out, whereas as always, I was intrigued. I searched on the web finding some information and a small map, and Di and I went up there with Eisa.

As with Iran's *qanats*, I reckoned if there was a tunnel, there had to be shafts, but finding one was like looking for the proverbial needle in a haystack. After a few false leads from the locals who thought we were looking for gold, we finally asked an olive farmer who was labouring with a horse-drawn wooden plough if he knew where the Roman tunnel was. Once again we got the answer we always got when wandering around Jordan on strange quests: 'I know you are looking for treasure. If you find any you should give me half' – but he knew where a tunnel entrance was and pointed across to a nearby shallow valley.

We scrambled up its far side to find a gaping hole with a steep shaft descending into the darkness. There were a few poor handholds in the walls, and poorly cut, uneven and sloping steps disappeared down into the gloom. The photos we had seen on the web showed a cave entrance that you could walk into. We hadn't come prepared to descend a steep shaft and I only had sandals. A slip on the steps would have led to an unstoppable fall into the unknown.

The next day we abandoned our climbing plans and went back on our new quest with better footwear and a rope. We abbed in to find two passages at the bottom, one filled with rubble, the other half-filled but still passable. Small holes had been cut through the rock below the shaft, presumably for tying ropes through, and a small cut niche a little further on looked like an oil lamp niche of the kind we had seen in Roman copper mines near Feynan. Continuing along the passage that unexpectedly twisted and turned (*why isn't it straight?*), we came to the top of another shaft. That was unexpected too.

Like the entrance shaft it had poorly cut steps and the bottom was out of sight. So that was the end of that as we had no more rope. Presumably it led down to the water tunnel but it was going to have to wait as we had a canyoning trip planned before returning home to the UK. We passed the information on to our Jordanian friends, but it still remains to be explored.

Four months later Jordan's first active cave was found not far from Salt, north of Amman, by Islam Ma'ani and friends, including Osama who said, 'It's a natural cave in limestone and mud stone … the water is running inside all year long, really big and amazing … an underground river … it looks like the tunnels fill up with water in winter. There are many chambers and tunnels and lots of crawls, the longest being around a hundred metres and only thirty centimetres high.'

A couple of days after our Roman tunnel exploration we were off down south again, this time to descend Wadi Hasa, the thousand-metre-deep canyon that cuts west through the mountains towards the south end of the Dead Sea. The Jordan Trail crossed it with a possible overnight at Burbeita hot springs. A few kilometres further downstream the water from the hot spring of Afra joins it. These two springs supply much of the permanently flowing warm water that we followed for two days downriver through some spectacular canyon scenery. Like the Petra to Humeima trek, Hasa was another of the few places in Jordan that we hadn't fully explored.

It's a magnificent and ever-changing canyon, always hemmed in by impossibly wild and barren mountains. Not a place you would want to be stuck in should there be heavy rains and a flash flood; its numerous narrow canyons were water-worn to a height of twenty metres. Even the cliffs of the more open stretches were washed clean to five metres or more. We found freshwater crabs there as we had in other canyons. The species had originally travelled up from the Nile, their shells having been found in archaeological sites dating back 7,000 years. We also saw the footprints of a large animal in the sand, perhaps a hyena or a jackal.

Late on the first day we were stopped by a group of Bedouin who had seen us and raced to catch us. It was a friend from Wadi Rum, Hamad Abu Sultan, the brother of Sabbah Eid's wife, Thria. It was strange to meet him far down in this remote canyon; he was fishing with his friends using a cast-net and had a good catch, certainly enough to feed them all. I didn't even know Wadi Rum Bedouin ate fish!

We left them to their sport and for two days we walked almost continuously in the river, sometimes almost waist deep in fast-flowing water, occasionally managing to escape on to its pebbly banks. The night was spent sleeping under the stars on a sandy shoulder some ten metres above the river, the croaking of frogs and the sound of the ever-rushing water being a rare serenade in this desert land. A cool night breeze heralded the dawn, rustling the hanging palms and carrying with it the sweet familiar smell of desert herbs. We rose early for the descent of the final dramatic cliff-bound canyon, at one point the river squeezing through a cavern of trapped boulders. Continuing downstream, cascades of yellow mimosa and pink oleanders peppered its shores. Just before reaching its western end, we met some German archaeologists. They were searching optimistically for signs of Neolithic man, though their Bedouin helpers were, unsurprisingly, hoping to find real treasure and not stone tools.

There are new discoveries all the time in Jordan. Soon after, a new temple of the Roman era was discovered in Petra and recent research published in the *Journal of Archaeological Science* by a team led by paleoanthropologist April Nowell of the University of Victoria revealed surprisingly sophisticated adaptations by early humans living 250,000 years ago in a former oasis near Azraq in north Jordan. Thousands of sophisticated stone tools retained protein residue from butchered animals.

Nowell said, 'The hominins in this region were clearly adaptable and capable of taking advantage of a wide range of available prey, from rhinoceros to ducks, in an extremely challenging environment.' It will be interesting to know what the German archaeologists discovered in Wadi Hasa where there have previously been finds from the Upper Paleolithic period around 40,000 years ago.

For us, descending the Hasa Canyon was almost the end of another trip to Jordan. The Jordan Trail Association had just been formed. Di and I were more than pleased when, in autumn 2016, Mohammad Zayyadeen and Mohammad Al Homran, a couple of young Bedouin of the Azazmeh tribe, became the first two Jordanians to walk the whole of the trail, completing it in thirty-nine days. Their tribe were refugees from Bir es'-Seba who, like the Jahalin Bedouin, had lost their land following the creation of Israel, when it was renamed Beersheba. The Jordan Trail couldn't have been completed by two more worthy people. They had no thought of self-aggrandisement. Having heard about the trail, they simply did it for fun, which is how it should be, rather than in search of celebrity, fame or fortune, which these days seems too often to be an insidiously creeping motivation for undertaking outdoor challenges.

Inshallah, the trail should now provide others with an unforgettable personal journey while bringing income to the villages along the way. It also offers an opportunity for people from around the world to experience

Jordanian hospitality at a time when there is so much fear and suspicion about the Middle East and its people. In 2016 Jordan was voted number four by Rough Guides in its list of best places to visit. I'll say it again: we have never met a more kindly and welcoming people, whether it be the queen or the friendly shepherds met at every turn in the trail. The Jordan Trail was, perhaps, a logical and fitting conclusion to our thirty years of exploration in Jordan, and we still find the people as welcoming and the country as exciting as when we first went there. Previously I could never understand people who repeatedly went back to the same place, but Jordan has kept us busy with mountain exploration for over thirty years, and every year we continue to make new friends and more discoveries.

This almost concludes my story. Alan Bennett commented in *The Lady in the Van*, 'Writing is talking to yourself' – it's time to get back to reality. Thanks to Di's encouragement and help it's what I've been doing here on and off for three years, writing these memoirs whenever I was home and the weather was inclement. I hope I can safely say that our explorations have in many cases been of benefit not simply to the climbers and trekkers who have followed in our footsteps and to the host countries and companies who helped sponsor our trips but, most importantly, to the mountain, jungle and desert people we met on our travels, who showed us friendship, kindness and hospitality, even when we were strangers.

As a Naga chief said to us when we arrived in his village and were welcomed as guests, with people vacating their beds for us, 'We have nothing to give, but you are welcome'. Being given beans from the field of a struggling Ethiopian farmer tilling poor stony ground with his wooden plough, or being offered what little food was available at a poor Bedouin camp, knowing that they would go without, or being greeted by a Palestinian with the words, 'I see you are English, you gave away my country, but you are welcome, come and have some tea', were humbling and salutary experiences. Our refusals were never accepted. In fact, almost everywhere we went, it seemed the poorer and simpler peoples' lives were, the warmer their welcome and hospitality to strangers.

I thank them all here for reminding us what life and humanity is really about.

POSTSCRIPT

In the spring of 2017 we were invited to join 'the official inaugural through-walk' of the Jordan Trail and happily accepted – not to walk the whole length as we knew the vast majority of it well, even variations of it, but simply to enjoy it with others. And what a pleasure it was. To our surprise there was a huge event at the start with a band and dancers and speeches by ambassadors and ministers, concluding with an award for us from the Jordan Trail Association.

Over the following six weeks we walked most of the route, being met along the way by Queen Rania, wife of King Abdullah, who wished everyone well and thanked Di and me for developing Jordan's adventure tourism. We also took time out to spend a few essential days with our friends in Wadi Rum and to explore a new route for the last day of the trail through the Aqaba mountains with Sabbah Eid. It worked out well. We found an easy ascent followed by the descent of a colourful granite valley, with tumbled pink, blue and orange granite boulders beneath a black basalt skyline and the Red Sea beckoning beyond. When we repeated it with the group a few days later, it was mid May and close to 40 °C, so we wasted no time in plunging into the Red Sea's welcoming waves while a band of drummers welcomed us and TV cameras recorded the event.

A celebratory party followed in Aqaba. The trail had been rated first in the world's new trails by *Wanderlust* magazine. Her Excellency Lina Annab, the Minister of Tourism and Antiquities, herself a keen walker, thanked us for everything we had done for Jordan. Hakim Tamimi, now a member of the Jordan Tourism Board as well as a keen climber, canyoner and trekker said, 'You guys showed us the beauty of our country,' and Muna Haddad, president of the Jordan Trail Association who had just walked the full 650 kilometres, commented, 'You are the catalysts behind this. Thank you for all the amazing things you have done for Jordan'.

At the subsequent international Adventure Travel Trade Association conference at the Dead Sea, the Jordan Trail was the talk of the show. It seemed we hadn't been wasting our time. In fact, as I write this now in 2018, I just heard the Jordan Trail has had 'an impact equivalent to six million US dollars on Jordan's economy'.

Which metaphorically brings me to the end of this part of my own particular trail: a quest into the unknown that has occupied me since I discovered climbing over sixty years ago on the very Peak District hills and crags I can see from my window at home as I write this. That's not to say I'm hanging my boots up, though in an increasingly troubled world my quest has become ever more difficult. But as I write this Di and I still have two possible projects to some little-known mountains.

You never know unless you go …

ACKNOWLEDGEMENTS

Thanks go to the following people for material used in this book:

Arne Larsen for permission to quote from his article in the Norwegian climbing magazine, *Klatring*, about Leif-Norman Patterson and the Troll Wall, and Anders I. Ourom for his English translation of it.

Barry Taylor, Keith Chadwick and Paul Seddon for permission to use abridged versions of their *Rimmon Journal* stories from the Cairngorms, Ben Nevis and the Dolomites.

Géraldine Chatelard for permission to use her quotes on Wadi Rum.

Tannith Howard for permission to use extracts from her childhood diaries.

Thanks also to the following for confirming my memories and sharing theirs:

Tom Allen, Steve Beswick, Philippe Brass, Géraldine Chatelard, Wilf Colonna, Sean Conway, Rowland and Mark Edwards, Ron Fawcett, John 'Fred' Finnigan, Adrian 'Aido' and Gill Garlick, Rob Holt, Geoff Hornby, Tannith Howard, Fred Husøy, Mark Khano, Tony Martin, Leon McCarron, Bruce Mills, Bob Orrell, Paul Seddon, Mike Searle, Mick Shaw, John Smith, Di Taylor, Mirella Tenderini, Graham Wolstencroft, Brian 'Smiler' Woods, and sincere apologies to anyone I have missed.

And finally, a big thanks to Jon Barton, Camilla Barnard, Jane Beagley and the Vertebrate Publishing team without whose support and help this book would never have happened.